The Gun Digest® Book of
DEER GUNS

ARMS & ACCESSORIES FOR THE DEER HUNTER

Edited by Dan Shideler

© 2004
by KP Books

Published by

kp books
An imprint of F+W Publications, Inc.

700 East State Street • Iola, WI 54990-0001
715-445-2214 • 888-457-2873

Our toll-free number to place an order or obtain a free catalog is 800-258-0929.

Manuscripts, contributions and inquiries, including first class return postage, should be sent to the DEER GUNS Editorial Offices, Krause Publications, 700 E. State Street, Iola, WI 54990-0001. All materials received will receive reasonable care, but we will not be responsible for their safe return. Material accepted is subject to our requirements for editing and revisions. Author payment covers all rights and title to the accepted material, including photos, drawings and other illustrations. Payment is at our current rates.

CAUTION: Technical data presented here, particularly technical data on the handloading and on firearms adjustment and alteration, inevitably reflects individual experience with particular equipment and components under specific circumstances the reader cannot duplicate exactly. Such data presentations therefore should be used for guidance only and with caution. Krause Publications, Inc., accepts no responsibility for results obtained using this data.

Library of Congress Catalog Number: 2004105223

ISBN: 0-87349-932-8

Designed by Patsy Howell and Tom Nelsen
Edited by Dan Shideler

Printed in the United States of America

About Our Covers...

On the cover of this inaugural edition of the GUN DIGEST® Book of Deer Guns, we're proud to feature three tried-and-true deer guns, each of them a modern classic:

The Sturm-Ruger Bisley Hunter in 44 Remington Magnum has won countless accolades–and collected nearly as many trophy bucks! A refinement of Ruger's orginal Super Blackhawk, the Bisley Hunter features a grip frame modeled after that of Colt's 1894 Bisley single-action target revolver, named in honor of the then-popular shooting matches held in Bisley, England. With its stainless steel construction and 7-1/2-inch barrel, Ruger's single-action Bisley Hunter is a hard-hitting buckbuster that always delivers the goods.

Introduced in 1936 and produced continuously ever since, the Winchester Model 70 needs no introduction. "The Rifleman's Rifle," it is one of the most admired, most sought-after, and most imitated rifles in firearms history. Chambered to take everything from prairie dogs to elephants, the Model 70 has probably harvested more deer than any other bolt-action rifle. The magnificent example on our cover, chambered in 270 Winchester Short Magnum, comes compliments of Winchester's Custom Shop.

Finally, a Winchester of quite another sort also graces our first cover. The Model 1300 pump is the legitimate inheritor of the crown once worn by Winchester's famed Model 12. Today, in its third decade, the Model 1300 features a short-action rotary bolt that allows as many as three shots in less than a second! This particular 1300 is the go-anywhere, do-anything Ranger Deer model in 12 gauge–a sure-fire deer-dropper at a price anyone can afford.

Dan Shideler
Editor, Firearms & Outdoors Books

The editor would like to thank Joel Marvin, Ken Ramage, and Kevin Michalowski of KP Books for their advice and assistance; and Joseph Shideler for always setting a good example.

Contents

DEER DROPPERS:
Today's *HOT* HANDGUNS

By Mark Hampton

It was the third day of deer season and I was looking forward to my wife's joining me in the blind for the evening hunt. I was carrying a Thompson/Center Encore chambered in 308 Winchester, topped by a Burris 3X-12X scope. Karen was hoping to get her first deer with a T/C Contender in 223 Remington. A weather front was moving in and I was hoping it would have the deer moving. So far, I hadn't fired a shot during the first three days. However, I watched a nice ten-pointer sneak past me the first morning without giving me an opportunity to fill my tag.

Waiting for a good shot that never did materialize, I was almost heartbroken when he disappeared. That's deer hunting and part of what keeps us coming back day after day.

Early in the afternoon we started seeing a few does. It was a good sign and kept us occupied. Later in the evening it began to sprinkle and more deer were seen. Then, right before dark, a doe came running through the woods and headed into a clearing we were watching. Right behind her was the ten-pointer I had seen the first morning. I placed the Encore on a solid rest and

waited impatiently. When he made it to the clearing I had the hammer cocked. He stood momentarily, looking around for his lady friend but it was too late. The hammer dropped and broke the evening silence. Karen and I were both thrilled when the buck didn't run 50 yards. The rain came but that didn't dampen our happiness.

Why were my wife and I both hunting with a handgun that evening? For the same reason thousands of other deer hunters take to the woods every year in pursuit of whitetail: the challenge. Handgun hunting can be one of the most rewarding methods of taking game. Every year we find more and more hunters choosing the short gun for their deer hunting endeavors. These hunters can choose from a wide variety of quality handguns to make their hunts more enjoyable and successful. Not all guns are created equal but there are many options that fill different applications and personal preference.

Every year, deer are hunted from one end of the country to another with a bewildering variety of handguns. Regulations vary from state to state, some basing theirs on case length, others on minimum caliber or muzzle energy. Some states allow muzzleloading handguns for

The author took this 10-pointer one rainy morning using an Encore chambered in 308 Winchester. The Burris 3X-12X scoped helped make it a one-shot affair.

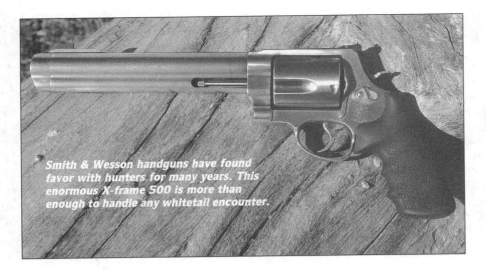

Smith & Wesson handguns have found favor with hunters for many years. This enormous X-frame 500 is more than enough to handle any whitetail encounter.

deer. It's the hunter's responsibility, of course, to know what's legal and what isn't in his neck of the woods, and to know his own limitations. There can be a difference between what's legal and what's wise.

I have to admit the vast majority of deer I have taken throughout my deer hunting career have fallen inside of 100 yards. Depending on what part of the country you hunt, the same could be true for many deer hunters. Deer are often found in the wide-open plains in some western states but, for most of us, are often pursued in some type of woods. For this type of hunting a good scoped revolver can handle most of the challenge. I say scoped because I feel optics assist hunters with making good, quality, clean shots, thus reducing the chance of wounding animals. There should be a great deal of emphasis on proper shot placement. We certainly owe it to the game we hunt. The scope allows you to see better in early and late evening conditions, when deer are most active. Mount a good scope on a quality revolver and you've got yourself a deer hunting handgun.

Long known for its dependable firearms, Ruger makes several good deer hunting revolvers. For several years I hunted not only whitetail but a variety of other big

game with the company's Super Blackhawk. It was a rugged, always dependable, efficient, single-action revolver that you could count on when you needed it most. The most popular barrel length for hunters was probably the 7 1/2-inch version but for some reason I like the longer 10 1/2 inch barrel. Obviously this gun was chambered in the

popular 44 Magnum, as are all Super Blackhawks.

Many of my Super Blackhawk revolvers were sent to Mag-Na-Port International for custom work. The quality gunsmiths at Mag-Na-Port do great work, making good guns even better. Most of the custom embellishments performed on my guns included muzzle crown, Mag-Na-Port process, trigger job, smoothing up the action, plus some other cosmetic work that added a special touch. The company's Stalker, which was a custom Super Blackhawk with scope, performed well in the field for me.

Today Ruger offers their new Super Blackhawk Hunter model that is also becoming popular with deer hunters. This new model comes equipped with a heavy solid-ribbed barrel machined to accept dovetail scope rings. This design puts the scope over the barrel, which

Freedom Arms (top) and Ruger (bottom) both make quality wheelguns for the whitetail fanatic. For hunting in the woods, these revolvers are ideal.

helps to balance the handgun very well. It also helps to reduce the amount of felt recoil somewhat. This is an excellent single-action revolver for deer hunting. When scoped properly it makes an ideal rig for whitetail. It is not uncommon for these guns to print three to four inch, one hundred yard groups when the right ammunition is found.

If for some reason you prefer double-action revolvers, Ruger offers the Redhawk and Super Redhawk models. These stoutly built, large-frame revolvers are capable of digesting a steady diet of heavy loads. Not that you need heavy loads for hunting whitetail. I have been shooting a Super Redhawk for many years now and it has always performed well. It has never let me down regardless of weather or how badly (blush!) I treated it.

These models come in different barrel lengths, and I seem to favor the longer tubes for hunting. Not necessary for success, just a personal preference. The swing-out cylinders on the double-action revolvers make for easy loading and unloading. You can see from the massive cylinder that this gun can handle any loads that are considered safe. The revolver is chambered for several rounds with the 44 Magnum being my favorite whitetail medicine. I haven't had the opportunity to hunt deer with the 480 Ruger but it sure helped me bag a 300 pound boar recently. Heck, if it will handle a big hog like that I know it will work wonders on whitetail.

Taurus provides deer hunters with the Raging Bull series in 44 Magnum, 480 Ruger, and 454 Casull. This big honkin' double-action revolver comes in several different barrel lengths. The cushion grip is extremely comfortable to shoot even with heavy kickers, the grip pushing back into the palm of your hand without discomfort. Another item that helped tame felt recoil is the Taurus factory muzzle brake. I was pleasantly surprised when shooting factory 44 Magnum ammunition. The eight-inch barrel helped add weight, which always reduces felt recoil, but the muzzle compensator really reduced muzzle flip. This made shooting a lot more enjoyable, allowing my shooting buddy and me to practice all afternoon without fatigue.

Freedom Arms makes one of the highest quality revolvers available today in their Model 83 Premium and Field grades. This well-built single-action wheelgun is a favorite among serious hunters with fatter-than-average wallets. While I don't consider the 357 Magnum an ideal whitetail cartridge, Bob Baker, President of Freedom Arms, took his first whitetail deer while hunting with me several years ago here in Missouri. Bob was using one of his revolvers in 357 Magnum when a nice ten point Show-Me State buck made the mistake of walking past his stand. The shot was around fifty yards and, being an excellent shot, Bob placed his one and only shot in the buck's vitals. It was a great way to start the opening morning! So if someone ever tells you that the 357 Magnum can't cut the mustard on whitetails, refer him to Bob Baker.

These fine handguns are available in most revolver cartridges suitable for deer hunting. The 454 Casull is one of the finest cartridges for close range hunting and is certainly a match for any whitetail regardless where they are hunted. The Freedom Arms 454 five-shooter is a top choice for any hunting application. When scoped, this gun is capable of accuracy as good as can be expected from any revolver. The company also offers a wide range of grips, ammunition, holsters, and even quality gun cases.

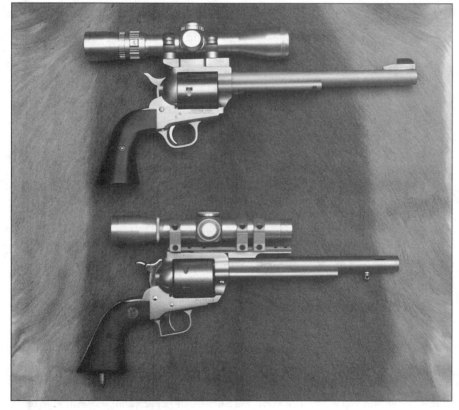

A quality scope simply helps the hunter to place his shots.

Another well-built single-action revolver is the BFR from Magnum Research. The BFR stands for Biggest Finest Revolver. Recently I was working with one of their hefty sixguns in 480 Ruger. This gun is pleasant to shoot even with the heavy kickers due to the weight and balance. Like the huge molybdenum bronze-frame custom revolvers of 30 years ago, the BFR is also available in 45-70 Government, and it wasn't too terribly uncomfortable to shoot. For single-action fans, the big BFR just might be the ticket to filling your deer tag this fall, especially if you believe, as General Nathan Bedford Forrest did, in getting there "fustest with the mostest."

Even before Dirty Harry hit the screen, Smith & Wesson was making its way into the hearts of handgun hunters. One of the company's favorite 44 Magnums is its famed Model 29. It was a good gun when Harry Callahan carried it, and it still is today. The blued version, the plain old Model 29, seems to have been dropped from S&W's rolls, but there are enough different stainless versions of the old classic to handle a forest-full of whitetails. It's also pleasing to note that S&W has reintroduced its Model 25 in 45 Colt. This 4-inch revolver has the guts to drop any deer foolish enough to wander into its range.

The reconstituted S&W firm is producing other models that can be found in the hands of serious deer hunters. Smith & Wesson's custom shop offers some neat handguns with features many hunters will find attractive. Their newest X-frame chambered for the mighty S & W 500, for example, cannot be manufactured fast enough to keep up with public demand. It is a very large five-shot revolver to say the least.

Recently I had the pleasure of shooting this massive wheelgun

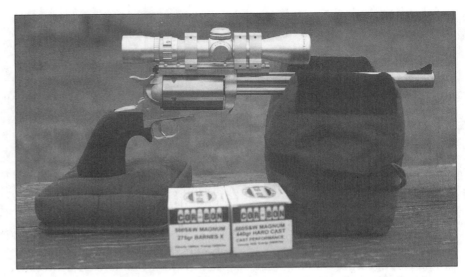

Magnum Research's BFR is a massive sixgun capable of digesting some fine deer medicine including 45-70 and 450 Marlin.

with a variety of Cor-Bon ammunition. The 275-gr. offering was surprisingly pleasant to shoot and broke every rock I connected with on the pond bank. The sheer weight of the gun, 72 ounces, helps reduce muzzle rise. The custom compensator is another reason that muzzle flip stays manageable. The Hogue Sorbothane grips didn't bite during recoil even with my small hands. The gun I was testing came with an 8 3/8 inch barrel. The 440-gr. hard-cast offering from Cor-Bon was quite different in the recoil department from the 275-grainers. While I haven't been able to hunt whitetail with this new offering from Smith & Wesson, it has already helped me take cape buffalo in Africa. I'm certain it will work fine on whitetail.

This discussion will not take a rigid stance on the superiority of

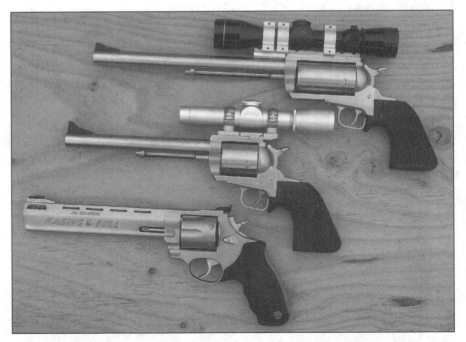

If you prefer hunting with a revolver, there are many great handguns available to fit the bill.

one type of handgun over the other. I do realize there are those out there who feel that if you're not hunting with a revolver, then you're really not handgun hunting. I don't agree with this line of thinking but I respect the opinion. If you feel, for whatever reason, you wish to hunt whitetail with a sixgun, by all means do so. There are many quality handguns already mentioned that will give you years of enjoyment. Earlier I admitted that the majority of the deer I have taken were inside of 100 yards. All of these opportunities could have been easily handled with a revolver.

Similarly, some may hunt deer with semi-auto pistols where legal. I do not. There are a few semi-auto pistols that can humanely put down a deer– Magnum Research's Desert Eagle comes to mind–but none is specifically marketed for deer hunting. Revolvers, single-shots, and bolt-actions fit the bill so well that they leave little room for anything else.

I do feel, however, that a 2X or 4X scope enhances any handgun's hunting performance. A good scoped pistol or revolver makes an ideal rig for hunting in the woods where shots may be limited to around 100 yards or less. Regardless of what firearm you choose, the ability to place your bullet where it belongs is vitally important. As responsible hunters, it is our duty to do so.

All of the above-mentioned revolvers are available in several good deer hunting rounds. The 357 Magnum has taken deer successfully but I don't consider it to be ideal compared to what else is out there on the market. The ancient 45 Colt can still put venison steak on the grill, as many deer have discovered to their sorrow when faced with an 1873 Colt single-action. The 41 Magnum is a fine whitetail cartridge, splitting the difference between the 357 and the 44. It

has never gained the popularity it should have received, however, and probably never will. It, like so many other cartridges, pales in comparison to the famed 44 Mag. Close to half-a-century old, the big 44 has found a secure place in the hearts of many handgun hunters and rightly so. A wide variety of quality bullets makes this round extremely versatile. If you don't handload, no sweat: there's a ton of high-performance factory ammunition available over the counter.

Stepping up in power, the 475 Linebaugh and 480 Ruger are also good choices. The question of which of these two "light heavyweight division" cartridges is better for deer hunting will probably be debated for years. You pays your money and takes your choice. Obviously, if you still have the need for more get up and go, the 454 Casull and 500 Smith & Wesson will fill the bill. Once you find the right bullet/load combination, a lot of practice will go a long way on increasing your chances in the field when deer season rolls around.

If you find yourself hunting in more open country where shots beyond 100 yards are a real possibility, don't despair. There are some truly accurate handguns that are capable of reaching out there and dropping the buck of your dreams. One of the most popular single shot handguns is the T/C Contender, or its newer version, the G2 (Generation 2). These guns have interchangeable barrel capability, allowing the shooter to own one frame and add as many different barrels as the heart desires or the spouse allows. The G2 will accept the older Contender barrels.

Some of the cartridges suitable for deer hunting in the Contender, G2, and Encore include the 7-30 Waters, 30-30 Winchester, 44 Magnum, 375

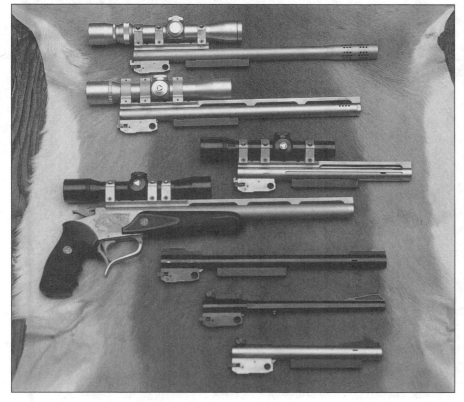

One of the great advantages of the T/C Contender is its interchangeable barrels.

JDJ, 45 Colt, and 45-70. The 375 JDJ is one of the newest offerings available thanks to a joint effort from Thompson/Center, JD Jones, and Hornady. And those are just the factory offerings! There are countless additional options if you consider custom barrel makers such as SSK Industries or On Target Technologies. These custom shops offer a variety of cartridge choices including wildcats.

The Encore is sort of a Contender on steroids. It is capable of handling a multitude of popular rimless deer hunting "rifle" cartridges including two of my favorites, the 7mm-08 Remington and 308 Winchester. I even have a 209X50 muzzleloading barrel for my Encore frame. This allows me to enjoy a few more days of deer hunting during the black powder

T/C's Encore can be chambered for a variety of rounds. This particular example sports a 375 JDJ barrel wearing a Bausch & Lomb 2X-6X scope.

season and still enjoy my favorite method of handgun hunting. I must warn you: these guns are addictive. Once you get hooked you'll be adding more barrels to your battery. If only I could keep my wife from finding all of my barrels!

Another handgun that offers long range capability is the Savage Striker. This bolt-action is also chambered in several

For long-range shooting, the Savage Striker is a good choice. This fine bolt-action repeater is available in the classic 308 Winchester.

The out-of-production Remington XP-100 can still be found in the hands of deer hunters. This is a very accurate handgun ideal for long-range shooting.

different options including 243 Winchester, 7mm-08, 308 Winchester and other bottle-necked cartridges. Sharing the same action as Savage's 110 bolt rifle, it will even handle the 300 Winchester Short Magnum, a stubby little scorcher that will reach into the next county. This type of handgun is ideal when sitting in a blind overlooking food plots or clearings where shots could range way out there. The bolt works from the left side so if you're right handed, you can keep a grip on the handgun while working the bolt with your left hand. The Striker is a lot of gun for the money. With a good trigger job and quality scope mounted on top, along with the right combination of bullet/load, this gun is a real shooter. It's a repeater, too, with a one- or two-shot magazine depending on caliber.

H-S Precision produces another bolt-action handgun that is unbelievably accurate. The company offers 11 calibers in its Pro-Series 2000 model. The trigger is fully adjustable from 2.5 to 3.5 pounds. The handgun comes with a center grip synthetic stock with bedding block system. The 2 1/2-inch wide fore-end rests wonderfully on sandbags or similar rest, making the handgun easy to shoot in this

manner. Just a couple of years ago I managed to drop a nice eight point Missouri buck one evening before dark using this handgun in .308 Winchester. The weight and balance of the gun makes shooting a 30-caliber handgun a piece of cake. For long range shooting the Pro-Series 2000 makes an excellent choice.

You may not be familiar with the German-made Blaser handgun but it's a unique bolt-action design. The handgun is based on the same design as the R93 rifle. The straight pull of the bolt, which is as smooth as oiled silk, makes for quick follow-up shots if necessary. No up-and-down bolt wagging here, just a pull-push back and then forward. The magazine holds two rounds. My test gun came in 308 and I took it to Africa for a workout. It is a shooter to say the least. The gun comes out of the box with a good trigger. This feature makes it easier to shoot the gun accurately without fighting the trigger. It balances nicely and everyone who shot this gun while hunting in Africa commented that it was easy to shoot even if they were not experienced with handguns. The Turkish walnut stock is pleasing to the eye and I hated the thought of putting a scratch on it. The Blaser has interchangeable barrel capability

and it, too, carries a multiple-round magazine.

The great-grandfather of all of these bolt-action pistols, Remington's XP-100, may be out of production, alas, but you can still shop around and find used specimens. Though its first chambering was the zippy 221 Fireball—hardly a deer cartridge—its later chamberings included a real deer cartridge, the 35 Remington. Many shooters appreciate the inherent accuracy this outstanding bolt action provides.

Like many other shooters, the XPs I own have gone through some custom refinements and rechambering. One of my favorite long range hunting guns is a custom XP topped with a 3X-12X Burris scope, McMillan stock, rechambered for 284 Winchester. There is another XP in my battery in 7BR with a nice looking Fajen thumbhole stock. It too shoots better than a vast majority of long guns. A friend of mine has one of the older Remington Custom Shop XP's in 7mm-08. That has got to be one fine deer hunting rig. It's normal with these handguns to shoot sub-MOA consistently. For hunting wide open spaces where shots are going to be one hundred and fifty yards and beyond, this type of handgun makes sense.

Keep in mind that all of these long range handguns have limitations. As hunters, we too have limitations on our capability. Just because Joe down the street can knock over a steel target at 400 yards doesn't mean I should be shooting deer at that range. Know your limitations as well as you know your handgun's capabilities.

It really doesn't matter much what type of handgun you choose for hunting as long as it fits your style, environment, and most importantly, your personal preference. The main requirement is to pick a gun that YOU like and then practice, practice, and then practice some more. There is no substitute for being familiar with your firearm. When that magic moment does happen and the buck of a lifetime steps out in the open, you want everything to come together. Whether your deer hunting finds you deep in the woods sitting on a stump or perched in an elevated blind overlooking a 300-yard clearing, there are handguns available to make your pursuit both enjoyable and successful.

Handgun hunting for whitetail is one of the most rewarding times spent in the field. Don't worry about having fun. You will.

Hunting with a handgun can be challenging. Hunters should always look for a rest on which to steady the crosshairs.

Taking a mature whitetail with a handgun is a rewarding experience. This T/C Contender chambered for 309 JDJ was responsible for filling the author's tag.

IT'S NOT YOUR DAD'S LEVER-ACTION

Recent developments in the centerfire lever-action rifle arena breathe new life into an old warrior

By Durwood Hollis

In an age where products become obsolete overnight, it's gratifying to see some things endure. The small metal hairpin, commonly known as a "bobby pin," has been with us seemingly forever. Since my wife and daughters still use them, apparently their function has not yet been outmoded. In some realms, functional application and sophisticated technology are part of a nexus from which neither is ready to retreat. And users are unwilling to depart from a pathway that has so often led to success. Maybe this explains why, despite the evolution of more sophisticated firearm designs, the lever-action rifle still remains popular among big game hunters.

As a callow adolescent, on what was to be a seminal deer hunt, I had occasion to use a Winchester Model 1895 lever-action rifle chambered in 30-40 Krag. This particular firearm had been a regular participant in the hunt. After a brief orientation in the care and feeding of the levergun, I set off in search of my first buck.

Toward the end of that first day, a deer suddenly appeared right in front of me. At that instant, every action became instinctual. The rifle came to my shoulder as though I'd been shooting it for years. And in one fluid movement, I thumbed back the hammer and lined the sights

This original Winchester Model 1895 in 30-40 Krag was one of the author's first deer rifles.

up on the buck. When the rifle hammer made contact with the cartridge primer, I though it was going to be all over. Like too many excited first-timers, however, I'd forgotten to bury the front sight blade in the buckhorn rear sight. Consequently, the 180-grain bullet flew harmlessly over the animal's back.

It didn't take any more than a second for the deer to realize that a teenager with a rifle wasn't a good thing. With near lightning speed, he fled the scene like his tail was on fire. Cranking the rifle lever quickly, I instantly chambered another round. This time, both the front and rear sights were precisely aligned. The moment the rifle muzzle caught up with the running target, I slapped the trigger and never stopped my swing. At the shot, the buck made a hooves-over-antlers roll, ending up in a heap at the base of a low rise. Needless to say, the hunt was over. And the buck that lay in the distance wasn't an ordinary deer. The headgear on that grizzled veteran was something to brag about. And did I brag–about the deer, the shot, and most of all, about the lever-action rifle!

The lever-action is a favorite in Michigan's deer woods, where a 30-30 or 35 Remington can still deliver the goods–and frequently do!

Even though lever-action rifles have been eclipsed by the popularity of bolt-action designs, they continue to have a commanding place in the firearms market. Modern manufacturers including Browning, Marlin, Ruger, Sako, Savage, Winchester and others have at one time or another all produced lever-action rifles. Some designs failed to garner interest, others were doomed because of manufacturing costs, but some survived and even flourished. Currently, Browning, Marlin, Ruger and Winchester are the only domestic makers of lever-action rifles. However, Legacy Sports International imports a lever-action based on the Winchester Model 92 design. A look at each product line will reveal some truly exciting new developments! Even if you're a levergun enthusiast, you may be surprised how a nineteenth-century tradition has leaped into the twenty-first century with a *bang*!

The Utah-based Browning Arms Company has cataloged for several years one of the most modern lever-action centerfire rifles ever designed. The Browning BLR (Browning Lever-Action Rifle) Lightweight 81 levergun uses an exceptionally smooth rack and pinion gear-operated system to load, chamber and eject cartridges (the trigger travels with the lever). And the ejection of the cartridge is to the side, rather than directly out of the top of the action. In addition, this unique design has a rotating head, a multiple-lug breech bolt

The perfect set-up shot for a lever action: up close and personal.

The compact Marlin 1895M in 450 Marlin: more than a ton and a half of muzzle energy in a very friendly package.

with a recessed face that allows the use of modern high-intensity chamberings.

An aluminum receiver is at the heart of the "lightweight" designation. Not only does this feature decrease the weight of the firearm, it also makes the gun easier to handle in the field. Moreover, both short-action and long-action configurations are available. One of the best features of this levergun is the flush-mounted, detachable magazine, which holds four magnum rounds or five standard caliber cartridges. It's the use of this type of cartridge containment, rather than the traditional tubular magazine and its need for flat-point projectiles (to prevent an accidental discharge in the magazine during recoil), that allows the BLR to use spire-point bullets. Therefore, when compared to other leverguns the Browning BLR is able to offer far better ballistic performance.

The BLR is provided in a wide range of modern, high-intensity calibers including 22-250, 243 Winchester, and 300 Winchester Magnum. Not since the demise of the lamented Savage 99 has a lever-action handled such long-range chamberings. The traditional straight-grip buttstock and a classic round forearm are crafted from American walnut and checkered for enhanced firearm control. To tame recoil, a deluxe black recoil pad has been added to the buttstock. This lever-action rifle

has a host of features, not the least of which it its ability to use modern standard and magnum chamberings without restriction on bullet configurations.

The Marlin Firearms Company has long been a player in the lever arena. Synonymous with functional dependability, impeccable performance and precision shot placement, their lever-action designs are true American classics. One of the most significant features of the Marlin design is the clean, flat, closed top receiver, which allows for top-mounted scope placement. A closed top receiver also keeps out environmental invectives, such as rain, snow and action-jamming debris. Moreover, this design affords true side-ejection of spent cartridges.

The Marlin Model 336SS lever-action, chambered in 30-30 Winchester, is just what foul weather hunters are looking for. The vast majority of its metal components, including the receiver and lever, are machined from stainless steel forgings. Other parts are nickel-plated for enhanced rust-resistance. Since most deer hunters will face inclement weather on occasion, combining the Marlin closed-receiver action design with rust-resistant metallurgy is an idea whose time has come. When it looks like tough weather outside, deer hunters won't have to think twice about taking their new stainless steel Marlin levergun to the field.

The Marlin Model 336C, available in either 30-30 Winchester or 35 Remington, has a special camouflage Mossy Oak Break-Up finish applied to its two-piece hardwood stock. Like its blued and stainless steel siblings, this model has a 20" Micro-Groove barrel, a tubular magazine that holds six shots and attached sling swivel studs. If you want to disappear in the woods, then this levergun has what it takes to make that happen.

In its Big Bore line, Marlin is offering seven remarkable models, chambered in extremely robust calibers: 480 Ruger, 475 Linebaugh, 450 Marlin Magnum, 444 Marlin and the venerable 45-70 Government. With the widest selection of centerfire leverguns of any manufacturer, it's obvious why Marlin continues to command center stage in the hunting arena.

The newest addition to this series is the Marlin Model 1895RL. This is a blued steel, carbine-length levergun, chambered for two of the most potent handgun cartridges in the world: the 480 Ruger and the 475 Linebaugh (both can be fired from the same rifle). Weighing just 7 pounds, this lever-action has a 18 1/2-inch barrel and a tubular magazine that can take six rounds of 480 Ruger or five of 475 Linebaugh. The stock is crafted from American black walnut, features a Mar-Shield finish and has cut checkering at the wrist and on the forearm. A ventilated rubber recoil pad and sling swivel studs are part of the package.

Marlin Models 1895M and 1895MR, chambered in the hard-hitting 450 Marlin Magnum, are both formidable contenders. This new belted cartridge, a modern version of the venerable old 45-70 Government, is the most powerful chambering ever offered in a Marlin levergun. The only difference between the two rifle models is barrel length: 18-1/2" (Model M) and 20" (Model MR). American black walnut buttstock and forend, as well as a ventilated recoil pad and sling swivel studs are standard on either rifle model.

Designed for the hunter who wants an easy-handling firearm with plenty of terminal bullet impact, the Marlin Model 1895G/GS Guide Gun is all that–and more. Chambered in the proven 45-70 caliber, this is a rifle that can handle everything from deer to grizzly bear. Available in your choice of blued steel (Model 1895G) or stainless steel (Model 1895GS) construction, this levergun weighs in at 7 pounds. Either rifle model has a 18-1/2" barrel, 4-shot tubular magazine, a semi-buckhorn folding rear sight and a ramp front sight with a brass bead and a Wide-Scan removable hood. Both the buttstock and the forend are American black walnut, protected with a Mar-Shield finish and checkered for enhanced rifle control. Sling swivels and a ventilated recoil pad are additional features.

The folks at Sturm, Ruger & Company may be the new guys on the block, but they have made their mark in the lever-action centerfire rifle realm. The Ruger Model 96 levergun, chambered in 44 Remington Magnum, is just what's needed in a compact, rugged and reliable firearm. Moreover, when a follow-up shot is called upon, all it takes to chamber another round is a simple flick of the wrist. This handy rifle is just 6 pounds in weight and measures 37-1/4" overall, which provides enhanced handling characteristics. Furthermore, the 18 1/2" barrel provides added velocity to the 44 Remington Magnum handgun cartridge chambering, making it the near equal of the respected 30-30 Winchester. The receiver is designed to accommodate over-the-bore, low scope mounting. Furthermore, the mounting bases are machined into the receiver and the rifle comes with a pair of scope rings at no extra cost. The short-throw lever (54 degrees of rotation) is color case finished and operates quickly and easily for near-instant access to additional shots. And the sliding cross-button safety is positioned just forward of the lever hinge point for easy access. The hardwood stock is one-piece and comes with a metal butt plate and barrel band. Like the famous Ruger 10/22 rimfire rifle, this centerfire levergun has a detachable rotary magazine made from high-impact polymer plastic, which holds a total of four extra rounds. When it comes to reliability, rugged construction and ready access, the Ruger Model 96 lever-action has it all.

One of the latest entries in the centerfire lever-action market is Legacy Sports International. Their handy little Puma Model 92 lever-action carbine is available in your choice of the powerful 454 Casull, the new 480 Ruger, or the 357 Remington Magnum chamberings. Based on the now famous Winchester Model 92 lever-action rifle, this new design uses modern materials and has been subjected to extensive testing for absolute safety. Available in either blued or stainless steel, with your choice of standard metallic or

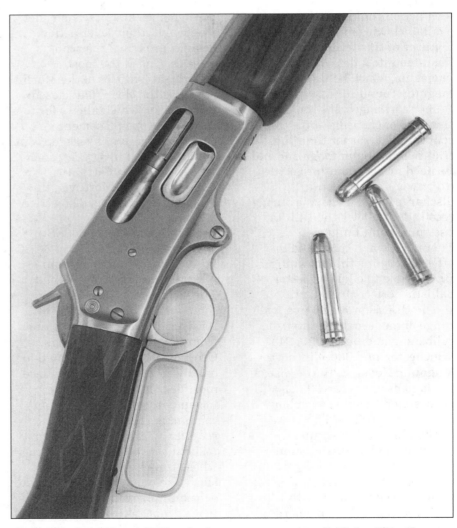

Marlin's poular 336 and 1895 series leverguns are now available in all-weather stainless steel and chamber a variety of bruiser-class cartridges.

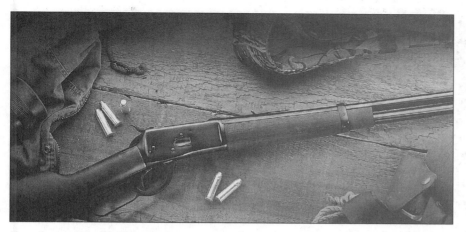

Based on a John M. Browning design of more than a century ago, the Puma Model 92 is engineered to safely handle powerhouses such as the 454 Casull and 480 Ruger.

Built for business: Winchester's Model 1894 Timber lever-action in 450 Marlin combines ease of handling and bone-crushing power.

high-visibility fiber-optic sights, this lightweight carbine-length rifle is just the ticket for hunting heavy cover. All of these rifles have 20" barrels, a tubular magazine tube and tropical hard wood buttstocks and forends. The carbines chambered in 454 and 480 calibers also have deeply-ventilated rubber buttstock recoil pads. And a low-profile, thumb-operated safety, mounted at the rear of the receiver provides an extra margin of safety for shooters. Affordable, light and quick-handling, the Puma Model 92 levergun is a rough and tumble carbine that's just plan fun to use in the field.

There are no more famous lever-action rifles than those by Winchester Arms. The Winchester lever-action Models 64, 71, 92, 94 and 95 set the standard for every levergun design that followed thereafter. Often copied, but seldom equaled, the Winchester Model 94 is still with us today. New to the line is the Winchester Model 94 Timber levergun, chambered in 450 Marlin Magnum. Designed for use in close cover, this carbine-length rifle is extremely maneuverable. This is accomplished in part by the use of a 18" barrel. Furthermore, the barrel is ported to control the recoil generated by the magnum chambering. Made from blued steel, the receiver is drilled and tapped for scope mounts. The top-tang mounted safety retains the clean, classical lines of the original Model 94 design. The three-quarter length magazine holds four extra rounds. And a fully adjustable XS brand ghost ring rear sight and ramp-style front sight provide everything you need for precise bullet placement, even on fast-moving targets. The checkered walnut stock buttstock has a semi-pistol grip for added control when shooting this hardhitting levergun. Likewise, the forend is

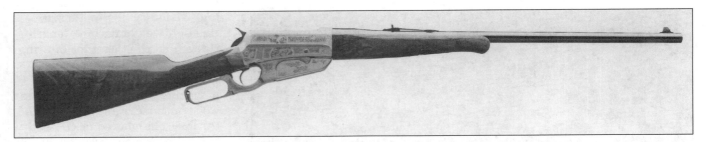

A grand old gun brought back to life: the Winchester 1895 in 405 Winchester is one of the most powerful lever-action rifles ever built.

also checkered for similar purposes. A thick Pachmayr recoil pad and sling swivel studs are part of this rifle package.

One of the preferred rifles of former President Theodore Roosevelt was the Winchester Model 95 lever-action. He actually took three of these rifles along on his 1909-1910 historic African safari. While the original rifle model has long been out of production, Winchester has once again produced a limited number of these rifles chambered in 405 Winchester. Available through the Custom Shop, these rifles are faithful to the original John Browning design. This unique lever-action has a deep box magazine, 24" barrel, steel buttplate, adjustable iron sights and a checkered walnut buttstock and forend. The only departure from the original design is the addition of a top-tang-mounted safety. It's gratifying to see this old warrior back in the game again, albeit in limited numbers and for a short time. Previous versions of the "new" 1895 chambered the 270 Winchester and 30-06.

The last shot: Despite rumors of its demise, the lever-action is flourishing. Many of the old traditional designs and chamberings are still with us. The popularity of the Marlin Model 336 and Winchester Model 94 leverguns, chambered in 30-30 Winchester and 35 Remington, is proof enough of these facts. Even the new Puma levergun is based on the venerable Winchester Model 92 motif. No doubt, the redesign of the Winchester Model 94 to accommodate side-ejection (in some models), with its availability in a much wider range of hardhitting calibers and a choice of wood or synthetic stocks, certainly has had a significant effect on the continuing interest in lever-action rifles. Likewise, Marlin has broadened its product line to include both stainless and a camouflage finish leverguns, making the lever-action concept more appealing to a wider range of shooters. And Browning and Ruger have redefined the entire lever-action concept: the former with the gear-driven action system, rotating bolt head and both short- and long-actions designed to accommodate corresponding modern chamberings, the latter with a one-piece stock design and detachable rotary magazine.

In the minds of many, the term deer rifle is defined by the lever-action concept. And despite advances in modern firearm design, that meaning persists. Part of the explanation is no doubt derived from the clean, classic lines of many lever-action rifles. And as these firearms evolved, the adaptation to changing technology has continued to endear the concept to subsequent generations of hunters.

Those of us who use a levergun in the deer woods know why this is true. All the rest are missing out on something special.

Whitetails, western creek bottoms and a fast-handling lever-action are three of the author's favorite things.

A TRULY CUSTOM LEVER-ACTION

The whole idea of a customized lever-action rifle would seem to be about as outlandish as mud flaps on a bullfrog. After all, the most salient features of a levergun are its clean lines, compact configuration and ready access to additional shots. To improve on this concept would seemingly be an impossible chore.

However, Jim West, the proprietor of Wild West Guns Inc., has done just that with his creation of the Alaskan Co-Pilot lever-action rifle. To accomplish the assignment, a Marlin Model 1895 levergun, chambered in 45-70 Government, is stripped down to its basic components. The barrel is recrowned (16-1/2, 18, or 20 inches in length), rechambered in 457 Alaskan or 50 Alaskan (proprietary magnum calibers) and new sights installed. The front sight is a Williams fiber optic (red or green) for high visibility under low light conditions. An aperture (ghost ring) sight, which allows instant target acquisition, is substituted for the original rear sight. The link between the barrel and action is engineered so the rifle can be easily taken-down into two individual component pieces. The action is tuned for total reliability. The ejector and trigger (3-lb pull) are replaced and the magazine tube is safety vented. After the stock is cut to length, a Pachmayr Decelerator recoil pad is added to ease the force of felt recoil (other options and accessories are available). And when the project is completed, MOA (minute-of-angle) accuracy at 100-yards is guaranteed. Considering that this is a take-down conversion, such a level of precision shot placement is remarkable. Those interested in a lightweight, easy handling and hardhitting lever-action rifle that can handle the biggest buck in the woods–and every other species of North American big game, for that matter–will instantly see the advantages that this custom take-down lever-action rifle can provide, regardless of the cost. For more information: contact Jim West at Wild West Guns Inc., 7521 Old Seward Hwy., Anchorage, Alaska, 99518, telephone 800-992-4570.

When nothing but the best will do: the Alaskan Co-Pilot levergun is custom-built on a Marlin chassis.

Faded into History

Gone but not forgotten, the Winchester Big Bore Angle Eject in 356 Winchester could punch out groups like this all day long.

Unfortunately, two extremely fine calibers, the 307 and 356 Winchester, have faded into the shadows of lever-action history. In 1983, Winchester brought out both chamberings in its Model XTR (Extra Range) Angle Eject Big Bore levergun, a brawnier version of the standard Model 94. Following this new trend, Marlin also marketed its Model 336ER in 307

Winchester. Both of these rounds were rimmed versions of the 308 and 358 Winchester calibers, respectively. Even though their ballistic performance (due to less case capacity and the necessity for flat-point bullets) is slightly below that of their rimless cousins, they exceed the performance of many other popular lever-action calibers, including 30-30 Winchester, 300 Savage,

30-40 Krag and the 35 Remington.

At this writing, neither the 307 nor the 356 Winchester is chambered in factory leverguns. And that's a shame. Both are quite capable of taking the lever-action rifle out of the category of a short-range brush gun and making it suitable for deer, bear, wild pigs and elk at longer ranges.

GIMME A LIGHT

Ultralight deer rifles pack a punch, but not pounds

By Wayne van Zwoll

The longer I hunt, the more I appreciate lightweight rifles – and not just because they're easier to carry. They're more responsive. A properly balanced bantam-weight rifle can help you shoot faster and hit more often.

Of course, lightweight rifles can punch you silly when they detonate cartridges the size of hot sauce bottles. But deer these days don't take any more killing than deer did a hundred years ago, when a 30-30 shooting a

160-gr. bullet at 1970 fps was considered potent. That's the other thing I like about lightweight rifles: they steer me to mild cartridges.

Early on, I found out why the Winchester 94 sold better than most deer rifles. I had one in hand when a buck barreled out of a thicket in western Oregon. I shot him as I might a grouse, following a miss with a marginal hit, then two solid hits. The 30-30 pointed itself. I had the same luck with a 99 Savage carbine decades later. This whitetail gave me time for only one shot, and the little 30 hurried to snatch the opportunity. A 150-gr. Power Point minced the deer's lungs. I've shot a few mule deer at long range in the last few years, and seldom carry lever rifles now. But it's clear to me that even in open country, deer hunters don't need magnum power or rifles as burdensome as bazookas.

Winchester trotted out a truly lightweight lever-action in 1924. The Model 53 was a half-magazine rifle derived from the Model 92, itself a nimble package. Its most potent chambering was 44-40, hardly fearsome by today's standards, but a match for the buckhorn sight on the 22-inch nickel-steel barrel. At just under 6 pounds, the 53 was lightning-quick to aim and, given its mild recoil and fine balance, fast on the follow-up.

By the time Winchester introduced its Model 70 in 1937, bolt-action rifles had been whittled down to 8 pounds or so. The Savage Model 1920, hardly

Still-hunters find lightweight rifles not only easy to pack, but quick on the shot.

Melvin Forbes built this New Ultra Light rifle in 6.5/284. It's a nail-driving lightweight.

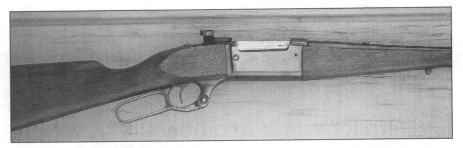

This petite Savage 99 in 250 is nicely balanced, with the weight low between the hands. It's also long out of production, unfortunately.

ever mentioned now, had the feel of more costly rifles and scaled only 7 pounds, about the heft of a Winchester 54 before the M70 replaced it. As optical sights and wildcat cartridges gave bolt guns a boost in popularity, shooters focused more on ballistic performance. Riflemen pined for greater reach; rifle weight mattered less. Remington offered its serviceable, affordable Models 721 and 722 (long and short actions) beginning in 1948. They weighed nearly a pound less than the 720, an earlier rifle on the 1917 Enfield action.

But they were no match for the Model 70 Featherweight that appeared in the early 1950s at 7 pounds. In 1962 Remington used alloy bottom metal to drop additional weight in its new Model 700. Weatherby, meanwhile, was sticking with 8 1/2-pound rifles. The Mark V *action* Roy Weatherby designed with Fred Jennie in 1957 had 36 ounces of steel! Roy's magnum cartridges needed long barrels to deliver top bullet speeds. At that time Browning was importing rifles on FN and Sako actions; only the small-action Sakos could be called light. In 1968, Bill Ruger announced his Model 77, at about 7 pounds. Some versions wore trim 22-inch barrels. Len Brownell stocks made these 77s especially responsive.

Four years earlier, Remington had introduced a strange-looking carbine, the Model 600. At 6 1/2 pounds, it was a handy deer rifle (chamberings: 222, 223, 243,

6mm, 308). A Model 600 Magnum in 6.5mm and 350 Remington Magnum offered more power. Dogleg bolt handles, square forends, pressed checkering and ventilated ribs earned these rifles no plaudits. They were succeeded in 1968 by 660-series rifles without the rib. These were dropped in 1971. Collectors pay handsomely now for the Magnums.

During the 1980s, lightweight rifles again began attracting hunters. Morgantown, W. Va., entrepreneur Melvin Forbes designed his Ultra Light action in 1984. It looked like a Remington 700, but bolt and receiver diameters were smaller. Says Melvin: "While the receiver has standard wall thickness, a smaller bolt body means less steel than in actions built to

accept magnums." Melvin designed the Model 20 around the 7x57 Mauser cartridge. "Its case is longer than that of the 308 Winchester," he points out. "So is the 6mm Remington, 257 Roberts and 284 Winchester. In a short-action magazine, their bullets must be seated deep. You forfeit case capacity. Our magazine box is 3 inches long, not 2.85 inches as in most short-action rifles."

Melvin didn't skeletonize the metal or cut barrels shorter than 22 inches. His Model 20 owes its feathery heft to a stock that weighs just 16 ounces. "Most synthetic stocks exhibit what I call boat-hull technology: they're fiberglass," says Melvin. "I came up with a stock comprising carbon fiber and Kevlar. It's actually stiffer than the barrel."

Winchester M70 Shadow rifles chambered for WSSM rounds combine light weight, great reach.

The M20 stock has no pillars; an aluminum sleeve over the front guard screw prevents over-tightening. The classic lines of this stock, and tight fit to the metal, hardly seem right for the striped camouflage pattern Melvin prefers. But color and pattern remain customer options. There's no checkering; a roughened Dupont Imron finish gives you a grip. Melvin now offers a longer (3 3/8-inch) action for the 30-06. A Model 28 for magnum cartridges is larger in diameter. A 3-inch M28 handles the 6.5mm and 350 Remington Magnums, plus the newer Winchester and Remington Short Magnums. The 3 3/8-inch version accommodates the likes of the 7mm Remington. M40 Ultra Lights swallow cartridges as big as the 416 Rigby. A midget version takes 223-size rounds.

In March, 1999 Melvin Forbes sold Ultra Light Arms to Colt, which had just bought Saco, a heavy weapons factory in Maine. Colt intended to build M28 rifles there while Melvin and his crew, working for Colt, produced stocks in Morgantown. But then Colt got into financial trouble. Municipal lawsuits directed at

the gun industry sapped money committed to debt service. Absurd though the lawsuits proved, Colt was compelled to scrap the Ultra Light project and sold Saco to General Dynamics. Melvin bought Ultra Light back. Due to litigation involving Colt, Melvin's firm is now *New* Ultra Light Arms.

New Ultra Light rifles mirror the originals, with a 4140 chrome-moly receiver, Douglas Premium barrel, Timney trigger, Sako-style extractor and thumb safety that can be pushed down to allow bolt cycling with the firing mechanism locked. Melvin makes 1 1/2-ounce scope rings that fit directly to the receiver.

In 1986, two years after the Ultra Light M20 debuted, Remington re-entered the lightweight rifle business with its nimble 6 1/2-pound Mountain Rifle. Of mass-produced rifles this is still the archetype, but similar models have followed. Remington's own Model 7, with its 20-inch barrel, is more a carbine than a lightweight rifle, but it weighs the same. Winchester offers a Compact Model 70 with 22-inch barrel and slightly stubbed stock. Ruger's

Ultra Light has a 20-inch barrel, as does Browning's A-Bolt Micro-Hunter and Savage's Model 10 FM Sierra. The Ruger 77UL weighs 6 1/2 pounds, the Savage and Browning 6 1/4.

Beginning with the introduction of a six-lug Mark V rifle for standard cartridges about six years ago, Weatherby has developed several lightweight rifles. The first, chambered for standard cartridges, weighed 6 1/2 pounds. Its 24-inch barrel delivered better balance and higher chronograph readings than shorter tubes. In 1999 Weatherby followed the Lightweight with a 5 3/4-pound Ultra Lightweight, also sporting a 24-inch barrel. Additional fluting and some alloy parts pared ounces. In 2001 this rifle became the first from a commercial firm to chamber the .338-06. Weatherby's Super Predator Master, initially fashioned as a rifle for the walking coyote hunter, sold so well in 243, 7mm-08 and 308 chamberings that Weatherby rightly assumed that many shooters were using it on deer. The predictable response: the Super Big Game Master, a mouthful of title for a rifle of elegant simplicity. Like the Super Predator Master, it features a tan, hand-laminated stock of Aramid, graphite and fiberglass. The 24-inch blackened, fluted stainless barrel is from John Krieger's shop. It is button rifled, contoured to keep the weight of standard SBGM rifles down to 5 3/4 pounds. Magnums (with the 9-lug action and a 26-inch hammer-forged tube) weigh nearly a pound more.

Another recent lightweight rifle hails from Kimber. The Clackamas, Ore., company got its start in the 1980s with a Model 82 22 rimfire. Almost as petite, the Model 84 was chambered for the 17s, 222 and 223. The Kimber 89 looked like a

Weatherby's Ultra Lightweight and Super Big Game Master feature 24- to 26-inch fluted barrels.

Winchester M70 and chambered standard big game rounds like the 30-06. All these rifles were discontinued when Kimber crumbled under Chapter 7 in 1989. Les Edelman became majority stakeholder in the new Kimber company that emerged.

In 1998, Kimber fielded a new rimfire designed by Nehemiah Sirkis: the Kimber 22. The firm's next rifle, a pet project for sales chiefs Dwight Van Brunt and Ryan Busse, was the 84M. Chambered in 243, 260, 7-08 and 308 (also 22-250), it weighs 5 3/4 pounds with a 22-inch barrel. Stockmaker Darwin Hensley shaped the trim Claro walnut stock. Checkered 20 lines to the inch, it is glassed and pillar-bedded to the action; the barrel floats. The 84M has a clean-breaking trigger, a claw extractor, steel bottom metal and an M70-style safety. The newer 8400 is similar but chambered for Winchester Short Magnum (WSM) cartridges. The latest Kimber is the Kevlar-stocked Montana, available in standard chamberings at less than 5 1/2 pounds.

The trend toward lighter rifles has had help from custom shops. Pleasanton, Texas gunmaker Lex Webernick (830-569-2055) has long specialized in lightweight rifles. Lex mates Winchester M70 and Remington M700 receivers to his "Rifles, Incorporated" stocks, and barrels of the customer's choosing. His muzzle brake is unobtrusive but effective. "Many hunters still want the reach of a 300 Winchester Magnum," Lex says. "And no matter how well-proportioned a stock, that much recoil will make a 5 1/2-pound rifle jump!" As do all the best custom makers, Lex trues the action so the bolt, barrel and receiver share the same axis, and so bolt lugs seat squarely.

A Webernick rifle I've used has an M70 action and a 24-inch barrel in 260 Remington. The ultra-slim grip is a trifle short for my hand, but its open shape makes for fast pointing. The short forend works fine because Lex had placed the front swivel stud on the forend's nose, where it won't hang up in cases or scabbards. You don't need forend beyond the swivel. This rifle proved ideal for a caribou hunt that took me miles from camp on foot. I found bulls that other hunters had not seen, and managed to sneak close to one with heavy beams and bezes. He dropped to a 120-gr. Nosler Ballistic Tip. I've since used Lex's rifles in my women's outdoor skills program, High Country Adventures. The slim grips fit small hands, and a thick, spongy butt-pad attenuates kick.

You can get custom and semi-custom rifles from many shops. Mark Bansner (717-484-2370) is a well-known name in Pennsylvania; Brown Precision (530-384-2506) qualifies as an institution on the West Coast. Kenny Jarrett (www.jarrettrifles.com), who built a reputation with super-accurate long-range rifles, now offers lightweights too. My friend, Texas gunmaker Charlie Sisk (936-258-4984), is leaning more and more to handier rifles, though he's still fussy about accuracy.

You can't truly appreciate carrying lightweight rifles until you've learned to shoot them. The key is to take control of the rifle. Heavy rifles require less of your participation. Be a good pedestal and don't wreck the shot, and the rifle will plant the bullet close to point of aim. Rifles that point like wands, on the other hand, must be *held*, not merely supported. The shot must be *pursued*, because you may not have time to wait for the rifle to fire itself. You must do more than bear the weight; you must tame the bounce, subdue the nervous energy between your hands.

Joe Arterburn killed this fine Texas whitetail with a lightweight Winchester 70 in 223 WSSM.

Remington's Alaska Wilderness Rifle delivers magnum punch in a featherweight package.

Balance with a slight tip to muzzle helps lightweight rifles point quickly and hold surely offhand.

To help a light rifle settle down, I favor a leather sling with an adjustable loop (Brownell's Latigo, for example: www.brownells.com). Bipods add weight and lack versatility. Stoney Point (507-354-3360) markets collapsible shooting sticks that I like better. For best results, plant the legs well forward and pull the intersection of the sticks toward you, using your left hand to keep the rifle's forend secure on the sticks.

Lightweight rifles can be very hard to shoot accurately if they have rough, heavy triggers. Indeed, unmanageable triggers are largely responsible for the myth that lightweight rifles aren't accurate. A trigger that requires muscle causes rifle movement, sending the shot astray. A consistent trigger that breaks like a slender glass shard is invaluable. I like a 2-pound trigger; it's stiff enough to prevent a cold, gloved finger from prematurely tripping the sear. But it's responsive enough that you can easily fire the rifle within a few seconds. (Hold the rifle too long, and your muscles will tire.) If your rifle doesn't have a suitable trigger, buy an aftermarket trigger from Shilen, Timney or Bold. In my rack is a 25 Souper from Charlie Sisk. It has a Jewell trigger. This rifle shoots well because it enables *me* to shoot as well as I can.

The contribution of a good trigger is hard to overestimate. Last winter I was shooting what may be the lightest rifle at market: a 3 3/4-pound take-down from Kifaru, International (800-222-6139). This wand is built on Remington's Model Seven action. My sample had fluted 18 1/2inch Shilen match-grade barrels in .260 and .308. Changing was easy: twist one out and the other in. Thin-walled barrels get hot quickly, so Patrick Smith, the rifle's designer, gave these barrels a half-length Kevlar sleeve that matches the stock. It's attractive, functional. A screw on the receiver ring locks into a detent in the threads so the barrel can't back out. After zeroing with the 260 barrel and a Kahles 3-9x scope, I sat on the ground and snugged up my sling. Three bullets went into a 1 3/4-inch cluster at 100 yards. I stood and loosed three more rounds. That group taped 3 7/8 inches. I seldom shoot much better than that, sitting or offhand. Patrick correctly attributes the rifle's fine performance from hunting positions to its crisp, light trigger.

Balance matters too, of course. Shoulder a best-quality English upland gun, and you'll think it's alive. You don't have to point it because it points itself. Balancing and profiling a rifle must be done at the same time if you are to get that uncanny pointability. It's more art than science, more than just getting to the proper fulcrum. Grip and forend must be relatively straight and ovoid in cross-section, with a slight flare low to keep your hand in place. But neither should be "hand-filling." Rather, they must be slim to allow the rifle to pivot easily and rotate slightly as you bring the rifle to your shoulder or swing on a deer that's moving fast.

You're smart to keep the center of gravity low in lightweight rifles, which means you'll use a trim, lightweight scope mounted tight to the receiver. You don't need a powerful scope for hunting deer anyway, and oversize front lenses are wasted in normal hunting light and at magnifications of less than 8x. I prefer a 4x32 scope for most of my big game hunting. A 6x with a 36mm objective gives you all the power you'll need and all the light your eye can use, even at long range at dusk. Prefer variables? Try a 2.5-8x Leupold VX-III or a Nikon or Kahles 2-7x, or a 3-9x36 Swarovski. Bushnell's 3200 and 4200 lines offer fine value, as does the Burris Fullfield II stable. Mount the scope so you catch a full field when your cheek lies as far forward on the comb as it comes when you shoulder the rifle quickly.

The trend toward lightweight rifles will continue as surely as hunters age. The new short magnum cartridges help fuel it by packing lots of horsepower into small actions. But recoil that leads to a flinch will impair your shooting. For this reason, it makes sense to stick with cartridges that don't beat you up. Truly, few animals get away because rifles or cartridges fall short. Many escape to die later because deer hunters shoot poorly. These loads deliver all the reach and power you need for deer, without cracking your scapula or dislodging your dentures.

	muz.	100 yds	200 yds	300 yds	400 yds
243 Winchester					
Federal 100 Sierra GameKing BTSP					
velocity, fps:	2960	2760	2570	2380	2210
energy, ft-lb:	1950	1690	1460	1260	1080
MRT:		+1.5	0	-6.8	-19.8
Hornady 100 BTSP LM					
velocity, fps:	3100	2839	2592	2358	2138
energy, ft-lb:	2133	1790	1491	1235	1014
MRT:		+1.5	0	-6.8	-19.8
Win. 95 Ballistic Silvertip					
velocity, fps:	3100	2854	2626	2410	2203
energy, ft-lb:	2021	1719	1455	1225	1024
MRT:		+1.4	0	-6.4	-18.9
6mm Remington					
Federal 100 Nosler Partition					
velocity, fps:	3100	2860	2640	2420	2220
energy, ft-lb:	2135	1820	1545	1300	1090
MRT:		+1.4	0	-6.3	-18.7

To keep recoil from causing a flinch, mate lightweight guns with manageable cartridges.

	muz.	100 yds	200 yds	300 yds	400 yds

6mm Remington (cont.)

Hornady 100 SPBT LM

	muz.	100 yds	200 yds	300 yds	400 yds
velocity, fps:	3250	2997	2756	2528	2311
energy, ft-lb:	2345	1995	1687	1418	1186
MRT:		+1.6	0	-6.3	-18.2

Rem. 100 PSP boat-tail

	muz.	100 yds	200 yds	300 yds	400 yds
velocity, fps:	3100	2852	2617	2394	2183
energy, ft-lb:	2134	1806	1521	1273	1058
MRT:		+1.4	0	-6.5	-19.1

240 Weatherby Mag.

Wby. 90 Barnes-X

	muz.	100 yds	200 yds	300 yds	400 yds
velocity, fps:	3500	3222	2962	2717	2484
energy, ft-lb:	2448	2075	1753	1475	1233
MRT:		+2.6	+3.3	0	-8.0

Wby. 95 Nosler Bal. Tip

	muz.	100 yds	200 yds	300 yds	400 yds
velocity, fps:	3420	3146	2888	2645	2414
energy, ft-lb:	2467	2087	1759	1475	1229
MRT:		+2.7	+3.5	0	-8.4

Wby. 100 Nosler Partition

	muz.	100 yds	200 yds	300 yds	400 yds
velocity, fps:	3406	3136	2882	2642	2415
energy, ft-lb:	2576	2183	1844	1550	1294
MRT:		+2.8	+3.5	0	-8.4
MRT:		+1.7	0	-7.6	-21.8

25-06 Remington

Federal 100 Nosler Bal. Tip

	muz.	100 yds	200 yds	300 yds	400 yds
velocity, fps:	3210	2960	2720	2490	2280
energy, ft-lb:	2290	1940	1640	1380	1150
MRT:		+1.2	0	-6.0	-17.5

Lightweight rifles can be very accurate. A Tikka fired this group.

Hornady 117 SP boat-tail LM

	muz.	100 yds	200 yds	300 yds	400 yds
velocity, fps:	3110	2855	2613	2384	2168
energy, ft-lb:	2512	2117	1774	1476	1220
MRT:		+1.8	0	-7.1	-20.3

25-06 Remington (cont.)

Win. 115 Ballistic Silvertip

	muz.	100 yds	200 yds	300 yds	400 yds
velocity, fps:	3060	2825	2603	2390	2188
energy, ft-lb:	2391	2038	1729	1459	1223
MRT:		+1.4	0	-6.6	-19.2

260 Remington

Federal 140 Sierra GameKing BTSP

	muz.	100 yds	200 yds	300 yds	400 yds
velocity, fps:	2750	2570	2390	2220	2060
energy, ft-lb:	2350	2045	1775	1535	1315
MRT:		+1.9	0	-8.0	-23.1

Rem. 120 Nosler Bal. Tip

	muz.	100 yds	200 yds	300 yds	400 yds
velocity, fps:	2890	2688	2494	2309	2131
energy, ft-lb:	2226	1924	1657	1420	1210
MRT:		+1.7	0	-7.3	-21.1

Rem. 125 Nosler Partition

	muz.	100 yds	200 yds	300 yds	400 yds
velocity, fps:	2875	2669	2473	2285	2105
energy, ft-lb:	2294	1977	1697	1449	1230
MRT:		+1.71	0	-7.4	-21.4

270 Winchester

Federal 130 Sierra GameKing

	muz.	100 yds	200 yds	300 yds	400 yds
velocity, fps:	3060	2830	2620	2410	2220
energy, ft-lb:	2700	2320	1980	1680	1420
MRT:		+1.4	0	-6.5	-19.0

Hornady 130 SST LM

	muz.	100 yds	200 yds	300 yds	400 yds
velocity, fps:	3215	2998	2790	2590	2400
energy, ft-lb:	2983	2594	2246	1936	1662
MRT:		+1.2	0	-5.8	-17.0

Rem. 130 Swift Scirocco

	muz.	100 yds	200 yds	300 yds	400 yds
velocity, fps:	3060	2838	2677	2425	2232
energy, ft-lb:	2702	2325	1991	1697	1438
MRT:		+1.4	0	-6.5	-18.8

7mm-08 Remington

Federal 140 Nosler Bal. Tip

	muz.	100 yds	200 yds	300 yds	400 yds
velocity, fps:	2800	2610	2430	2260	2100
energy, ft-lb:	2440	2135	1840	1590	1360
MRT:		+1.8	0	-7.7	-22.3

Rem. 140 Nosler Bal. Tip

	muz.	100 yds	200 yds	300 yds	400 yds
velocity, fps:	2860	2670	2488	2313	2145
energy, ft-lb:	2543	2217	1925	1663	1431
MRT:		+1.7	0	-7.3	-21.2

Win. 140 Power-Point Plus

	muz.	100 yds	200 yds	300 yds	400 yds
velocity, fps:	2875	2597	2336	2090	1859
energy, ft-lb:	2570	1997	1697	1358	1075
MRT:		+2.0	0	-8.8	26.0

	muz.	100 yds	200 yds	300 yds	400 yds
280 Remington					
Federal 140 Sierra Pro-Hunt.					
velocity, fps:	2990	2740	2500	2270	2060
energy, ft-lb:	2770	2325	1940	1605	1320
MRT:		+1.6	0	-7.0	-20.8
Rem. 140 Nosler Bal. Tip					
velocity, fps:	3000	2804	2616	2436	2263
energy, ft-lb:	2799	2445	2128	1848	1593
MRT:		+1.5	0	-6.8	-19.0
Win. 140 Ballistic Silvertip					
velocity, fps:	3040	2842	2653	2471	2297
energy, ft-lb:	2872	2511	2187	1898	1640
MRT:		+1.4	0	-6.3	-18.4

	muz.	100 yds	200 yds	300 yds	400 yds
308 Winchester					
Hornady 150 SP LM					
velocity, fps:	2980	2703	2442	2195	1964
energy, ft-lb:	2959	2433	1986	1606	1285
MRT:		+1.6	0	-7.5	-22.2
Rem. 150 Swift Scirocco					
velocity, fps:	2820	2611	2410	2219	2037
energy, ft-lb:	2648	2269	1935	1640	1381
MRT:		+1.8	0	-7.8	-22.7
Win. 150 Ballistic Silvertip					
velocity, fps:	2810	2601	2401	2211	2028
energy, ft-lb:	2629	2253	1920	1627	1370
MRT:		+1.8	0	-7.8	-22.8

MRT = mid-range trajectory in inches

No matter your choice of rifle and cartridge, you'll find deer hunting most pleasant when the load on your shoulder is light, both during carry and recoil. You'll stay fresh longer, cover more country – and shoot better too.

◇◇◇◇◇◇◇◇◇◇

ECONOMICAL LIGHTWEIGHTS

Factory-built bolt guns haven't changed much in the last 40 years, but variations have proliferated. The main models have been trimmed and given lightweight barrels and stocks. Not all of the resulting rifles balance well or point like a fine grouse gun. But they do ease your burden on the trail, and you can get 'em for not much more than a standard bolt-action. Other lightweights have been designed from the ground up to carry all day. Here are a few of both types:

Lever Actions:
Marlin Model 1894, 6.5 lbs.
Winchester Model 94 Trapper or Traditional, 6.3 lbs.

Bolt Actions:
Remington Model 700 Mountain Rifle, 6.5 lbs.
Remington Model 700 Titanium, 5.5 lbs.
Remington Model Seven AWR (short Ultra Mag), 6.5 lbs.
Ruger Model 77 Mark II Ultra Light, 6.0 lbs.
Ruger Model 77/44RS, 6.0 lbs.
Savage Model 16FSS, 6.0 lbs.
Tikka Model T3 Lightweight, 6.0 lbs.
Weatherby Mark V Super Big Game Master, from 5.8 lbs.
Winchester Model 70 Classic Compact, 6.0 lbs.
Winchester Model 70 Ultimate Shadow (WSM), 6.5 lbs.

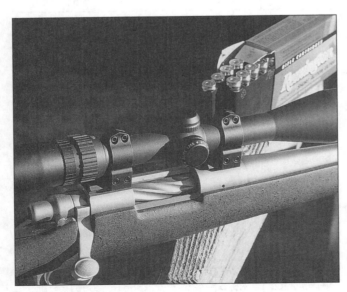

Remington's Titanium M700 weighs less than 6 pounds but offers fine accuracy.

HIT—OR MISS?

Simple tips and techniques to help you hit what you're aiming at

By Rick Sapp

It was cold already in Minnesota's early gun season. Despite my straining and squirming and pinching myself, my eyelids were creeping downward. The solution? Coffee, of course. Lots of coffee.

For every cause there is an effect, however, and coffee's diuretic properties are a vexation. Soon nature wasn't merely calling; she was hollering. I placed the shotgun in the gun rack, fumbled for the pee bottle and stood up. It was only then that I saw antlers. With a hunter's belated instinct, I instantly froze.

It was a dandy buck and not 75 yards away, angling from left to right in front of me. Because the deer was so close, I believed it would notice the movement if I risked standing up completely or sitting down again.

My hand slid toward the Winchester 1300 pump and, still in a half-crouch, I carefully lifted it upward, mounted it against my right shoulder and flicked off the safety. Shooting at less than 75 yards, I was confident of a quick, clean kill.

When the buck reached an open spot about 60 yards away and 30 degrees to my right, I

Flinching from an unexpected noise, a stunning flash or a physical shock is natural. Whatever kind of gun you shoot, you must learn to control your reaction to the explosion of the shot if you plan to consistently achieve tight groups.

squeezed the trigger. It took me by complete surprise when the deer bounded away. I fired again. Inspecting the deer's path a few minutes later confirmed two clean misses.

I was more than disappointed. I was puzzled. I was familiar with the gun and confident of the shot. What could have gone wrong?

Plenty, that's what. While it may be a poor carpenter who blames his tools, sometimes misses can be traced to the gun or the scope. Sometimes, however, the shooter is responsible, either because of poor technique, bad habit, or good old-fashioned bad luck. Whatever the cause, missing is obviously no fun. It pays to understand how misses happen and what can be done to avoid them.

No matter whether you're shooting a rifle, a shotgun, a handgun, or a muzzleloader, failure to score in the field can be attributed to only two causes: hardware (i.e., the gun and its accoutrements) or operator error. Fortunately, remedies exist for both of them.

Hardware

The Heartbreak of Flinching

Flinching, the fearful anticipation of the hefty muzzle blast and recoil of a deer gun, may seem to be an operator error, but it always starts with the gun itself. No one ever flinches when shooting a Daisy Red Ryder. Flinching is a learned habit and it can be overcome, but it requires serious attention to loads, comfort accessories and the gun itself.

It doesn't take a .458 Winchester Magnum or a .454 Casull to cause flinch. A friend in Oregon has experimented with dropping from a 170-grain Speer to a 165-grain Barnes and then to a 150-grain Speer to reduce the shock from his 30-30 Winchester. If you're flinching and suspect that recoil is to blame, perhaps you should outfit your shooting iron with a recoil-reducing item such as the C & H Mercury Recoil Reducer (rifles), a Kick Eez Sorbothane recoil pad (shotguns), or a new set of better-fitting grips (handguns).

If you miss deer occasionally because you cannot seem to pull the trigger and, when you do pull it, you flinch, you may be over-gunned. Try – at least temporarily – shooting a smaller caliber. Lay aside your 300 Winchester Magnum and begin shooting groups with a .22 or even a Daisy or a Crosman. Get used to pulling the trigger again without experiencing the blast and shock of your deer rifle. Build a good habit.

If recoil is causing you to flinch, options include extending the forcing cone on your current rifle barrel or having it ported, although these may be more effective at reducing muzzle rise and making a second shot easier than reducing recoil. More extreme suggestions are to bore holes in the butt behind the plate and fill them with lead or, on a shotgun, to replace the plastic magazine plug with a heavy steel plug on the assumption that heavier firearms absorb more recoil energy.

If excessive noise is the source of your flinch, porting certainly isn't the answer. Hearing protection is. Gunfire causes sharp bursts of high levels of noise. The human "pain threshold" is considered to be 125

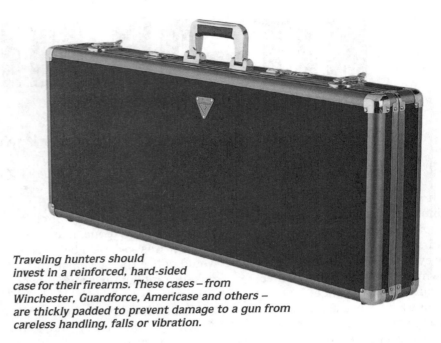

Traveling hunters should invest in a reinforced, hard-sided case for their firearms. These cases – from Winchester, Guardforce, Americase and others – are thickly padded to prevent damage to a gun from careless handling, falls or vibration.

dB. Your first .22? Figure 140 dB. Your 12 gauge slug gun? Figure a whopping 152 dB, and that astonishing noise level is immediately adjacent to your ear. A jet engine winding up is only 140 dB. (Only?)

Several companies, notably Bob Walker's Game Ear, have approached the problem scientifically. Their Game Ear II, for instance, features adjustable frequency tuning. This means you can amplify specific sound frequencies and modify or eliminate others. Thus you can hear a deer walking, but when you put the .243 to your cheek and pull the trigger, the tiny, built-in electronic interruption circuit will muffle the noise of the blast. This saves your hearing and reduces the flinch reaction.

No Wiggle Room

A scoped gun must be re-sighted each year or before every hunt, whichever comes first. Even if it travels to deer camp in a thickly padded, hard-sided case, you should arrive in deer camp in time to verify its accuracy. Scopes shift. Airport baggage handlers are merciless with luggage, especially luggage marked "Fragile."

A more subtle cause for scope misalignment may be the slight, continuous vibration of being carried in a car. A drop of LocTite (not the permanent kind) on the scope's base screws and eternal vigilance in the field will keep your scope positioned squarely

Travel by any means causes unaccountable changes in your scope alignment. You should always arrive at a hunting destination in time to check your zero.

The shooting range before hunting season is where you iron any of the kinks out of your shooting system: gun, scope, mounts and rings, recoil pads and ammo. Once you have tight groups at your chosen distance, find a place to practice some of those odd and unexpected shot presentations that deer will inevitably give you in the woods.

imagine this strategy maximizes their dollar. It does not.

Practicing and hunting with different types of ammo is foolish. Buy the best ammunition your ego requires and your wallet can afford. Remington Premier and Safari Grade, Federal Premium High Energy, and Black Hills Gold, among others, are premium rifle loads from premium manufacturers. Premium shells have top-shelf features such as corrosion-resistant nickel plating and lacquered primers for absolute moisture resistance. In my experience, you cannot consistently and economically handload a shell as good as these.

On the other hand, you may not need an expensive, premium bullet for deer. Even a big buck is a small creature compared to an elk or a moose. For deer, you want a fast-opening bullet for immediate disruption of the vitals and in this category, bullets such as the Hornaday SST or Sierra GameKing may be excellent for your shooting needs.

My friend, Canadian writer Ian McMurchy says, "Every barrel makes its own rules." It is true. Shoot a variety of ammo

on its mounts. Changes in altitude and temperature can also affect the zero because scope mounts, especially aluminum or see-through models, can expand and contract at different rates from the scope tube or the gun barrel. So zero your gun at a shooting range near your hunting site and check it often.

Ammo

I know hunters who use old or just plain cheap ammo for zeroing their gun but upgrade to more expensive ammo for hunting. Apparently, the idea is that they can burn a couple boxes of shells zeroing their gun, but they may only get one shot all season at a trophy deer. They

Practice with the same loads or shells with which you will hunt. Although it might be scientifically accurate to think of a gun as a soulless mechanical device, individual guns express preferences for particular loads and you can unlock their secret language by studying down-range performance. (Photo courtesy Tim Hooey)

and you will find one or two that perform best in your gun. Remember however that if you spend several thousand dollars on the hunt of a lifetime, there is no possible justification for saving a few bucks on ammo. So practice and zero your gun with the same ammo with which you intend to take your trophy.

Let's Keep It Clean, Guys

Dave Meredith, director of customer service for CVA, says the formula for shooting accuracy is simple: Clean-Clean-Clean and Practice-Practice-Practice. Of course, CVA means black powder shooting, but the principles of cleaning and practice apply to any gun, from your synthetic-stocked Remington 700 chambered for .270 Winchester or your six-round Ruger Redhawk in .44 magnum.

Dirty guns shoot dirty. There is no reason not to perform at least the minimum acceptable level of cleaning, i.e., wiping the gun's surface to remove the skin oil, dirt and debris that a hot gun attracts naturally and swabbing a de-leading patch through its bore and chamber. Shotgunners and muzzleloader hunters may find that they have to periodically remove the plastic fouling deposited in the bore by sabots.

Rifles and handguns are subject to lead and copper fouling. These literally plate the bore of your gun, interfering with the rifling, and they can be tough to remove. The Outers Foul Out System is one excellent way to remove metal fouling. A less attractive alternative is to spend half a day with a brass or bronze brush and a bottle of solvent.

Operator Error

Flashback to those Minnesota woods, me standing with my shotgun in hand, watching an unscathed buck escape through the scrub: There's got to be something wrong here, I thought. But what?

Before I began to tinker with my shotgun, I discussed the problem of accurate shooting with NRA Pistol Instructor Phillip Suggs at Bradford Sportsman's Farm in Graham, Florida. I did not want to miss another fine buck, especially on an easy shot. Suggs, who knocks spinning aspirin out of the air at a hundred yards and shoots skeet with a handgun, was a voice of wisdom and experience.

"It usually isn't the gun that is shooting poorly," Suggs said, "unless it is damaged … and it takes a lot of carelessness to bang up a modern gun so that it won't shoot straight. Usually, it is the guy behind the gun who needs the help."

Certainly, things can go wrong with a gun, Suggs said, shaking his head. "Drop a gun on a cement floor or use it for a hammer – I've seen guys do that – and you can bend its sights or cause a round to jam and will certainly knock the scope out of alignment. In these cases, you may be able to fix the problem yourself … or you may need a certified gunsmith to have a look. Unless you have broken a lens,

NRA Pistol Instructor Phillip Suggs says it is not usually the gun that is at fault when a shot misses its target. "Usually, it is the guy behind the gun who needs the help," he says.

you can re-mount a scope; sights you can bend back into place."

In Suggs' experience, inconsistent, inaccurate shooting is a shooter matter, not a gun matter. "It doesn't matter what kind of gun you shoot," he said, "pistol, black powder, rifle or shotgun. If you begin to tinker in any fundamental way, keep the telephone number of a competent gunsmith handy. You'll need it."

Here are a couple of tips to help you build deer-hunting accuracy with any firearm:

Your Eyes

If you are unhappy with your accuracy, have your eyes checked. It is not just baseball umpires who need glasses. Unless you can see your target clearly, in crisp definition, you certainly should not hunt with a gun. A local optician's office may be your first, best stop.

My eye protection preference is a pair or prescription contact lenses under a pair of impact-resistant sunglasses specifically made for shooting. This combination maximizes protection and visual acuity. Olympic Optical manufactures polycarbonate-lens shooting glasses for Smith & Wesson. A pair of their frameless, wrap-around Ozone gray-tinted glasses give you superb coverage and UV protection, too. If you can see well, there is no reason that you should not be able to shoot well.

Additionally, the combination of contact lenses and shooting glasses gives you the most versatility in lens tints for any kind of weather. Yellow and orange tints brighten and block the day's muddy blues; reds increase contrast; gray and green cut glare without altering basic colors. As long as you keep your lenses clean and scratch-free, you will go a long way to shooting accuracy.

Unless you are a superb stalker or have one killer ground blind location, even an excellent shot will need to put a scope on a handgun for deer hunting. Depending upon the power and size of the handgun, a low power, fixed-magnification, fully multi-coated scope such as a Burris 2X in non-reflective black matte can be a good choice. According to Burris, this scope's "Ballistic Plex" reticle style is designed to deal with a handgun's "more lofty trajectories."

If you can't see it, you can't hit it. It's as simple as that.

Your Shooting Form

The second major operator-induced cause for missing a trophy buck is improper shooting form. This is the most likely reason for my spectacular misses in the Minnesota woods. At the time, I was scrunched around a treestand, twisting to my "wrong side" and shooting offhand, but that's just an excuse. Practice beforehand could have saved the day.

You must practice for an awkward target presentation. In deer hunting, you know, the typical shot will not give you much time to savor a deep, calming breath, then carefully aim and squeeze one off.

Unless you are hunting a planted green field, your shot at a buck moving through the woods will normally be quick and dirty. If you practice shooting from unusual positions and

at odd angles, you should be sufficiently prepared when some impertinent book buck suddenly boogies into view. Practice replaces nervous tension with confidence. So, practice, practice, practice.

Tommy Brown, a Florida optometrist and pistol shooter, reminds us that on a moving deer, our eyes focus on only one thing at a time. They will either focus on the deer's vitals or they will focus on the gun's sights. If you have practiced mounting your gun and shooting at unusual angles, when the "moment of truth" arrives your sights will align automatically.

Of course, just what constitutes correct shooting form depends on the type of gun we're using. Take shotguns, for instance. Normally we think of a scattergun as a pointing weapon, not an aiming weapon like a rifle or handgun. A shotgunner leans forward, into his target. A rifleman or handgun shooter is

Sean Hooey's first deer by muzzleloader. If you teach your youngsters proper shooting form, equip them with gear that fits, show them responsible hunting skills and how to care for their equipment, you will have done your part to pass along the American hunting tradition. (Photo courtesy Tim Hooey)

The result of paying attention to the details is a buck hanging from the skinning pole. The secret – if it can officially be called a secret – is clean – clean – clean and practice – practice – practice.

centered, with weight equally distributed or even slightly back.

When you scope a shotgun, however, you transform it into a powerful but less accurate rifle, one that is not capable of precision shooting beyond a couple hundred yards. For a scoped slug- or sabot-loaded shotgun, you must learn to squeeze the trigger as you would a rifle rather than snap it as if you were shooting a clay game.

Instructors for trap or upland game bird hunting, for example, train you to keep both eyes open.

Rely on a permanent cheek-stock spot, they insist, to place your dominant eye view straight along the sighting plane of the rib. With a scoped gun, you want only your dominant eye behind the crosshairs. The other eye will typically be closed.

Whatever you are shooting, keep your head down and into the shot. A habit of peeking or looking around the gun when you pull the trigger will cause a miss.

Accurate shooters take care of the three most critical parts of their gun: sights or scope, barrel

and ammo. Accurate shooters take care of themselves by protecting their vision and hearing. Accurate shooters pay attention to basic principles of good shooting form, applying them wherever possible in hunting situations.

In a perfect world, accuracy would be a matter simply of tightening a screw or pushing a switch. That's not the case, obviously. In this world, deer-hunting accuracy is as much a quality of the person behind the gun as it is of the gun itself. ✦

Professional Gunsmiths Recommend

The gunsmiths at Pickett Weaponry in Newberry, Fla., have worked on thousands of guns since the shooting sports store opened in 1978. "Our philosophy," says co-owner Carl Pickett, "is to stock the store with people who love and understand guns. In that respect, we are different from a shoe store where virtually anyone can work. We have a hands-on business. Customers can come here to browse or ask for help, whatever they want."

Carl's work, and that of gunsmith Nick Garrett as well, does not take place "out front" with customers, but in small, cluttered rooms in the back of the store. Their job is to make guns shoot straight and smooth. In this respect, they stress two points: 1) "firelapping" a new gun and 2) giving it the best possible trigger.

Firelapping, Nick says, is the term for "shooting-in" or polishing a barrel—actually burnishing the bore—with the projectile. It can be an effective accuracy-enhancing technique for rifles, handguns, or rifled shotguns. Although guns usually come from the manufacturer in excellent condition, tiny irregularities left in the barrel when its lands and grooves are machined will cause shooting irregularities. Copper and moisture-collecting grime build up at

these points and cause "hot spots," points of high friction. The result is a less-than-consistent accuracy.

To fire-lap your deer gun, Garrett suggests that you take about 30 rounds of your favorite ammo plus plenty of cleaning patches and go to the range. Fire a round and then pull a patch with solvent through the barrel, drawing the patch from the chamber to the muzzle. Repeat this shoot-and-clean process 10 times and then clean your barrel thoroughly. Advance to two rounds before pulling a patch and solvent followed now by a dry patch through the barrel, halting after 10 rounds. Re-clean the barrel. Repeat the whole process again with three shots and the wet-dry patch routine. That's all there is to it.

Firelapping is designed to complete the barrel polishing and smoothing process for shooters who are interested in true minute of angle accuracy (and of course, this should be all hunters). Both Garrett and Pickett, plus thousands of independent testimonials, verify that the process almost always tightens your groups, and sometimes it tightens them dramatically.

The second action you can take to increase accuracy – according to Garrett it is the number one thing – is adjusting the trigger. Both Pickett and Garrett tell

horror stories however, about trigger systems that customers had "fixed" or "adjusted" themselves.

"The trigger is a delicate mechanism," Garrett says. "Although it isn't terribly complicated, it is a very balanced system. Too many things can go wrong if you don't know exactly what you are doing."

Manufacturers set most triggers between six and nine pounds pull. A relatively easy and inexpensive adjustment by a gunsmith can reduce the pull to around three pounds and smooth out the action at the same time.

"If you sight on a deer and begin to pull the trigger," Garrett says, "you don't want to have to pull forever and you don't want bumps in the pull or friction between the trigger and the frame as this can throw the firing pin off its track. The point of trigger work is to allow the gun to go off when you want it to."

The gunsmiths at Pickett Weaponry insisted that such attention to detail as firelapping and refining the trigger pull provide small increases in accuracy. "Take them all together though," Pickett says, "and they can add up to the difference between venison on the table and a long track after a gut-shot deer."

Carl Pickett (left) and Nick Garrett are the gunsmiths at Pickett Weaponry in Newberry, Florida. They say a shooter can take two important measures to help their bullets arrive consistently at a deer's vitals. One of these, which long gun owners themselves can (and should) perform themselves, especially with new guns, is called "firelapping." The second, applicable to both long guns and handguns, is trigger refurbishing, but this, they insist, should be left to a competent and experienced gunsmith.

The Hammer of THOR

Rooted in the past, today's semi-auto deer guns pack a sophisticated punch

By Dan Shideler

The day dawned crunchy-cold on November 21, 2001, in the remoteness of Missaukee County, Michigan. My assignment that morning was to bring back an antlerless camp deer to feed an increasingly resentful band of hunters who had begun making hurtful remarks about my beanie-weenies.

Okay, then. I donned my blaze orange, picked up my rifle, and headed into a sugar maple grove a few hundred yards from camp. A light scattering of snow had settled on the ground, and the bare maple branches clacked and clattered in the stiff breeze. I clambered into my blind and waited to see what the well-worn deer trails might bring me.

I didn't have long to wait. Not two minutes later, a gray-brown blur entered the grove stage right and trotted toward me. Perfect. A medium-sized doe, one that hunters in my circle would call "a good eatin' deer."

I raised my rifle and squeezed off. *Ka-blang!* An intervening maple sapling blew out at its waist and toppled over. That was more than enough excitement for the doe, who hoisted her flag, popped her clutch, and lit out for the territories. As she angled away from me, I brought the bead down and squeezed the trigger. *Ka-blang!* again, and the doe flipped bum over tea kettle and came to rest in a heap.

Even a 90-year-old Winchester Model 1910 semi-auto can still feed a deer camp.

Out of habit, I bent down to retrieve my empties. One was lost forever, but the bright brass headstamp of the other winked up at me from the snow: 401 WSL. The mighty 401 Winchester Self Loading.

That doe was probably the first deer taken in Michigan with a 401 Winchester semi-auto rifle in decades. Back before WWII, however, you didn't have to spend much time at all in the deer woods before someone would show up with one-a them new-fangled repeaters. In those dim distant days, semi-autos (known then as self-loaders or autoloaders) were one of the greatest technological marvels ever to grace the deer woods. And nowadays, even in this age of GPS and laser sights, they still are.

For a quick follow-up shot, nothing beats a semi-auto. True, a skilled operator of a lever- or bolt-action can deliver two, three, or even more targeted shots surprisingly fast. But some of us need all the help we can get, and the semi-auto can provide that winning edge.

Some may deride semi-autos as clunky, unreliable, and ugly. However, a survey of the market reveals that today's semi-auto deer rifles have reached the pinnacle of efficiency, performance, and, yes, even of style. But it was a different picture entirely at the start of the twentieth century, when semi-autos made their appearance.

The great-grand-daddy of all modern semi-auto deer guns was the Remington model 8, patented by—who else?—John M. Browning in 1903. The model 8 hit the market in 1906, and it immediately created a furor. Bearing the trademark humpbacked receiver of Browning's revolutionary Auto-5 shotgun, the Model 8 operated on a long-recoil principle that required the barrel to blow backward against the bolt under recoil, thus ejecting the fired case and cocking the hammer as the bolt raced forward to scoop up a fresh round from the magazine and re-lock itself. Whew.

The Model 8 worked, though it functioned with all the delicacy of two Penn Central freightcars coupling. Chambered in 25, 30, 32, and 35 Remington (all but the 35 being rimless knockoffs of well-established Winchester rimmed cartridges), the Model 8 was successful enough to receive a facelift in 1936 as the Model 81 and keep its place in the Remington line until 1950.

Winchester, meanwhile, was busy reworking its Model 1903 22 rimfire self-loader (the first successful American sporting semi-auto) into something suitable for deer. Doing the best they could on short notice, they rolled out the Model 1905 self-loader. The Model 1905 chambered two dubious pipsqueaks, the 32 and 35 Winchester Self Loading. These anemic cartridges looked, and were, underpowered for deer at ranges greater than 10 feet, so in 1907 the good folks in New Haven introduced the Model 1907 in 351 WSL, basically a longer version of the 35 WSL. The 351 case was just a smidge longer than that of today's 357 Magnum, and ballistics of the two are roughly comparable.

Since John Browning's long-recoil patents were locked up tighter than a Chubb bank vault, Winchester's self-loaders were based on a blowback design that used a fairly substantial breechblock to balance out the recoil generated by the cartridges. It wasn't the best possible solution–blowback actions are suited for rimfires, not centerfires–but it got Winchester into the game.

The problem with the 1907 was the cartridge, not the rifle. The 351 WSL was an okay deer-killer at short range, no more than that, and it was hampered by a 180-gr. hard-nosed bullet that obstinately refused to expand. Also, the little cartridge looked mighty unimpressive to serious deer hunters. In those days, if you entered the woods with a gun chambering a cartridge much smaller than a 30-30, you were looked on as a sissy-boy who drank coffee with your pinky lifted. The 1907 was tolerated in the deer woods, but it couldn't compete with Remington's Model 8.

Frustrated at missing out on a seat on the semi-auto bandwagon, Winchester rolled up its sleeves, said enough's enough, and introduced the Model 1910 chambered for the mighty 401 WSL. Advertised with the unforgettable tagline "It Hits Like the Hammer of Thor," the 401 really delivered the goods with power equivalent to today's 44 Magnum cartridge.

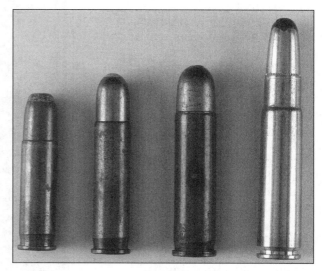

(Left to right): The 35 Winchester Self Loading gave way to the 351 WSL and finally the 401 WSL. The 35 Remington, though, was still the cartridge to beat.

Like the cartridge it chambered, the Model 1910 wasn't dainty. Its massive recoil-balancing breechblock, housed in the rifle's wooden forearm, looked like something that fell off a tank. For some reason, however, the 1910 never really caught on. By 1937, only the Model 1907 in the marginal 351 remained in the Winchester semi-auto line, where it rested complacently for another 20 years.

All of the Winchester self-loaders shared the same general appearance and takedown design. They also shared an unlovely tendency to split their forearms, the nearly inevitable result of the battering effect of their blowback action. Today, they earn footnotes in the reference books chiefly for two reasons: 1) the entire 1903/1905/1907/1910 family was designed by Thomas C. Johnson, who would go on to design Winchester's outstanding Model 12 pump shotgun; and 2) the Model 1905's lowly 32 Self-Loading cartridge actually served as the inspiration for the U. S. Ordnance Department's "Cartridge, Cal. .30, Carbine, Ball, M1." You guessed it: the much-maligned 30 Carbine round.

Unlike today's semi-autos, neither the Remington nor the Winchester selfloaders incorporated the principle of gas operation. In a gas-operated arm, a small portion of the rapidly-expanding gases generated by the burning propellant is siphoned off through a port in the barrel. From there, the gas is brought to bear on a piston, which thrusts backward toward the receiver to initiate the ejection/recocking/reloading cycle.

Back before the turn of the century, John Browning had modified a lever-action Winchester carbine so that its lever was attached to a rod that was in turn linked to a primitive flap valve mounted over a hole near the barrel's muzzle. When the gun was fired, gases bled through the hole to bear against the flap valve. The flap valve then flapped backward to operate the lever automatically.

If this sounds primitive, it is. Yet, like all of John Browning's inventions, it worked and worked well. So well, in fact, that the design was incorporated into the famous Colt Model 1898 "Potato Digger" machine gun, America's first true gas-operated gun. The nickname came from the flap valve, which toggled downward from the barrel enthusiastically enough to carve a trench in the ground if fired from a prone position.

The Potato Digger was an all-business kind of gun, the darling of the U. S. Marines during the Spanish-American War. But as far as sporting arms were concerned, gas was deemed a malignant genie best left in the bottle. It fell to the now-forgotten Standard Arms

The Hammer of Thor.

Company of Wilmington, Delaware, to introduce America's first gas-operated deer semi-auto, the ill-fated Model G, around 1910.

Talk about unique! Bearing a sculpted cast-brass forearm that allowed it to function either as a semi-auto or a pump gun, the Standard Model G could be had in 25, 30, or 35 Remington. But these loads were too powerful for the Standard gun, sad to say: the Model G routinely sheared off its flimsy bolt extensions, thus effectively turning the gun into a long, ornate paperweight.

For one or two shots, the Model G worked just fine if you held your mouth right. But its bad press soon caught up with it, and Standard Arms sank without a ripple. It remained for John C. Garand's famed M1 30-06 military rifle of 1936 to demonstrate that the force of expanding gas could indeed be harnessed into a workable high-power semi-auto.

The M1, in fact, prepared a whole generation of post-WWII hunters for gas-operated semi-autos. After selling off existing inventories of its grand but aging Model 81, Remington capitalized on this wartime familiarity in 1955 with its Model 740 autoloader in 30-06. The 740 was a novelty: a high-powered, gas-operated, semi-auto deer gun that actually worked.

What made Remington's 740 the most successful semi-auto to date was its self-regulating gas system: it would function reliably with most hunting loads, even those of different bullet weights. The earlier long-recoil and blowback systems functioned with one standard factory load only. A too-light load wouldn't cycle the action, while a too-heavy load might part your hair with a runaway breechblock. The Model 740, however, let you shoot the full gamut of 30-06 deer loads without a hitch, all the way from the plain-vanilla 150-grainers to the big 220-gr. "woods loads." The 740's flexibility made long-recoil and blowback centerfire deer autos seem quaint and old-hat. Gas operation was the wave of the future.

Ultimately offered in 30-06, 280, 244, and 308, the 740 was freshened up in 1960 as the Model 742, which dominated the semi-auto deer rifle market until 1980, when it was ultimately succeeded by a number of variations on the same theme: the Models 74, Four, and 7400. All of these descendants of the 740 proved that the gas gun was here to stay.

During this time, Winchester wasn't exactly asleep at the switch. In 1961, it introduced the Model 100, a rotary-bolt autoloader chambered in 243, 284, and 308. The Winchester's sleek lines made it very popular

The ill-fated Standard Model G (right), the first gas-operated semi-auto, couldn't compete with Remington's Model 8 (left).

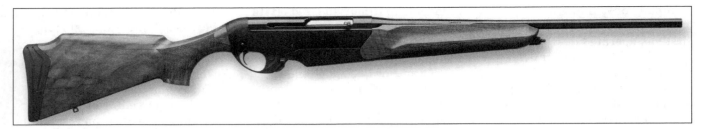

Benelli's R1 autoloader is probably the most stylish semi-auto ever produced.

for a time, as did its high-performance cartridges. Be aware, however, that the Model 100's firing pin was later the subject of an accidental-discharge safety recall. If you have a Model 100, ask a competent gunsmith to examine it before you fire it.

Simultaneously, Bill Ruger was tinkering away in his Connecticut workshop. He emerged with the aptly-named Ruger Model 44 "Deerstalker" carbine. This nifty gas-operated semi-auto picked up where the Winchester Model 1910 left off, offering a slap-you-silly woods cartridge in a handy little package. The Ruger's only weak point was its gas ports, which could become fouled if fed a steady diet of unjacketed-lead 44 Magnum ammunition, which was practically all that was available back then. This problem evaporated as more ammunition makers adopted jacketed offerings, and the Model 44 held its place in the Ruger lineup until 1985.

From across the Atlantic, Browning watched these developments with interest. In a real wowser of a move, the Belgium-based manufacturer introduced its BAR (Browning Automatic Rifle) High Power Rifle in 1967. Not to be confused with the military BAR, the sporting BAR was a masterpiece of good taste and practicality. Offered in chamberings as mild as the 243 and as imposing as the 338 Winchester Magnum, the BAR quickly earned a reputation as the Rolls-Royce of semi-autos. In a slightly modified form, it still occupies an honored niche in the Browning line.

So where do things stand today? Though it seems sometimes that bolt-actions get all the press, the gas-operated semi-auto deer gun is not merely alive, but thriving. In fact, today's semi-auto deer gun offerings are richer than ever before. Among the great manufacturers of self-loaders, only Winchester has discontinued that action type, preferring instead to concentrate on its excellent line of bolt- and lever-action rifles. As for the rest of the market, American deer hunters have never had it so good!

Benelli

Just when you thought you couldn't possibly need another gun, here comes Benelli with its R1. Chambered for 30-06, 308 Winchester, and 300 Winchester Magnum, this 2003 offering boasts a first for a self-loader: interchangeable free-floating 20-, 22-, and 24-inch barrels. A three-lug bolt provides powerful lockup while paired short-action action bars reduce felt recoil, thus aiding target re-acquisition when fast follow-up shots are required. The R1's removable magazine holds three or four rounds, depending on caliber, and optional recoil pads provide various lengths of pull.

But the most striking attribute of the RS1 is its styling. Resembling Benelli's rakish Super Black Eagle shotgun, the RS1 is a pleasure to behold. From the graceful sweep of the RS1's magazine assembly to its ergonomically-placed triggerguard safety, not a single line looks out of place. Its satin walnut forearm blends so gracefully with its aluminum receiver that it looks as though the wood were somehow melted and poured into place.

The 7-pound RS1 is the latest word in sporting semi-autos and it carries a price tag that reflects its novelty. Its no-nonsense chamberings combine with its

A BAR by any other name would shoot as sweet! The synthetic Browning Lightweight Stalker is tailor-made for the deer woods.

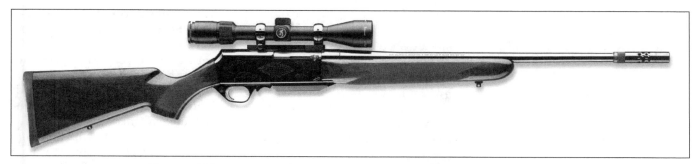

Browning's Safari is the crown jewel of the BAR line and is available with the BOSS accuracy system.

sleek good looks to make a package that is easily the most dynamic autoloader to hit the market so far this century.

Browning

The ageless BAR is still with us in four tasteful models: the Lightweight Stalker, the Long Trac, the Short Trac, and the Safari.

Weighing less than 8 pounds even in its stiffest chamberings, the Lightweight Stalker eschews fine wood in favor of an aluminum receiver and a durable synthetic stock and forearm that shave a few ounces of weight. But it's still pure BAR, available in 243, 308, 270, 7mm Magnum, 30-06, 300 and 338 Winchester Magnum, and even three of the Winchester Short Magnums (7mm, 270, and 300). As with all BARs, a seven-lug bolt provides more than adequate lockup even in the heaviest chamberings. Iron sights are standard on the Lightweight Stalker, and if there ever was a deer gun, this is it.

The BAR Long Trac is a long-action autoloader that handles four proven woods and plains cartridges: 270, 30-06, and 300 and 338 Winchester Magnum. Sightless but drilled and tapped for scope mounts, the Long Trac lets you reach right out there when you have to. With the right scope, though, it's equally at home in the woods. Sporting an aircraft-grade aluminum receiver, the Long Trac has a satin-finished walnut stock and forearm. Retail is about the same as its brethren. The Short Trac is a short-action version of the Long Trac. It's chambered for the 243, 308, and the 270, 7mm, and 300 Winchester Short Magnums.

Remington designed the first successful semi-auto gas rifle, the Model 740, half a century ago. Today the tradition continues with the Model 7400, the 7400 Synthetic, and the new 7400 Weathermaster.

BAR barrel lengths range from 20 inches to 26 inches.

The BAR Safari is the real thoroughbred of Browning's autoloader line. With an all-steel receiver and 16 different chamberings, it is the only BAR with Browning's BOSS (Ballistic Optimizing Shooting System) anti-harmonics accurizing device available as an option. The Safari is intended for use with a scope and does not carry iron sights.

Remington

It should be no surprise that Remington's current Model 7400 is one of the most popular semi-auto deer guns. After all, it's a lineal descendant of America's first successful gas-operated deer gun, the Model 740.

The 7400 is available in three flavors: the traditional 7400, the 7400 Synthetic, and the 7400 Weathermaster. The satin-finish walnut-stocked 7400 is available in 243, 270, 308, and 30-06 with a high-gloss version available in 270 and 30-06. All of these models carry 22-inch barrels and tip the scales at 7 1/2 pounds, except for the carbine model. The 7400 carbine, a real ear-ringer for sure, has an 18 1/2-inch barrel and weighs 7 1/4 pounds. Magazine capacity for all 7400s is four rounds.

The 7400 Synthetic is just what its name implies: a synthetic-stocked version of the traditional 7400. Barrel lengths and overall weights are the same. The 7400 will appeal to those who, as I do, die a little every time they drag a walnut stock over a barbed-wire fence.

The 7400 Weathermaster is a striking rifle inspired, no doubt, by Remington's 870 Marine Magnum 12-ga. pump shotgun. Available only in 270 and 30-06, the Weathermaster features synthetic stocks and a matte nickel-plated barrel, receiver, and magazine. The matte nickel plating minimizes glare and offers that extra little bit of protection against rain and snow. In my experience, no deer hunting trip is complete without a 45-mph sleet storm, so the Weathermaster should be just the ticket.

Ruger

As noted, Ruger's original Model 44 in 44 Magnum was a fixture in that manufacturer's line for two and a half decades. When it was dropped in 1985, I for one wept copiously. But happy days returned in 2000 with the introduction of the 99/44 Deerfield in 44 Magnum. Based on a beefier version of Ruger's Mini-14 platform, the Deerfield features a detachable four-round rotary magazine similar to that of the 10/22. With its hardwood stock, 18 1/2-inch barrel, 6 1/4 pound weight, and front handguard, the Deerfield is perhaps the most unconventional of all modern semi-auto deer guns. It isn't as sexy as the Benelli R1, and it won't reach over into the middle of next week like the BAR. For ranges up to 100 yards, however, this little five-shooter is unique in today's market: a no-frills working carbine chambered for a yee-hah woods cartridge.

Kissin' cousin to the Deerfield is Ruger's Mini-Thirty. When this carbine was introduced in 1987, some sneered at its 7.62x39mm chambering, saying that it was "no better than a 30-30." *"No better than a 30-30"?!* Them's fightin' words! When loaded with softpoint bullets, the 7.62x39 will punch a hole through the biggest whitetail that ever lived, assuming a realistic range. So will the 30-30, for that matter.

Ruger offers three versions of the Mini-Thirty: stainless metal with hardwood furniture; blued metal with hardwood furniture; and stainless metal with synthetic furniture. All versions feature an 18 1/2-barrel, removable five-round magazine, adjustable sights, and an overall weight of between 6 1/2 and 7 pounds.

OVER THE PAST CENTURY, semi-auto deer guns have evolved more than any other type of American sporting rifle. However, what was true in 1906 is still true today: a self-loader will never substitute for good markmanship or true sportsmanship. We may load four rounds into our semi-auto magazines before we head out into the woods and fields, but we always hope that we'll come back with three of them left. On those occasions when circumstance demands a speedy second shot, however, the semi-auto is still the hammer of choice. 🦌

Any deer within 100 yards should feel plenty nervous if someone's holding a Ruger Mini-Thirty.

BOLT ACTION SLUGFEST

*Once derided as "farmer's guns," bolt-action shotguns
may be the most accurate slug guns on the market*

By Dave Henderson

If your formative years as a deer hunter were spent east of the Mississippi and you are at least a little gray at the temples, chances are you knew someone who started with a slug-loaded, inexpensive bolt-action shotgun–or maybe you toted one yourself. Seems like there was always somebody serving an in-woods apprenticeship with a Polychoked Mossberg 195, Marlin 55, J.C. Higgins, Stevens, Sears 140 bolt gun, or the like.

Back then the turnbolt shotgun was a "starter" reserved for kids–an inexpensive stepping stone to Ithaca or Remington

pumps or autoloaders. Or they were multi-purpose ordnance used by frugal folks who weren't as serious about dedicating a particular gun to deer hunting as they were in simply having some firepower handy in the truck or behind the farmhouse door that could be of use in all seasons.

Suffice to say the bolt actions of those days were at the lower end of the shotgun spectrum. But you've also got to remember that shotguns and slugs *per se* weren't accurate back then, either. Put three out of five in a gallon can at 40 paces and you had a tack driver. Firepower had far more

appeal and usefulness than that kind of accuracy.

But, as I say, that was then. This is now. Modern bolt-action slug guns are definitely not reinventions of the wheel. Comparisons between them and yesterday's simple actions are about as valid as racing the Spirit of St. Louis against a Stealth bomber. Slug shooting has evolved eons in the last 10 years. Today there are five modern production bolt-action rifled barrel slug guns in general circulation, "modern" being the operative word here. Not all are currently in production, but all are widely available on the secondary market.

The Renaissance Begins

"Years ago the bolt action was simply an inexpensive shotgun with little more than reliability to justify its existence," says Mossberg CEO Alan "Iver" Mossberg, whose company was one of the prime providers of entry-level bolt shotguns decades ago. "The growing popularity of the pump and autoloading shotguns nearly retired the bolt action. Oddly enough, when bolt-action interest was waning and many states were changing their deer seasons to 'shotgun only,' slug ammunition was improving ten-fold. Suddenly the bolt action

Author with Illinois buck taken with a Tar-Hunt RSG-12 slug gun and Lightfield Commander slugs.

was reborn and repositioned." The growing market for slug guns gave a new lease on life to the tired old bolt-action shotgun.

In a way, it was inevitable that the bolt-action gun would re-emerge in this Renaissance of slug shooting. After all, like arrow speed in archery, lane grip in bowling and shaft flex in golf, accuracy has become the Holy Grail of shotgun slug shooting.

I mean, stop and think, folks. Are you expecting something less than a two-inch group with a pump shotgun? Get real. If you're looking for a super-accurate rifle do you look at a pump? Hardly. A lever action? Nope. Autoloader? Certainly not your first choice.

Go to a benchrest rifle match and look at what the competitors are shooting. Remember, these are the test pilots of the firearms industry. These riflemen are perfectionists. They're apt to retire a gun if they can't cover its last five-shot group with a dime.

What do they shoot? Bolt actions and single shots. No exceptions. Show up with any other action and be prepared for snickers, smirks and an out-of-the-money finish.

Why are bolts so inherently accurate, compared to other actions?

"Because all operations are in a straight line and the barrels are screwed into the receiver for the most solid mounting, which also allows them to be free-floated," said Randy Fritz, of Bloomsburg, Pennsylvania, a world-class bench rest rifle shooter and builder of the Tar-Hunt custom slug guns.

Those features dampen accuracy-robbing off-line movement and other vibration in the gun. The trigger mechanisms are also simpler and more adjustable, since they don't have to incorporate creep or slop to offset potential accidental fire during recoil as they do in looser-

constructed pumps and autoloaders.

Fritz and fellow Pennsylvania custom gunsmith Mark Bansner began building high-quality bolt-action slug guns, the SSG models, in 1990. Fritz's RSG 12- and later 20-gauge bolt-guns are based on Remington 788- and 700-style actions of his design and fitted with E.R. Shaw barrels. Bansner's SSG guns were first built on Mauser-style actions and later on one of his design, fitted with heavy-walled Hastings barrels.

Bolt-Actions Go Mainstream

But the rifled barrel bolt-action market got a bit crowded when, at the 1994 Shooting, Hunting and Outdoor Trades (S.H.O.T.) Show in Dallas, Marlin introduced the 512 Slugmaster and Browning unveiled the A-Bolt slug gun.

Marlin 512

Word around the industry is that *Outdoor Life* shooting writer Jim Carmichel—well aware that the bolt action is more inherently accurate than any other action and that no one was making a bolt-action slug

Custom sluggers: Bansner SSG-12 (left) and Tar-Hunt RSG-12.

gun—suggested to the Marlin folks that the company's clubby entry-level Model 55 bolt shotgun had the makings of a fine slug gun if it were fitted with a quality rifled barrel.

The original Marlin 512 was thus exactly that: a birch-stocked

The forward placement of the Marlin's bolt handle necessitated a unique side-mounted scope base.

The Browning A-Bolt was probably the best factory-made slugger but its lofty price tag drove it out of the market.

Model 55 Goose Gun with its famed 38-inch smoothbore barrel replaced by a 21-inch, 1:28 twist rifled barrel. The original 512 was actually a closer cousin to the Model 55S that Marlin marketed in the 1960s. That version featured a 24-inch smoothbore barrel, rifle sights and sling swivels.

The Marlin 512 bolt is mounted well forward, Mannlicher style, and notches in a slot in the receiver top, necessitating a side scope mount (Weaver 10M). A heavy recoil lug is anchored between the receiver and barrel into a recess in the stock.

If you are a fan of the 3-inch slug be advised that 1) not all

3-inch slugs are the same length, and 2) the Marlin clip can't handle the longest 3-incher, the Winchester, which tends hang up on the front edge of the magazine and not align with the chamber. To its credit, Marlin warned of this situation in its owner's manual.

The Marlin was upgraded appreciably from its debut model, evolving into the sleeker synthetic-stocked, ported, fiber-optic sighted Model 512P. Since it came to market as a modified version of an existing 12-gauge action design, there were never any plans for a 20-gauge version, which would have required a design of its own.

The A-Bolt

Browning's A-Bolt, built under contract by Miroku of Japan, was essentially one of the company's A-Bolt rifles chambered for 12 gauge and fitted with a synthetic stock. In fact, the original version was a smoothbore fitted with a rifled choke tube.

The Marlin, with an original suggested retail of less than $350, quickly became an affordable option for those who wanted an accurate gun dedicated to slug shooting. The A-Bolt, meanwhile, endured two years of minor design manipulation between Utah and Tokyo. It was never really competitive from a retail standpoint when it finally reached these shores in 1996 with a rifled barrel, optional walnut stock and a near-$800 pricetag.

Nevertheless, one would get few arguments that the Browning A-Bolt was the best commercial bolt-action slug gun ever made. It was a terrific performer with its short, crisp, 60-degree bolt throw, front-locking bolt lugs, 1:32 twist barrel and hinged floor plate for its detachable box magazine.

Meanwhile, Savage and Mossberg—which already had bolt-action designs among their longstanding patents—also jumped onto the bolt-action bandwagon.

The Savage 210F

Originally called the 210F Master Shot, the Savage 210F Slug Warrior (and its Realtree-clad clone, the 210F Camo Slug Warrior) is a 12-gauge version of the company's accurate and economically popular 110 series bolt-action rifles. Like the Browning A-Bolt, the 210F features a 60-degree bolt rotation, 24-inch rifled barrel (1:35 twist) and black glass-filled polymer synthetic stock with a ventilated recoil pad.

The rifle-style bolts of the Browning A-Bolt (top) and the Savage 210.

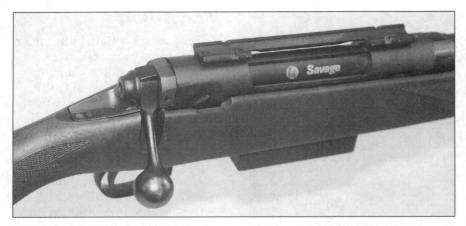

The Savage 210 slugger is actually a shotgun version of the company's well-respected 110 rifle series.

Like their rifle counterparts, neither the Savage nor Browning bolt slug guns had sights—a unique concession to the fact that scopes are essential on today's rifled barrel slug guns. Without the benefit of a scope the shooter can never aim fine enough to discern the true accuracy potential of today's guns.

The clip-fed, 7.5-pound Savage 210F is built around a front-locking rifle-style bolt that features controlled feed with left- and right-hand extractors. The original suggested retail was only a slightly plusher neighborhood than the original Marlin 512 and today is only in the sub-$500 neighborhood.

Probably with an eye toward the future and possibly toward handloading, the 210F's bolt was designed with three front-locking lugs like the Browning (unlike Mauser-based traditional rifle bolts that feature twin-opposed lugs) and a 60-degree bolt rotation.

The Savage extractor is a slender, hook-like affair that rotates with the bolt head and is housed in a slot just above the bottom locking lug. Extraction is theoretically via inertia with a blade contacting the case rim though a slot in the bolt head as the bolt reaches the last half-inch of travel.

The Savage's 24-inch rifled barrel (1:35 twist) is threaded to the receiver and held by a locking collar *a la* the 110 rifle. The receiver ring is well-vented. The action and stock are mated via two screws, one threading into the bottom surface of the recoil lug, the other just ahead of the trigger guard bow. The gun features a black glass-filled polymer synthetic stock with a ventilated recoil pad.

The Savage is one of the two modern bolt guns that does not use a detachable clip (Tar-Hunt's newest RSG-12 and -20 series is the other). Instead, the Savage features a two-shot integral box magazine that juts from the bottom of the forearm. The gun thus must be loaded from the top, which is a cumbersome task, given the bulkiness of shotgun shells. The Savage is the only bolt gun that can be fed from either the left or right side.

Mossberg's 695

The recently-discontinued Mossberg 695 is actually a spruced-up version of the smoothbore, fixed-choke Maverick 95 bolt gun that was introduced around 1995. The gun's synthetic-stocked, internal box magazine (no clip) 3-shot 12-gauge is obviously an evolution of the old Mossberg Model 195/395 series of Polychoked, 26-inch-barreled smoothbores that were popular 12-gauge starter guns in the 1960s.

The 695 has basically the same stock and dimensions as the Maverick Model 95 but features a 22-inch fully rifled barrel (1:34 twist) that was ported in a unique X-pattern near the muzzle. The gun came with a two-shot clip similar to the Marlin and Savage, but, unlike the Savage, offers Tru-Glo rifle sights in addition to Weaver-style scope bases and optional Bushnell scopes. Like the Savage, the Mossberg 695 features a black synthetic stock with a schnabel-nose forend.

The Mossberg's two-piece, rear-rotating bolt, similar to that found in rimfire rifles, is locked when the bolt handle lowers into a cut in the receiver wall. The trigger, in a unique design, is tensioned by an expansion spring rather than the compression type normally used. The safety is similarly unique, a turn-bolt affair affixed to the rear of the bolt like the Japanese Arisaka war rifles.

The 7.5-pound Mossberg gun comes with a two-shot clip similar to the Marlin and Browning, but has to win the "Ugly" award for the manner in which the forearm swells in a goiter-like protuberance to accommodate the bulky clip. The Mossberg offers a front post and rear folding leaf rifle sights in addition to Weaver-style scope bases. The Mossberg 695 features a black synthetic stock with a schnabel-nose forend.

The uniquely ported muzzle of a Mossberg 695.

Both the Savage and Mossberg designs also overcame early feeding problems with slight bolt re-designs in the late 1990s.

Savage has essentially the same outlook, riding an existing design as far as it will go with no desire to retool for smaller bore that might interest less than 20 percent of the existing market.

Whereas the Browning, Tar-Hunt and Savage designs feature rifle-like locking lugs (front lugs in the Browning and Savage, rear lugs on the Tar-Hunt) to assure fortress-like lock-up when the bolt is closed, the Marlin and Mossberg models lock merely by sliding the bolt handle into a recess in the receiver and stock.

It can be argued that given the low chamber pressures in shotguns (SAAMI limit for slugs is 11,500-12,000 foot pounds per square inch as compared to around 20,000 psi for the old blackpowder .45-70 Government loading), the added security of locking lugs is overkill. Modern high-performance centerfire rifles need locking lugs because their bolts must be built to withstand 55,000-60,000 foot psi.

But while commercial slug loads will always be limited as to their pressures, the age of handloading slugs isn't far away and the sturdier lock up will be a necessity for adventuresome private loaders. Tar-Hunt's Fritz, for instance, worked up a personal slug load for elk hunting that provides the same terminal energy at 100 yards that a .30-06 has at the muzzle. Hulls are destroyed in one firing but the "overbuilt" Tar-Hunt RSG-12 stands up to the challenge.

The Rolls-Royce: The Tar-Hunt

The vaunted $2,000 Tar-Hunt custom bolt-action guns, which are considered the ultimate in slug-shooting ordnance, usually don't see 100 units sold in a year, including those made for SWAT teams and other law enforcement entities. The Tar-Hunt's two-piece bolt locks in the a rear receiver ring rather than the front so that the non-rotating front half has room to incorporate a very narrow extractor cut in the actual chamber. The two stamped steel extractors are virtually identical to Marlin's and the ejector is a spring plunger type.

Since Day One Fritz has used Shaw's 21.5-inch heavy barrels. While he'll build your Tar-Hunt in a variety of rifling twist rates, most are cut at 1:28 inches, which is currently considered ideal for stabilizing sabot slugs. The interior diameter measures a SAAMI specs .728" in the grooves and .718" at the lands. The barrel walls are .120-inch thick while the Sniper or Tactical model Tar-Hunts sport straight-tapered .150-inch wall barrels. All Tar-Hunt barrels are ported 360 degrees at the muzzle to

State of the art (top to bottom): Savage 210, Mossberg 695, Browning A-Bolt, and Marlin 512 bolt guns shown with an H&R Model 980 single-shot.

The Tar-Hunt custom slug gun looks like an old Remington 788 on steroids.

reduce barrel jump and to help loosen sabots on the exiting slugs, which apparently allows them to drop off simultaneously, thus improving accuracy.

The Bloomsburg, Pa., shooter-gun builder has achieved several sub-half inch, 100-yard, five-shot groups with the 45-pound bench version of the gun and currently supplies barreled actions to all major slug manufacturers for their R&D work.

The word "accuracy" in slug shooting is a relative term. The vast majority (more than 95 percent) of deer taken with a slug gun are shot at distances inside of 100 yards. In fact, the typical shot in the slug woods is well inside of 75 yards. Thus the general slug-shooting populace is hesitant to dedicate a gun to deer hunting. A shotgun with a fixed rifled barrel is useless for anything but shooting slugs, which is the reason the accurate but limited-application bolt-action guns are shrinking from the market.

The Market Shakes Out

Mark Bansner's SSG bolt-action slugger, the first serious gun of its type, was driven out of the gun market in 1996 by the low-priced commercial models. Similarly, despite its quality, the Browning A-Bolt was discontinued in 1999 because it

simply couldn't compete in a retail sense. The average slug shooter didn't see sufficient difference in performance between the Browning and the fine-shooting Mossberg at one-third the price, or the similarly acceptable but only slightly more expensive Marlin and Savage bolts.

While the Marlin 512 and Mossberg 695 were popular, the latter being referred to as a "retail home run" in its first few years on dealer shelves, both have since been discontinued due to flagging sales. Mossberg may have discontinued the 695 to make room in its line for the SSi-One top-break slug-gun, while Marlin's only current slug gun

offerings are to be found in the lineup of its sister company H&R 1871/NEF.

Today only the Savage and Tar-Hunt guns remain, despite the fact that Savage sells fewer than 1,000 of its 210 annually. The others are still available, in varying degrees of scarcity, since the Mossberg wasn't discontinued as a production gun until 2003, the Marlin in 2001. The A-Bolt, in fact, has developed a bit of a cult following since it was discontinued late in the last century. Its design and accuracy are seemingly appreciated more now in its absence, and the guns command a healthy price on the used gun market.

But the fact remains, if you are seeking accuracy in slug-shooting, the bolt-action guns should be your first stop.

The bolt-action slug is state-of-the-art in slug guns. This hunter is using a Tar-Hunt 20-gauge Mountaineer.

ACCURACY WITHOUT A SCOPE

THINK YOU NEED A SCOPE? NOT ALWAYS!

By Wayne van Zwoll

Few hunters rely on iron sights these days. In the past half century, scope use has become all but universal. During its first years of production in the late 1930s, Winchester's Model 70 had no provision for scope mounts; now most versions of the 70 wear no sights. But good shooting is still possible with iron sights, and some people have worked magic with them.

Thirty years ago in Mishawaka, Indiana, I stepped to the firing line for a go at a spot on the U.S. Olympic Team. In the middle of the black scoring area that appeared as a dot at 50 feet was the *real* target, a 10-spot the

For quick shooting at deer, open-sighted carbines are still a top choice.

diameter of a finishing nail surrounded by a 9-ring you could obliterate with a 22 bullet. Centering the black in the iron sight, I assumed my precisely zeroed Anschutz rifle and its super-accurate Eley ammunition would deliver 10s. To reach the final qualifying stage, I'd have to fire the equivalent of a one-hole 60-shot group in a bullseye I couldn't even see! Luck was with me that day, my prone position as good as it's ever been. Fifty-one bullets took out the middle dot, and the other nine cut deep into 9-ring. A .45 pistol bullet would have covered the group.

The best iron sights for bullseye shooting are an aperture (peep) rear and a globe front with an insert that's the equivalent of a scope's reticle. For a long time, my favorite insert was an orange plastic disc with a hole in the middle just big enough to admit a narrow rim of white around the black target. The hole's bevel showed dark, to provide a crisp sight picture. Later I went to a black steel ring (no plastic) because it was recommended by the best shooters. Still, I shoot as well under most conditions with the orange plastic. It's important that the disc be big enough to allow sufficient light around the target – but not so much light that you're working hard to center it. Some riflemen "shade" with a front aperture, moving it slightly to one side or the

other to compensate for wind. This tactic has always given me the willies. I've succeeded at times but have also blundered by over-correcting. My eyes weren't (and aren't) sharp enough to shade irons on small targets. I'd rather hold center and dial in the required windage or elevation adjustments.

An aperture rear sight is also a good hunting sight, though you'll want a bead or blade rather than a ring up front, for quick aim at big, irregularly shaped targets. You'll also want a wide aperture in the rear, to help you find the target right away and to deliver more light to your eye. On a hunt, you be compelled to shoot in shadow or failing light. I've taken the aperture out of the Redfield sight on my Model 70 375 H&H; now the threaded hole in the sight frame serves as my aperture. It is more precise than it looks, because my eye automatically centers the front bead in the middle. That's where most of the light is.

Close to the eye, aperture sights like this Williams deliver surprising precision.

The longer the sight radius (distance between sights), the greater the degree of precision. The closer the rear sight to your eye, the smaller and more accurate it can be. Field of view, depth perception and brightness are greatest when your eye is up against the aperture. Of course, recoil prevents such intimacy; but target shooters do crowd the sight. That's why rifles for nineteenth-century Schuetzen matches had tang-mounted rear sights. Winchester and Marlin lever rifles and single-shot hunting rifles routinely wore tang sights before scopes became so popular; now Cowboy Action shooters have rediscovered the value of these long-stemmed Marbles and Lyman "peeps." Cocking-piece sights on bolt rifles have become as rare as crank-handles on automobile engines; however, they're among my favorite sights because they're close to your eye and compact. The bolt-mounted peep on Winchester's 71 lever-action rifle has the modest size of a cocking-piece sight, though it sits well forward. You get plenty of precision from either, despite the moving bases. (For hard-kicking rifles like the 348, any tang sight can put the aperture *too* close to your eye.)

My first hunting rifle, a restocked 303 British SMLE, had a barrel-mounted Williams open sight with a shallow V "African" notch. It proved faster than the popular U or deep V notches and didn't obscure the target as much as buckhorn or semi-buckhorn sights then common on lever rifles. I still like the shallow V, with or without an eye-catching white center-line. It's popular on double rifles. So is an "Express" sight with folding leaves zeroed for different yardages. I prefer a single fixed leaf filed to a 100-yard zero. Then there's no choosing the wrong leaf, or having the right one collapse

during recoil or rough handling. An open sight is properly a close-range sight. Few marksmen shoot well enough with one to justify its use beyond 150 yards. With a single rear notch, you should be able to hold center and count on a lethal hit on big animals out to at least 150 yards.

Whether you have an open sight or aperture sight on a hunting rifle, the front sight should be big enough to catch your eye right away, even at the expense of precision. There's no magic bead size, because barrel length affects *apparent* size and subtention. There's no perfect bead material or color either. I like ivory except in snow. Gold works well against a variety of backgrounds. Fluorescent sights are very fast but under bright conditions get fuzzy. In shadows they can give you a halo effect, much like that of a street lamp at night. Too much brightness not only blurs sight edges; it can hide the target. Even metal beads can degrade a sight picture by scattering light. Avoid spherical bead faces, as they reflect incident light off the edge, shifting the bead's apparent position and causing you to miss. A bead should be flat-faced but angled toward the sky to catch light.

Redfield's Sourdough front sight featured a square red insert, angled up. You could employ it as a bead or a post. A black steel post can get lost against thick timber. It also mandates a 6-o'clock hold – fine for bullseyes on white paper but obstructive on game and slower than a bead you can slap on a target.

Someone is always cooking up new iron sights. Bob Fulton of Glenrock, Wyoming has experimented with globe sights on hunting rifles. His Ruger Number One in 411 Hawk has a globe front sight holding a clear plastic insert etched with a crosswire. The rear sight is a modified Krag. At the end of the

Wayne removed the aperture from the sight on his 375 and uses the frame only for fast aim.

27-inch barrel the flared rear end of the globe sight fits almost perfectly in the aperture of the rear sight. There's a thin ring of daylight around the globe so you can tell instantly if it's out of center. "It's a good sight against mottled backgrounds," says Bob. "Unlike a blade, the vertical and horizontal wires obscure almost none of the target. The sight picture is like that of a scope."

Bob has also built barrel-mounted rear aperture sights. The rear sight on his Winchester 95 has a platinum-lined ring arcing over the factory notch. "That's the fastest sight I've ever used," he told me. "It accounted for piles of jackrabbits when I was in the Army, stationed in the Southwest. Surplus '06 ammo was cheap!"

Wayne mounted a receiver sight on his pellet rifle, for inexpensive practice.

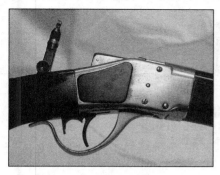
The tang sight on this 19th-century single-shot rifle increases sight radius and precision.

Some innovative sights have gone commercial, like the "Little Blue" peep sight, a dainty folding aperture that screwed to the back of a Redfield scope base as an auxiliary sight. Alas, it is no longer available.

There's nothing wrong with a standard Lyman or Redfield or Williams receiver sight and a gold bead over the muzzle. Traveling to Alaska some seasons back, I carried only one rifle: a 1903 Springfield with a Lyman rear aperture sight and a fine gold bead up front. With that old 30-06 I made a one-shot kill on a moose at 120 yards, and toppled a Dall ram at 70. A scope would have allowed me to shoot at longer range – but it also would have denied me the thrill of a sneak. Iron sights give you a feeling of personal contact with the game, more intimate than one artificially conjured in a lens. It's similar to the feeling you get stalking animals with a bow and arrow.

A few years ago, a tall, rough-hewn Texan handed me a Marlin lever rifle with a perforated peg perched on the receiver. Its stem threaded into a small block that dovetailed into a larger base block and moved across it for lateral adjustment. To raise or lower the sight you simply screwed the ring out or in. "How about that, partner?" he bellowed. "Kinda slick, huh?" It was indeed slick. So was the front blade, angled like a Sourdough but all the way to the base and with a white line down its middle.

The Texan founded Ashley Outdoors to make his sights, then left. The company has grown and now goes by the name of XS Sights. It builds aperture sights and front blades for bolt rifles, shotguns and muzzleloaders, as well as for lever-actions. I use them on my Marlin Guide Gun, and on a Mauser 98. They seem to me the best rear sights available for hunting rifles these days, though I still prefer Sourdoughs or flat-faced beads up front. The XS white line does stand out in dark conditions, and against a light background the entire blade is easy to see.

The key to effectiveness with any sight is practice.. Here are some things to keep in mind after you zero:

Focus on the front sight. Your eye can't focus at three distances simultaneously, so it's best to get a sharp view of the middle image.

This novel open sight is skeletonized so as not to obscure the target.

That way, you won't have to put two fuzzy images together. The rear sight can be out of focus, and the target not quite as clear as you'd like – and you'll still hit center if the front sight is distinct and in the proper relationship to the other two images.

Remember that every shot is practice, and that the more you shoot the better you'll shoot if you take care with every sight picture and let-off. Sloppy shooting is just practicing bad form. Honestly, good shooting takes focused effort – more with iron sights than with a scope because your eye must do more work.

Don't assume that a scope will always help you shoot better. Scopes help mainly when a target is too small or distant or indistinct to see clearly. Iron sights take weight off the top of your rifle, improving its balance and enabling you to point it more easily. Irons also give you a horizon-wide field and are unaffected by the snow and rain that cloud a scope lens.

Sometimes scopes are simply superfluous.

XS Sights, formerly Ashley, offers a sleek, trim rear aperture sight with bases for most rifles.

The XS front sight has a stout blade with eye-catching white line.

Bob Fulton fashioned this novel globe front sight for his Ruger Number One.

Annie Oakley and Ad Topperwein: Iron-Sight Artists

In an age before telescopic sights were common, two old-fashioned shootists showed the world what could be done with iron sights.

Phoebe Ann Moses, born in a log cabin in Darke County, Ohio, in August, 1860, had a hard childhood. But subsistence hunting would propel her to fame. She shot her first game, a squirrel, at age eight. Soon Annie began shooting quail on the wing with her 22, and dominating turkey shoots. Then, at a local match, she beat visiting sharpshooter Frank Butler – who apparently did not know at first that his opponent was a 15-year-old girl. A year later they married, and

Phoebe Ann Moses, aka Annie Oakley

Annie joined Frank's traveling show under the stage name of Annie Oakley. Sioux Chief Sitting Bull called her "Watanya cicilia," or "Little Sure-Shot." When exhibition shooter Captain A.H. Bogardus left Buffalo Bill's Wild West Show, Annie got on the docket, aiming into a mirror to shoot over her shoulder at glass balls Frank threw in the air.

Petite at 100 pounds and sweet-tempered, Annie became an audience favorite. The German Crown Prince, later to become Kaiser Wilhelm II, asked her to shoot a cigarette from his lips. She obliged, allowing in the wake of World War I that a miss might have changed history. Annie shot coins from Frank's fingers and split playing cards edgewise with bullets. In 1884, using a Stevens 22 at an exhibition in Tiffin, Ohio, she hit 943 glass balls out of 1,000 tossed. She could make one ragged hole in the middle of a playing card, firing 25 shots in 25 seconds with a repeater. Johnny Baker, another Wild West Show marksman, tried for 17 years to outshoot Annie Oakley, and never did. "She wouldn't throw a match," he said ruefully. "You had to *beat* her, and she wasn't beatable."

Annie used iron sights for exhibition shooting. At age 62, after an automobile accident crippled her, she could still hit with rifle bullets 25 airborne pennies in a row.

Equally amazing were the stunts of **Ad Topperwein**, born in 1869 near New Braunfels, Tex. With a 22 Winchester 1890 pump rifle, Ad began his career shooting aerial targets. Ad later replaced the 1890 with a Winchester 1903 autoloader, then with its successor, a Model 63. In 1887, at age 18, he landed a job as a cartoonist in San Antonio. But he

practiced his marksmanship during off-hours and wound up shooting for a circus. In 1894 he used a rifle to break 955 of 1,000 clay 2 1/4-inch disks tossed in the air. Dissatisfied with the score, he repeated twice, shattering 987 and 989. Standard clay shotgun targets proved too easy; he broke 1,500 straight, the first 1,000 from 30 feet, the last 500 from 40.

By his late 20s, Ad was also a showman, hired by Winchester as an exhibition shooter. After firing at a washer tossed aloft, he'd tell onlookers that the bullet went through the middle. Challenged by the audience, Ad would stick a postage stamp over the hole for another toss, and perforate the stamp.

And all of this without a scope!

Ad Topperwein

Bridging the Gap

Today's muzzleloaders are edging closer to centerfire performance

By Peter R. Schoonmaker

In great-great-grandpaw's day, all balls were round; all powder was black; a cap was a cap was a cap; every muzzleloader had a hammer; and when you put all of these together and squeezed the trigger, your gun fired. Or it didn't.

Things have changed—boy howdy, have they changed! In this sneak preview of Successful Muzzleloader Hunting, *published in Fall 2004 by KP Books, muzzleloading authority and author Peter R. Schoonmaker describes some of the latest, most exciting developments in muzzleloaders for the deer hunter.*

They've come a long way, baby.

A far cry from the smokepoles of yesteryear, modern muzzleloading rifles have the look and feel of a center-fire rifle. Gun designs have come a long way in providing accuracy and hunting trajectories by matching bullets, powder charges and barrels twists for optimum performance.

Sales figures indicate that many muzzleloader hunters today aren't concerned with nostalgia. They're concerned with efficiency, accuracy, convenience and performance. Even Traditions' PA Pellet Flintlock and the Thompson/Center Firestorm Flintlock, which externally resemble "traditional" designs, feature latest-and-greatest innovations such as removable breech plugs, synthetic stocks and fiber optic sights. Today's modern muzzleloading rifles of also feature adjustable triggers and sights; synthetic, wood and laminated stocks; and 209 shotgun primer ignitions.

The undeniable lure of tradition notwithstanding, the results are in. Hunters are voting with their wallets, and consumer interest and sales speak for themselves. Muzzleloader hunting with modern muzzleloading rifles geared towards the big game hunter is at an all-time high. And the following models are a big reason why.

Knight Rifles

Tony Knight raised the bar on muzzleloading performance in 1985 with the introduction of his modern muzzleloading rifle, the MK-85. The MK-85 featured an in-line plunger-style ignition, a 1-in-28 barrel twist to handle modern projectiles such as saboted pistol bullets, and a double safety system. My father and I have taken a fair amount of game with our .50-caliber MK-85 Knight Hawk with a thumbhole stock shooting 100 grain Hodgdon charges behind 250-grain Barnes MZ all-copper bullets, the most notable of this being two Iowa bucks on the same day with the same MK-85.

Tony Knight raised the bar again with his bolt-action Disc (Disc Ignition System Concept) Rifle in 1997. This 43-inch 8-pound Knight .50-caliber offering features a 24-inch barrel with a 1-in-28 barrel twist with the emphasis on accurately pushing sabot bullets with stiff charges. Charges range from 100-grain volume loads of FFg blackpowder or Pyrodex to three 50-grain Pyrodex Pellets, a winning load in this rifle. The composite Monte Carlo stock is available in black or camouflage. Other advanced features include blued or stainless Green Mountain barrels, adjustable Timney triggers, removable stainless steel breech plugs, receivers drilled and tapped for scope mounts, the Knight patented double safety system, fully adjustable rear sights,

In 1985, Tony Knight's series of inline muzzle loaders revolutionized blackpowder deer hunting.

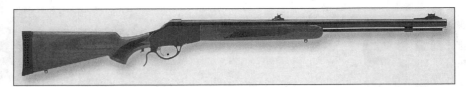

Reminiscent of the classic Winchester High Wall, Knight's .50 Revolution DISC rifle will shoot 2 1/2" groups at 100 yards.

rubber recoil pads, and instructional videos.

The Disc Rifle revolves around a bolt-action ignition system that uses unique plastic ignition discs that carry a #11 percussion cap or the more popular and hottest muzzleloading ignition available, a 209-shotshell primer. The action of lifting the bolt and sliding it to the rear of the action exposes a priming port where the disc with the primer is placed. The motion of sliding the bolt forward and down mates the disc with the breech plug as well as providing a weatherproof ignition system.

Knight also offers the DISC rifle in .45-caliber. My father and I scoped one with a BSA 4.5-14 Big Cat and took it to the shooting range and put it through the paces. Three 50-grain Pyrodex Pellets pushed a 125-grain bullet at over 2500 fps. Barnes' 150- and 180- grain Red Hot bullets are also available in .45 caliber. All three bullets have a downrange drop within an inch of each other out to 200 yards. Any of these loads will punch the ticket of the biggest whitetail that ever lived if placed properly.

Knight also offers the Master Hunter DISC rifle. This .50 cal. DISC features gold-plated trigger and guard, a jeweled bolt, a tooled laminated stock with a thumbhole grip and aMonte Carlo cheek piece. Many hunters found that the Disc Rifles often performed best with loose Pyrodex and blackpowder charges. A real bruiser, the .52-caliber Disc Extreme rifle was built to shoot a heavy 375-grain bullet at high velocity with the addition of the innovative

Powerstem breechplug that enhances powder charge combustion in the barrel.

But even the revolutionary DISC rifles seem tame compared to Knight 's all-new Revolution. The Revolution is the latest introduction from this creative muzzleloading pioneer. If you think all the new breed of muzzleloaders look alike, think again. No plunger or bolt-action here. Not hardly.

The Revolution has the look and feel of a sporterized Winchester 1885 Hi-Wall single shot, one of the most beautiful rifles of all time. A pivoting breechblock design lies at the heart of this .50-caliber muzzleloader. Jacking the trigger guard forward allows you to cock the hammer and open the primer chamber. Knight's full plastic jacket DISC 209 primer slips into

the breechplug. Pull the trigger guard back in place and you're locked and ready.

Easy, straight-through cleaning is achieved by removing the rifle's Quick Detachable Action. The precision Green Mountain rifle barrel with a 1-in-28 twist comes with a 2 1/2-inch, three-shot group at 100-yards guarantee. The Knight Revolution is available in blued or stainless finish with synthetic (black or camo), walnut, or laminated stocks.

Thompson/Center Arms

Thompson/Center's Encore 209X50 magnum muzzleloader was introduced in the late 1990s. When closed, its simple, convenient break-action seals the 209-shotshell primer for waterproof hunting. The removable breech plug with the EZ Tip extractor introduced easy maintenance for cleaning and removing unfired charges. The Encore is a very handy rifle that is easy to prime and shoot. When used with the Shock Wave bullet,

T/C's primer-fired Encore 209X50 Magnum will wax big bucks without missing a beat.

The swinging-breech T/C Omega whacked this fine whitetail at 100 yards.

co-developed with Hornady Manufacturing, you're shooting a hard-hitting hunting bullet from an easy-handling rifle. T/C's new, short Katahdin carbine with 20-inch ported barrel makes the Encore 209x50 a mighty convenient hunting partner.

In early 2003 I received a first-run .45 caliber T/C Omega Rifle. Oh boy, I thought, another blue barreled, black synthetic stocked muzzleloader. Whoopee. But it didn't take long to realize that this rifle redefines the in-line muzzleloader. It features a totally new concept of breech that simply swings down and away, exposing the in-line breech plug for a) installing a 209-shotgun primer and b) easy removal of the breech plug for uninhibited, straight-through barrel cleaning. And although modern in concept, the Omega rifle is a back-hammer percussion gun. T/C rifles have always possessed the feel of a north woods deer gun, but how would the Omega perform in the field?

In the fall of 2003, on two occasions I had observed both bucks and does entering the corner of a woodland opening at sunset. I thought this would be an excellent opportunity for my father to take a crack at them. The field's open ground had a roll in it so the hunter would have to have some height to see over the rise. By using one section of a ladder stand, I could get my father eight feet off the ground.

On Halloween eve I tucked my father and the .45 Omega into the tree line opposing the trail entrance at 3:00 p.m. As the sun's disc prepared to do its daily disappearing act, a lone deer appeared at the far corner trail entrance 125 yards away. The Bushnell Elite 3200 scope that we had mounted on the Omega gathered the fading light as my father settled the crosshairs on the moving buck at 100 yards.

I heard the report of the Omega and headed down the trail with great expectations. From the edge of the opening I could see a large cloud of Triple Seven smoke as it hung in the evening air. The expression on my dad's face indicated that, yes indeed, the Omega is a mighty fine deer gun.

Remington

Throughout its 180+-year history, the Remington Arms Company has always produced appealing and dependable firearm designs. In 1996, the company introduced a muzzleloader that responded to the needs of a new generation. Based on the tried and true Model 700 bolt action, the 700 ML features a 24" barrel on a 44-inch rifle that weighs in at 7 3/4 lbs. The 700 ML shoulders like an old friend with its 1/2" drop at the comb, 3/8" drop at the heel, and a 13 3/8" length of pull. Except for the visible ramrod, the Model 700 in-line black powder rifle looks and feels like a standard center fire Model 700 short action. The 700 ML is offered in blued carbon steel, while the stainless version is the 700 MLS. Both are cradled by a synthetic stock to the design of its predecessor.

Unlike the klatch-poof-boom of the lock of the very first Remington flinter in 1816, the new 700 ML features a completely modern in-line striker design with a lock time of 3.0 milliseconds. Instead of pulling the hammer back to cock this muzzleloader, you simply work the bolt action to cock the firing pin. The open breech design features a stainless steel breech plug that can accept a #11 percussion cap, a musket cap, or a 209-primer. The safety is at easy thumb reach at the rear of the bolt. Barrel rifling today is geared towards elongated projectiles that require a fast rate of twist. Remington chose a 1-in-28 rifling twist for its ultra high-quality 700ML.

Winchester

Last April, dad and I also had the opportunity to test a .45-caliber Winchester X-150 muzzleloader. This attractive rifle features a blued barrel with a stainless steel bolt action and breech. A 26-inch fluted barrel with a 1-in-28 rifling twist and a well-designed composite stock complete the package. At 8 pounds and 45 inches long, this

This .50 Winchester X-150 wears Advantage Timber High Definition camo.

In keeping with the company's reputation, Austin & Halleck's 420-series bolt actions are exquisitely finished as well as practical in the field.

rifle is well balanced. Shotgun 209 primer ignition, fiber optic sights, and removable breech plug complete the package.

The fiber optic sights seemed minimal in size, so my father mounted a T/C Hawken Hunter 4x32 Center Plex Reticle scope on the rifle, gathered powder and projectiles, and headed for the shooting range. By the time hunting season rolled around, the load of choice was two 50-grain Pyrodex Pellets pushing a 225-grain PowerBelt Aero Tip bullet at 1968 fps with 1935-fpe PowerBelt Bullets.

With this load, the Winchester X-150 proved to be a nice-shooting, comfortable rifle, with a smooth working bolt and quick, reliable ignition. My father dropped a whitetail with this set-up at 60 yards.

Austin & Halleck

Coming from a company that is renowned for its traditional muzzleloaders, Austin & Halleck's 420 series bolt-action rifles are the handsomest guns on the market. They feature octagon-to-round barrels and nicely figured wood stocks with classic 20:1 checkering. A large receiver makes it a natural for 209 priming, and fully adjustable triggers facilitate comfortable and accurate shooting with 150-grain charges in the 1-in-28 twist 26-inch barrel. Hodgdon's Triple Seven and Barnes Bullets provide consistent 1-inch groups at 100 yards. For the discriminating muzzleloader

shooter and hunter, these rifles are the last word.

Savage's 10ML-II

Savage Arms set the world of muzzleloading a-buzz in late 2000 when they introduced the first smokeless powder muzzleloader, the 10ML-II. This .50-caliber, bolt-action 209-primed high performance muzzleloader features a removable breech plug with vent liner, a receiver drilled and tapped for scope installation as well as fiber optic sights. But the use of non-corrosive smokeless powder sets it apart.

Because the rifle is built to handle the pressures of smokeless powder producing over 2300 fps velocity and 3000 ft. lbs. of energy, blackpowder, Pyrodex, and replica powders can be used was well. DO NOT–let me repeat that: DO NOT–NEVER–EVER–use smokeless powder in any other muzzleloading firearm unless expressly recommended for such by the manufacturer. The 10ML-II was specifically designed to handle smokeless powder. Try this trick in any other frontstuffer and you'll earn yourself a one-way ride in a long black station wagon.

The Savage 10ML-II has proven itself as a well-constructed and very accurate muzzleloading firearm featuring a unique ignition module that is seated into chamber of the rifle like a cartridge. Top whitetail photographer and writer Charlie Alsheimer swears by his Savage smokeless muzzleloader. And he should know.

Other Notables. . .

Thompson/Center's Black Diamond is a real workhorse that appealed to many hunters for their "special" one a year muzzleloader hunt. CVA's Firebolt 209 Ultra Magnum is a lot of bolt-action for the money. The MDM Buckwacka Magnum is another break-open action that is a well-built, all-business hunting rifle. Traditions new Evolution long-distance bolt-action rifle also joins the ranks of hard-hitting rifles with magnum load capacity. And the new Winchester Apex Magnum 209 features a swing action design on a 44-inch 81/2-pound rifle in .45 or .50 caliber. It's Winchester's answer to the T/C Omega.

With so many choices, we're truly living in the Golden Age of muzzleloading. Writing in 1874, American author Sarah Orne Jewett had this to say about muzzleloaders: "[In my youth] some very ingenious person invented percussion caps, and those were thought as near perfection as anything could be." Oh, Sarah! If you could only see how far things have come!

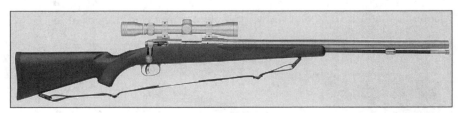

Blackpowder, Pyrodex, pellets, smokeless powder, you name it–Savage's unique 10ML-II will handle virtually any propellant in the right doses without a hitch.

TESTFIRE:
THE MODEL 710

REMINGTON'S MOST UNUSUAL RIFLE

By Wayne van Zwoll

In 1948, Remington announced its Models 721 and 722 bolt rifles. With uncheckered walnut and stamped bottom metal, they didn't offer the class of a Winchester 70, then barely a decade old. But those Remingtons sold well because they sold for less than the Winchester and performed just fine afield. They were accurate, durable and reliable. They even handled well. In 1962 Remington replaced the 721 and 722 with the Model 700, a more refined rifle that's since been offered in myriad configurations.

To shooters who remembered its forebears and saw Remington's commitment to affordable big game rifles, the Model 710 couldn't have been much of a surprise. This bolt-action, announced early in 2001, was intended to fill a price niche left vacant by the expansion of the 700 line into specialty rifles for connoisseurs. The 710 came to deliver Model 700 performance in a package beginning shooters could afford. You can now buy 710s in 7mm Remington and 300 Winchester Magnum, as well as in its charter chamberings, 270 and 30-06.

"We began working on the 710 early in 1999," says Mike Keeney, the project's chief engineer. "It was a just a concept then: a new entry-level rifle that offered great value for the dollar. We had to put it on the dealer's rack at low cost, so he could sell it cheap. Beyond that, we were constrained by a tight capital expenditures budget that limited purchase of new tooling. Our goal was to save money and produce a rifle that would be as strong as a Model 700, as reliable and as accurate. The 710 was the result."

This rifle is not simply a 700 in sackcloth. It's truly different, with a receiver made from seamless steel tubing. The 700 receiver, in comparison, starts out as bar stock, which is then drilled, reamed and broached before the mills go to work cutting the sear slot, ejection port, magazine mouth and other features.

"We saved some money with the tubing," says Mike, "because machining bar stock is costly. The tubing is not 4140 chrome-moly, not strong enough for locking lug recesses. If we were to specify chrome-moly in seamless tubes, the price would be exhorbitant."

Well, if seamless tubing won't hold a bolt in place upon firing, how can it be used on the 710?

Mike explains that the 710 receiver has no lug recesses. "They're in the barrel. We cut them right after we finish the

The 710's profile reflects its 700 and 721-722 ancestry. Mechanical differences are substantial.

chambering, on the same machine. It takes about a minute per barrel longer." Therein is the main difference between the 710 and the 700 – and just about every other bolt rifle. The 710 bolt locks directly into the barrel. The receiver serves only as a bolt race and a feeding mechanism; it holds the trigger group and supports the scope. No heavy lifting there!

The bolt-barrel mating idea is not new. In fact, Remington employs it in 7400 autoloader and 7600 pump rifles. They feature a separate shank extension with lug recesses. The extension is threaded onto the barrel. In contrast, the new 710 has an integral extension. "It's very strong," says Mike. "It also preserves our reputation for three rings of steel around the cartridge head. The 710 will stand any proof load a Model 700 can digest."

The 710 bolt head has the recessed clip-style extractor familiar to anyone who's looked at a 700. The plunger ejector is also the same. But there are three locking lugs, not two. "That gave us a couple of advantages," says Mike. "First, it reduces bolt lift to 60 degrees, making for fast repeat shots. Secondly, it enables us to make each lug a little less proud – we got plenty of total bearing surface without having to cut deep bolt races."

Speaking of bolt races, the 710's tube receiver doesn't have any. Instead, there's a fiberglass-reinforced nylon insert, with the lug races molded in. Impregnated with Teflon and silicon, the races are self-lubricating.

"We made one mistake with this sleeve," says Mike. "Maybe two. Our tests showed the race did indeed deliver slick bolt operation – but only after some shooting. At the lab, 100 shots go through our test rifles before we even think about it. The once-a-

year hunters likely to buy the 710 might not shoot a box of ammo in a year. Those who bought the first rifles complained about the stiff bolt. They just didn't do the shooting needed to seat it." The other miscalculation: "We thought the public would look favorably on a bolt that wasn't so sloppy as to fall open if you tipped the rifle up. The 710's bolt definitely does not. But shooters were used to bolts dropping free, and they didn't like one that required a pull."

Remington subsequently changed the bolt specs, reducing body diameter by about .003". Engineers also installed reinforcing strips on the back side of the insert, between the lug races. "We found part of the binding problem was due to over-rotation of the bolt," explains Mike. "Though required bolt lift was only 60 degrees, a lot of shooters used to two-lug bolts kept lifting as they withdrew the bolt. That caused a slight cavitation in the lug race, and consequent sticking." The stiffer inserts and looser bolt fit ensure effortless bolt travel on rifles from the current production run – though a little manipulation still helps the bolt move easier. I've had three 710s in my hands,

The 710 has good balance. It's not a lightweight rifle, but you'll find few more durable.

one made early, another with the reinforced insert, and a current-run magnum. All three actions can seem stiff compared to a Mauser 98's, but only the early 710 seemed *difficult* to operate.

The Model 700-style trigger group on the 710 hangs from the insert. The left-hand sideplate, steel on the 700, is nylon here and integral with the insert. The right-hand sideplate is steel,

The 710 in .300 Winchester Magnum balances well, feels surprisingly lightweight. It's all Remington, inside and out!

riveted to the rest of the trigger group. To take the trigger off the receiver, you have to remove a small screw just below the bolt release and under the stock-line on the receiver's left side. The screw is cemented in. So are the adjustment screws: one in the back for sear engagement, two up front for weight (bottom) and over-travel (top). "We don't recommend that owners adjust triggers," Mike says. "You have to know what you're doing, or you could make the trigger unsafe." That's true. It's why I think Remington, Ruger, Winchester and every other gunmaker frightened by threat of litigation into making triggers that will lift a small engine block should reconsider. *The trigger is a firing device*, not a handle. If it's made so stiff as to impede accurate shooting, riflemen will *have* to resort to adjustment. Better that the factory do it in the first place. Making triggers foolproof is tantamount to making them unusable. A crisp 3 pounds will satisfy most hunters. A 3-pound trigger offers enough resistance to prevent accidental discharge by cold-stiffened fingers. But it is light enough that applying necessary pressure won't make the rifle tremble unduly.

The 710's safety is in the same place as the 700s but has, as Mike says, a different geometry. It operated as intended on the rifles I shot. A friend had trouble engaging the safety on his 710. He sent the rifle back to the factory and got it repaired. Mike suspects that, like snug bolts, tight safeties on the first rifles probably frustrated some shooters. "The 710s coming off the line now are user-friendly. No break-in required!"

There's a second safety on the 710 – and, for that matter, on all Remington 700s these days. It's a small button on the left side of the cocking piece. A J-shaped slot in the button takes a J-shaped key. Want to render the rifle inoperable? Just lock the bolt open with the key. It's safe. Want to make it safe forever? Just lose the key. Or you can ensure function by unlocking the device, then throwing the key away.

The 710 was initially cataloged in 270 and 30-06 but is now available in 7mm Magnum and 300 Winchester Magnum as well. The first rifles to ship were '06s. They wore 22-inch barrels, button-rifled with six right-hand grooves, a 1-in-10 twist. "Remington 700s have hammer-forged rifling," adds Mike. In my experience, there's no difference in accuracy potential between the two rifling types. Most barrel-makers agree that dimensional uniformity and finish have a bigger effect on accuracy than does rifling method. The 710 barrel has a slot in its belly that mates with a steel recoil lug in the stock, which is made of fiberglass-reinforced polypropylene. The trigger guard is integral. There's a black rubber recoil pad. I like the gray, rough-textured stock finish. The top of the comb is properly straight, with a modest cheekpiece. Mike says the stock walls are heavier than they need to be "to eliminate the hollow sound a lot of shooters object to." Those thick walls add weight, but the rifle still scales a manageable 7 1/8 pounds.

The 710's detachable box magazine features a generous bottom plate and a forward latch. It holds four 30-06 cartridges, three magnums. "We designed it for central feed," says Mike. "Again, reliability was a primary goal from the start, and a cartridge coming up from the middle has a straighter shot into the chamber than one rising from the left or right." Cartridges below form a staggered stack. I ask Mike why Remington didn't employ a blind magazine, as on the 700 ADL and the Model 78

Wayne fired this 1 1/2-inch group with a first-run 710 in 30-06.

that had a brief moment in the sun. I like blind magazines.

"First," Mike replies, "detachable magazines are convenient. Push a latch, and the cartridges drop into your hand in one neat package. If you're in a vehicle with the rifle unloaded and you suddenly spot a buck, you can jump out, snap the magazine in, and go after him. No fumbling with numb fingers for loose rounds in your pocket. No jams.

"The second advantage is cost. It's less with a box because the feed lips are bent into pressed steel. That's easy to do. A blind magazine still has a metal box to ensure correct internal dimensions, but the feed lips are part of the receiver. As you know, they have to be just right for a smooth feed. Machining them into the magazine mouth isn't easy or cheap." The 30-06 I plucked from the first run of 710s fed reliably but not easily. In contrast, the 300 Winchester Magnum that's in my rack now feeds with the eagerness of a well-aged 700. From the box or single-loaded from the hand, the bolt slicks each round smoothly

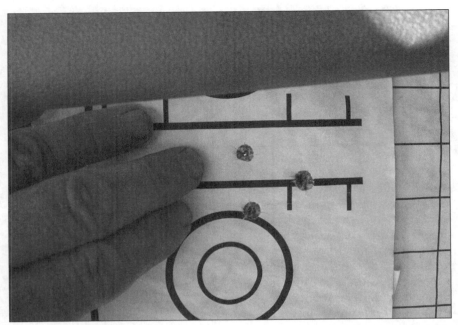

The 710 in .300 Winchester Mag printed just over an inch groups at 100 yards. Not bad for an out-of-0the-box "no frills" rifle!

into the chamber. Extraction is snappy and positive.

I recall that Remington's 788, the last entry-level rifle Mike will acknowledge, wore a detachable box. It was a short-action rifle with interrupted-thread lockup. Made from 1967 to 1984, it was modestly successful at market. I owned a 308 for awhile, and it shot just over an inch. "Those were fine rifles," he concedes, "but more expensive to make than we anticipated."

What level of accuracy can you expect from 710s? The early 30-06 I shot delivered groups of about 1 1/2 inches. That's quite good for a big game rifle – certainly adequate for the longest shooting you're likely to do at deer. It's better accuracy than most of us can use from hunting positions. The 300 Winchester Magnum I had at the range this week printed a 1-inch group and doubled holes a couple of times but averaged between 1 and 2 inches – that with 190-grain Match loads from Black Hills. Mike says most accuracy reports have been favorable. He reminds me this rifle was

designed to perform alongside an off-the-shelf 700.

Next to its lockup and the bolt race insert, the most unusual feature of the 710 is its packaging. Buy one of these rifles, and you get a scope too. Bushnell's 3-9x40 Sharpshooter scope comes mounted in rings machined to Remington's specifications – an "OEM" or "original equipment manufacturer" product, as opposed to an item bought or contracted from outside sources selling existing product.

"*Most* 710 rifles are shipped with these scopes," says Mike Keeney. "The barrels are undrilled for sights. But we install iron sights as an alternative. The price is the same."

Price. That's important to the customers Remington targeted with its new rifle. It retails for about $425, But many have been sold at discount.

Some early 710s went out the door for less than $350. These days, that's very cheap for a big game rifle with a variable scope.

The 710 is not for the connoisseur. It lacks the refinements of more expensive rifles, and the level of finish once lavished on even entry-level rifles. There's no walnut here, and the pad fit could be better. The cast bolt handle is not to my taste. But to be fair, this rifle fulfills the requirements company engineers specified before it took shape. The bolt-to-barrel lockup is certainly strong. The straight-line feed and 700-style bolt face promise sure-fire reliability, and the button-rifled barrel has delivered accuracy better than what you'll get with some more costly guns. The bomb-proof stock, durable metal finish and a scope that adds essentially nothing to the price are bonuses. If you're not an entry-level shooter, maybe you need a rifle for the truck, a knock-about gun for trips into the back-country on unproven horses and in ill-fitting scabbards, a foul-weather smokepole that lets you focus on hunting instead of shielding an expensive stick of French walnut.

Come to think of it, the market for rugged, no-frills rifles like Remington's rough-and-ready 710 is bound to be with us for a long time. 🦌

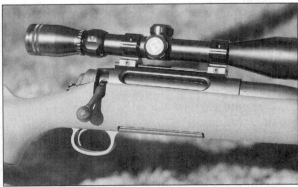

Factory-packaged with a 3-9x Bushnell scope, the 710 is a real bargain at around $425.

Reports from the Field

What's Hot in the World of Deer Guns and Accessories

By the Contributing Editors of GUN DIGEST© 2005

RIFLES

Benelli

Last year, the sleek R1 autoloading rifle from Benelli was available in 30-06 and 300 Winchester Magnum. This year, the 308 Winchester chambering has been added to the list but, unfortunately, the 7mm-08 Remington has not.

Ed Brown

I recently examined the new lightweight Damara from Ed Brown and found it to be a very nice rifle. Built on Brown's short action, it has a McMillan fiberglass stock and 22-inch barrel and it weighs just over six pounds. Available chamberings include about anything you can squeeze into a short-action rifle, from the 243 Winchester to the short magnums from Remington and Winchester. You can buy this one with a right- or left-hand action.

Browning

With their racy European styling, the new ShortTrac and LongTrac versions of the BAR autoloader were obviously spooked from the bushes by last year's introduction of the R1 rifle by Benelli. As you might have guessed, one is chambered for short cartridges such as the 243 Winchester, 308 Winchester and the three WSM cartridges in 270, 7mm and 300 calibers while the other is offered in 270 Winchester, 30-06, 7mm Remington Magnum and 300 Winchester Magnum. Both variations have lightweight aluminum receivers and their trigger guards and floorplates are synthetic. Depending on caliber and barrel length, nominal weights range from 6-3/4 to 7-1/2 pounds. Weights for the standard BAR run from 7-1/4 to 8-1/2 pounds.

With its titanium receiver, lightweight 23-inch stainless steel barrel and synthetic stock, the new Mountain Ti version of the A-Bolt rifle is rated at only 5-1/2 pounds. For now, it is available in the three WSM chamberings of 270, 7mm and 300.

Harrington & Richardson/NEF

The break-action H&R single-shot Handi-Rifle is both adult and youth rifles in 7mm-08 and stainless steel rifles in 30-06 and 270 Winchester. Then we have the Huntsman Combos. The

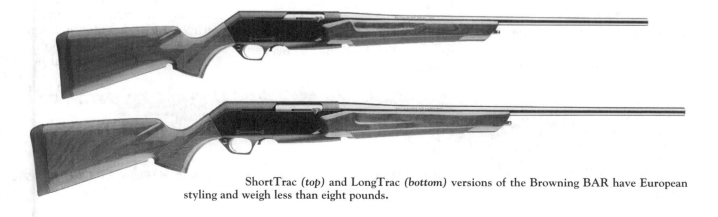

ShortTrac *(top)* and LongTrac *(bottom)* versions of the Browning BAR have European styling and weigh less than eight pounds.

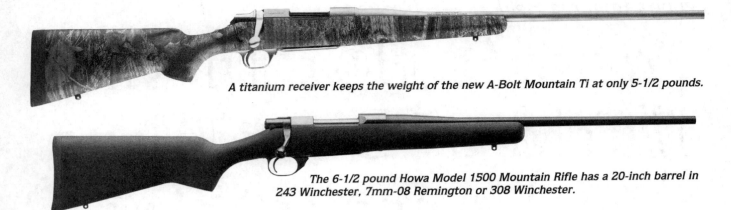

A titanium receiver keeps the weight of the new A-Bolt Mountain Ti at only 5-1/2 pounds.

The 6-1/2 pound Howa Model 1500 Mountain Rifle has a 20-inch barrel in 243 Winchester, 7mm-08 Remington or 308 Winchester.

Pardner and Handi-Rifle sets come with interchangeable shotgun and muzzleloader barrels in 12-gauge and 50-caliber, while the Handi-Rifle set has barrels in 243 Winchester and 50- caliber. Regardless of which you choose, all represent excellent buys and are surprisingly accurate considering their cost

Legacy Sports International

The 6-1/2 pound Howa Model 1500 Mountain Rifle is available with a 20-inch barrel in 243 Winchester, 7mm-08 Remington and 308 Winchester. The action has a hollowed bolt handle knob and lightening cuts along the receiver and bolt shroud for weight reduction. All metal has a dark, non-glare finish and the stock is hardwood with a black, rough-textured finish. With the exception of its 12-5/8 inch length of pull the new Youth Rifle is quite similar to that one. As for new chamberings, the Hunter and Lightning rifles are now available in 25-06 Remington.

Marlin

The New Model Marlin 1895 is now available in five chamberings. Joining the 444 Marlin, 45-70 Government and 450 Marlin are the 480 Ruger and 475 Linebaugh. Called the Model 1895RL, it has an 18 1/2-inch barrel with six-groove rifling with a 1:20 twist and its magazine holds six 480s or five 475s. Nominal weight is seven pounds, same as for rifles in the other three calibers.

Remington

For several years now I have urged Remington decision-makers to offer the 8x57mm Mauser chambering in the limited edition Model 700 Classic. After all, what could be more classic than an old cartridge that continues to be more popular among American hunters than a whole slew of American-designed cartridges? I finally get my wish in 2004. Number 24 in a series that started back in 1981 with the 7x57mm Mauser, the Model 700 Classic in 8x57mm has a 24-inch barrel and weighs just over seven pounds.

They call it the Model 700 CDL (Classic Deluxe) but to me it looks like a reintroduction of the original Model 700 Mountain Rifle. Which is okay by me because the Model 700 MR is one of the best-looking, best-handling and best- feeling big-game rifles I have ever carried in the field. The new version does have a longer barrel: 24 inches in 243 Winchester, 7mm-08, 270 Winchester and 30-06, and 26 inches in 7mm Remington Magnum, 7mm Remington Ultra Mag, 300 Winchester Magnum and 300 Remington Ultra Mag. Weights run around 7-1/2 pounds in standard chamberings and 7-3/4 pounds for the magnums. All metal has a satin blued finish and the classically styled stock has cut checkering, black forearm tip and gripcap and Remington's own R3 recoil pad.

The Model 700 Titanium, which is America's first affordable rifle with a titanium receiver, is now available in a short-action magnum version with 24-inch barrel in 7mm and 300 Remington Short Action Ultra Mag. Nominal weight is

The New Model 1895 from Marlin is now available in 480 Ruger and 475 Linebaugh.

The Remington Model 700 CDL.

The Remington Model Seven YS (Youth Synthetic).

6-3/8 pounds which means that its field-ready weight with scope, lightweight carrying sling and loaded magazine should not greatly exceed eight pounds. That's darned light for a rifle capable of squeezing maximum performance from Remington's two ultra-short magnum cartridges.

Considered by many who own it to offer the most performance for the least amount of money, the Model 710 is now available in a magnum version with a 24-inch barrel in 7mm Remington Magnum or 300 Winchester Magnum. Its detachable magazine holds three rounds and the rifle comes with a Bushnell 3-9X Sharpshooter scope riding up top. Nominal weight is 7-1/4 pounds.

As its name implies, the Model Seven YS (Youth Synthetic) has a synthetic stock and a 12 3/8-inch length of pull for short arms. Surface texturing on the grip and forearm are just the thing for slippery hands and the R3 recoil pads tames what little recoil is generated by the 223 Remington, 243 Winchester, and 7mm-08 cartridges. The satin-blued barrel is 20 inches long and nominal weight is 6-1/4 pounds. A long-action version with a 22-inch barrel in 270 Winchester

and 30-06 might represent the best of all deals. The young hunter can start out with Remington's new Managed Recoil loadings of those two cartridges and then after a few deer seasons have come and gone he or she can graduate to standard-power loadings.

Rifles, Incorporated

Among my proudest possessions is a trio of Lightweight Strata rifles built by Lex Webernick on Remington Model 700 actions in 257 STW, 6.5 STW and 7mm STW. Those rifles weigh around five pounds each. Even lighter at 4-1/2 pounds is the Titanium Strata built on the Model 700 titanium action in most chamberings up to and including the 300 Weatherby Magnum. One of those rifles on the short action in 243 Winchester, 6mm Remington or 257 Roberts would be especially nice for rough-country deer.

Rossi

Last year, Rossi introduced its "Matched Pairs" combo set version of its single-shot gun with both centerfire rifle and shotgun barrels. This year, you can buy a three-barrel set with those—plus a muzzleloader

barrel. One combination is made up of barrels in 17 HMR, 270 Winchester and 50-caliber. In case you are not familiar with the Rossi, it is an economy-grade, break-action, knockabout gun with exposed hammer *(replete with hammer-block safety)*. To break down its barrel for loading and unloading you simply press down on a lever located at the side of its receiver.

Sako

New Model 75 variants from Sako for 2004 include the Hunter and Stainless Synthetic in 270 WSM and 300 WSM. Three additional chambering options for the Model 75 Deluxe are 416 Remington Magnum and the two just-mentioned Winchester shorty magnums. Also new is the Custom Single-Shot in 308 Winchester with heavy, fluted, stainless-steel barrel, laminated wood stock replete with beavertail forearm.

Savage

I am no great fan of muzzle brakes but if ever I become one the adjustable brake from Savage is the one my rifles will wear. Twist the brake one way to open its gas ports and your rifle

The Savage Safari Express.

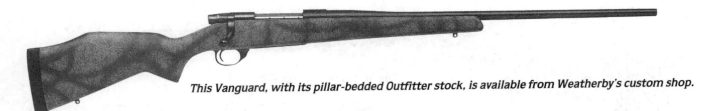

This Vanguard, with its pillar-bedded Outfitter stock, is available from Weatherby's custom shop.

is ready for a shooting session at the benchrest or practice range. Twist it in the opposite direction and you are ready to head for the field. The AMB is presently available on the Model 116FSAK and the Safari Express. The relatively new AccuTrigger is something Savage bolt guns have needed for a very long time and I am glad to see it standard issue on practically every model variation, including the in-line muzzleloader. Weight of pull on most rifles is owner-adjustable from 2-1/2 to 6 pounds.

Schuerman Arms, Ltd.

For the second year in a row, the Model SA40 from Schuerman Arms has received my vote as the bolt-action rifle with the smoothest action. Somewhat like the Colt Sauer rifle of yesteryear, it has three pivoting locking lugs–but in this case they are located quite close to the front of the bolt. The bolt glides to and fro in the receiver like hot grease on glass. It is available in about any chambering you can think of, from 22-250 to 416 Remington Magnum.

Thompson/Center

The G2 Contender rifle will be offered in 375 JDJ , and the Encore rifle is now available in 280 Remington, 375 JDJ, and 405 Winchester. Also available from Thompson/Center is 375 JDJ ammo loaded with a 220-grain flatnose bullet at about 2200 fps in Encore and Contender pistols, and 2300 to 2400 fps in rifle versions of those guns. The new carbine variation of the Encore 209x50 muzzleloader has a 20-inch barrel.

I had never hunted with the Encore in anything except its handgun form until the performance I was getting out of a 26-inch custom shop barrel in 6mm-06 and the new 90-grain Swift Scirocco bullet indicated it was time I did. I later used that same Encore receiver and stock along with a 205x50 muzzleloader barrel to take a 140s-class whitetail while hunting with Judd Cooney in Iowa.

Tikka

The T3 Lite Stainless is my favorite Tikka big-game rifle. It has a stainless-steel barreled action, a black synthetic stock and weighs a mere 6-1/4 pounds in standard chamberings, and 6-1/2 pounds in the magnums. Barrel lengths are 22-1/2 and 24-1/2 inches. Chambering options range from the 223 Remington to the 338 Winchester Magnum. My pick for this rifle is the 7mm-08 Remington. Latest in the lineup is the T3 Laminated Stainless with those same barrel lengths and calibers.

USRAC

Those who shoot from the left shoulder will surely be pleased to learn that the Featherweight and Sporter versions of the Model 70 now come with the bolt handle over on their side. The left-hand Featherweight is available in three WSM chamberings: 270, 7mm and 300, while Sporter options include those three, plus 270 Winchester, 30- 06, 7mm Remington Magnum and 300 Winchester Magnum. Believe it or not, USRAC now offers seven variations of the Model 9410 with the Semi-Fancy Traditional being

the latest. It gets its name from– you guessed it–its stock of semi-fancy walnut. The latest version of the Model 94 lever action is called the Timber *(who comes up with these names?)*. It has an 18-inch ported barrel in 450 Marlin and, even more interesting, it comes from the factory wearing an aperture sight.

Weatherby

Who'd ever have thought we'd see a Weatherby big-game rifle with a fully adjustable trigger priced at $476? That's retail for the Vanguard Synthetic and I've seen them go for a bit less. The one I took on a deer hunt in Texas proved to be better than accurate enough with Federal Premium ammo. The latest Vanguard synthetic stock is the Monte Carlo style and it is injection-molded of lightweight composite materials for maximum durability and stability. Also new for 2004 is the Vanguard Sporter with walnut stock replete with rosewood forend tip, 18 lines-per-inch cut checkering and a nice rubber recoil pad. It has a 24- inch barrel and is chambered for a variety of cartridges. Both new variations have Monte Carlo-style stocks simply because a Weatherby doesn't look or feel like a Weatherby unless it has a Monte Carlo stock. Others have attempted to copy the design but nobody has managed to capture the true essence of the Monte Carlo stock like Weatherby.

Up until now the Vanguard has been available in 223 Remington, 22-250, 243 Winchester, 270 Winchester, 308 Winchester, 30-06, 7mm

Remington Magnum, 300 Winchester Magnum, 300 Winchester Short Magnum, 300 Weatherby Magnum and 338 Winchester Magnum. A new chambering this year is the 257 Magnum—which just happens to be one of the most popular Weatherby cartridges. Loaded to respective velocities of 3825, 3600 and 3400 fps with 87-, 100- and 117-grain bullets, it also just happens to be the fastest 25-caliber factory cartridge available. I simply cannot imagine a better long-range antelope/deer/caribou/sheep/goat rifle for the money than the Weatherby Vanguard in 257 Weatherby Magnum. For those who simply cannot be satisfied by an off-the-shelf rifle, the Weatherby custom shop offers a number of modifications to the Vanguard. They include hand-bedded synthetic stocks in various camo patterns, replete with pillar bedding. Special metal finishes such as black Teflon and titanium nitride are also available.

Before leaving the subject of things Weatherby I must mention that I survived another cold winter hunting season in large part due to the warmth of excellent wool clothing sold by this company. Its most severe test of 2003 came during a muzzleloader hunt for deer in Iowa. Sitting on a deer stand all day long in temperatures that drop below zero is not very high up on my list of fun things to do and had I not been wearing extremely warm wool clothing I could not have done it. I managed to survive by wearing the Double Yoke Shirt, the Heavyweight Parka and the Late Season Cargo Pant over several layers of long underwear. Anytime it snowed or the wind blew I wore a Browning rain jacket and pant on the outside. I also wore the Weatherby Heavyweight Gloves with

chemical warmers placed inside. Like Ralphie's little brother in "The Christmas Story", I had on so much clothing I could hardly lower my arms but I stayed warm and just as important, I got my buck. – *Layne Simpsonl*

NOTE: Autographed copies of Layne's full-color, hardback books, *"Shotguns and Shotgunning"* and *"Rifles and Cartridges For Large Game"*, are available for $39.95 plus $6 for shipping and handling each from High Country Press, 306 Holly Park Lane, Dept. GD, Simpsonville, SC 29681. Also available is a softcover edition of his *"The Custom 1911 Pistol"* for $30.95 plus $4 s&h.

HANDGUNS

It was 50 years ago, in 1955, when Smith & Wesson produced the first 44 Magnum. Everyone knew we had reached the top; there was simply no way six-guns could ever be made more powerful. Then, in 1983 Freedom Arms produced their first 454 Casull. John Linebaugh arrived on the scene giving us the 475 and 500 Linebaughs and then stretching both to approximately 1.60 inches for "Maximum" versions of the same two cartridges. Custom revolver-builders offered heavy-duty, five-shot 45 Colt six-guns to allow heavy loading of this grand old cartridge, and Hornady and Ruger collaborated on the 480. Had we reached the end of powerful six-gun cartridge development?

Not quite. The big news last year was the 500 S&W Magnum cartridge and the new Smith & Wesson X-frame revolver. We have now had a year to test this largest of all double-action six-guns, as well as the 500 cartridge. Other manufacturers have joined with Smith & Wesson in supplying 500-chambered revolvers—with Magnum Research offering a

single action BFR revolver while Taurus has countered with their Raging Bull version in 500 S&W Magnum. Two custom makers, Gary Reeder Custom Guns and SSK Industries, have offered their 500 Magnums in revolver and single-shot form, respectively. It has been my good (?) fortune to have test-fired the 500 Magnum extensively over the past year, chambered in the original 8 3/8-inch Smith & Wesson Model 500, a 10 1/2-inch BFR, an SSK Custom Encore, and a Gary Reeder single action. The cartridge has proven to be extremely accurate, as well as speaking with authority and finality when used on game.

One might think this would be the end of cartridge development; however, I have been shown three new cartridges that will be arriving on the scene this year. As this is written they must remain as "mystery cartridges", however I can share the fact that two of them will be standard length 50-caliber cartridges for use in single-action revolvers, while the other will be a "Maximum"-length 45-caliber cartridge. We are still looking and hoping for a five-shot Ruger single action in 480 Ruger or 50-caliber, however none of these will be in handguns marked with the Ruger label.

Colt

At one time Colt had a whole stable full of snakes. The Viper, Cobra, King Cobra, and

Colt's Python celebrates its 50th anniversary this year as the Python Elite.

Diamondback are all gone; however, the Anaconda and the Python remain. Although originally offered in both 45 Colt and 44 Magnum, currently the Anaconda is offered only in a stainless steel 44 Magnum with barrel lengths of 4, 6, and 8 inches, complete with fully adjustable sights and finger-groove rubber grips. It has proven to be a sturdy, reliable, accurate hunting handgun. Many shooters would argue that the Python is the finest double-action revolver ever offered at any time. I don't argue; I just enjoy shooting the Python. It continues in the Colt lineup as the Python Elite, in either blue or stainless with a 4- or 6-inch barrel.

Freedom Arms

Last year Freedom Arms introduced their Model 97 five-shot 44 Special, which I have now had a pleasurable year shooting. Since its inception in 1907, the 44 Special has been chambered in some of the finest revolvers ever produced. From Smith & Wesson we have the Triple-Lock, the Model 1926, the 1950 Target and, in more recent times, the Model 24 and Model 624—as well as a five-shot 296 and 696. Colt waited a while to chamber the 44 Special; however, when they finally moved in that direction they gave us the New Service, the Single Action Army, and the New Frontier. All great six-guns; however, the 44 Special Triple-Lock is most often considered the finest 44 Special––if not the finest revolver-period––ever manufactured. It now has a rival. The 44 Special Model 97 from Freedom Arms is surely the finest single-action 44 Special ever offered, and may just be every bit as good as that first Special 44.

Hartford Armory

A new six-gun manufacturer has arrived on the scene.

Hartford Armory is now offering the Remington 1890 and 1875 Single Actions. Go back 125 years. Colt, Remington, and Smith & Wesson all made beautiful single-action revolvers. The Colt handled blackpowder extremely well, while the Remington and Smith & Wesson had such tight tolerances they were actually smokeless-powder guns in a blackpowder age. In other words, they were so tightly fitted and closely machined they fouled easily when used with blackpowder. Fast- forward to today and we have the return of the Remington at a time when most shooters use them with smokeless powder. At last we will find out what excellent six-guns the Remingtons actually were. Hartford Armory is building truly authentic versions of the originals that have, at least in my hand, a different feel from the Italian replicas. Both the 1875 and 1890 will be offered in a full blue finish, classified as Hartford Armory Dark Blue, or with a Turnbull case-colored frame; and also in stainless steel. Stocks are two-piece walnut.

Now comes the real surprise: this new version of the old Remington Single Action is chambered in 45 Colt and rated for +P loads; and is also offered in 44 Magnum. Other calibers will be 357 Magnum and 44-40. Although sights are the traditionally fixed single-action style; the front sight, which screws into the barrel, will be offered in different heights for sighting-in heavy-duty hunting loads. I am definitely looking

forward to fully testing of this new/old revolver.

Magnum Research

Magnum Research offers the all-stainless steel BFR (*Biggest Finest Revolver*). The BFR looks much like a Ruger Super Blackhawk; the grip frames will accept the same grips—however, unlike Ruger six- guns, the BFR has a freewheeling cylinder that rotates either clockwise or counter-clockwise when the loading gate is opened. It is offered in two versions: the Short Cylinder chambered in 454 Casull and 480 Ruger/475 Linebaugh, and 22 Hornet; the Long Cylinder is offered in 444 Marlin, 450 Marlin, 45-70, a special 45 Colt that also accepts 3- inch .410 shotgun shells, and–new for this year–500 S&W Magnum.

All BFR revolvers are American-made with cut-rifled, hand-lapped, recessed-muzzle-crowned barrels; tight tolerances; soft brushed stainless steel finish; and are normally equipped with an adjustable rear sight mated with a front sight with interchangeable blades of differing heights. They can be ordered from the factory set up with a scope and an SSK base. The SSK mounting system is the strongest available anywhere for scoping hard-kicking handguns. For the past year I have been extensively testing two BFR six-guns in 480/475 Linebaugh and 500 S&W Magnum. They have proven to be exceptionally accurate and have performed flawlessly.

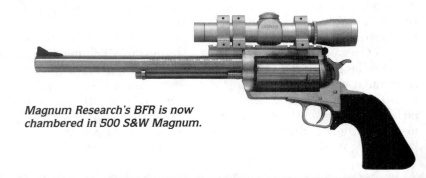

Magnum Research's BFR is now chambered in 500 S&W Magnum.

Ruger

Ruger single actions have always been favorites of handgun hunters—especially their Hunter Models which continue to be offered in both the Super Blackhawk and Bisley models, in stainless steel, chambered in 44 Magnum, and wearing 7 1/2-inch heavy-ribbed barrels set up to accept Ruger scope rings.

Ruger continues to offer their excellent lineup of six-guns: the Blackhawk, the Bisley Model, the Vaquero, the Bisley Vaquero, the Redhawk, the Super Redhawk, the GP-100, and the Single-Six. This year marks the Golden Anniversary of the immensely popular Ruger 357 Blackhawk. Also new this year from Ruger is the Ruger Studio of Art and Decoration for providing engraved versions of Ruger firearms. There will be no set patterns; rather, each firearm will be individually embellished to fit the desires of the owner. The work will be performed only on new Ruger firearms. In the past this service has only been available for special presentations or occasions, and for the late Bill Ruger's personal collection.

Savage

Savage continues to offer their excellent Striker series of bolt-action pistols. The stainless steel Striker comes with a black synthetic stock, muzzle brake, left-hand bolt, and chambered in 223 Remington, 270 WSM, 7-08 Remington, 7mm WSM, 308 Winchester, and 300 WSM.

Smith & Wesson

Thousands of the Model 500 X-Frame 500 S&W Magnum were sold in its first year of production and now a new, easier-packing version is offered. The newest Model 500 has a 4-inch barrel—actually 3 inches of barrel, plus a compensator. This could be just the ticket for those who regularly travel areas where four- legged

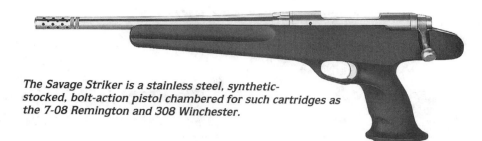

The Savage Striker is a stainless steel, synthetic-stocked, bolt-action pistol chambered for such cartridges as the 7-08 Remington and 308 Winchester.

beasts can be mean and nasty. This new version also wears the finger-grooved rubber grips of the original 8 3/8-inch Model 500.

As far as grips go, I have found a better way—I should say the better way has been shown to me by Rod Herrett of Herrett's Stocks.

Some shooters experience a phenomenon when shooting the 500 Magnum in that the cylinder unlocks and rotates backwards. One of the reasons for this—and it does not happen with every shooter—is the rubber grips cause the Model 500 to bounce off the web of the hand, resulting in the trigger hitting the trigger finger—which naturally causes the trigger to start backwards and the cylinder to unlock. The solution from Rod Herrett was a pair of smooth-finished walnut Jordan stocks. These grips fill in the backstrap and do not bounce off the hand, as the rubber grips

have a tendency to do with some shooters.

The extremely popular Mountain Gun with its tapered 4-inch barrel is back, this time as a 45 Colt with the Model 25; the Model 686 is offered as a seven-shot 357 Magnum with a 5-inch standard barrel *sans* the heavy underlug; the Model 327 is offered as an eight-shot 357 Magnum with a 2-inch barrel. Hopefully, these special 25 and 686 Models will start a trend back to standard barrels.

Taurus

The Taurus Raging Bull arrives in a new version with a longer cylinder and frame to accommodate the 500 S&W Magnum, and a couple of lightweight versions are now offered for easy carrying, with the Instant Backup smaller Model 85 in a five-shot 9mm and an eight-shot 17 HMR—viable

Two of the greatest bargains offered to handgun hunters are Ruger's Hunter Model 44 Magnum in the Bisley and Super Blackhawk versions.

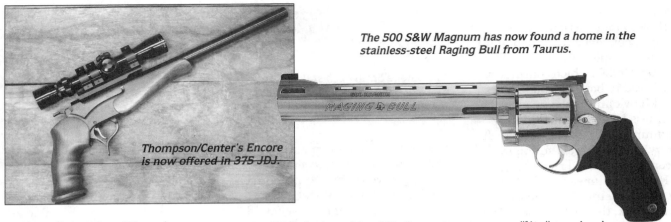

The 500 S&W Magnum has now found a home in the stainless-steel Raging Bull from Taurus.

Thompson/Center's Encore is now offered in 375 JDJ.

options for senior citizens' defensive use. At the other end of the power spectrum, Taurus offers the Hip Carry, a 28-ounce, 4-inch barreled Raging Bull chambered in 44 Magnum. Grips are the recoil-reducing cushioned insert grips found on the standard Raging Bull.

Thompson/Center

Thompson/Center single-shot pistols have long been favorites both at long-range silhouette matches and in the hunting field. They have been chambered for dozens of factory and wildcat cartridges for those looking for long-range accuracy and adequate power for either target shooting or taking big game. T/C offers two versions of their break-open, single-shot pistols: the standard Contender now in its second phase with the easier-opening G2, and the Encore. The G2 will handle cartridges in the 30-30 and 44 Magnum range, while the larger, heavier Encore feels quite at home with the higher-pressure cartridges such as the 308 and 30-06. Some cartridges, such as the 45-70, are offered in both versions.

Two new cartridges have been added this year, both chambered in the Contender and the Encore. The first cartridge is the new 20-caliber varmint cartridge, the 204 Ruger; while the second is capable of taking any big-game animal found anywhere in the world. The latter cartridge is the

375 JDJ, designed by J.D. Jones of SSK Industries. J.D. is a longtime friend and the absolute authority when it comes to many things concerned with firearms, especially with single-shot pistol cartridges. The 375 JDJ is to single-shot pistols what the 375 H&H is to bolt-action rifles. It may be larger than necessary for some critters and a little light for others, but in capable hands it will always do the job with authority. If I could have only one—and wouldn't that be terrible—single-shot pistol for hunting big game, it would be chambered in 375 JDJ. I have been using my custom SSK 375 JDJ with great satisfaction for nearly two decades now. The introduction of this cartridge in a standard factory handgun should increase its popularity even more. – *John Taffin*

SHOTGUNS

Ithaca

For slug shooters, Ithaca has a rifled 24-inch barrel with a 1:34 twist that fits Remington, Browning and Benelli shotguns. The barrels have either a steel cantilever scope mount or TRUGLO fiber-optic sights. Ithaca states two-inch groups at 100 yards should not be uncommon.

Last year's introduction of the Storm series of 12-gauge guns was so well received that a 20-

gauge "lite" version is now available. The Deerslayer has a 24-inch rifled barrel with open sights. All metal parts have a Parkerized finish to go along with a black synthetic stock and forearm. A Sims Limb Saver recoil pad takes the sting out of recoil. The Turkeyslayer wears a 24-inch ported barrel with TRUGLO fiber-optic sights and a screw-in Full choke tube designed for Remington's Hevi-Shot loads. The camo pattern is HD Hardwoods Green. The Upland wears a 26-inch ventilated rib barrel with a Raybar front sight. The Parkerized metal and synthetic stock and forearm will withstand any foul weather. The gun can also be cloaked in Realtree Advantage MAX-4 HD camo.

Mossberg

The 935 Magnum is Mossberg's new gas-operated autoloader, which handles the 12-gauge 3 1/2-inch shell. The 935's synthetic stocks come in basic black or dressed in various camo patterns. The gun includes a ventilated rib on a 22-, 24-, 26-, or 28-inch barrel with three screw-in Accu-Mag choke tubes. Nice touches include stock spacers, a button to quickly empty the magazine and a fiber-optic front bead.

The Grand Slam series includes the 935 and the 835 Ultra-Mag and 500 pumps. The 935 Grand Slam has a 22-inch barrel; 20-inch barrels are on the 835s and 500s. All the guns are covered in a variety of camouflage patterns and come with a camo-colored sling. Adjustable fiber-optic sights are standard, along with an Extra Full extended choke tube for turkey hunting.

The 835 pump 12-gauge comes in several additional models. The Field wears hardwood stocks and a 26-inch ventilated rib barrel. The Synthetic is the same gun with a matte metal finish and synthetic stocks. The Turkey/Waterfowl Combo is dressed in camo with 24- and 28-inch barrels. Adjustable fiber-optic sights are attached to the shorter barrel. The longer barrel wears a fiber-optic front bead. The Turkey/Deer Combo comes with a 24-inch barrel with an Ulti-Full choke tube screwed in. The deer barrel is 24 inches long, rifled for slugs and has a cantilever scope ring base.

The 500 pump Waterfowl wears Mossy Oak Obsession camo with a 20-gauge 28-inch barrel and Advantage Max 4 camo with the 12-gauge's 28-inch barrel. The Bantam Slug 20-gauge has a rifled barrel 24 inches long. The stock has a 13-inch length of pull, grip closer to the trigger and forearm set closer to the receiver. The Bantam Field/Slug Combo has a 20-gauge 22-inch barrel for birds, and a 24-inch rifled slug barrel. The regular size Field/Slug Combo 12-gauge has a 24-inch rifled barrel with adjustable sights and a 28-inch smoothbore barrel that accepts choke tubes. The Muzzleloader/Slug Combo has a 50-caliber muzzleloader barrel and a 24-inch rifled slug barrel.

Remington

The Model 870 pump has been around in one version or another since ducks were invented. This year an 870 Special Purpose Shotgun in 20-gauge has a fully rifled 18 1/2-inch barrel, black synthetic stocks, R3 recoil pad and a cantilever scope base that is attached to the barrel and reaches back over the receiver to allow using a scope, or other optic sight with normal eye relief.

Rossi

Rossi has added a fully rifled 12-gauge barrel to its hinge action. To take the sting out of shooting slugs, the barrel is ported back of the front sight. Adjustable rear and front dot TRUGLO fiber-optic sights are standard, as is a scope ring base.

Tristar

Tristar imports the HP and HP Marine join the TR-Diana line of semi-autos. Both models have synthetic black handles and a 19-inch barrel with three extended 12-gauge choke tubes. An adjustable rear sight and front blade are for shooting slugs and buckshot. – *John Haviland*

BLACKPOWDER

Prairie River Arms

This innovative company is marketing a modern-type muzzleloader that is about as far from the traditional long rifle as one can get. They have incorporated the inline principle into a bullpup design that is truly unique. The bullpup design, where the action is moved back into the buttstock under the shooter's cheek, surfaced in the mid-1900s in custom centerfire varmint rifles. It is most recently seen in the current British military assault rifle. The advantage is a standard length barrel in a very short rifle.

The Prairie River rifle features a 28-inch barrel, and an overall length of 31-1/2 inches. This is accomplished by moving the action back into the buttstock, and moving the trigger forward. The stock design is a thumbhole type: very straight, putting the shoulder directly in line with the barrel. This makes recoil very manageable with little or no muzzle raise on firing. Balance is very good, putting the weight of the gun between the hands. The short length makes it a very handy gun in brush or tree stands. The rifle is available with a hardwood stock in either a natural or an "all weather" black epoxy finish. It can be had in either 50- or 54-caliber. The 1:28 rifling twist is correct for conical bullets or sabotted projectiles.

The rifle uses standard #11 caps. The nipple is reached by pushing up a door in the offside of the buttstock. After capping, this door is pushed back down, effectively sealing the ignition system from moisture, dirt, etc.– – as well as containing any cap fragmentation or blowback. The nipple sets in a drum that protrudes from the bottom of the barrel, which assures the drum will fill with powder via gravity when the gun is loaded. The cocking handle is just to the rear of the trigger and has two safety positions. There is an additional safety inside the trigger guard that blocks trigger movement. An

The Prairie River Arms "Bull Pup" inline; note the nipple access door in the buttstock.

The Knight Disc Extreme in 52-caliber gives superior ballistics at ranges of 200 yards.

anodized hard aluminum ramrod fits into the stock under the barrel. The mechanism is very simple, just two moving parts, and takedown is by the removal of one screw.

The guns are available with Williams Guide-type sights, front and rear, or an optional M-16-type carrying handle that contains a M-16 national match sight, matched with a Williams front. The carrying handle will also accept standard M-16/AR-15 scope mounts, if you are so inclined. With the carrying handle installed and the tall front sight–*a la* assault rifles– this one is certainly not your grandfather's muzzleloader!

Knight Rifles

Knight never rests on its laurels. has a couple of things for the in-line shooter also. First, they have added something to their Disc Extreme rifles. The new offering is a 52-caliber with a totally redesigned breech plug called the Power Stem. The breech plug is made with a thin, hollow extension on the front that channels the fire from the 209 primer to the front of the powder charge. By igniting the front of the powder charge first, the bullet gains more uniform acceleration, yielding higher velocities, increased energy and less punishing recoil, according to Knight. To further add to shooter comfort, the gun comes with an Xcoil recoil pad by HiViz shooting systems. This pad is said to dampen felt recoil by 33 percent more than conventional recoil pads. The recommended charge of 150 grains of FFg loose blackpowder, or its equivalent, gives velocities approaching 2000 fps with a 375-grain bullet.

Pellets or charges less than 90 grains are not recommended. The 52-caliber outperforms the 54-caliber due to the bullet/sabot fit. The thinner petals on the 52-cal. sabot allow it to release from the bullet quicker, enhancing accuracy. The rifle uses the Full Plastic Jacket ignition system, with 209 primers, found on the other Disc Supreme rifles.

The other new offering from Knight is a revolutionary in-line that looks, at first glance, like a Winchester High Wall without a hammer. This rotating-block action is activated by pulling the trigger guard down and forward to expose the breech plug. A full plastic jacket is inserted into the breechblock and raising the trigger guard closes the action. The gun, assuming a loaded barrel, is ready to fire. The hammer is enclosed in the swinging-action block.

For cleaning, the trigger guard is rotated forward and the entire action block — trigger, hammer, springs, etc. — can be removed from the rifle without tools. Called the Knight Revolution, the new rifle features a 27-inch barrel in either blued or stainless finish, a two-piece synthetic stock and fully adjustable metallic fiber optic sights. Caliber is .50. The trigger is fully adjustable for both creep and pull weight. With an overall length of 43-1/2 inches and a weight of just under 8 lbs., this is a handy rifle that will find favor with hunters everywhere, I predict.

Hornady Manufacturing Co.

This Nebraska-based outfit that has been one of the leaders in developing projectiles for the muzzle-loading hunter, is out

with a new sabot that should simplify things in the hunting field. Called the Lock and Load Speed Sabot, this is a typical plastic sabot–but with a "tail."

A plastic stem, cast in the center of the bottom of the sabot, is designed to fit into the hole in the center of the Pyrodex or new Triple 7 pellets from Hodgdon. The stem will hold three of the 50-grain pellets or it can be cut off if two pellets are required for the favorite load. This is the closest anyone has come to bringing the convenience of cartridge loading to muzzleloading since the days of combustible paper cartridges. The sabots are combined with Hornady's SST-ML bullet. This bullet, developed specifically for muzzleloading, features a polymer tip that increases ballistic efficiency and initiates expansion of the jacketed bullet to twice its diameter upon impact. Hornady claims true 200-yard performance from this bullet, properly loaded. The Lock and Load Speed Sabot is available in 50- caliber with two 45-caliber bullet weights, 250- and 300-grain. It is packaged in 5-load pocket field packs that will hold the sabots, with pellets attached; keeping them clean and moisture-free until needed. A real handy system for the hunter.

One can't help but be amazed by the wide selection of both traditional and modern-type blackpowder guns being made. It seems that every year we see major improvements in the modern hunting muzzleloading firearms and the ammunition available for them. Manufacturers and suppliers are continually improving and upgrading. We have taken the

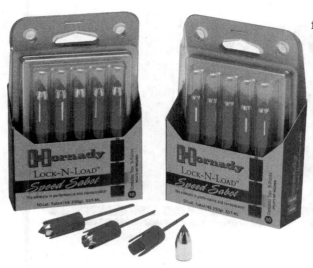

Hornady packages their Speed Sabot in handy 5-shot packages.

muzzleloading firearm to levels never dreamed of by our forefathers. The muzzleloading hunter has a vast selection of guns and supplies to choose from – a larger selection than at any time in our history, including the era when the muzzleloader reigned supreme. Traditional firearm reproductions also cover darn near everything that was made during the heyday of this type firearm. Quality and authenticity of these reproductions is very good. If you are a muzzleloading hunter, re-enactor, or lover of these old guns, it's a great time to be alive. Life is good. – *Doc Carlson*

KNIVES

Today's hunting knife scene is a good mix of mass-produced working knives and specialized limited-run blades meant to last the deer hunter a lifetime (at least). Fixed-blade designs seem to rule the roost these days, though there are a number of excellent folders on the market, too.

The Kershaw Majesty combines a 3 1/4-inch blade, a cocobolo handle, finger notches along the back half of the blade spine and a gut hook. "It has finger notches to prevent index

fingers and thumbs from slipping onto the blade," a Kershaw spokeman says. "The cocobolo handle is rounded and tapered instead of square, so it better fits the hand."

Anticipating heavy cutting and field use, Buck Knives offers a full-tang blade in the Buck 196 Mini Alpha Hunter. It sports a 2 1/2-inch, modified-drop-point blade and a resin-impregnated rosewood handle.

The TOPS Knives Pasayten Lite Traveler sports a 5 1/4-inch cryogenically-heat-treated blade, a black-linen-Micarta handle and a Kydex sheath with a revolving spring steel pocket clip.

Katz offers several versions of its Kagemusha fixed blade. Handle choices include white Micarta, cherrywood and Kraton, and each model comes standard with a 3 1/2-inch, full-tang stainless steel blade in plain or gut-hook "Ninja-Point" configurations.

From the "and now for something totally different" department is the Puma System Hunt Set. Integral to an aluminum handle with a stag insert is a locking system that secures each of the three blades in place. By lifting a locking lever, one blade can be extracted from the handle and replaced with one of a different style. Blades include a drop point, a saw blade and a large, big-bellied "White Hunter."

To fashion what he believes is the ultimate hunting knife, Edmund Davidson developed Max's Crooked Skinner, a one-piece hunter with a desert-ironwood grip. The hand-rubbed blade stretches 3 3/4 inches. The knife retails for about as much as a deer rifle. A *nice* deer rifle.

At the other e spectrum is the System II fixed knife. It featur stainless stee handle and a neck sheath. The the Blackie Collins-design sheath until it is released via a spring-loaded mechanism. Retail is about the same as a box of centerfire rifle ammo.

Gerber's Freeman Hunter sports a pear-wood grip complemented by a 440C blade with gut hook and a leather sheath. The company says the wood grain gives the knife style and appeals to more mature customers as a throwback to days before plastic and rubber knife grips became so popular.

The Swamp Rat D-2 Hunters have rubber (Resiprene C) handle, and they are anything but throwbacks to an earlier time. There are six D-2 Hunter models with 3 1/2- and 4 1/2-inch satin-finished blades in several configurations. Each comes in a limited edition of 300 pieces, and they retail in ranges under $100, depending on size.

Other notable new knives for the deer hunter include the Bear MGC Feathermate; Benchmade Model 190 drop-point hunter; Browning Buck Mark Silhouette; Case Ridgeback Wood Caper; Cold Steel Pendleton Hunter; Columbia River Knife & Tool Alaska Pro Hunter; Fallkniven H1 Hunter's Knife; Ka-Bar Dozier Folding Skinner; Kellam Voyager; Knives Of Alaska Light Hunter Mini Skinner/Cleaver; Lone Wolf Loveless Traditional Semi-Skinner Green Micarta®; Marble's Sport with Safe Grip handle; Outdoor Edge Kodi-Caper; A.G. Russell's Folding Gent's Hunter; Schrade Badger SX21; Spyderco Impala Gut Hook; and Columbia Sportswear/United Cutlery Gallatin Range Hunting Knife. – *Joe Kertzman*

TAKEDOWN: Winchester Model 70

Similar/Identical Pattern Guns

The same basic assembly/disassembly steps for the Winchester Model 70 also apply to the following guns:

Winchester Model 70 Featherweight

Winchester Model 70 H.B. Varmint

Winchester Model 70 Lightweight Carbine

Winchester Model 70 Lightweight Rifle

Winchester Model 70 Mannlicher

Winchester Model 70 Sporter

Winchester Model 70 Super Express

Winchester Model 70 Winlite

Winchester Model 70 Win-Tuff Featherweight, Lightweight

Winchester Model 70A

Winchester Model 670

Winchester Model 670 Carbine

Winchester Model 770

Winchester Ranger

Data: Winchester Model 70
Origin: United States
Manufacturer: Winchester Repeating Arms New Haven, Connecticut
Cartridges: From 222 to 458, including several magnum rounds
Magazine capacity: Varies with cartridges
Overall length: 42-1/2 to 44-1/2 inches
Barrel length: 22 and 24 inches
Weight: About 7-1/2 pounds

The original Model 70 first appeared in 1936, and was made until 1963. An "economy" version was made between 1964 and 1972, and since that time the original quality was resumed, with some of the innovations of the 1964 version retained. Collectors, and some shooters, treasure the pre-1964 "originals," but in some ways, the later guns, as now currently made, are mechanically superior. A list of the calibers and model variations of the Model 70 would nearly fill an entire page. The gun covered here is a late standard model. On the pre-1964 guns, the bolt detail is quite similar to the standard Mauser pattern. As many readers will be aware, the Model 70 is now made under license by the U.S. Repeating Arms Co.

Disassembly:

1. To remove the bolt, the safety must be in the off-safe position. Open the bolt, and depress the bolt stop, located at the left rear of the receiver. Hold it down, and withdraw the bolt toward the rear. For clarity, the bolt stop is indicated with a drift punch in the photo. It is depressed with a fingertip.

2. Remove the screws on the underside at the front and rear of the trigger guard. Note that on some Model 70 guns the magazine is a through-type, with a hinged cover plate. The one shown in the photos is a closed (blind) type, with a solid stock underside. After the guard screws are removed, the guard can be taken off downward.

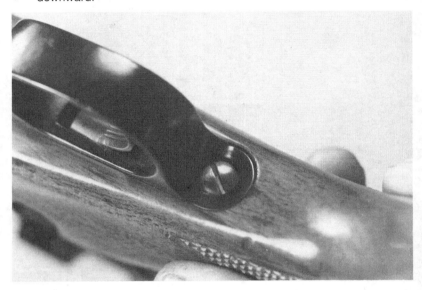

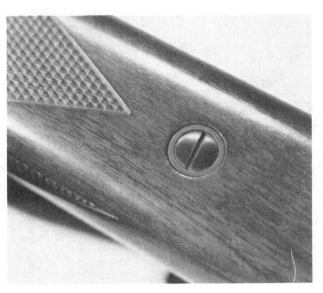

3. Remove the main stock mounting screw, on the underside below the chamber area. If the gun is a through-magazine type, this screw will be in the forward base of the magazine floorplate. When all three screws are removed, the action can be taken out of the stock.

4. If the gun is a blind magazine type, the magazine follower, spring, and internal floorplate can be taken out upward. If the gun has an external floorplate, the floorplate and front hinge plate can be taken off downward. The plate is attached to its base with a cross pin. A cross pin also retains the floorplate catch and its spring in the front of the trigger guard.

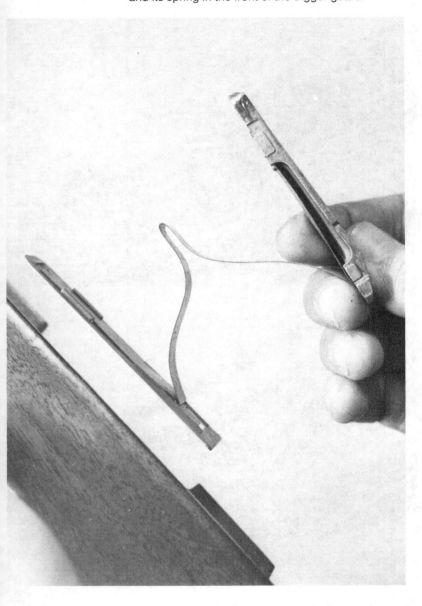

5. The magazine box, or housing, is usually a tight press fit on the bottom of the receiver, and can be removed by exerting downward pressure while working it gently from side to side.

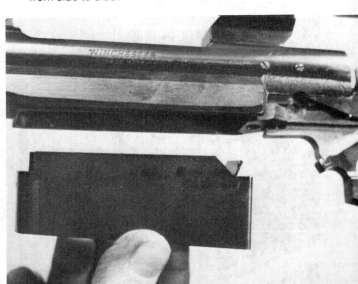

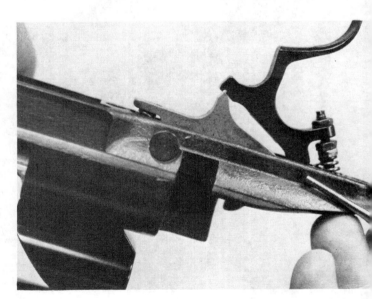

6. A cross pin retains the trigger assembly on the underside of the receiver. Note that the trigger, its spring, and adjustment system can be removed downward without disturbing the adjustment. The cross pin must be drifted out toward the left.

7. Note that the trigger pin has an enlarged head on the left side, and is also the pivot and retainer for the bolt stop and its spring. Before removal, note the relationship of the bolt stop, its spring, and the trigger, to aid reassembly. Restrain the spring as the pin is drifted out, and ease it off.

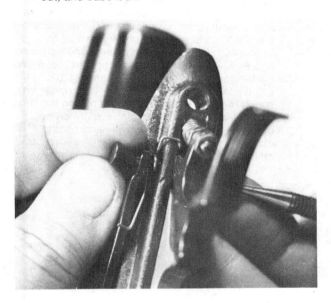

8. The bolt stop is moved downward and toward the rear for removal.

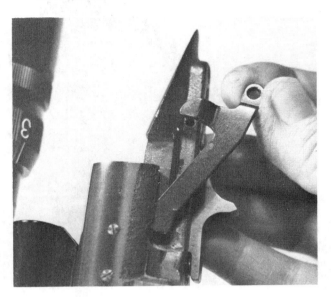

9. The sear is retained on the underside of the receiver by a cross pin which must be drifted out toward the right. Restrain the sear against the tension of its strong spring, and remove the sear and spring downward.

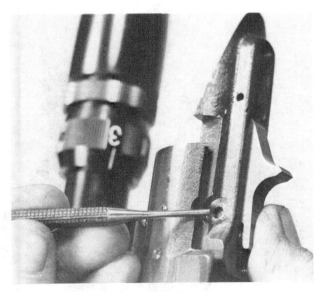

10. Grip the lower lug of the cocking piece firmly in a vise, and move the bolt forward until the safety can be turned back to the safe position. Depress the bolt sleeve lock plunger, located on the left side of the bolt, and unscrew the rear section, the bolt sleeve. During this operation, take care that the safety is not tripped to the fire position.

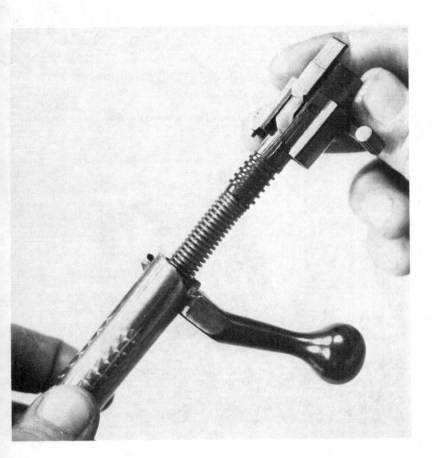

11. When the sleeve and striker assembly has cleared its internal threads, withdraw it toward the rear.

12. Grip the forward portion of the striker firmly in a vise, with the spring retaining C-clip and compression washer just above the vise jaws. Pry the compression washer upward, remove the C-clip, and allow the washer and spring to come down on the vise. With a firm hold on the bolt sleeve, open the vise, and slowly ease the assembly upward, releasing the tension of the spring. Take care not to lose the compression washer. If the gun is an older one, spring removal is done by simply pulling the firing pin sleeve slightly toward the rear, giving it a quarter-turn in either direction, and easing it off toward the front. After the tension is relieved, take off the spring toward the front.

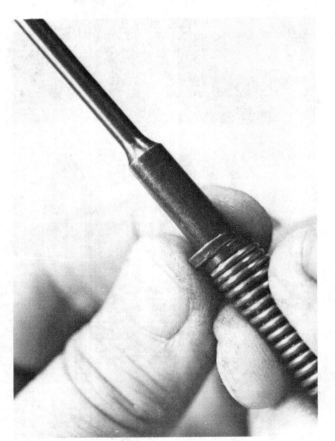

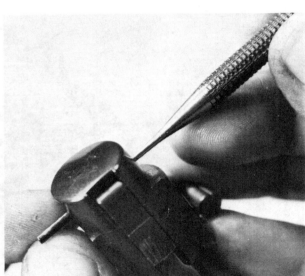

13. Drift out the cross pin in the bolt end piece, at rear of the bolt sleeve.

14. Remove the bolt end piece toward the rear. If it is tight, it can be tapped off by sliding the striker assembly against it.

15. Remove the striker assembly from the rear of the bolt sleeve.

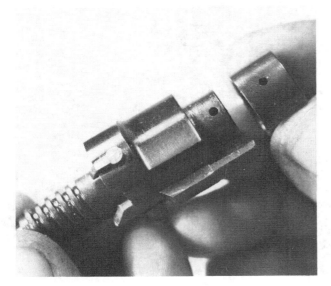

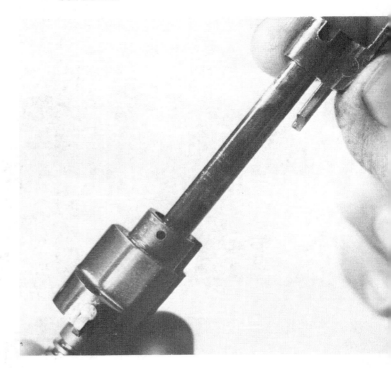

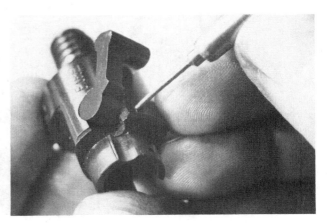

16. To remove the bolt sleeve lock plunger and spring, push out the retaining pin, which runs lengthwise in the sleeve, and take off the plunger and spring toward the side.

17. Use a very small drift punch to push the small pin beside the safety inward, into the interior of the bolt sleeve. The safety-lever should be in the off-safe position. ·

18. Turn the safety around toward the rear, then move it upward and out of the bolt sleeve. **Caution:** *The safety positioning spring and plunger will be released as the safety clears the sleeve, so restrain them and ease them out.*

19. To remove the ejector, drift out the angled cross pin at the front of the bolt. **Caution:** *The strong ejector spring will expel the ejector as the drift is removed, so ease the ejector out toward the front, and remove the spring.*

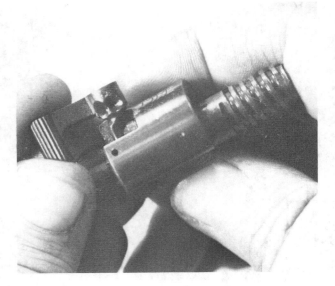

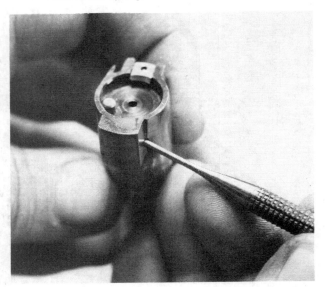

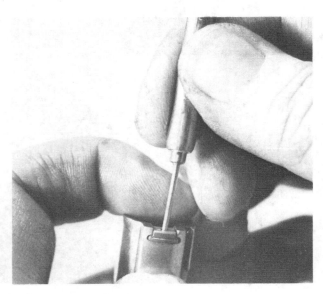

20. To remove the extractor, use a small-diameter drift punch to depress the extractor plunger, accessible through a small hole in the front face of the extractor. While keeping the plunger depressed, move the extractor out of its T-slot in the bolt lug. **Caution:** *Restrain the plunger and spring, and ease them out.* If the gun is an older one, it will have a long external Mauser-style extractor. For removal details on this type, see the Mauser or Springfield sections.

Reassembly Tips:

1. When replacing the striker spring, note that the retaining C-clip has a recess on one side. This side must go toward the front. With the forward part of the striker gripped in a vise (as in disassembly), this means that the recess on the C-clip should be installed downward, toward the vise jaws.

2. Before the bolt sleeve and striker assembly can be installed in the bolt body, the striker must be locked to the rear by placing the safety in the on-safe position. Grip the lower lug of the striker firmly in a vise, push the bolt sleeve toward the front, and set the safety. When the sleeve and striker assembly are back in the bolt body, the safety must be released to the off-safe position before the bolt can be reinserted in the receiver.

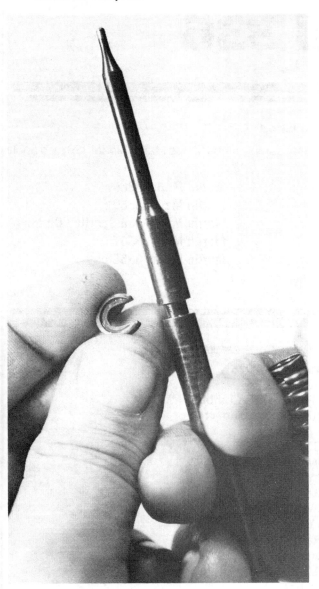

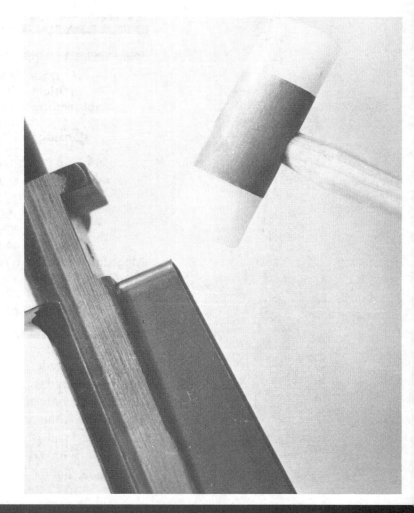

3. If the magazine housing has been removed, insert its rear edge into the recess first, then tap the front gently inward and toward the rear until it is in place.

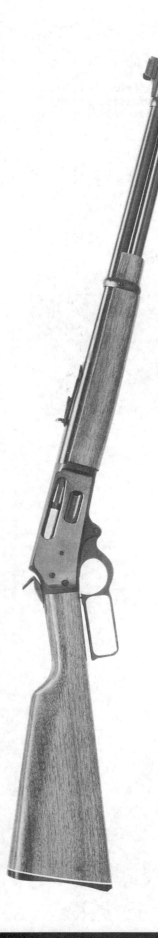

TAKEDOWN: Marlin Model 336

Similar/Identical Pattern Guns

The same basic assembly/disassembly steps for the Marlin Model 336 also apply to the following guns:

Marlin Model 30AS
Marlin Model 336L
Marlin Model 336 LTS
Marlin Model 336 Zipper
Marlin Model 336 Marauder
Marlin Model 336 Extra-Range

Marlin Model 336C
Marlin Model 336DL
Marlin Model 336 Sporting Carbine
Marlin Model 336T
Marlin Model 336CS

Data:	Marlin Model 336
Origin:	United States
Manufacturer:	Marlin Firearms Company North Haven, Connecticut
Cartridge:	219 Zipper, 30-30 Winchester, 32 Winchester Special, 307 Winchester, 35 Remington, 356 Winchester, 375 Winchester, 44 Remington Magnum
Magazine capacity:	6 rounds
Overall length:	38-1/2 inches
Barrel length:	20 inches
Weight:	7 pounds

An extensive redesign of the Marlin Model 36 (1936) rifle, the Model 336 was first offered in 1948. It was initially available in several calibers, but in recent years only the 30-30 and 35 Remington chamberings have been in production. Although most lever-action guns are generally more complicated than other manually-operated types, the Model 336 has a relatively easy takedown, with no really difficult points. Several sub-models of this gun were made, and the instructions will apply to any of these.

Disassembly:

1. Partially open the lever, and take out the lever pivot cross screw. Remove the lever downward.

2. Remove the bolt toward the rear.

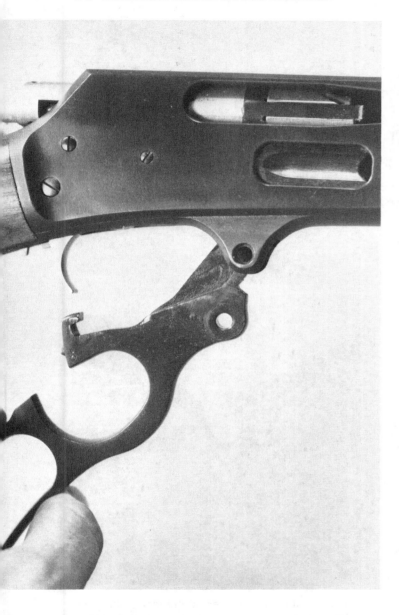

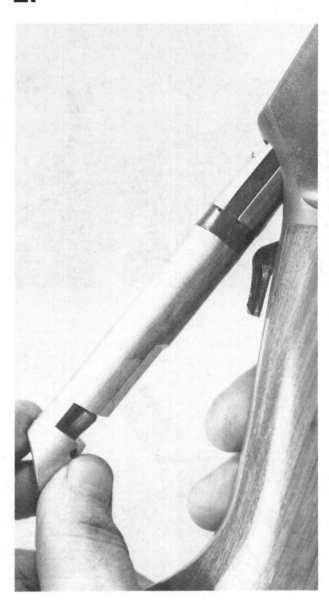

3. Push the ejector mounting stud inward, and remove the ejector from inside the receiver. The ejector spring is staked in place, and removal in normal disassembly is not advisable, except for repair.

4. Drifting out the vertical roll pin at the rear of the bolt will release the rear firing pin and its spring for removal toward the rear.

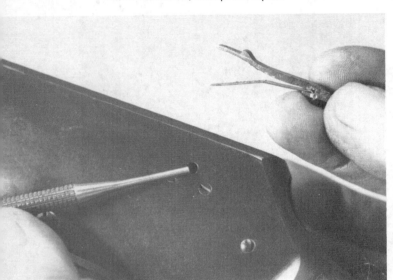

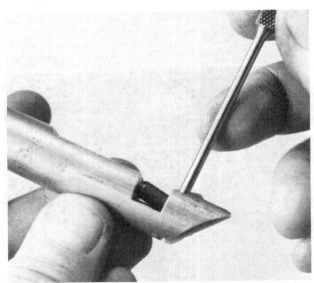

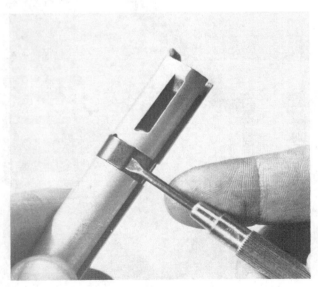

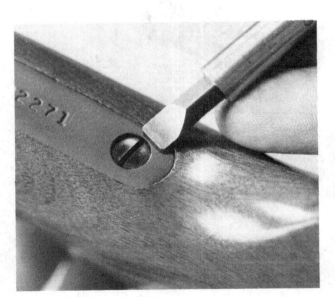

5. Use a small screwdriver to pry the extractor clip off its recess on the front of the bolt, using a fingertip to lift the front of the extractor out of its channel. Removal of the extractor will give access to the vertical pin that retains the front firing pin. After the pin is drifted out, the firing pin is removed toward the rear.

6. Remove the vertical screw at the rear of the upper tang, and take off the stock toward the rear. If the stock is tight, bump the front of the comb with the heel of the hand to start it off.

7. Depress the trigger-block (arrow), on the underside behind the trigger, and gently lower the hammer to the fired position. With smooth-jawed pliers or strong fingers, grip the upper portion of the hammer spring base plate, tilt it forward, and slide it toward the side, moving its lower end out of its groove in the lower tang. Keep a firm grip on the plate, as the spring is under some tension, even when at rest. Remove the plate, and the hammer spring, toward the rear.

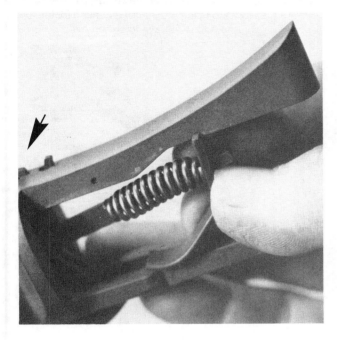

8. Remove the hammer pivot screw, and take out the hammer upward. Drifting out the cross pin at the rear of the hammer will release the hammer spring strut, but in normal takedown it is best left in place.

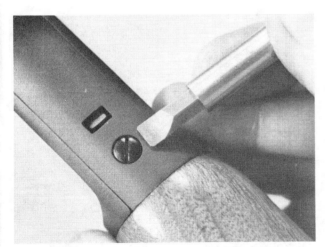

9. Remove the vertical screw on the underside at the forward end of the trigger housing.

10. Remove the screw on the left side of the receiver at lower center.

11. Remove the trigger housing downward and toward the rear. If it is very tight, it may be necessary to tap it with a plastic hammer to start it out.

12. Drifting out the trigger cross pin will allow the trigger and sear to be removed downward. The small pin just forward of the trigger is the contact for the lever latch, and does not have to be removed.

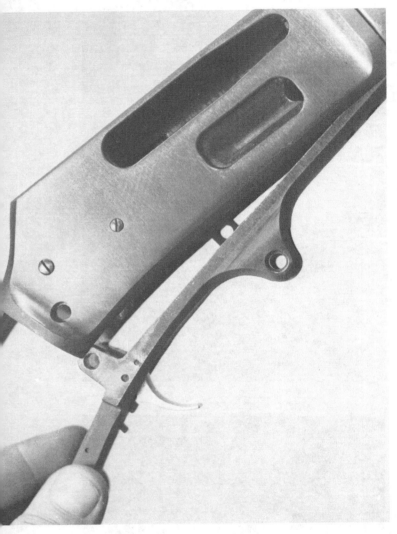

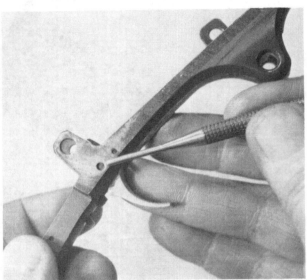

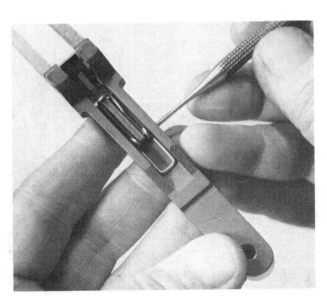

13. A small cross pin in the lower tang portion of the trigger housing retains the trigger safety-block and the combination spring that powers the block and the trigger/sear system. After the pin is drifted out, the block and spring are removed upward. **Caution:** *The spring is under tension. Control it, and ease it out.*

14. The lever latch plunger and its spring are retained in the lever by a cross pin, and are removed toward the rear. The short coil spring is quite strong, so control it and ease it out.

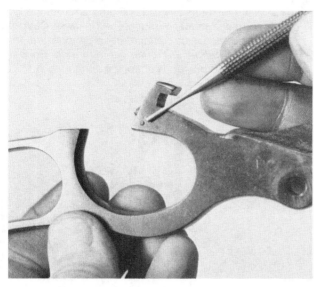

15. After the trigger housing plate is taken off, the bolt-locking block can be moved downward out of the receiver.

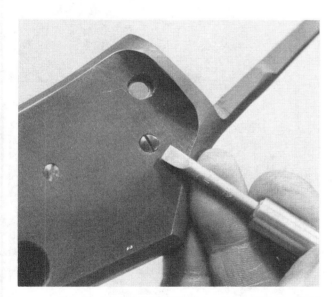

16. Remove the carrier pivot screw, located on the right side of the receiver at center rear.

17. Remove the carrier downward. The carrier rocker and its spring are retained on the left side of the carrier by a vertical pin.

18. Remove the small screw on the right side of the receiver to the rear of the loading port, and take out the loading gate from inside the receiver.

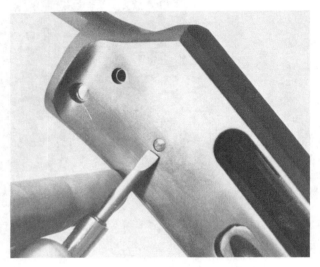

19. Remove the screw on the underside of the magazine tube at its forward end, and take out the tube end piece, magazine spring, and follower. **Caution:** *Some magazine springs are more powerful than others, and all are under some tension. Ease the end piece out, and control the spring.*

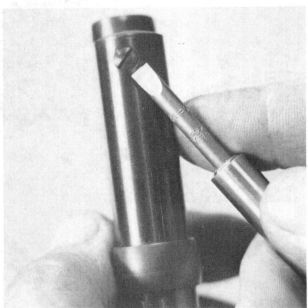

20. Slide the front sight hood off toward the front, remove the two vertical screws in the front sight base, and take off the front sight upward.

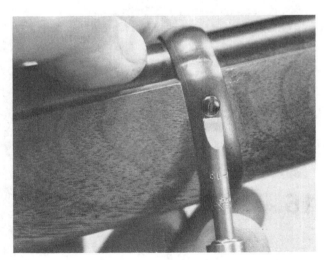

21. Take out the cross screw in the front barrel band. Take out the cross screw in the rear barrel band, and slide the barrel band off toward the front.

22. Move the forend wood forward to free the magazine tube, then slide the magazine tube, forend wood, and front barrel band off toward the front.

Reassembly Tips:

1. When replacing the magazine tube, be sure its rear tip enters the well in the front of the receiver. Be sure it is oriented at the front so its screw groove will align with the hole in the front barrel band.

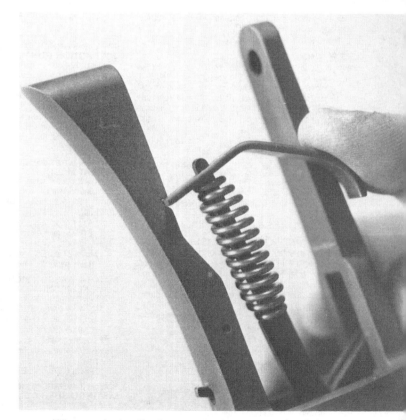

2. When replacing the hammer spring system, hook the lower end of the spring plate in its groove in the lower tang, tip the top of the plate forward, beneath the upper tang, and slide the plate across into place.

MODERN GUN VALUES

Handguns

Colt Anaconda
Colt Python
Colt Python Stainless
Freedom Arms 44 Magnum Casull
Freedom Arms 454 Casull
Savage Striker Bolt-Action Hunting Handgun
Smith & Wesson Model 19 Combat Magnum
Smith & Wesson Model 66 Combat Magnum
Smith & Wesson Model 586 Distinguished Combat Magnum
Smith & Wesson Model 610 Classic Hunter Revolver
Smith & Wesson Model 657
Smith & Wesson Model 686
Smith & Wesson Model 686 Magnum PLUS
Smith & Wesson Model 686 Midnight Black

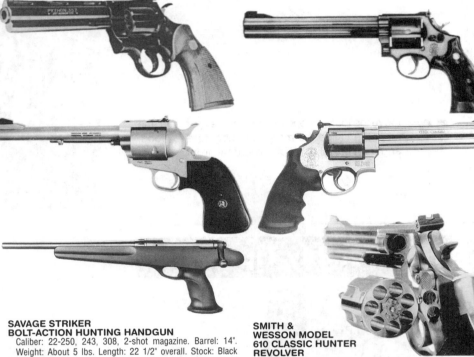

COLT ANACONDA
Revolver; double action; 44 Rem. Mag., 45 LC; 6-shot cylinder; 4", 6", 8" barrel; 11-5/8" overall length; weighs 53 oz.; red insert front sight, white-outline adjustable rear; finger-grooved black neoprene combat grips; stainless steel construction; ventilated barrel rib; offset bolt notches in cylinder; full-length ejector rod housing; wide spur hammer. Introduced 1990; still produced.

New: $500	**Perf.:** $425	**Exc.:** $375

COLT PYTHON
Revolver; double action; 357 Mag.; 6-shot swing-out cylinder; made first appearance in 6" barrel later with 2 1/2", 3", 4", 8"; checkered walnut grips contoured for support for middle finger of shooting hand; vent-rib barrel; ramp front sight, fully-adjustable rear; full-length ejector rod shroud; wide-spur hammer; grooved trigger; blued, nickel finish; hand-finished action. Introduced 1955; still in production.

Perf.: $550	**Exc.:** $475	**VGood:** $400

Nickel finish

Perf.: $550	**Exc.:** $475	**VGood:** $400

Colt Python Stainless
Same specs as standard Python except stainless steel construction; 4", 6" barrel lengths only. Introduced 1983; still produced.

Perf.: $675	**Exc.:** $550	**VGood:** $475

FREEDOM ARMS 44 MAGNUM CASULL
Revolver; single action; 44 Mag.; 5-shot cylinder; 4 3/4", 6", 7 1/2", 10" barrel; 14" overall length (7 1/2" barrel); weighs about 59 oz.; blade front sight on ramp, fully-adjustable rear; Pachmayr rubber grips; Field Grade with matte stainless finish; Premier Grade with brushed stainless finish; impregnated hardwood grips, Premier Grade sights. Made in U.S. by Freedom Arms. Introduced 1992; still in production.

Field Grade

New: $1100	**Perf.:** $875	**Exc.:** $825

Premier Grade

New: $1500	**Perf.:** $1200	**Exc.:** $900

FREEDOM ARMS 454 CASULL
Revolver; single action; 454 Casull; 5-shot cylinder; 4 3/4", 6", 7 1/2", 10", barrels; weighs 50 oz. (7 1/2" barrel) impregnated hardwood stocks; blade front sight, notch or adjustable rear; stainless steel; sliding bar safety. Introduced 1983; still in production.

Fixed sights

Perf.: $1250	**Exc.:** $950	**VGood:** $800

Adjustable sights

Perf.: $1300	**Exc.:** $1000	**VGood:** $850

SAVAGE STRIKER BOLT-ACTION HUNTING HANDGUN
Caliber: 22-250, 243, 308, 2-shot magazine. Barrel: 14". Weight: About 5 lbs. Length: 22 1/2" overall. Stock: Black composite ambidextrous mid-grip; grooved forend; "Dual Pillar" bedding. Sights: None furnished; drilled and tapped for scope mounting. Features: Short left-hand bolt with right-hand ejection; free-floated barrel; uses Savage Model 110 rifle scope rings/bases. Introduced 1998. Made in U.S. by Savage Arms, Inc.

New: $350	**Perf.:** $300	**Exc.:** $250

SMITH & WESSON MODEL 19 COMBAT MAGNUM
Revolver; double action; 357 Mag.; 6-shot; 2 1/2", 4", 6" barrel; available with 4" barrel; 9 1/2" overall length; weighs 35 oz.; 1/8" Baughman quick-draw front plain ramp, fully-adjustable S&W micrometer-click rear; checkered Goncalo Alves grips with S&W medallion; S&W bright blue or nickel finish; built on the lighter S&W K-frame as used on the K-38, et al., rather than on the heavier N-frame used for the Model 27 and 28. Introduced about 1956; dropped 1999.

New: $350	**Perf.:** $300	**Exc.:** $225

SMITH & WESSON MODEL 66 COMBAT MAGNUM
Revolver; double action; 357 Mag., 38 Spl.; 6-shot cylinder; 2 1/2", 4", 6" barrel; 9 1/2" overall length (4" barrel); weighs 36 oz.; stainless steel construction; checkered Goncalo Alves target stocks; Baughman Quick Draw front sight on plain ramp, micro-click adjustable rear; grooved trigger, adjustable stop; satin finish. Introduced 1971; still in production.

Perf.: $375	**Exc.:** $325	**VGood:** $250

SMITH & WESSON MODEL 586 DISTINGUISHED COMBAT MAGNUM
Revolver; double action; 357 Mag.; 4", 6" heavy barrel; weighs 46 oz. (6" barrel), 41 oz. (4" barrel); L-frame design; ejector rod shroud; combat-type trigger; semi-target hammer; Baughman red ramp front sight, micrometer-click rear; soft rubber or Goncalo Alves target stocks; blued or nickel finish. Introduced 1981; dropped 1999.

New: $350	**Perf.:** $300	**Exc.:** $275
New: $350	**Perf.:** $300	**Exc.:** $275

SMITH & WESSON MODEL 610 CLASSIC HUNTER REVOLVER
Revolver; double action; 10mm, 6-shot cylinder. Barrel: 6 1/2" full lug. Weight: 52 oz. Length: 12" overall. Stocks: Hogue rubber combat. Sights: Interchangeable blade front, micro-click rear adjustable for windage and elevation. Features: Stainless steel construction; target hammer, target trigger; unfluted cylinder; drilled and tapped for scope mounting. Introduced 1998.

New: $550	**Perf.:** $450	**Exc.:** $375

SMITH & WESSON MODEL 657
Revolver; double action; 41 Mag., 6-shot. Barrel: 6". Weight: 48 oz. Length: 11 3/8" overall. Stocks: Soft rubber; wood optional. Sights: Pinned 1/8" red ramp front, micro-click rear adjustable for windage and elevation. Features: Stainless steel construction.

New: $450	**Perf.:** $375	**Exc.:** $325

SMITH & WESSON MODEL 686
Revolver; double action; 357 Mag.; 2 1/2", 4", 6" heavy barrels; weighs 46 oz. (6" barrel); L-frame design; stainless steel construction; ejector rod shroud; combat-type trigger; semi-target hammer; Baughman red ramp front sight, micrometer-click rear; soft rubber or Goncalo Alves target stocks; satin finish. Introduced 1981; still in production.

Perf.: $400	**Exc.:** $325	**VGood:** $250

Smith & Wesson Model 686 Magnum PLUS
Similar to the Model 686 except has 7-shot cylinder, 2 1/2", 4" or 6" barrel. Weighs 34 1/2 oz., overall length 7 1/2" (2 1/2" barrel). Hogue rubber grips. Introduced 1996.

New: $450	**Perf.:** $375	**Exc.:** $325

Smith & Wesson Model 686 Midnight Black
Same specs as Model 686 except black finish; semi-target hammer; red ramp front sight, plain or white-outline micro rear; speedloader cut-out; full lug barrel; Goncalo Alves target stocks. Introduced 1989; no longer in production.

Exc.: $400	**VGood:** $350	**Good:** $250

SMITH & WESSON 41 MAGNUM (MODEL 57)
Revolver; 41 Mag.; 6-shot; 4", 6", 8 3/8" barrel; 11 3/8" overall length (6" barrel); weighs 48 oz.; wide, grooved target

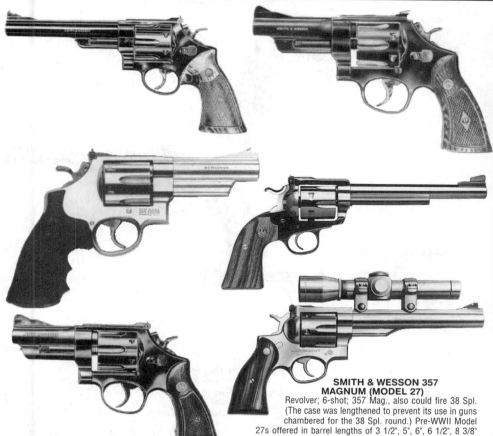

Handguns

SMITH & WESSON
41 MAGNUM (MODEL 57)
SMITH & WESSON
44 MAGNUM (MODEL 29)
SMITH & WESSON
44 MAGNUM MODEL 629
SMITH & WESSON
357 MAGNUM (MODEL 27)
SMITH & WESSON
357 MAGNUM (MODEL 627)
SMITH & WESSON HIGHWAY
PATROLMAN (MODEL 28)
SMITH & WESSON MODEL 25-5
STURM RUGER BISLEY
STURM RUGER BLACKHAWK
STURM RUGER
BLACKHAWK NEW MODEL
STURM RUGER REDHAWK

trigger and broad-spur target hammer; 1/8" red ramp front, S&W micro-adjustable rear with white-outline notch; special oversize target-type of Goncalo Alves grips with S&W medallion; bright blue or nickel finish. Introduced as a sporting companion to the fixed-sight Model 58, both being chambered for a new cartridge developed especially for them at that time, carrying a bullet of .410" diameter. The old 41 Long Colt cartridge cannot be fired in guns chambered for the 41 Magnum, nor can any other standard cartridge. Introduced 1964; dropped 1993.

4" and 6" barrels
   Perf.: $300   **Exc.:** $250   **VGood:** $200
83/8" barrel
   Perf.: $325   **Exc.:** $275   **VGood:** $225

SMITH & WESSON 44 MAGNUM (MODEL 29)
Revolver; 44 Mag.; also handles 44 Spl., 44 Russian; 6-shot; 4", 5", 6 1/2", 8 3/8"; 11 7/8" overall length (6 1/2" barrel); weighs 43 oz. (4" barrel), 47 oz. (6 1/2" barrel), 51 1/2 oz. (8 3/8" barrel); 1/8" red ramp front sight, S&W micro-adjustable rear; target-type Goncalo Alves grips with S&W medallion; broad, grooved target trigger; wide-spur target hammer; bright blue or nickel finish. As with the Model 27, the Model 29 was developed to take a new cartridge developed by lengthening the 44 Special case by 0.125" to prevent use of 44 Magnum ammo in guns chambered for the 44 Special. The 44 Magnum is loaded to pressures approximately twice that of the 44 Special. Introduced in 1956; still in production as Model 27 minus the cost-raising frills such as the checkered topstrap.
   Exc.: $525   **VGood:** $375   **Good:** $250

SMITH & WESSON 44 MAGNUM MODEL 629
Revolver; 44 Mag.; 6-shot; 4", 6", 8 3/8" barrel; 11 3/8" overall length (6" barrel); weighs 47 oz.; 1/8" red ramp front; S&W micro-adjustable rear sight; same as Model 29 Stainless except steel construction; target-type Goncalo Alves grips; broad grooved trigger; wide spur target hammer; satin finish. Still in production.
   New: $500   **Perf.:** $400   **Exc.:** $300

SMITH & WESSON 357 MAGNUM (MODEL 27)
Revolver; 6-shot; 357 Mag., also could fire 38 Spl. (The case was lengthened to prevent its use in guns chambered for the 38 Spl. round.) Pre-WWII Model 27s offered in barrel lengths of 3 1/2", 5", 6", 6 1/2", 8 3/8" and 8 3/4"; could be custom-ordered with barrels of any length up to 8 3/4"; 11 3/8" overall length (6" barrel); weighs 41 oz. (3 1/2" barrel), 42 1/2 oz. (5" barrel), 44 oz. (6" barrel), 44 1/2 oz. (6 1/2" barrel), 47 oz. (8 3/8" barrel); could be ordered with any of S&W's standard target sights; 3 1/2" version usually furnished with Baughman quick-draw on a plain King ramp; finely checkered topstrap matched barrel rib, with vertically grooved front and rear grip straps and grooved trigger; S&W bright blue or nickel finishes; checkered Circassian square or Magna-type walnut stocks, with S&W medallion. Retail price at beginning of WWII was $60. Post-WWII production similar, with hammer redesigned to incorporate a wider spur and inclusion of the present pattern of S&W click-micrometer rear sight; blue or nickel finish. Post-WWII models can be identified by S or N serial number prefix. Model 27 was the first centerfire revolver with recessed cylinder; 1935-1938 guns were registered to owner with registration number stamped in yoke of frame; about 6000 made before registration stopped. The papers, themselves, have some collector value without the gun.
Pre-WWII registered
   Exc.: $1750   **VGood:** $1350   **Good:** $900
Pre-WWII not registered
   Exc.: $850   **VGood:** $600   **Good:** $450
Post-WWII model
   Perf.: $350   **Exc.:** $300   **VGood:** $200

SMITH & WESSON 357 MAGNUM (MODEL 627)
Revolver; 357 Mag; 6-shot; 5 1/2" barrel; stainless steel variation of Model 27; limited production with 5276 manufactured. Introduced 1989.
   Perf.: $500   **Exc.:** $400   **VGood:** $300

SMITH & WESSON HIGHWAY PATROLMAN (MODEL 28)
Revolver; 357 Mag.; 6-shot; 4", 6" barrel; 11 1/4" overall length (6" barrel); weighs 41 3/4 oz. (4" barrel); 44 oz. (6" barrel); 1/8" Baughman Quick Draw front sight on plain ramp, S&W micro-adjustable rear; checkered walnut, Magna-type grips with S&W medallion; target stocks at extra cost; blued finish with sandblast stippling on barrel rib and frame edging. Introduced in 1954 as a functional version of the Model 27 minus the cost-raising frills such as the checkered topstrap.
   Exc.: $225   **VGood:** $175   **Good:** $150

SMITH & WESSON MODEL 25-5
Revolver; 45 Colt; 6-shot; 4", 6", 8 3/8" barrel; adjustable sights; square-butt, checkered, target-type Goncalo Alves grips; blue or nickel finish. Introduced in 1978 and called the 25-5 to distinguish it from the Model 25-2 in 45 ACP. Available with presentation case. Discontinued 1987.
   Exc.: $350   **VGood:** $300   **Good:** $250

STURM RUGER BISLEY
Revolver; single action; 22, 32 H&R Mag., 357, 41 Mag., 44 Mag., 45 Colt; 7 1/2" barrel; 13" overall length; flat-top frame; low hammer with deeply checkered wide spur; wide, smooth trigger; longer grip frame; unfluted cylinder; roll engraved with Bisley marksman, trophy. Introduced 1985; still in production.
   New: $325   **Perf.:** $275   **Exc.:** $225
22, 32 H&R
   New: $275   **Perf.:** $225   **Exc.:** $185

STURM RUGER BLACKHAWK
Revolver; single action; 357 Mag., 41 Mag., 45 LC; 6-shot; 4-5/8", 6 1/2" (357, 41 Mag.) barrel; 12" overall length (6 1/2" barrel); large frame; checkered hard rubber or uncheckered walnut grips; hooded adjustable rear sight, ramp front; blued. Introduced 1965; dropped 1972.
   New: $300   **Perf.:** $250   **Exc.:** $200

STURM RUGER BLACKHAWK NEW MODEL
Revolver; single action; 30 Carbine, 357 Mag./38 Spl., 41 Mag., 45 LC; 6-shot cylinder; 4-5/8", 6 1/2" barrel; 7 1/2" barrel (30 Carbine, 45 LC); 12 1/2" overall length (6 1/2" barrel); weighs 42 oz.; new Ruger interlocked mechanism; transfer bar ignition; hardened chrome-moly steel frame; wide trigger music wire springs; independent firing pin; blue, stainless or high-gloss stainless finish. Introduced 1973; still in production.
   New: $300   **Perf.:** $250   **Exc.:** $200
Stainless finish
   New: $400   **Perf.:** $325   **Exc.:** $250
High-gloss stainless finish
   New: $375   **Perf.:** $300   **Exc.:** $250

STURM RUGER REDHAWK
Revolver; double action; 41 Mag., 44 Mag.; 6-shot; 5 1/2", 7 1/2" barrel; 5 1/2" barrel added 1984; 13" overall length (7 1/2" barrel); weighs 54 oz.; stainless steel brushed satin or blued finish; Patridge-type front sight, fully-adjustable rear; square-butt Goncalo Alves grips. Introduced 1979; still in production.
Blue
   New: $450   **Perf.:** $375   **Exc.:** $300
Stainless
   New: $475   **Perf.:** $400   **Exc.:** $350

Handguns

Colt Anaconda
Colt Python
Colt Python Stainless
Freedom Arms 44 Magnum Casull
Freedom Arms 454 Casull
Savage Striker Bolt-Action Hunting Handgun
Smith & Wesson Model 19 Combat Magnum
Smith & Wesson Model 66 Combat Magnum
Smith & Wesson Model 586 Distinguished Combat Magnum
Smith & Wesson Model 610 Classic Hunter Revolver
Smith & Wesson Model 657
Smith & Wesson Model 686
Smith & Wesson Model 686 Magnum PLUS
Smith & Wesson Model 686 Midnight Black

STURM RUGER SUPER BLACKHAWK
Revolver; 44 Mag.; 5 1/2", 7 1/2", 10 1/2" barrel; 13 3/8" overall length (7 1/2" barrel); weighs 48 oz.; 1/8" ramp front, micro-click fully-adjustable rear; American walnut grips; interlock mechanism; non-fluted cylinder; steel grip and cylinder frame; square back trigger guard; wide serrated trigger; wide spur hammer. Introduced 1985; still in production.

New: $350   **Perf.:** $300   **Exc.:** $250

Stainless

New: $400   **Perf.:** $350   **Exc.:** $300

Sturm Ruger Blackhawk Hunter
Same specs as Super Blackhawk except stainless finish; 7 1/2"; scope rings. Introduced 1992; still in prduction.

New: $450   **Perf.:** $400   **Exc.:** $325

STURM RUGER SUPER REDHAWK
Revolver; double action; 44 Mag.; 6-shot; 7 1/2", 9 1/2" barrel; 13" overall length (7 1/2" barrel); weighs 54 oz.; heavy extended frame with Ruger Integral Scope Mounting System; wide topstrap; ramp front with interchangeable sight blades, adjustable rear; Santoprene grips with Goncalo Alves panels; satin polished stainless steel finish. Introduced 1987; still in production.

New: $475   **Perf.:** $400   **Exc.:** $300

TAURUS MODEL 454 RAGING BULL
Revolver; double action; 454 Casull, 5-shot. Barrel: 5", 6 1/2", 8 3/8". Weight: 53 oz. (6 1/2" barrel). Length: 12" overall (6 1/2" barrel). Stocks: Soft black rubber. Sights: Patridge front, micrometer click adjustable rear. Features: Ventilated rib; integral compensating system. Introduced 1997. Imported by Taurus International.

Blue finish

New: $650   **Perf.:** $550   **Exc.:** $450

Stainless steel

New: $725   **Perf.:** $650   **Exc.:** $550

TAURUS MODEL 607
Revolver; double action; 357 Mag.; 7-shot; 4", 6 1/2" barrel; weighs 44 oz.; Santoprene I grips with finger grooves; serrated ramp front sight, fully-adjustable rear; ventilated rib with built-in compensator (6 1/2" barrel). Imported by

Taurus International. Introduced 1995; still imported.

Blue finish, 4" barrel

New: $350   **Perf.:** $300   **Exc.:** $250

Blue finish, 6 1/2" barrel

New: $350   **Perf.:** $300   **Exc.:** $250

Stainless steel, 4" barrel

New: $400   **Perf.:** $350   **Exc.:** $300

Stainless steel, 6 1/2" barrel

New: $425   **Perf.:** $375   **Exc.:** $325

TAURUS MODEL 608
Revolver; double action; 357 Mag., 8-shot. Barrel: 4", 6 1/2", 8 3/8". Weight: 44 oz. Length: NA. Stocks: Soft black rubber. Sights: Serrated ramp front, fully adjustable rear. Features: Ventilated rib with built-in compensator on 6 1/2" barrel. Available in blue or stainless. Introduced 1995. Imported by Taurus international.

Blue finish, 4"

New: $375   **Perf.:** $300   **Exc.:** $250

Stainless steel, 4"

New: $425   **Perf.:** $350   **Exc.:** $275

Blue finish, 6 1/2", 8 3/8"

New: $400   **Perf.:** $325   **Exc.:** $275

Stainless steel, 6 1/2", 8 3/8"

New: $450   **Perf.:** $375   **Exc.:** $300

THOMPSON/CENTER CONTENDER
Single shot; break-open action; chambered for 29 calibers; 8 3/4", 10", 14" round, heavy, octagon barrel; adjustable sights; checkered walnut grip, forearm; interchangeable barrels; detachable choke for shot cartridges; blued finish. Introduced 1967; still in production.

New: $350   **Perf.:** $300   **Exc.:** $275

THOMPSON/CENTER CONTENDER HUNTER
Single shot; break-open action; chambered for 8 calibers; 12", 14", barrel with muzzlebrake; 2 1/2x scope with illuminated reticle; walnut grips with rubber insert; interchangeable barrels; sling with studs and swivels; carrying case; blued finish. Introduced 1990; still in production.

New: $650   **Perf.:** $575   **Exc.:** $525

THOMPSON/CENTER ENCORE
Single shot, break-open action; 22-250, 223, 260 Rem., 7mmBR, 7mm-08, 243, 7.62x39, 308, 270, 30-06, 44 Mag., 444 Marlin single shot. Barrel: 10", 15", tapered round. Weight: NA. Length: 19" overall with 10" barrel. Stocks: American walnut with finger grooves, walnut forend. Sights: Blade on ramp front, adjustable rear, or none. Features: Interchangeable barrels; action opens by squeezing the trigger guard; drilled and tapped for scope mounting; blue finish. Announced 1996.

New: $475   **Perf.:** $400   **Exc.:** $325

WESSON FIREARMS HUNTER SERIES
Revolver; double action; 357 Supermag, 41 Mag., 44 Mag., 445 Supermag; 6-shot cylinder; 6", 7 1/2" fixed barrel; 14" overall length; weighs 64 oz.; Hogue finger-groove rubber or wood presentation grips; blade front sight, dovetailed Iron Sight Gunworks rear; 1:18.75" twist barrel; Alan Taylor two-stage forcing cone; non-fluted cylinder; bright blue or satin stainless. Introduced 1994; dropped 1995.

7 1/2" barrel, blue finish

New: $700   **Perf.:** $650   **Exc.:** $600

7 1/2" barrel, stainless steel

New: $750   **Perf.:** $700   **Exc.:** $650

6" compensated barrel, 7" shroud), blue finish

New: $725   **Perf.:** $675   **Exc.:** $625

6" compensated barrel, 7" shroud), stainless steel

New: $775   **Perf.:** $725   **Exc.:** $675

6" compensated barrel, 7" shroud, scope rings on shroud, blue finish

New: $775   **Perf.:** $725   **Exc.:** $625

6" compensated barrel, 7" shroud, scope rings on shroud, stainless steel

New: $800   **Perf.:** $750   **Exc.:** $700

Price: Open Hunter (open sights, 7 1/2" barrel), blue $805.00

Price: As above, stainless $849.00

Price: Compensated Open Hunter (6" compensated barrel, 7" shroud), blue $837.00

Rifles

SMITH & WESSON
41 MAGNUM (MODEL 57)
SMITH & WESSON
44 MAGNUM (MODEL 29)
SMITH & WESSON
44 MAGNUM MODEL 629
SMITH & WESSON
357 MAGNUM (MODEL 27)
SMITH & WESSON
357 MAGNUM (MODEL 627)
SMITH & WESSON HIGHWAY
PATROLMAN (MODEL 28)
SMITH & WESSON MODEL 25-5
STURM RUGER BISLEY
STURM RUGER BLACKHAWK
STURM RUGER
BLACKHAWK NEW MODEL
STURM RUGER REDHAWK

BERETTA MATO DELUXE BOLT-ACTION RIFLE

Bolt action; 270, 280 Rem., 30-06, 7mm Rem. Mag., 300 Win. Mag., 338 Win. Mag., 375 H&H. 23.6" barrel; weighs 7.9 lbs. 44.5" overall. XXX claro walnut stock with ebony forend tip, hand-rubbed oil finish. Bead on ramp front, open fully adjustable rear sights; drilled and tapped for scope mounting. Mauser-style action with claw extractor; three-position safety; removable box magazine; 375 H&H has muzzle brake; premium for 375 caliber. Introduced 1997, dropped 2003. From Beretta U.S.A. **LMSR: $2470**

Perf: $2000   **Exc.: $1500**   **VGood: $1000**

BRNO CZ 537 SPORTER

Bolt action; 270, 30-06 (internal 5-shot magazine), 243, 308 (detachable 5-shot magazine); 23 5/8" barrel; 44 3/4" overall length; weighs 7 lbs. 9 oz.; checkered walnut stock; hooded ramp front sight, adjustable folding leaf rear; improved standard-size Mauser-style action with non-rotating claw extractor; externally adjustable trigger; American-style safety; streamlined bolt shroud with cocking indicator. Imported from the Czech Republic by Magnum Research. Introduced 1992. **LMSR: $649**

Perf: $550   **Exc.: $475**   **VGood: $375**

With full stock, 308, 30-06

Perf: $650   **Exc.: $575**   **VGood: $475**

BROWNING A-BOLT HUNTER

Bolt action; 25-06, 270, 30-06, 280, 7mm Rem. Mag., 300 Win. Mag., 338 Win. Mag., 375 H&H (long action); 22-250, 243 Win., 257 Roberts, 22-250, 7mm-08, 308 Win., also 223 WSSM, 243 WSSM, 270 WSM, 7mm WSM, 300 WSM (short action); 22", 24", 26" barrel; 44 3/4" overall length; weighs 6 1/2 to 7 1/2 lbs.; recessed muzzle; magnum and standard action; classic-style American walnut stock; recoil pad on magnum calibers; short throw fluted bolt; three locking lugs; plunger-type ejector; adjustable, grooved gold-plated trigger; hinged floorplate; detachable box magazine; slide tang safety; rosewood grip, forend caps. Made in Japan. Introduced 1985; redesigned in 1994 as A-Bolt II.

Perf: $415   **Exc.: $375**   **VGood: $300**

BROWNING A-BOLT II HUNTER

Bolt action; 223, 223 WSSM, 22-250, 243, 243 WSSM, 25-06, 270, 270 WSM, 280, 7mm-08, 7mm Rem. Mag., 308, 30-06, 300 Win. Mag., 338 Win. Mag., 375 H&H Mag.; 4-shot (standard calibers), 3-shot (magnum calibers) detachable box magazine; 22" medium sporter weight barrel with recessed muzzle; 26" on magnum calibers; 44 3/4" overall length, 41 3/4" (short action); weighs 6 1/2 to 7 1/2 lbs.; classic-style American walnut stock; recoil pad standard on magnum calibers; short-throw (60-degree) fluted bolt; three locking lugs; plunger-type ejector; grooved and gold-plated adjustable trigger; hinged floorplate; slide tang safety; glossy stock finish, rosewood grip and forend cap; high polish blue; BOSS barrel vibration modulator and muzzlebrake system not available in 375 H&H. Imported from Japan by Browning. Introduced 1994; still imported. **LMSR: $652**

Perf: $450   **Exc.: $400**   **VGood: $350**

With open sights

Perf: $500   **Exc.: $450**   **VGood: $380**

With BOSS

Perf: $540   **Exc.: $480**   **VGood: $400**

BROWNING ACERA STRAIGHT-PULL RIFLE

Bolt action; straight pull; 30-06, 300 Win. Mag.; barrel length 22"; 24" for magnums; weighs 6 lbs., 9 oz. 41 1/4" overall. American walnut stock with high gloss finish. Optional blade on ramp front, open adjustable rear sights. Straight-pull action; detachable box magazine; Teflon coated breechblock; drilled and tapped for scope mounting. Introduced about 1999. No longer imported.

Perf: $850   **Exc.: $700**   **VGood: $600**

BROWNING BAR

Semi-automatic; 243 Win., 308 Win., 270 Win., 280 Rem., 30-06, 7mm Rem. Mag., 300 Win. Mag., 338 Win. Mag., also 270 WSM, 7mmWSM, 300 WSM; 22" barrel; 4-shot detachable box magazine (standard calibers), 3-shot (magnum calibers); adjustable folding leaf rear sight, gold bead hooded ramp front; receiver tapped for scope mounts; checkered walnut pistol-grip stock forearm. weighs 7 1/2 to 8 1/2 lbs. Not to be confused with the military Browning fully-automatic rifle. Grades I, II introduced in 1967; Several grades still in production. Grades vary according to amount of checkering, carving, engraving, inlay work. Premium for Belgian marked.

Grade I

Perf: $600   **Exc.: $475**   **VGood: $400**

Grade I Magnum

Perf: $610   **Exc.: $485**   **VGood: $410**

Grade II

Perf: $700   **Exc.: $620**   **VGood: $550**

Grade II Magnum

Perf: $725   **Exc.: $650**   **VGood: $595**

Grade III

Perf: $1100   **Exc.: $900**   **VGood: $700**

Grade III Magnum

Perf: $1300   **Exc.: $1100**   **VGood: $900**

Grade IV

Perf: $1500   **Exc.: $1300**   **VGood: $900**

Grade IV Magnum

Perf: $1600   **Exc.: $1400**   **VGood: $1000**

Grade V

Perf: $3000   **Exc.: $2600**   **VGood: $2100**

Grade V Magnum

Perf: $3300   **Exc.: $2900**   **VGood: $2300**

BROWNING BAR STALKER AUTO RIFLE

Semiautomatic; 243, 308, 270, 270 WSM, 7mm WSM, 30-06, 7mm Rem. Mag., 300 Win. Mag., 338 Win. Mag. Barrel: 20", 22" and 24"; weighs 6 lbs., 12 oz. (243) to 8 lbs., 2 oz. (magnum cals.) 41" to 45" overall. Black composite stock and forearm. Sights: Hooded front and adjustable rear or none. Optional BOSS (no sights); gas-operated action with seven-lug rotary bolt; dual action bars; 3- or 4-shot magazine (depending on caliber). Introduced 2001. Still imported by Browning. Premium for magnum calibers. **LMSR: $825**

Perf: $775   **Exc.: $650**   **VGood: $600**

BROWNING MODEL 81 BLR

Lever action; 223, 22-250, 243, 257 Roberts, 284 Win., 7mm-08, 308 Win., 358 Win.; 4-shot detachable box magazine; 20" round, tapered barrel; 39 3/4" overall length; weighs 7 lbs.; gold bead front sight, hooded ramp, square-notch adjustable rear; drilled, tapped for scope mounts; oil-finished, checkered, straight-grip walnut stock; recoil pad; half-cock hammer safety; wide, grooved trigger. Introduced 1971; made only in Japan after 1972; still imported by Browning. **LMSR: $696**

Belgian manufacture

Perf: $600   **Exc.: $550**   **VGood: $400**

Japanese manufacture

Perf: $500   **Exc.: $450**   **VGood: $330**

Browning Model 81 BLR Long Action

Same specs as Model 81 BLR except long action; 270, 30-06, 7mm Rem. Mag.; 22", 24" barrel; weighs 8 1/2 lbs.; six-lug fluted, rotary bolt. Made in Japan. Introduced 1991; still imported by Browning. **LMSR: $696**

Perf: $500   **Exc.: $450**   **VGood: $330**

Rifles

Browning Model 1885 Low Wall Traditional Hunter
Similar to the Model 1885 Low Wall except chambered for 357 Mag., 44 Mag. and 45 Colt; steel crescent buttplate; 1/16" gold bead front sight, adjustable buckhorn rear, and tang-mounted peep sight with barrel-type elevation adjuster and knob-type windage adjustments. Barrel is drilled and tapped for a Browning scope base. Oil-finished select walnut stock with swivel studs. Introduced 1997. Imported from Japan. **LMSR: $$1289**
    Perf: $850   **Exc.:** $700   **VGood:** $575

BROWNING BPR PUMP RIFLE
Pump-action; 243, 308 (short action); 270, 30-06, 7mm Rem. Mag., 300 Win. Mag., 4-shot magazine (3 for magnums); 22" barrel; 24" for magnum calibers; weighs 7 lbs., 3 oz. 43" overall (22" barrel). Select walnut stock with full pistol grip, high gloss finish. Gold bead on hooded ramp front sight, open click adjustable rear. Slide-action mechanism cams forend down away from the barrel on the rearward stroke. Seven-lug rotary bolt; cross-bolt safety behind trigger; removable magazine; alloy receiver. Introduced 1997. Imported from Belgium by Browning; no longer imported. **LMSR: $718.00**
    Perf: $700   **Exc.:** $600   **VGood:** $500

HARRINGTON & RICHARDSON ULTRA HUNTER
Single shot; 25-06, 308 Win., 450 Marlin; 26" (25-06), 22" (308 and 450 Marlin) barrel; weighs about 7 1/2 lbs.; no sights furnished; drilled, tapped for scope mounting; cinnamon-colored laminate stock and forend; hand-checkered grip and forend; break-open action with side-lever release; positive ejection; comes with scope mount; swivel studs; blued receiver and barrel. From H&R 1871, Inc. Introduced 1995; still produced. Premium for 450 Marlin. **LMSR: $250**
    Perf.: $200   **Exc.:** $150   **VGood:** $110

HARRINGTON & RICHARDSON MODEL 300 ULTRA
Bolt action; 22-250, 243 Win., 270 Win., 30-06, 308 Win., 300 Win. Mag., 7mm Rem. Mag.; 3-shot magazine (magnums), 5-shot (others); 22", 24" barrel; FN Mauser action; with or without open rear sight, ramp front; hand-checkered American walnut stock; cheekpiece, full pistol grip; pistol-grip cap, forearm tip of contrasting exotic wood; rubber buttplate, sling swivels. Introduced 1965; discontinued 1978.
    Exc.: $350   **VGood:** $295   **Good:** $250

MARLIN MODEL 336C
Lever-action; 30-30, 35 Rem., 32 Spl.; 6-shot tubular magazine; 20" barrel; 38 1/2" overall length; weighs 7 lbs.; updated version of Model 36 carbine; semi-buckhorn adjustable folding rear sight, ramp front with Wide-Scan hood; receiver tapped for scope mounts; round breech bolt; gold-plated trigger; offset hammer spur; top of receiver sandblasted to reduce glare. Introduced 1948; discontinued 1983; updated version still in production. **LMSR: $529**
    Exc.: $250   **VGood:** $230   **Good:** $170

Marlin Model 336A
Same specs as Model 336C except 24" round barrel; two-thirds magazine tube; 6-shot; blued forearm cap; sling swivels. Introduced 1950; temporarily discontinued 1962. Reintroduced 1973; discontinued 1980, updated version still offered. **LMSR: $451**
    Exc.: $290   **VGood:** $250   **Good:** $200

Marlin Model 336A Lever-Action Carbine
Same as the Marlin 336C except 20" barrel; has cut-checkered, walnut-finished hardwood pistol grip stock with swivel studs, 30-30 only, 6-shot. Hammer-block safety. Adjustable rear sight, brass bead front. **LMSR: $441**
    Perf: $290   **Exc.:** $250   **VGood:** $200

Marlin Model 336A-DL
Same specs as Model 336A except sling; swivels; hand-checkered stock, forearm. Discontinued 1962.
    Exc.: $470   **VGood:** $370   **Good:** $290

Marlin Model 336CC
Same as the Marlin 336A except has Mossy Oak Break-Up camouflage stock and forearm. 30-30 only, 6-shot; receiver tapped for scope mount or receiver sight. Introduced 2001, still in production. Made in U.S.A. by Marlin. **LMSR: $503**
    Perf: $465   **Exc.:** $410   **VGood:** $375

Marlin Model 336CS
Same specs as Model 336A except 30-30, 35 Rem.; 6-shot two-thirds tube magazine; 20" barrel; 38 1/2" overall length; weighs 7 lbs.; select black walnut stock; capped pistol grip; hammer-block safety; tapped for scope mounts; offset hammer spur. Introduced 1984; discontinued 2001. **LMSR: $493**
    Perf.: $310   **Exc.:** $240   **VGood:** $190

Marlin Model 336SS Lever-Action Carbine
Same as the 336C except receiver, barrel and other major parts are machined from stainless steel. 30-30 only, 6-shot; receiver tapped for scope. Still offered. **LMSR: $640**
    Perf.: $520   **Exc.:** $430   **VGood:** $170

Marlin Model 336W Lever-Action Rifle
Similar to the Model 336CS except has walnut-finished, cut-checkered Maine birch stock; blued steel barrel band has integral sling swivel; no front sight hood; comes with padded nylon sling; hard rubber butt plate. Introduced 1998, still offered. Made in U.S.A. by Marlin. **LMSR: $457**
    Perf: $310   **Exc.:** $230   **VGood:** $170

Marlin Model 336 Sport Carbine
Same specs as Model 336A rifle except 20" barrel; weighs 7 lbs.; two-thirds 6-shot magazine. Introduced 1948; discontinued 1963.
    Exc.: $300   **VGood:** $250   **Good:** $180

Marlin Model 336SD
Same specs as Model 336A except 20" barrel; checkered pistol grip, forend; 38 1/2" overall length; weighs 7 1/2 lbs.; leather sling; deluxe sports carbine. Introduced 1954; discontinued 1962.
    Exc.: $550   **VGood:** $325   **Good:** $220

MARLIN MODEL 444 RIFLE
Lever action; 444 Marlin; 5-shot tube magazine; 24" barrel; 42 1/2" overall length; weighs 7 1/2 lbs.; open elevation-adjustable rear sight, hooded ramp front; action is strengthened version of Model 336; straight-grip Monte Carlo stock of uncheckered American walnut; recoil pad; carbine forearm; barrel band; sling; sling swivels. Introduced 1965; discontinued 1972.
    Exc.: $325   **VGood:** $250   **Good:** $190

Marlin Model 444 Sporter
Same specs as Model 444 Rifle except 22" barrel, 40 1/2" overall length; folding rear, brass bead front sight; Model 336A-type pistol-grip stock, forearm; recoil pad; detachable

MOSSBERG MODEL 472 CARBINE
Lever action; 30-30, 35 Rem.; 6-shot tubular magazine; 20" barrel; adjustable buckhorn rear sight, ramp front; with gold bead; barrel tapped for scope mounting; off-set hammer spur; side-ejecting; pistol-grip or straight stock; barrel band on forearm; sling swivels on pistol-grip style, removable saddle ring on straight-stock model. Manufactured 1972 to 1980.
    Exc.: $200   **VGood:** $170   **Good:** $130

REMINGTON MODEL FOUR
Semi-automatic; 243 Win., 6mm Rem., 270, 7mm Express Rem., 280 Rem., 308 Win., 30-06; 4-shot clip magazine; 22" round tapered barrel; 42" overall length; weighs 7 1/2 lbs.; gold bead ramp front sight, windage-adjustable sliding ramp rear; checkered American walnut Monte Carlo pistol-grip stock; cartridge head inset on receiver bottom denotes caliber; positive cross-bolt safety; tapped for scope mount. Redesign of Model 742. Introduced 1981; discontinued 1988.
    Exc.: $395   **VGood:** $350   **Good:** $320
D Peerless Grade
    Perf.: $1995   **Exc.:** $1695   **VGood:** $995
F Premier Grade
    Perf.: $4195   **Exc.:** $3795   **VGood:** $2695
F Premier Gold Grade
    Perf.: $6495   **Exc.:** $4995   **VGood:** $3995

REMINGTON MODEL 74 SPORTSMAN
Semi-automatic; 30-06; 4-shot magazine; 22" barrel; weighs 7 1/2 lbs.; open adjustable sights; walnut-finished hardwood stock, forend; cartridge head inset on receiver bottom denotes caliber; positive cross-bolt safety; tapped for scope mounts. Introduced 1984; discontinued 1987.
    Exc.: $295   **VGood:** $260   **Good:** $210

REMINGTON MODEL 81, 81A WOODSMASTER
Semi-automatic; 30, 32, 35 Rem., 300 Savage; 5-shot non-detachable box magazine; 22" barrel; 41 1/2" overall length; weighs 8 lbs.; white metal bead front sight, step-adjustable rear; takedown; hammerless; solid breech; unchecked American walnut pistol-grip stock, forearm; shotgun-style buttplate. Introduced 1936 to replace Model 8; discontinued 1950.
    Exc.: $425   **VGood:** $350   **Good:** $275

REMINGTON MODEL 740A
Semi-automatic; 244, 280, 308 Win., 30-06; 4-shot detachable box magazine; 22" barrel; 42 1/2" overall length; weighs 7 1/2 lbs.; white metal bead ramp front sight, step-adjustable, semi-buckhorn rear; hammerless; solid frame; side ejection; unchecked American walnut pistol-grip stock; grooved semi-beavertail forearm. Introduced 1955; discontinued 1960.
    Exc.: $295   **VGood:** $260   **Good:** $210

---

swivels; sling. Introduced 1972; discontinued 1983; updated version still offered. **LMSR: $631**
    Perf.: $285   **Exc.:** $230   **VGood:** $200

Marlin Model 444P Outfitter Lever-Action
Similar to the 444 with 18 1/2" ported barrel; weighs 6 3/4 lbs.; overall length 37". Available only in 444 Marlin. Introduced 1999, dropped 2003. **LMSR: $631**
    Perf.: $550   **Exc.:** $450   **VGood:** $400

Marlin Model 444SS
Same specs as Model 444 Sporter except 22" barrel with deep-cut Ballard-type rifling; fully-adjustable semi-buckhorn rear sight; hammer-block safety; offset hammer spur; Mar-Shield finish. Introduced 1984; dropped 2001. **LMSR: $582**
    Perf.: $390   **Exc.:** $330   **VGood:** $230

MARLIN MODEL 1894
Lever action; 41 Mag., 44 Mag., 45 Colt; 10-shot tube magazine; 20" carbine barrel; 37 1/2" overall length; weighs 6 lbs.; hooded ramp front sight, semi-buckhorn adjustable rear; unchecked straight grip black walnut stock, forearm; gold-plated trigger; receiver tapped for scope mount; offset hammer spur; solid top receiver sand blasted to reduce

glare. 41 Mag. produced 1985-1988; 45 Colt produced 1989-1990. Introduced 1969; later production as Model 1894S.
    Perf.: $350   **Exc.:** $300   **VGood:** $250

Marlin Model 1894C
Same specs as Model 1894 except 357 Mag.; 9-shot tube magazine; 18 1/2" barrel; 35 1/2" overall length; weighs 6 lbs. Introduced 1979; discontinued 1985. Improved version still offered. **LMSR: $556**
    Perf.: $380   **Exc.:** $290   **VGood:** $225

MARLIN MODEL 1895
Lever action; 45-70; 4-shot tube magazine; 22" round barrel; 40 1/2" overall length; weighs 7 lbs.; offset hammer spur; adjustable semi-buckhorn folding rear sight, bead front; solid receiver tapped for scope mounts, receiver sights; two-piece unchecked straight grip American walnut stock, forearm of black walnut; rubber buttplate; blued steel forend cap. Meant to be a recreation of the original Model 1895 discontinued in 1915. Actually built on action of Marlin Model 444. Introduced 1972; discontinued 1979. Updated version still in production. **LMSR: $631**
    Exc.: $320   **VGood:** $280   **Good:** $230

Marlin Model 1895SS
Same specs as Model 1895 except full pistol-grip stock; hammer-block safety. Introduced 1984; discontinued 2001. **LMSR: $582**
    Perf.: $350   **Exc.:** $290   **VGood:** $230

Rifles

REMINGTON MODEL 742A
Semi-automatic; 6mm Rem., 243 Win., 280 Rem., 308 Win., 30-06; 4-shot box magazine; 22" barrel; 42" overall length; weighs 7 1/2 lbs.; gold bead front sight on ramp, step-adjustable rear; versions in 1960s with impressed checkering on stock, forearm; later versions, cut checkering. Introduced 1960; discontinued 1980.

    Exc.: $300   **VGood: $275**   **Good: $250**

Remington Model 742C Carbine
Same specs as Model 742A except 280, 308 Win., 30-06; 18 1/2" barrel; 38 1/2" overall length; weighs 6 1/2 lbs.

    Exc.: $350   **VGood: $300**   **Good: $260**

REMINGTON MODEL 7400
Semi-automatic; 6mm Rem., 243, 270, 280, 30-06, 308, 35 Whelen; 4-shot detachable magazine; 22" barrel; 42" overall length; weighs 7 1/2 lbs.; gold bead ramp front sight, windage-adjustable sliding ramp rear; tapped for scope mounts; impressed checkered American walnut pistol-grip stock; positive cross-bolt safety. Introduced 1981; still in production. **LMSR: $612**

    Perf.: $485   **Exc.: $370**   **VGood: $310**

With black synthetic stock, matte black metal, rifle or carbine, **LMSR: $509**

    Perf: $450   **Exc.: $350**   **VGood: $275**

Remington Model 7400 Carbine
Same specs as Model 7400 except 30-06 only; 18 1/2" barrel; weighs 7 1/4 lbs. Introduced 1988; no longer in production. **LMSR: $612**

    Perf.: $485   **Exc.: $370**   **VGood: $310**

Remington Model 7400 Special Purpose
Same specs as Model 7400 except 270, 30-06; non-glare finish on the American walnut stock; all exposed metal with non-reflective matte black finish; quick-detachable sling swivels; camo-pattern Cordura carrying sling. Made in U.S. by Remington. Introduced 1993; discontinued 1994.

    Perf.: $430   **Exc.: $350**   **VGood: $290**

REMINGTON MODEL 78 SPORTSMAN
Bolt action; 223, 243, 308, 270, 30-06; 4-shot magazine; 22" barrel; 42 1/2" overall length; weighs 7 1/2 lbs.; open adjustable sights; straight-comb walnut-finished hardwood stock; cartridge head inset on receiver bottom denotes caliber; positive cross-bolt safety; tapped for scope mount. Introduced 1984; discontinued 1989.

    Exc.: $285   **VGood: $235**   **Good: $195**

REMINGTON MODEL 600
Bolt action; 222 Rem., 6mm Rem., 243, 308, 35 Rem.; 5-, 6-shot (222 Rem. only) magazine; 18 1/2" round barrel with ventilated nylon rib; 37 1/4" overall length; weighs 5 1/2 lbs.; blade ramp front sight, fully-adjustable open rear; drilled, tapped for scope mounts; checkered walnut Monte Carlo pistol-grip stock. Introduced 1964; discontinued 1967.

    Exc.: $400   **VGood: $320**   **Good: $275**

223 Rem. Caliber Rare.

    Exc.: $500   **VGood: $400**   **Good: $300**

REMINGTON MODEL 660
Bolt action; 222 Rem., 6mm Rem., 243, 308; 5-, 6-shot (222 Rem. only) magazine; 20" barrel; 38 3/4" overall length; weighs 6 1/2 lbs.; brass bead front sight on ramp, open adjustable rear; checkered Monte Carlo stock; black pistol-grip cap, forearm tip. Introduced 1968; discontinued 1971.

    Exc.: $525   **VGood: $450**   **Good: $350**

REMINGTON MODEL 700ADL
Bolt action; 222, 222 Rem. Mag., 22-250, 243, 25-06, 264 Win. Mag., 6mm Rem., 270, 280, 7mm Rem. Mag., 308, 30-06; 4-shot (264, 7mm), 6-shot (222, 222 Rem. Mag.), 5-shot (others); 20", 22", 24" round tapered barrel; 39 1/2" overall length (222, 222 Rem. Mag., 243 Win.); removable, adjustable rear sight with windage screw, gold bead ramp front; tapped for scope mounts; walnut Monte Carlo stock, with pistol grip; originally introduced with hand-checkered pistol grip, forearm; made for several years with RKW finish, impressed checkering; more recent models with computerized cut checkering. Introduced 1962; still in production. **LMSR: $585**

    Perf.: $400   **Exc.: $320**   **VGood: $285**

With optional laminated stock.

    Perf.: $400   **Exc.: $350**   **VGood: $300**

Remington Model 700 ADL Synthetic
Similar to the 700 ADL except has a fiberglass-reinforced synthetic stock with straight comb, raised cheekpiece, positive checkering, and black rubber butt pad. Metal has matte finish. Available in 22-250, 223, 243, 270, 308, 30-06 with 22" barrel, 300 Win. Mag., 7mm Rem. Mag. with 24" barrel. Introduced 1996. Still offered. **LMSR: $511**

    Perf: $350   **Exc.: $300**   **VGood: $260**

REMINGTON MODEL 700BDL
Bolt action; 17 Rem., 22-250, 222 Rem., 222 Rem. Mag., 243, 25-06, 264 Win. Mag., 270, 280, 300 Savage, 30-06, 308, 35 Whelen, 6mm Rem., 7mm Rem. Mag., 7mm-08, 300 Win. Mag., 338 Win. Mag., 8mm Mag.; 4-shot magazine; 20", 22", 24" barrel; stainless barrel (7mm Rem. Mag., 264, 300 Win. Mag.); with or without sights; select walnut, hand-checkered Monte Carlo stock; black forearm tip, pistol-grip cap, skip-line fleur-de-lis checkering; matted receiver top; quick-release floorplate; quick-detachable swivels, sling. Still in production. **LMSR: $576**

    Perf.: $465   **Exc.: $400**   **VGood: $325**

Left-hand model

    Perf.: $525   **Exc.: $450**   **VGood: $350**

Remington Model 700 LSS Rifle
Similar to 700 BDL except stainless steel barreled action, gray laminated wood stock with Monte Carlo comb and cheekpiece. No sights furnished. Available in 7mm Rem. Mag., 7mm Rem. Ultra Mag., 375 Rem. Ultra Mag., LH 7mm Rem. Ultra Mag., 300 Rem. Ultra Mag., and 338 Rem. Ultra Mag. in right-hand, and 30-06, 300 Rem. Ultra Mag., 338 Rem. Ultra Mag. in left-hand model; premium for left-hand. Introduced 1996, still offered. **LMSR: $803**

    Perf: $600   **Exc.: $485**   **VGood: $410**

REMINGTON MODEL 700 CAMO SYNTHETIC
Bolt action; 22-250, 243, 7mm-08, 270, 280, 30-06, 308, 7mm Rem. Mag.; 4-shot, 3-shot (7mm, 300 Wea. Mag.) magazine; open adjustable sights; synthetic stock, stock and metal (except bolt and sights) fully camouflaged in Mossy Oak Bottomland camo; swivel studs. Made in U.S. by Remington. Introduced 1992; discontinued 1994.

    Perf.: $450   **Exc.: $375**   **VGood: $330**

REMINGTON MODEL 700 CLASSIC
Bolt action; 22-250, 6mm Rem., 243, 270, 7mm Mauser, 30-06, 7mm Rem. Mag., 350 Rem. Mag., 375 H&H, 300 Win. Mag.; 24" barrel; 44 1/2" overall length; weighs 7 3/4 lbs.; no sights; drilled and tapped for scope mounting; American walnut straight-comb stock with 20 lpi checkered pistol grip, forend; rubber recoil pad; sling swivel studs; hinged floorplate. Introduced 1978. **LMSR: $576**

    Perf.: $500   **Exc.: $450**   **VGood: $400**

SMITH & WESSON
41 MAGNUM (MODEL 57)
SMITH & WESSON
44 MAGNUM (MODEL 29)
SMITH & WESSON
44 MAGNUM MODEL 629
SMITH & WESSON
357 MAGNUM (MODEL 27)
SMITH & WESSON
357 MAGNUM (MODEL 627)
SMITH & WESSON HIGHWAY
PATROLMAN (MODEL 28)
SMITH & WESSON MODEL 25-5
STURM RUGER BISLEY
STURM RUGER BLACKHAWK
STURM RUGER
BLACKHAWK NEW MODEL
STURM RUGER REDHAWK

REMINGTON MODEL 710
Bolt action; 270 Win., 30-06; 22" barrel; weighs 7-1/8 lbs.; 42 1/2" overall length; Gray synthetic stock; Bushnell Sharpshooter 3-9x scope mounted and bore-sighted. Unique action locks bolt directly into barrel; 60-degree bolt throw; 4-shot dual-stack magazine; key-operated Integrated Security System locks bolt open. Introduced 2001. Still offered.
LMSR: $425
    Perf.: $ 295   **Exc.: $250**   **VGood: $175**

REMINGTON MODEL 720A
Bolt action; 257 Roberts, 270, 30-06; 5-shot detachable box magazine; 22" barrel; 42 1/2" overall length; weighs 8 lbs.; bead front sight on ramp, open rear; models available with Redfield No. 70RST micrometer or Lyman No. 48 receiver sights; checkered American walnut pistol-grip stock; modified Model 1917 Enfield action. Made only in 1941 as factory facilities were converted to wartime production. Note: Most 720s were made in 30-06; few in 270; and only a handful in 257 Roberts. Add premium for rarer calibers.
    Exc.: $1250   **VGood: $1000**   **Good: $700**

REMINGTON MODEL 721A
Bolt action; 270, 280, 30-06; 4-shot box magazine; 24" barrel; 44 1/4" overall length; weighs 7 1/4 lbs.; white metal bead front sight on ramp, step-adjustable sporting rear; uncheckered American walnut sporter stock with pistol grip; semi-beavertail forend; checkered shotgun-style buttplate; thumb safety; receiver drilled, tapped for scope mounts, micrometer sights. Introduced 1948; discontinued 1962.
    Exc.: $300   **VGood: $235**   **Good: $200**

REMINGTON MODEL 722A
Bolt action, short action version of Model 721; 222 Rem., 222 Rem. Mag., 243 Win., 244 Rem., 257 Roberts, 300 Savage, 308; 4-, 5-shot (222 Rem.) magazine; 24", 26" (222 Rem., 244 Rem.) barrel; 43 1/4" overall length; weighs 7 lbs.; shorter action than Model 721A; white metal bead front sight on ramp, step-adjustable sporting rear; receiver drilled,

tapped for scope mounts or micrometer sights; uncheckered walnut sporter stock. Introduced 1948; discontinued 1962.
    Exc.: $360   **VGood: $310**   **Good: $275**

REMINGTON MODEL 725ADL
Bolt action; 222 Rem., 243, 244, 270, 280, 30-06; 4-, 5-shot (222 Rem.) box magazine; 22", 24" (222 Rem.) barrel; 42 1/2", 43 1/2" (222) overall length; weighs 7 lbs.; removable hood ramp front sight, adjustable open rear; Monte Carlo comb, walnut stock; hand-checkered pistol grip, forearm; hinged floorplate; swivels. Some calibers bring premium. Introduced 1958; discontinued 1961.
    Exc.: $395   **VGood: $290**   **Good: $200**

REMINGTON MODEL 788
Bolt action; 222, 22-250, 223, 6mm Rem., 243, 7mm-08, 308, 30-30, 44 Mag.; 3-, 4-shot (222) detachable box magazine; 22", 24" (222, 22-250) barrel; 41"-43 5/8" overall length; weighs 7-7 1/2 lbs.; open fully-adjustable rear sight, blade ramp front; receiver tapped for scope mounts; American walnut or walnut-finished hardwood pistol-grip stock, uncheckered with Monte Carlo comb; thumb safety; artillery-type bolt. Introduced 1967; discontinued 1983.
    Exc.: $330   **VGood: $275**   **Good: $240**
44 Mag., 7mm-08.
    Exc.: $395   **VGood: $330**   **Good: $275**

REMINGTON MODEL SEVEN
Bolt action; 17 Rem., 222 Rem., 223 Rem., 243, 7mm-08, 6mm, 308; 4-shot magazine, 5-shot (222 only) 18 1/2" barrel; 37 1/2" overall length; weighs 6 1/4 lbs.; ramp front sight, adjustable open rear; American walnut stock; modified Schnabel forend; machine-cut checkering; short action; silent side safety; free-floated barrel. Introduced 1983; still in production. **LMSR: $549**
    Perf.: $450   **Exc.: $370**   **VGood: $320**

REMINGTON MODEL SIX
Slide action; 6mm Rem., 243, 270, 308 Win., 308 Accelerator, 30-06, 30-06 Accelerator; 4-shot detachable clip magazine; 22" round tapered barrel; 42" overall length; weighs 7 1/2 lbs.; gold bead front sight on matted ramp, open adjustable sliding ramp rear; cut-checkered Monte Carlo walnut

stock with full cheekpiece; cross-bolt safety; tapped for scope mount; cartridge head medallion on receiver bottom to denote caliber. Special version of Model 760. Introduced 1981; discontinued 1988.
    Perf.: $395   **Exc.: $350**   **VGood: $300**
D Peerless Grade.
    Perf.: $1995   **Exc.: $1795**   **VGood: $1095**
F Premier Grade.
    Perf.: $4195   **Exc.: $3795**   **VGood: $2695**
F Premier Gold Grade.
    Perf.: $6495   **Exc.: $5195**   **VGood: $3995**

REMINGTON MODEL 76 SPORTSMAN
Slide action; 30-06; 4-shot magazine; 22" barrel; 42" overall length; weighs 7 1/2 lbs.; open adjustable sights; walnut-finished hardwood stock, forend; cartridge head inset on receiver bottom denotes caliber; cross-bolt safety; tapped for scope mounts. Introduced 1984; discontinued 1987.
    Perf.: $300   **Exc.: $270**   **VGood: $225**

REMINGTON MODEL 141, 141A GAMEMASTER
Slide action; 30, 32, 35 Rem.; 5-shot tube magazine; 24" barrel; 42 3/4" overall length; weighs 7 3/4 lbs.; hammerless; takedown; white metal bead ramp front sight, step-adjustable rear; uncheckered American walnut half-pistol-grip stock; grooved slide handle. Introduced 1936; discontinued 1950.
    Exc.: $400   **VGood: $325**   **Good: $270**

REMINGTON MODEL 760
Slide action; 222 Rem., 223 Rem., 6mm Rem., 243 Win., 244 Rem., 257 Roberts, 270 Win., 280 Rem., 30-06, 300 Savage, 308 Win., 35 Rem.; 4-shot magazine; 22" barrel; 42 1/4" overall length; weighs 7 1/2 lbs.; hammerless; white metal bead front sight on ramp, step-adjustable, semi-buckhorn rear. Models from mid-'60s to early '70s with impressed checkering; others hand-checkered on pistol grip, slide handle; early versions with grooved slide handle, no checkering on stock. Introduced 1952; discontinued 1980.
    Perf.: $375   **Exc.: $320**   **VGood: $250**
222 Rem., 223 Rem.
    Perf.: $1295   **Exc.: $995**   **VGood: $695**
257 Roberts.
    Perf.: $810   **Exc.: $670**   **VGood: $475**

REMINGTON MODEL 7600
Slide action; 6mm Rem., 243, 270, 280, 30-06, 308, 35 Whelen; 4-shot detachable magazine; 22" barrel; 42" overall length; weighs 7 1/2 lbs.; removable gold bead ramp front, windage-adjustable sliding ramp rear sight; tapped for scope mount; impressed checkered American walnut pistol-grip stock; positive cross-bolt safety. Introduced 1981; still in production in a number of variations. **LMSR: $588**
    Perf.: $425   **Exc.: $350**   **VGood: $275**

Rifles

Savage Model 110C
Same specs as Model 110 except 22-250, 243 Win., 25-06, 270 Win., 30-06, 308 Win., 7mm Rem. Mag., 300 Win. Mag.; 3-shot (Magnums), 4-shot detachable box magazine; 22", 24" (22-250, Magnums) barrel; open folding leaf rear sight, gold bead ramp front; hand-checkered Monte Carlo American walnut pistol-grip stock; recoil pad (Magnums). Introduced 1966.
 Exc.: $265   **VGood: $230**   **Good: $200**
Left-hand model.
 Exc.: $270   **VGood: $240**   **Good: $210**

SAVAGE MODEL 340
Bolt action; 22 Hornet, 222 Rem., 30-30; 3-, 4-shot detachable box magazine; 20", 22", 24" medium-weight barrel; 40" overall length (20" barrel); weighs 6 3/4 lbs.; click-adjustable middle sight, ramp front; uncheckered one-piece American walnut pistol-grip stock; thumb safety at right rear of receiver. Introduced 1950; discontinued 1986.
 Exc.: $230   **VGood: $200**   **Good: $170**

Savage Model 99C
Same specs as late production Model 99 except detachable clip magazine replaces rotary type; 22-250, 243 Win., 284 Win., 308 Win. (284 dropped in 1974); 4-shot detachable magazine, 3-shot (284); 22" barrel; 41 3/4" overall length; weighs 6 3/4 lbs.; hammerless; solid breech; Damascened bolt; case-hardened lever; blue receiver; gold-plated trigger; top tang safety; hooded gold bead ramp front, adjustable folding ramp rear sight; receiver tapped for scope mounts; walnut stock with checkered pistol grip, forend; Monte Carlo comb; swivel studs. Introduced in 1965; last variation of the Model 99; production discontinued 1998.
 Exc.: $530   **VGood: $430**   **Good: $370**

Savage Model 99E (Late Model)
Same specs as Model 99 except 243, 250 Savage, 300 Savage, 308; 20", 22", 24" medium-weight barrel; weighs 7 1/4 lbs.; hardwood pistol-grip stock; trigger guard safety. Introduced 1960 as "economy" version; discontinued 1982.
 Exc.: $320   **VGood: $270**   **Good: $190**

Savage Model 99EG (Late Model)
Same specs as Model 99 except 243, 250-3000, 250 Savage, 300 Savage, 308, 358 Win.; 24" barrel; 43 1/4 overall length; weighs 7 1/4 lbs.; checkered pistol-grip stock. Introduced 1946; discontinued 1960.
 Exc.: $390   **VGood: $330**   **Good: $230**

Savage Model 99F Featherweight (Late Model)
Same specs as Model 99 except 243, 250-3000, 284 Win., 300 Savage, 308, 358 Win.; 22" lightweight barrel; 41 1/4" overall length; weighs 6 1/2 lbs.; solid breech; polished Damascened finish bolt; case-hardened lever; blued receiver; grooved trigger; checkered walnut pistol-grip stock; feather-

weight solid frame model. Introduced 1955; discontinued 1972.
 Exc.: $395   **VGood: $320**   **Good: $210**

SAVAGE MODEL 170
Slide action; 30-30, 35 Rem.; 3-shot tubular magazine; 22" barrel; 41 1/2" overall length; weighs 6 3/4 lbs.; folding leaf rear sight, gold bead ramp front; receiver drilled, tapped for scope mount; select checkered American walnut pistol-grip stock; Monte Carlo comb, grooved slide handle; hard rubber buttplate. Introduced 1970; discontinued 1981.
 Exc.: $200   **VGood: $170**   **Good: $140**

STURM RUGER DEERFIELD 99/44 CARBINE
Semiautomatic; 44 Mag., 4-shot rotary magazine; 18 1/2" barrel; weighs 6 1/4 lbs.; 36 7/8" overall length; Hardwood stock; Gold bead front, folding adjustable aperture rear sights; Semi-automatic action; dual front-locking lugs lock directly into receiver; integral scope mount; push-button safety; marketed with 1" rings and gun lock. Introduced 2000. Made in U.S.A. by Sturm, Ruger & Co. **LMSR: $675**
 Perf.: $600   **Exc.: $500**   **VGood: $400**

STURM RUGER MINI THIRTY RIFLE
Semi-automatic; 7.62x39mm Russian; 5-shot detachable staggered box magazine; 18 1/2" barrel; weighs 7 1/4 lbs.; six-groove barrel; Sturm Ruger integral scope mount bases; folding peep sight; blued or stainless finish. Introduced 1987; still in production. **LMSR: $649**
 Perf.: $460   **Exc.: $390**   **VGood: $340**
Stainless finish
 Perf.: $480   **Exc.: $400**   **VGood: $355**

STURM RUGER MODEL 44
Semi-automatic; 44 Mag.; 4-shot tube magazine; 18 1/2" barrel; magazine release button incorporated in 1967;

uncheckered walnut pistol-grip carbine stock; barrel band; receiver tapped for scope mount; folding leaf rear sight, gold bead front. Introduced 1961; dropped 1985.
 Perf.: $395   **Exc.: $350**   **VGood: $300**

STURM RUGER MODEL 77R
Bolt-action; 22-250, 220 Swift, 243 Win., 7mm-08, 6.5 Rem. Mag., 280 Rem., 284 Win., 308 Win., 300 Win. Mag., 338 Win. Mag., 350 Rem. Mag., 25-06, 257 Roberts, 250-3000, 6mm Rem., 270 Win., 7x57mm, 7mm Rem. Mag., 30-06; 3-, 5-shot magazine, depending upon caliber; 22" tapered barrel; hinged floorplate; adjustable trigger; hand-checkered American walnut stock; pistol-grip cap; sling swivel studs; recoil pad; integral scope mount base; optional folding leaf adjustable rear sight, gold bead ramp front. Introduced in 1968; no longer in production. Replaced by the Model M77 Mark II.
 Perf.: $400   **Exc.: $330**   **VGood: $300**
350 Rem. Mag. caliber
 Perf.: $450   **Exc.: $390**   **VGood: $330**

Sturm Ruger Model 77RL Ultra Light
Same specs as Model 77R except 243, 308, 270, 30-06, 257, 22-250, 250-3000; 20" light barrel; Sturm Ruger 1" scope rings. Introduced 1983; **LMSR: $592**
 Perf.: $420   **Exc.: $350**   **VGood: $300**

Sturm Ruger Model 77RS
Same specs as Model 77R except magnum-size action; 257 Roberts, 25-06, 270 Win., 30-06, 7mm Rem. Mag., 300 Win. Mag., 338 Win. Mag.; 3-, 5-shot, depending upon caliber; 22" barrel (270, 30-06, 7x57, 280 Rem.); 24" barrel (all others).
 Perf.: $410   **Exc.: $350**   **VGood: $300**

SMITH & WESSON
41 MAGNUM (MODEL 57)
SMITH & WESSON
44 MAGNUM (MODEL 29)
SMITH & WESSON
44 MAGNUM MODEL 629
SMITH & WESSON
357 MAGNUM (MODEL 27)
SMITH & WESSON
357 MAGNUM (MODEL 627)
SMITH & WESSON HIGHWAY
PATROLMAN (MODEL 28)
SMITH & WESSON MODEL 25-5
STURM RUGER BISLEY
STURM RUGER BLACKHAWK
STURM RUGER
BLACKHAWK NEW MODEL
STURM RUGER REDHAWK

Sturm Ruger Model 77 RSI International
Same specs as Model 77R except 18 1/2" barrel; full-length Mannlicher-style stock; steel forend cap; loop-type sling swivels; open sights; Sturm Ruger steel scope rings; improved front sight; 22-250, 250-3000, 243, 308, 270, 30-06; weighs 7 lbs; 38 3/8" overall length. Introduced 1986; still in production. **LMSR: $713**

Perf.: $475	**Exc.:** $390	**VGood:** $330

STURM RUGER MODEL 77R Mark II
Bolt-action; 223, 22-250, 243 Win., 25-06, 257 Roberts, 270 Roberts, 270 Win., 280 Rem., 6mm Rem., 6.5x55, 7x57, 30-06, 308 Win. Mag., 7mm Rem. Mag., 300 Win. Mag., 338 Win. Mag.; 4-shot magazine; 20" barrel; 39 1/2" overall length; weighs 6 1/2 lbs.; American walnut stock; no sights; Ruger integral scope mount base; marketed with 1" scope rings; three-position safety; redesigned trigger; short action. Introduced 1989; still in production. **LMSR: $634**

Perf.: $390	**Exc.:** $350	**VGood:** $300

Sturm Ruger Model 77 Mark II All-Weather Stainless
Same specs as Model 77R Mark II except all metal parts of stainless steel; fiberglass-reinforced Zytel stock; 223, 243, 270, 308, 30-06, 7mm Rem. Mag.; fixed blade-type ejector; new triggerguard; patented floorplate latch; three-position safety; integral scope base, 1" Sturm Ruger scope rings; built-in swivel loops. Introduced 1990; **LMSR: $574**

Perf.: $495	**Exc.:** $450	**VGood:** $400

STURM RUGER NO. 1B
Single-shot; 22-250, 220 Swift, 243 Win., 223, 257 Roberts, 280, 6mm Rem., 25-06, 270 Win., 30-06, 7mm Rem. Mag., 300 Win. Mag., 338 Mag., 270 Weatherby, 300 Weatherby; 26" barrel with quarter rib; American walnut, two-piece stock; hand-checkered pistol grip, forearm; open sights or integral scope mounts; hammerless falling-block design; automatic ejector; top-tang safety. Introduced 1967; still in production. **LMSR: $774**

Perf.: $540	**Exc.:** $420	**VGood:** $365

THOMPSON/CENTER CONTENDER CARBINE
Single shot; 22 LR, 22 Hornet, 223 Rem., 7mm TCU, 7-30 Waters, 30-30, 357 Rem. Max., 35 Rem., 44 Mag., 410; 21" barrel; 35" overall length; weighs 5 1/8 lbs.; open adjustable rear sight, blade front; drilled, tapped for scope mounts; checkered American walnut stock; rubber buttpad; built on T/C Contender action; interchangeable barrels. Introduced 1985; still in production. **LMSR: $592**

Perf.: $420	**Exc.:** $325	**VGood:** $270

THOMPSON/CENTER ENCORE RIFLE
Single shot, breakopen; 22-250, 223, 243, 25-06, 270, 7mm-08, 308, 30-06, 7mm Rem. Mag., 300 Win. Mag.; 24", 26" barrel; weighs 6 lbs., 12 oz. (24" barrel); 38 1/2" overall length (24" barrel); American walnut stock, Monte Carlo style, with Schnabel forend, or black composite stock; Ramp-style white bead front, fully adjustable leaf-type rear sights; Interchangeable barrels; action opens by squeezing trigger guard; drilled and tapped for T/C scope mounts; polished blue finish. Introduced 1996, still in production. **LMSR: $627**

Perf.: $550	**Exc.:** $450	**VGood:** $410

With black composite stock and forend

Perf.: $500	**Exc.:** $400	**VGood:** $350

THOMPSON/CENTER TCR '87 HUNTER
Single shot; 22 Hornet, 222 Rem., 223 Rem., 22-250, 243 Win., 270, 308, 7mm-08, 30-06, 32-40 Win., 375 H&H, 416 Rem. Mag.; 12-gauge slug; 23" (standard), 25 7/8" heavy barrel; break-open; no sights; checkered American black walnut stock; interchangeable barrels; single-stage trigger; cross-bolt safety. Introduced 1987; discontinued 1992.

Perf.: $420	**Exc.:** $380	**VGood:** $310

WEATHERBY MARK V ACCUMARK
Bolt action; 223, 22-250, 243, 25-06, 240 Wea Mag, 257, 270, 7mm, 300, 340 Wea. Mags., 338-378 Wea. Mag., 30-378 Wea. Mag., 7mm STW, 7mm Rem. Mag., 300 Win. Mag.; 26", 28" barrel; weighs 8 1/2 lbs.; 46-5/8" overall length; Bell & Carlson stock with full length aluminum bedding block. Drilled and tapped for scope mounting. Uses Mark V action with heavy-contour stainless barrel with black oxidized flutes, muzzle diameter of .705". Introduced 1996; still offered. Made in U.S.A. From Weatherby. **LMSR: $1507**

Perf.: $1200	**Exc.:** $1000	**VGood:** $850

WEATHERBY MARK V DELUXE
Bolt-action; 22-250, 30-06, 224 Weatherby Varmintmaster (standard); 240, 257, 270, 7mm, 300, 340, 378, 460 (magnum); 2-, 5-shot box magazine, depending on caliber; 24", 26" barrel; avaiable in right- or left-hand model; some

actions made by Sauer in Germany to Weatherby specs; no sights; drilled, tapped for scope mounts; Monte Carlo stock with cheekpiece; skip checkering on pistol grip, forearm; forearm tip, pistol grip cap, recoil pad; quick-detachable sling swivels. Introduced in 1958; made in U.S. from 1958 to 1960, then production transferred to Germany, later to Japan; still in production. **LMSR: $1715**

Standard calibers, German-made

Exc.: $1295	**VGood:** $1095	**Good:** $820

Standard calibers, Japan-made

Exc.: $995	**VGood:** $895	**Good:** $750

Magnum calibers, German-made

Exc.: $1495	**VGood:** $1195	**Good:** $995

Magnum calibers, Japanese-made

Exc.: $1095	**VGood:** $995	**Good:** $850

WEATHERBY MARK V LAZERMARK
Bolt action; 240, 257, 270, 7mm Wea. Mag., 300, 340, 378 WM, 416 WM, 460 WM, 300 WM; 3-, 5-shot magazine; 24", 26" round tapered barrel; checkered pistol-grip American walnut stock; rosewood forearm, pistol grip; lazer carved stock, forend. Introduced 1981; still in production. (Add $250 for 416 WM & 460 WM calibers.) **LMSR: $1923**

Perf.: $1200	**Exc.:** $1100	**VGood:** $875

WEATHERBY MARK V SYNTHETIC
Bolt action; 7mm Rem Mag, 300 Win Mag, 338 Win Mag; 24" barrel; weighs 7 1/2 lbs.; synthetic stock with raised Monte Carlo comb, dual-taper checkered forend; low-luster blued metal; uses Mark V action. Right-hand only. Made in U.S. From Weatherby. Introduced 1995; still produced. **LMSR: $923**

Perf.: $650	**Exc.:** $540	**VGood:** $475

WEATHERBY VANGUARD
Bolt action; 25-06, 243, 270, 30-06, 308, 264, 7mm Rem. Mag., 300 Win. Mag.; 3-, 5-shot magazine, depending on caliber; 24" hammer-forged barrel; 44 1/2" overall length; weighs 7 7/8 lbs.; no sights; receiver drilled, tapped for scope mounts; American walnut stock; pistol-grip cap; forearm tip; hand checkered forearm, pistol grip; adjustable trigger; hinged floorplate. Introduced 1970; discontinued 1983.

Perf.: $450	**Exc.:** $375	**VGood:** $325

WEATHERBY WEATHERMARK
Bolt action; 240, 257, 270, 7mm, 300, 340 Wea. Mags, 7mm Rem. Mag., 270 Win., 30-06; 22", 24" barrel; weighs 7 1/2 lbs.; impregnated-color black composite stock with raised point checkering; Mark V action; right-hand only. Introduced 1992; no longer made.

Perf.: $600	**Exc.:** $520	**VGood:** $465

375 H&H

Perf.: $695	**Exc.:** $620	**VGood:** $570

Rifles

WINCHESTER MODEL 70 (1936-1963)
Bolt action; 22 Hornet, 220 Swift, 243, 250-3000, 7mm, 257 Roberts, 264 Win. Mag., 270, 7x57mm, 300 Savage, 300 H&H Mag., 300 Win. Mag., 30-06, 308, 338 Win. Mag., 35 Rem., 358 Win., 375 H&H Mag., (other calibers on special order such as 9x57mm and 7.65mm); 4-shot box magazine (magnums); 5-shot (other calibers); 20", 24", 25", 26" barrel; claw extractor; hooded ramp front sight, open rear; hand-checkered walnut pistol-grip stock; Monte Carlo comb on later productions. Introduced 1936; discontinued 1963. In many cases, the value depends largely on the caliber of the rifle.
Note: 300 Savage, 35 Rem., 7.65mm, 9x57mm very rare-see appraiser.
Pre-WWII (1936-1945)
Standard calibers

Exc.: $1100	**VGood:** $850	**Good:** $650

220 Swift, 257 Roberts, 300 H&H Mag.

Exc.: $1300	**VGood:** $900	**Good:** $700

375 H&H Mag., 7x57mm, 250-3000

Exc.: $1600	**VGood:** $1100	**Good:** $900

Post-WWII (1946-1963)
Standard calibers

Exc.: $900	**VGood:** $800	**Good:** $600

220 Swift, 243, 257 Roberts

Exc.: $1100	**VGood:** $900	**Good:** $650

22 Hornet, 300 H&H Mag.,

Exc.: $1600	**VGood:** $1300	**Good:** $1100

300 Win. Mag., 338 Win. Mag., 375 H&H Mag.

Exc.: $1500	**VGood:** $1200	**Good:** $1000

Note: 250-3000, 300 Savage, 358, 35 Rem., 7x57mm Very rare-see appraiser.

Winchester Model 70 Featherweight
Same specs as Model 70 (1936-1963) except 243, 264 Win. Mag., 270, 308, 30-06, 358 Win.; 22" lightweight barrel, 24" (special order); weighs 6 1/2 lbs.; lightweight American walnut Monte Carlo or straight comb stock; checkered pistol grip, forend; aluminum triggerguard, checkered buttplate, floorplate; 1" swivels. Introduced 1952; discontinued 1963. Calibers 243, 270, 30-06, 308

Exc.: $990	**VGood:** $800	**Good:** $650

264 Win. Mag., 358 Win.

Exc.: $1500	**VGood:** $1300	**Good:** $1000

WINCHESTER MODEL 70 (1964-1971)
Bolt action; 22-250, 222, 225, 243, 270, 308, 30-06, (standard calibers); 5-shot box magazine; 22" heavy barrel; 42 1/2" overall length; weighs 7 lbs.; plunger-type extractor; hooded ramp front sight, adjustable open rear; checkered walnut Monte Carlo stock, cheekpiece; sling swivels. Introduced 1964; discontinued 1971.

Exc.: $395	**VGood:** $325	**Good:** $300

WINCHESTER MODEL 70 (1972 to present)
Bolt action; 22-250, 222, 25-06, 243, 270, 308, 30-06; 5-shot box magazine; 22" swaged, floating barrel; removable hooded ramp bead front sight, open rear; tapped for scope mounts; walnut Monte Carlo stock; cut checkering on pistol grip, forearm; forend tip; hinged floorplate; steel grip cap; sling swivels. Introduced 1972; discontinued 1980.

Perf.: $360	**Exc.:** $300	**VGood:** $220

Winchester Model 70 Classic SM
Same specs as Model 70 (1972 to present) except 264 Win. Mag., 270, 30-06, 7mm Rem. Mag., 300 Win. Mag., 300 Weatherby Mag., 338 Win. Mag., 375 H&H Mag.; 3-shot magazine (magnum), 5-shot (others); 24", 26" barrel; weighs 7 3/4 lbs.; with or without sights; scope bases and rings; black composite, graphite-impregnated stock; black matte-finished metal; pre-'64-type action with controlled feeding; BOSS barrel vibration modulator and muzzle brake system optional. Introduced 1994; still in production. **LMSR: $602**

Perf.: $475	**Exc.:** $410	**VGood:** $360

375 H&H

Perf.: $550	**Exc.:** $460	**VGood:** $390

With BOSS (270, 30-06, 7mm Rem. Mag., 300 Win. Mag., 338 Win. Mag.)

Perf.: $600	**Exc.:** $510	**VGood:** $440

Winchester Model 70 Featherweight Classic
Same specs as Model 70 (1972 to present) except 22-250, 223, 243, 270, 280, 30-06, 308, 7mm-08; no sights; scope bases and rings; standard-grade walnut stock; claw extractor; controlled-round feeding system. Introduced 1992; still in production. **LMSR: $680**

Perf.: $570	**Exc.:** $510	**VGood:** $330

Winchester Model 70 Classic Stainless
Same specs as Model 70 (1972 to present) except 22-250, 243, 308, 270, 30-06, 7mm Rem. Mag., 300 Win. Mag., 300 WSM, 300 Weatherby Mag., 338 Win. Mag., 375 H&H Mag.; 3-shot magazine (magnum), 5-shot (others); 22", 24", 26" stainless steel barrel; weighs 6 3/4 lbs.; no sights; drilled, tapped for scope mounts; black fiberglass/graphite composite stock; matte gray finish; stainless steel pre-'64-type action with controlled feeding; BOSS barrel vibration modulator and muzzlebrake system optional. Introduced 1994.
LMSR: $785

Perf.: $525	**Exc.:** $420	**VGood:** $360

375 H&H Mag., with sights

Perf.: $575	**Exc.:** $470	**VGood:** $410

With BOSS (all except 300 Wea. Mag., 375 H&H Mag.)

Perf.: $635	**Exc.:** $535	**VGood:** $430

Winchester Model 70 XTR
Same specs as Model 70 (1972 to present) except 222, 22-250, 25-06, 243, 270, 308, 30-06, 264 Win. Mag., 7mm Rem. Mag., 300 Win. Mag., 338 Win. Mag.; 3-shot magazine (magnum), 5-shot (others); 22", 24" (magnum) barrel; satin-finished stock. Introduced 1978; discontinued 1989.

Perf.: $395	**Exc.:** $340	**VGood:** $300

Winchester Model 70 Black Shadow
Bolt action; 270, 30-06, 7mm Rem Mag, 300 Win Mag; 22" or 24" barrel; black composite stock, matte blue barrel and action. Push-feed bolt design; hinged floorplate. Made in U.S.A. by U.S. Repeating Arms Co. Introduced in 2000. **LMSR: $512**

Perf.: $425	**Exc.:** $350	**VGood:** $300

WINCHESTER RANGER Model 70
Bolt action; 223, 243, 270, 30-06, 7mm Rem. Mag.; 3-shot magazine (7mm Rem. Mag.), 4-shot (others); 22", 24" barrel; weighs 7 1/8 lbs.; economy version of Winchester Model 70; American hardwood stock; no checkering; composition buttplate; matte blue finish. Introduced 1985; **LMSR: $503**

Perf.: $370	**Exc.:** $320	**VGood:** $235

WINCHESTER MODEL 64 (EARLY PRODUCTION)
Lever action; 219 Zipper, 25-35, 30-30, 32 Spl.; 20", 24" barrel; weighs 7 lbs.; Winchester No. 22H open sporting or Lyman No. 56 (20" barrel) open rear sight, hooded ramp bead front; uncheckered American walnut pistol-grip stock, forend. Originally manufactured 1933 to 1957. Collector value on original production.

Exc.: $1295	**VGood:** $895	**Good:** $540

Winchester Model 94 Timber Carbine
Similar to the Model 94 Big Bore. Chambered for 444 Marlin; 18" ported barrel; half-pistol grip stock with butt pad; checkered grip and forend. Introduced 1999; no longer offered. Made in U.S.A. by U.S. Repeating Arms Co., Inc. **LMSR: $573**

> **Perf:** $500   **Exc.:** $400   **VGood:** $330

WINCHESTER MODEL 94 TRADITIONAL-CW
Lever action; 30-30 Win., 6-shot; 44 Mag., 11-shot tubular magazine; 20" barrel; weighs 6 1/2 lbs.; 37 3/4" overall length; Straight grip checkered walnut stock and forend; hooded blade front, semi-buckhorn rear. Drilled and tapped for scope mount; forged steel receiver; side ejection, exposed rebounding hammer with automatic trigger-activated transfer bar. Introduced 1984, still offered. **LMSR: $481**

> **Perf:** $400   **Exc.:** $350   **VGood:** $300

WINCHESTER MODEL 1886 LEVER-ACTION RIFLE (Recent Manufacture)
Lever action; 45-70, 4-shot magazine; 22" round tapered barrel; 40 1/2" overall length; weighs 7 1/4 lbs.; Smooth walnut stock; Bead front sight, ramp-adjustable buckhorn-style rear. Recreation of the Model 1886 lightweight rifle. Polished blue finish; crescent metal butt plate; metal forend cap; pistol grip stock. Reintroduced 1998. From U.S. Repeating Arms Co., Inc.

Grade I, **LMSR: $1152**

> **Perf:** $1100   **Exc.:** $900   **VGood:** $650

High Grade, **LMSR: $1440**

> **Perf:** $1350   **Exc.:** $1200   **VGood:** $900

WINCHESTER MODEL 100
Semi-automatic; gas-operated; 243 Win., 284 Win., 308 Win.; 3-shot magazine (284 Win.), 4-shot (others); 22" barrel; 42 1/2" overall length; weighs 7 1/2 lbs.; hooded bead front sight, folding leaf rear; tapped for receiver sights, scope mounts; one-piece walnut with checkered pistol-grip stock, forearm; sling swivels. Introduced 1960; discontinued 1974. 284 chambering brings a premium.

Pre-1964 Model

> **Exc.:** $525   **VGood:** $490   **Good:** $380

Post-1964 Model

> **Exc.:** $475   **VGood:** $450   **Good:** $325

WINCHESTER MODEL 1907
Semi-automatic; 351 Win. Self-Loading; 5-, 10-shot box magazine; 20" barrel; takedown; open rear sight, bead front; uncheckered walnut pistol-grip stock, forend. Introduced 1907; discontinued 1957. Collector value.

> **Exc.:** $495   **VGood:** $430   **Good:** $285

Winchester Model 64 Deer Rifle
Same specs as Model 64 except 30-30, 32 Spl.; weighs 7 3/4 lbs.; hand-checkered pistol-grip stock, forend; 1" sling swivels; sling; checkered steel buttplate; discontinued 1957.

> **Exc.:** $1295   **VGood:** $950   **Good:** $650

WINCHESTER MODEL 88
Lever action; 243 Win., 284 Win., 308 Win., 358 Win.; 5-shot detachable box magazine; 22" barrel; 39 1/2" overall length; weighs 6 1/2 lbs.; hammerless; hooded white metal bead front sight, Lyman folding leaf middle sight; one-piece checkered walnut stock with steel-capped pistol grip, fluted comb, sling swivels; three-lug bolt; crossbolt safety; side ejection. Introduced 1955; discontinued 1974.

308 Win.

> **Exc.:** $495   **VGood:** $450   **Good:** $380

243 Win. (pre-1964)

> **Exc.:** $595   **VGood:** $500   **Good:** $400

243 Win. (post-1964)

> **Exc.:** $495   **VGood:** $450   **Good:** $380

284 Win. (pre-1964)

> **Exc.:** $825   **VGood:** $650   **Good:** $540

284 Win. (post-1964)

> **Exc.:** $620   **VGood:** $495   **Good:** $420

358 Win.

> **Exc.:** $1200   **VGood:** $920   **Good:** $730

WINCHESTER MODEL 94 (Post-1964 production)
Lever action; 30-30, 25-35, 32 Spl., 7-30 Waters, 44 Mag.; 6-tube magazine; 20", 24" barrel; weighs 6 1/4 lbs.; open rear sight, ramp front; plain American walnut straight-grip stock; barrel band on forearm; saddle ring; side or angle ejection (post-1982); blued finish. Introduced 1964; modified variations still in production. **LMSR: $352**

> **Exc.:** $240   **VGood:** $170   **Good:** $130

Side or Angle Eject Model

> **Exc.:** $250   **VGood:** $185   **Good:** $140

Winchester Model 94 Classic
Same specs as Model 94 except 30-30; 20", 26" octagonal barrel; semi-fancy American walnut stock, forearm; steel buttplate; scrollwork on receiver. Introduced 1967; discontinued 1970.

> **Exc.:** $310   **VGood:** $250   **Good:** $200

Winchester Model 94 Legacy
Same specs as Model 94 except 30-30; half-pistol-grip walnut stock; checkered grip and forend. Introduced 1995; still in production. **LMSR: $477**

> **Perf:** $400   **Exc.:** $300   **VGood:** $250

Winchester Model 94 Ranger
Same specs as Model 94 except economy version; 30-30; 5-shot magazine; 20" barrel; uncheckered hardwood stock, forearm. Introduced 1985; still in production. **LMSR: $371**

> **Perf:** $230   **Exc.:** $200   **VGood:** $170

Shotguns

BENELLI BLACK EAGLE SLUG GUN
Recoil-operated semi-auto; 3" 12-ga.; 24" rifled barrel; no rib; weighs 7 1/8 lbs.; two-piece steel/alloy receiver; drilled, tapped for scope mount; marketed with scope mount. Made in Italy. Introduced 1989; discontinued 1991.

Perf.: $750   **Exc.:** $495   **VGood:** $410

Benelli Black Eagle Super Slug
Same specs as Benelli Black Eagle Slug Gun except 3-1/2" chamber; 24" E.R. Shaw Custom rifled barrel; 45-1/2" overall length; weighs 7 1/2 lbs.; scope mount base; matte-finish receiver; wood or polymer stocks available. Imported from Italy by Heckler & Koch, Inc. Introduced 1992; still imported.
With wood stock; **LMSR: $1335**

Perf.: $1120   **Exc.:** $920   **VGood:** $785

With polymer stock; **LMSR: $1,320**

Perf.: $1110   **Exc.:** $910   **VGood:** $775

24" barrel, Timber HD Camo; **LMSR: $1,450**

Perf.: $1235   **Exc.:** $1035   **VGood:** $900

BENELLI M1 SUPER 90 MONTEFELTRO SLUG
Rotating-bolt autoloader; 12-ga.; 3" chamber; 4-shot magazine; 24" barrel; Cylinder choke; 45 1/2" overall length; weighs 7 lbs.; checkered European walnut drop-adjustable stock with satin finish; matte blue metal finish. Made in Italy. Introduced, 1988; discontinued, 1992.

Perf.: $590   **Exc.:** $340   **VGood:** $290

Benelli M1 Super 90 Slug
Same specs as M1 Super 90 Montefeltro Slug except 5-shot magazine; 18 1/2" Cylinder barrel; open or aperture (ghost ring) rifle-type sights; polymer straight stock; matte black finish. Introduced 1986; still imported. **LMSR: $785**

Perf.: $615   **Exc.:** $310   **VGood:** $280

BENELLI NOVA PUMP RIFLED SLUG GUN
Pump gun chambered in 12-ga. 3"; 24" barrel and rifled bore; open rifle sights; synthetic stock; weighs 8.1 pounds. **LMSR: $575**

Perf.: $425   **Exc.:** $385   **VGood:** $350

BROWNING A-500G BUCK SPECIAL
Gas-operated autoloader; 12-ga.; 24" barrel; 45-1/2" overall length; weighs 7 3/4 lbs.; screw adjustable rear sight, contoured ramp front with gold bead. Made in Japan. Introduced 1990; discontinued 1992.

Perf.: $540   **Exc.:** $360   **VGood:** $320

BROWNING A-500R BUCK SPECIAL
Recoil-operated counterpart to the A-500G; same specs otherwise as A-500G. Made in Belgium. Introduced 1987; discontinued 1993.

Perf.: $470   **Exc.:** $370   **VGood:** $330

BROWNING AUTO-5 LIGHT BUCK SPECIAL (Miroku)
Slug gun version of A-5 recoil-operated autoloader; similar to Auto-5 Light (FN) except 24" barrel; choked for slugs; vent rib; adjustable rear sight, gold bead front on contoured ramp; detachable swivels, sling optional on current model. Made by Miroku of Japan. Introduced 1976; discontinued 1985; reintroduced 1989; still in production. **LMSR: $790**

Perf.: $600   **Exc.:** $400   **VGood:** $350

BROWNING B-2000 BUCK SPECIAL
Transitional autoloader in 2 3/4 12-ga.; 24" slug barrel; no rib; open rear sight, front ramp. Introduced 1974; discontinued 1982.

Perf.: $350   **Exc.:** $280   **VGood:** $250

BROWNING A-BOLT HUNTER
Bolt action; 12-ga.; 3" chamber; 2-shot detachable magazine; 22" fully rifled barrel or 23" barrel with 5" Invector choke tube; weighs 7 1/8 lbs.; 44 3/4" overall length; blade front sight with red insert, open adjustable rear, or no sights; drilled and tapped for scope mount; walnut stock with satin finish; A-Bolt rifle action with 60° bolt throw; front-locking bolt with claw extractor; hinged floorplate; swivel studs; matte finish on barrel, receiver. Imported by Browning. Introduced 1995; still imported. **LMSR: $790**
Rifled barrel

Perf.: $650   **Exc.:** $470   **VGood:** $400

Invector barrel

Perf.: $600   **Exc.:** $420   **VGood:** $350

Browning A-Bolt Stalker Shotgun
Same specs as A-Bolt Hunter except black, non-glare composite pistol-grip stock, forend. Imported by Browning. Introduced 1995; still imported. **LMSR: $710**
Rifled barrel

Perf.: $600   **Exc.:** $450   **VGood:** $400

Invector barrel

Perf.: $550   **Exc.:** $400   **VGood:** $350

Browning BPS Buck Special
Same specs as BPS except 24" Cylinder barrel; no Invector choke tubes. Introduced 1977; reintroduced 1989; still in production. **LMSR: $495**

Perf.: $375   **Exc.:** $240   **VGood:** $200

10-ga.

Perf.: $525   **Exc.:** $375   **VGood:** $340

Browning BPS Game Gun Deer Special
Same specs as BPS except 12-ga.; 3" chamber; heavy 20 1/2" barrel with rifled choke tube; rifle-type sights with adjustable rear; solid receiver scope mount; "rifle" stock dimensions for scope or open sights; gloss or matte finished wood with checkering; newly designed receiver/magazine tube/barrel mounting system to eliminate play; sling swivel studs; polished blue metal. Made by Miroku in Japan. Introduced 1992; still imported. **LMSR: $575**

Perf.: $430   **Exc.:** $240   **VGood:** $200

Shotguns

SMITH & WESSON
41 MAGNUM (MODEL 57)
SMITH & WESSON
44 MAGNUM (MODEL 29)
SMITH & WESSON
44 MAGNUM MODEL 629
SMITH & WESSON
357 MAGNUM (MODEL 27)
SMITH & WESSON
357 MAGNUM (MODEL 627)
SMITH & WESSON HIGHWAY
PATROLMAN (MODEL 28)
SMITH & WESSON MODEL 25-5
STURM RUGER BISLEY
STURM RUGER BLACKHAWK
STURM RUGER
BLACKHAWK NEW MODEL
STURM RUGER REDHAWK

FRANCHI SLUG GUN
Recoil-operated autoloader; 12-, 20-ga.; 5-shot magazine; 22" Cylinder-bore barrel; raised gold bead front sight, Lyman folding leaf open rear; hand-checkered European walnut pistol-grip stock, forearm; sling swivels. Introduced 1955; no longer in production.
   Exc.: $300   **VGood:** $250   **Good:** $200

**HARRINGTON & RICHARDSON
MODEL 162 SLUG GUN**
Single barrel; sidelever breakopen; exposed hammer; takedown; 12-, 20-ga.; 3" chamber; 24" Cylinder choke barrel; rifle sights; uncheckered hardwood pistol-grip stock, forend; recoil pad. Introduced 1968; discontinued 1985.
   Perf.: $105   **Exc.:** $85   **VGood:** $75

Ithaca Model 51 Deerslayer
Same specs as Model 51 except 12-, 20-ga.; special 24" slug barrel; Raybar front sight, open adjustable rear; sight base grooved for scope. Introduced 1972; discontinued 1983.
   Perf.: $330   **Exc.:** $270   **VGood:** $220

Ithaca Model 37 Deerslayer
Same specs as Model 37 except 20", 26" barrel bored for rifled slugs; open rifle-type rear sight, ramp front. Introduced 1969; discontinued 1986.
   Perf.: $290   **Exc.:** $200   **VGood:** $175

Ithaca Model 37 Super Deerslayer
Same specs as Model 37 except 20", 26" barrel bored for rifled slugs; open rifle-type rear sight, ramp front; improved wood in stock, slide handle. Introduced 1962; discontinued 1979.
   Exc.: $310   **VGood:** $240   **Good:** $180

ITHACA MODEL 66RS BUCK BUSTER
Lever-action single shot in 12-, 20-ga.; 22" Cylinder barrel; rifle sights. Introduced 1967; 12-ga. discontinued 1970; 20-ga. discontinued 1979.
   Perf.: $140   **Exc.:** $100   **VGood:** $80

MARLIN MODEL 512 SLUGMASTER
Bolt action; 12-ga.; 3" chamber; 2-shot detachable box magazine; 21" rifled barrel with 1:28" twist; weighs 8 lbs.; 44 3/4" overall length; ramp front sight with brass bead and removable hood, adjustable folding semi-buckhorn rear; drilled and tapped for scope mounting; press-checkered, walnut-finished Maine birch stock; ventilated recoil pad. Uses Model 55 action with thumb safety. Designed for shooting saboted slugs. Introduced 1994; still in production. **LMSR: $353**
   Perf.: $275   **Exc.:** $210   **VGood:** $180

Mossberg Model 500ALS Slugster
Slug version of pump-action Model 500; 12-ga.; 2 3/4", 3" chamber; 18 1/2", 24" Cylinder-bore barrel; rifle sights; game scene etched in receiver. Introduced 1977; no longer in production.
   Perf.: $230   **Exc.:** $160   **VGood:** $130

Mossberg Model 500ASG Slugster
Identical to regular Model 500 except 12-, 20-ga.; 2 3/4", 3" chamber; 18 1/2", 24" slug barrel; ramp front sight, open adjustable folding leaf rear; running deer etched on receiver. No longer in production.
   Perf.: $225   **Exc.:** $180   **VGood:** $150

Mossberg Model 500 Trophy Slugster
Identical to regular Model 500 pump except 12-ga.; 3" chamber; 24" smooth or rifled bore; 44" overall length; weighs 7 1/4 lbs.; scope mount; walnut-stained hardwood stock;

swivel studs; recoil pad; Introduced 1988; still in production. **LMSR: from $398**
   Perf.: $285   **Exc.:** $200   **VGood:** $180

MOSSBERG MODEL 695 SLUGSTER
Gauge: 12, 3" chamber; 22" barrel, fully rifled, ported; weighs 7 1/2 lbs.; black synthetic, with swivel studs and rubber recoil pad; blade front, folding rifle-style leaf rear sights; fiber optic; Weaver-style scope bases; matte metal finish; rotating thumb safety; detachable 2-shot magazine; Mossberg cablelock. Made in U.S. by Mossberg. Introduced 1996. **LMSR: $345**
   Perf.: $275   **Exc.:** $220   **VGood:** $185
With Fiber Optic rifle sights LMSR: $367
   Perf.: $297   **Exc.:** $242   **VGood:** $207
With woodlands camo stock, Fiber Optic sights LMSR: $397
   Perf.: $327 \   **Exc.:** $272   **VGood:** $237

MOSSBERG SSi-ONE SLUG
Gauge: 12, 3" chamber; 24", fully rifled barrel; weighs 8 lbs.; 40" overall; walnut, fluted and cut checkered; sling-swivel studs; drilled and tapped for scope base; no sights (scope base supplied); frame accepts interchangeable rifle barrels (see Mossberg SSi-One rifle listing); lever-opening, break-action design; ambidextrous, top-tang safety; internal eject/extract selector. Introduced 2000. **LMSR: $480**
   Perf.: $390   **Exc.:** $310   **VGood:** $250

REMINGTON MODEL 11-48 RSS SLUG GUN
Recoil-operated 12-ga. slugger; adjustable rifle-type gold bead front sight, step-adjustable rear. Introduced 1959; no longer in production.
   Exc.: $350   **VGood:** $265   **Good:** $200

REMINGTON MODEL 11-87 PREMIER SPECIAL PURPOSE DEER GUN
21" barrel; rifled and Improved Cylinder choke tubes; rifle sights; cantilever scope mount, rings; gas system handles all 2 3/4" and 3" slug, buckshot, high-velocity field and magnum loads; not designed to function with light 2 3/4" field loads; dull stock finish, Parkerized exposed metal surfaces; bolt and carrier have blackened color. Introduced 1987; discontinued 1995.
   Perf.: $500   **Exc.:** $350   **VGood:** $260

**Remington Model 11-87 Premier
SPS-BG-Camo Deer/Turkey**
Same specs as Model 11-87 Premier except 21" barrel; Improved Cylinder, Super-Full Turkey (.665" diameter with knurled extension) Rem-Choke tubes and rifled choke tube insert; rifle sights; synthetic stock, forend; quick-detachable swivels; camo Cordura carrying sling; all surfaces Mossy Oak Bottomland camouflage-finished. Introduced 1993; discontinued 1995.
   Perf.: $525   **Exc.:** $365   **VGood:** $300

Shotguns

Colt Anaconda
Colt Python
Colt Python Stainless
Freedom Arms 44 Magnum
 Casull
Freedom Arms 454 Casull
Savage Striker Bolt-Action
 Hunting Handgun
Smith & Wesson Model 19
 Combat Magnum
Smith & Wesson Model 66
 Combat Magnum
Smith & Wesson Model 586
 Distinguished Combat
 Magnum
Smith & Wesson Model 610
 Classic Hunter Revolver
Smith & Wesson Model 657
Smith & Wesson Model 686
Smith & Wesson Model 686
 Magnum PLUS
Smith & Wesson Model 686
 Midnight Black

Remington Model 11-87 Premier SPS-Deer
Same specs as Model 11-87 Premier except fully-rifled 21"
barrel; rifle sights; black non-reflective synthetic stock,
forend; black carrying sling. Introduced 1993; still in production; **LMSR: $824**

| Perf.: $525 | Exc.: $375 | VGood: $290 |

With wood stock (Model 11-87 SP Deer Gun) Rem-Choke,
21" barrel w/rifle sights; **LMSR: $756**

REMINGTON MODEL 1100 DEER
Gas-operated autoloader; hammerless; takedown; 12-,
20-ga.; 5-shot magazine; 20", 21", 22" Improved Cylinder
barrel; rifle sights; checkered walnut pistol-grip stock,
forend; recoil pad. Still in production. **LMSR: $565**

| Perf.: $400 | Exc.: $290 | VGood: $235 |

Left-hand model

| Perf.: $450 | Exc.: $340 | VGood: $285 |

Remington Model 870 Brushmaster Deluxe
Slug version of Remington's famous 870 Wingmaster pump
gun except 12-, 20-ga.; 2 3/4", 3" chamber; 20" barrel;
Improved Cylinder or choke tube; adjustable rear sight, ramp
front; satin-finished checkered wood stock, forearm; recoil
pad; right- or left-hand model. Discontinued 1994.
Right-hand model

| Perf.: $340 | Exc.: $240 | VGood: $190 |

Left-hand model

| Perf.: $380 | Exc.: $270 | VGood: $220 |

Remington Model 870 Express Deer
Similar to Model 870 but with hardwood stock and
non-reflective matte finish; recoil pad; 12-ga.; 20" smooth
bore or rifled barrel; fixed Improved Cylinder choke; open
iron sights; Monte Carlo stock. Introduced 1991; still in production. **LMSR: $332**
Smooth bore barrel

| Perf.: $240 | Exc.: $175 | VGood: $140 |

Rifled barrel

| Perf.: $270 | Exc.: $205 | VGood: $170 |

Remington Model 870 Express Rifle-Sighted Deer Gun
Same as Model 870 Express Deer except 20" barrel with
fixed Imp. Cyl. choke, open iron sights, Monte Carlo stock.
Introduced 1991. **LMSR: $332**

| Perf.: $265 | Exc.: $215 | VGood: $180 |

W/fully rifled barrel; **LMSR: $365**

| Perf.: $298 | Exc.: $248 | VGood: $213 |

Synthetic Deer (black synthetic stock, black matte metal);
LMSR: $372

| Perf.: $295 | Exc.: $225 | VGood: $185 |

REMINGTON MODEL 870 SPS DEER
Fully-rifled 20" barrel; rifle sights; black non-reflective synthetic stock, forend; black carrying sling. Introduced 1993;
still in production. **LMSR: $407**

| Perf.: $340 | Exc.: $240 | VGood: $190 |

Savage Model 30 Slug Gun
Pump gun chambered in 12-, 20-ga.; 22" slug barrel; rifle
sights. Introduced 1964; discontinued 1982.

| Perf.: $180 | Exc.: $150 | VGood: $130 |

THOMPSON/CENTER ENCORE RIFLED SLUG GUN
Gauge: 20, 3" chamber; 26" barrel, fully rifled; weighs about
7 lbs.; 40 1/2" overall; walnut with walnut forearm; steel,
click-adjustable rear and ramp-style front, both with fiber
optics; break-open design uses interchangeable barrels;
composite stock and forearm available. Introduced 2000.
LMSR: $637

| Perf.: $540 | Exc.: $435 | VGood: $375 |

WINCHESTER MODEL 1400 DEER GUN
Gas-operated autoloader chambered for 2 3/4 12-ga.; 22"
barrel for slugs or buckshot; rifle sight; walnut stock, forearm. Introduced 1965; discontinued 1974.

| Perf.: $250 | Exc.: $200 | VGood: $180 |

Winchester Model 1400 Slug Hunter (Recent)
Updated version of Model 1400 Deer Gun; 12-ga.; 22"
smoothbore barrel; Improved Cylinder, Sabot Winchoke
tubes; adjustable open sights; drill, tapped for scope
mounts. Introduced 1990; no longer in production.

| Perf.: $345 | Exc.: $275 | VGood: $235 |

Winchester Model 1200 Deer
Slug version of the successor to the Model 12 pump
gun;12-ga.; 22" barrel for rifled slugs or buckshot; rifle-type
sights; walnut stock only; sling swivels. Introduced 1965;
discontinued 1974.

| Perf.: $210 | Exc.: $150 | VGood: $140 |

Winchester Model 1300 Black Shadow Deer
Successor to the Model 1200 pump gun; 12-ga.; 3" chamber; 22" vent-rib barrel; Improved Cylinder WinChoke tube;
ramp-type front sight, fully adjustable rear; receiver drilled
and tapped for scope mounts. Introduced 1994; still in production. **LMSR: $344**

| Perf.: $270 | Exc.: $210 | VGood: $180 |

With rifled barrel; **LMSR: $366**

| Perf.: $301 | Exc.: $231 | VGood: $186 |

With cantilever scope mount; **LMSR:$409**

| Perf.: $344 | Exc.: $274 | VGood: $229 |

Combo (22" rifled and 28" smoothbore bbls.); **LMSR: $442**

| Perf.: $395 | Exc.: $325 | VGood: $280 |

Compact (20-ga., 22" rifled barrel, shorter stock);
LMSR: $409

| Perf.: $295 | Exc.: $225 | VGood: $165 |

Winchester Model 1300 Ranger Deer
Economy version of the Model 1300 Deer Gun; 22" Cylinder
smoothbore or rifled deer barrel with rifle-type sights; drilled
and tapped; for scope mounts; rings and bases. Introduced
1983; still in production. **LMSR: $343**

| Perf.: $300 | Exc.: $245 | VGood: $200 |

Winchester Model 1300 Slug Hunter
Same specs as Model 1300 Ranger except 12-ga.; 22"
smoothbore or rifled barrel; Improved Cyinder, Sabot choke
tubes (smoothbore only); adjustable open sights; receiver
drilled and tapped for scope mounts; scope bases;
cut-checkered walnut stock, forend. Introduced 1990;
smoothbore dropped 1992; still in production as Model
1300 Slug Hunter Deer. **LMSR: $404**

| Perf.: $350 | Exc.: $265 | VGood: $200 |

Many manufacturers do not supply suggested retail prices. Others did not get their pricing to us before press time. All pricing can vary dependent on the exact brand and style of ammo selected and/or the retail outlet from which you make your purchase. Pricing has been rounded to the nearest dollar and represents our best estimate of average pricing. An * after the cartridge means these loads are available with Nosler Partition or Swift A-Frame bullets. Listed pricing may or may not reflect this bullet type. ** = these are packed 50 to box, all others are 20 to box. Wea. Mag.= Weatherby Magnum. Spfd. = Springfield. A-A-Sq. = A-Square. N.E.=Nitro Express.

Cartridge	Bullet Weight	VELOCITY (fps)					ENERGY (ft. lbs.)					TRAJ. (in.)				Price
		Muzzle	100 yds.	200 yds.	300 yds.	400 yds.	Muzzle	100 yds.	200 yds.	300 yds.	400 yds.	100 yds.	200 yds.	300 yds.	400 yds.	
243 Winchester	90	3120	2871	2635	2411	2199	1946	1647	1388	1162	966	1.4	0.0	-6.4	-18.8	NA
243 Winchester	100	2960	2697	2449	2215	1993	1945	1615	1332	1089	882	+2.5	+1.2	-6.0	-20.0	$16
243 Winchester	105	2920	2689	2470	2261	2062	1988	1686	1422	1192	992	+2.5	+1.6	-5.0	-18.4	$21
243 Light Mag.	100	3100	2839	2592	2358	2138	2133	1790	1491	1235	1014	+1.5	0.0	-6.8	-19.8	NA
243 WSSM	55	4060	3628	3237	2880	2550	2013	1607	1280	1013	794	0.6	0.0	-3.9	-12.0	NA
243 WSSM	95	3250	3000	2763	2538	2325	2258	1898	1610	1359	1140	1.2	0.0	-5.7	-16.9	NA
243 WSSM	100	3110	2838	2583	2341	2112	2147	1789	1481	1217	991	1.4	0.0	-6.6	-19.7	NA
6mm Remington	100	3100	2829	2573	2332	2104	2133	1777	1470	1207	983	+2.5	+1.6	-5.0	-17.0	$16
6mm Remington	105	3060	2822	2596	2381	2177	2105	1788	1512	1270	1059	+2.5	+1.1	-3.3	-15.0	$21
6mm Rem. Light Mag.	100	3250	2997	2756	2528	2311	2345	1995	1687	1418	1186	1.59	0.0	-6.33	-18.3	NA
240 Wea. Mag.	100	3395	3106	2835	2581	2339	2559	2142	1785	1478	1215	+2.5	+2.8	-2.0	-11.0	$43
25-35 Win.	117	2230	1866	1545	1282	1097	1292	904	620	427	313	+2.5	-4.2	-26.0	0.0	$24
250 Savage	100	2820	2504	2210	1936	1684	1765	1392	1084	832	630	+2.5	+0.4	-9.0	-28.0	$17
257 Roberts	100	2980	2661	2363	2085	1827	1972	1572	1240	965	741	+2.5	-0.8	-5.2	-21.6	$20
257 Roberts+P	117	2780	2411	2071	1761	1488	2009	1511	1115	806	576	+2.5	-0.2	-10.2	32.6	$18
257 Roberts+P	120	2780	2560	2360	2160	1970	2060	1750	1480	1240	1030	+2.5	+1.2	-6.4	-23.6	$22
257 Roberts	122	2600	2331	2078	1842	1625	1831	1472	1169	919	715	+2.5	0.0	-10.6	-31.4	$21
257 Light Mag.	117	2940	2694	2460	2240	2031	2245	1885	1572	1303	1071	+1.7	0.0	-7.6	-21.8	NA
25-06 Rem.	100	3230	2893	2580	2287	2014	2316	1858	1478	1161	901	+2.0	+0.8	-5.7	-18.9	$17
25-06 Rem.	117	2990	2770	2570	2370	2190	2320	2000	1715	1465	1246	+2.5	+1.0	-7.9	-26.6	$19
25-06 Rem.*	120	2990	2730	2484	2252	2032	2382	1985	1644	1351	1100	+2.5	+1.2	-5.3	-19.6	$17
25-06 Rem.	122	2930	2706	2492	2289	2095	2325	1983	1683	1419	1189	+2.5	+1.8	-4.5	-17.5	$23
25 WSSM	115	3060	284	2639	2442	2254	2392	2066	1778	1523	1398	1.4	0.0	-6.4	-18.6	NA
25 WSSM	120	2990	2717	2459	2216	1987	2383	1967	1612	1309	1053	1.6	0.0	-7.4	-21.8	NA
Wea. Mag.	100	3555	3237	2941	2665	2404	2806	2326	1920	1576	1283	+2.5	+3.2	0.0	-8.0	$32
6.5x55mm Light Mag.	129	2750	2549	2355	2171	1994	2166	1860	1589	1350	1139	+2.0	0.0	-8.2	-23.9	NA
6.5x55mm Swe.*	139/140	2850	2640	2440	2250	2070	2525	2170	1855	1575	1330	+2.5	+1.6	-5.4	-18.9	$18
6.5x55mm Swe.	156	2650	2370	2110	1870	1650	2425	1950	1550	1215	945	+2.5	0.0	-10.3	-30.6	NA
260 Remington	125	2875	2669	2473	2285	2105	2294	1977	1697	1449	1230	1.71	0.0	-7.4	-21.4	NA
260 Remington	140	2750	2544	2347	2158	1979	2351	2011	1712	1448	1217	+2.2	0.0	-8.6	-24.6	NA
6.5 Rem. Mag.	120	3210	2905	2621	2353	2102	2745	2248	1830	1475	1177	+2.5	+1.7	-4.1	-16.3	Disc.
264 Win. Mag.	140	3030	2782	2548	2326	2114	2854	2406	2018	1682	1389	+2.5	+1.4	-5.1	-18.0	$24
270 Winchester	130	3060	2776	2510	2259	2022	2702	2225	1818	1472	1180	+2.5	+1.4	-5.3	-18.2	$17
270 Win. Supreme	130	3150	2881	2628	2388	2161	2865	2396	1993	1646	1348	1.3	0.0	-6.4	-18.9	NA
270 Winchester	135	3000	2780	2570	2369	2178	2697	2315	1979	1682	1421	+2.5	+1.4	-6.0	-17.6	$23
270 Winchester*	140	2940	2700	2480	2260	2060	2685	2270	1905	1590	1315	+2.5	+1.8	-4.6	-17.9	$20
270 Win. Light Magnum	130	3215	2998	2790	2590	2400	2983	2594	2246	1936	1662	1.21	0.0	-5.83	-17.0	NA
270 Winchester*	150	2850	2585	2336	2100	1879	2705	2226	1817	1468	1175	+2.5	+1.2	-6.5	-22.0	$17
270 Win. Supreme	150	2930	2693	2468	2254	2051	2860	2416	2030	1693	1402	1.7	0.0	-7.4	-21.6	NA
270 WSM	130	3275	3041	2820	2609	2408	3096	2669	2295	1564	1673	1.1	0.0	-5.5	-16.1	NA
270 WSM	140	3125	2865	2619	2386	2165	3035	2559	2132	1769	1457	1.4	0.0	-6.5	-19.0	NA
270 WSM	150	3120	2923	2734	2554	2380	3242	2845	2490	2172	1886	1.3	0.0	-5.9	-17.2	NA
270 Wea. Mag.	130	3375	3119	2878	2649	2432	3287	2808	2390	2026	1707	+2.5	-2.9	-0.9	-9.9	$32
270 Wea. Mag.*	150	3245	3036	2837	2647	2465	3507	3070	2681	2334	2023	+2.5	+1.2	-1.8	-11.4	$47
7mm Mauser*	139/140	2660	2435	2221	2018	1827	2199	1843	1533	1266	1037	+2.5	0.0	-9.6	-27.7	$17
7mm Mauser	145	2690	2442	2206	1985	1777	2334	1920	1568	1268	1017	+2.5	+0.1	-9.6	-28.3	$18
7mm Mauser	154	2690	2490	2300	2120	1940	2475	2120	1810	1530	1285	+2.5	+0.8	-7.5	-23.5	$17
7mm Mauser	175	2440	2137	1857	1603	1382	2313	1774	1340	998	742	+2.5	-1.7	-16.1	0.0	$17
7x57 Light Mag.	139	2970	2730	2503	2287	2082	2722	2301	1933	1614	1337	+1.6	0.0	-7.2	-21.0	NA
7x30 Waters	120	2700	2300	1930	1600	1330	1940	1405	990	685	470	+2.5	-0.2	-12.3	0.0	$18
7mm-08 Rem.*	140	2860	2625	2402	2189	1988	2542	2142	1793	1490	1228	+2.5	+0.8	-6.9	-21.9	$18
7mm-08 Rem.	154	2715	2510	2315	2128	1950	2520	2155	1832	1548	1300	+2.5	+1.0	-7.0	-22.7	$23
7mm-08 Light Mag.	139	3000	2790	2590	2399	2216	2777	2403	2071	1776	1515	+1.5	0.0	-6.7	-19.4	NA
7x64mm Bren.	154	2820	2610	2420	2230	2050	2720	2335	1995	1695	1430	+2.5	+1.4	-5.7	-19.9	NA
7x64mm Bren.*	160	2850	2669	2495	2327	2166	2885	2530	2211	1924	1667	+2.5	+1.6	-4.8	-17.8	$24
284 Winchester	150	2860	2595	2344	2108	1886	2724	2243	1830	1480	1185	+2.5	+0.8	-7.3	-23.2	$24
280 Remington	140	3000	2758	2528	2309	2102	2797	2363	1986	1657	1373	+2.5	+1.4	-5.2	-18.3	$17
280 Remington*	150	2890	2624	2373	2135	1912	2781	2293	1875	1518	1217	+2.5	+0.8	-7.1	-22.6	$17
280 Remington	160	2840	2637	2442	2556	2078	2866	2471	2120	1809	1535	+2.5	+0.8	-6.7	-21.0	$20
280 Remington	165	2820	2510	2220	1950	1701	2913	2308	1805	1393	1060	+2.5	+0.4	-8.8	-26.5	$17
7x61mm S&H Sup.	154	3060	2720	2400	2100	1820	3200	2520	1965	1505	1135	+2.5	+1.8	-5.0	-19.8	NA
7mm Dakota	160	3200	3001	2811	2630	2455	3637	3200	2808	2456	2140	+2.1	+1.9	-2.8	-12.5	NA

Cartridge	Bullet Weight	VELOCITY (fps) Muzzle	100 yds.	200 yds.	300 yds.	400 yds.	ENERGY (ft. lbs.) Muzzle	100 yds.	200 yds.	300 yds.	400 yds.	TRAJ. (in.) 100 yds.	200 yds.	300 yds.	400 yds.	Price
7mm Rem. Mag. (Rem.)	140	2710	2482	2265	2059	NA	2283	1915	1595	1318	NA	0.0	-4.5	-1.57	0.0	NA
7mm Rem. Mag.*	139	3150	2930	2710	2510	2320	3085	2660	2290	1960	1670	+2.5	+2.4	-2.4	-12.7	$21
7mm Rem. Hvy Mag	139	3250	3044	2847	2657	2475	3259	2860	2501	2178	1890	1.1	0.0	-5.5	-16.2	NA
7mm Rem. Mag.	150	3110	2830	2568	2320	2085	3221	2667	2196	1792	1448	+2.5	+1.6	-4.6	-16.5	$21
7mm Rem. Mag.*	160/162	2950	2730	2520	2320	2120	3090	2650	2250	1910	1600	+2.5	+1.8	-4.4	-17.8	$34
7mm Rem. Mag.	165	2900	2699	2507	2324	2147	3081	2669	2303	1978	1689	+2.5	+1.2	-5.9	-19.0	$28
7mm Rem. SA UM	140	3175	2934	2707	2490	2283	3033	2676	2277	1927	1620	1.3	0.0	-6	-17.7	NA
7mm Rem. SA UM	150	3110	2828	2563	2313	2077	3221	2663	2188	1782	1437	2.5	2.1	-3.6	-15.8	NA
7mm Rem. SA UM	160	2960	2762	2572	2390	2215	3112	2709	2350	2029	1743	2.6	2.2	-3.6	-15.4	NA
7mm Rem. WSM	140	3225	3008	2801	2603	2414	3233	2812	2438	2106	1812	1.2	0.0	-5.6	-16.4	NA
7mm Rem. WSM	160	2990	2744	2512	2081	1883	3176	2675	2241	1864	1538	1.6	0.0	-7.1	-20.8	NA
7mm Wea. Mag.	140	3225	2970	2729	2501	2283	3233	2741	2315	1943	1621	+2.5	+2.0	-3.2	-14.0	$35
7mm Wea. Mag.	154	3260	3023	2799	2586	2382	3539	3044	2609	2227	1890	+2.5	+2.8	-1.5	-10.8	$32
7mm Wea. Mag.*	160	3200	3004	2816	2637	2464	3637	3205	2817	2469	2156	+2.5	+2.7	-1.5	-10.6	$47
7mm Wea. Mag.	165	2950	2747	2553	2367	2189	3188	2765	2388	2053	1756	+2.5	+1.8	-4.2	-16.4	$43
7mm Wea. Mag.	175	2910	2693	2486	2288	2098	3293	2818	2401	2033	1711	+2.5	+1.2	-5.9	-19.4	$35
7mm STW	140	3325	3064	2818	2585	2364	3436	2918	2468	2077	1737	+2.3	+1.8	-3.0	-13.1	NA
7mm STW Supreme	160	3150	2894	2652	2422	2204	3526	2976	2499	2085	1727	1.3	0.0	-6.3	-18.5	NA
7mm Rem. Ultra Mag.	140	3425	3184	2956	2740	2534	3646	3151	2715	2333	1995	1.7	1.60	-2.6	-11.4	NA
303 Savage	190	1890	1612	1327	1183	1055	1507	1096	794	591	469	+2.5	-7.6	0.0	0.0	$24
30 Remington	170	2120	1822	1555	1328	1153	1696	1253	913	666	502	+2.5	-4.7	-26.3	0.0	$20
7.62x39mm Rus.	123/125	2300	2030	1780	1550	1350	1445	1125	860	655	500	+2.5	-2.0	-17.5	0.0	$13
30-30 Win.	150	2390	1973	1605	1303	1095	1902	1296	858	565	399	+2.5	-3.2	-22.5	0.0	$13
30-30 Win. Supreme	150	2480	2095	1747	1446	1209	2049	1462	1017	697	487	0.0	-6.5	-24.5	0.0	NA
30-30 Win.	160	2300	1997	1719	1473	1268	1879	1416	1050	771	571	+2.5	-2.9	-20.2	0.0	$18
30-30 Win.*	170	2200	1895	1619	1381	1191	1827	1355	989	720	535	+2.5	-5.8	-23.6	0.0	$13
300 Savage	150	2630	2354	2094	1853	1631	2303	1845	1462	1143	886	+2.5	-0.4	-10.1	-30.7	$17
300 Savage	180	2350	2137	1935	1754	1570	2207	1825	1496	1217	985	+2.5	-1.6	-15.2	0.0	$17
30-40 Krag	180	2430	2213	2007	1813	1632	2360	1957	1610	1314	1064	+2.5	-1.4	-13.8	0.0	$18
307 Winchester	180	2510	2179	1874	1599	1362	2519	1898	1404	1022	742	+2.5	-1.6	-15.6	0.0	$20
7.5x55 Swiss	180	2650	2450	2250	2060	1880	2805	2390	2020	1700	1415	+2.5	+0.6	-8.1	-24.9	NA
308 Winchester	150	2820	2533	2263	2009	1774	2648	2137	1705	1344	1048	+2.5	+0.4	-8.5	-26.1	$17
308 Winchester	165	2700	2440	2194	1963	1748	2670	2180	1763	1411	1199	+2.5	0.0	-9.7	-28.5	$20
308 Winchester	168	2680	2493	2314	2143	1979	2678	2318	1998	1713	1460	+2.5	0.0	-8.9	-25.3	$18
308 Win. (Fed.)	170	2000	1740	1510	NA	NA	1510	1145	860	NA	NA	0.00	0.0	0.0	0.0	NA
308 Winchester	178	2620	2415	2220	2034	1857	2713	2306	1948	1635	1363	+2.5	0.0	-9.6	-27.6	$23
308 Winchester*	180	2620	2393	2178	1974	1782	2743	2288	1896	1557	1269	+2.5	-0.2	-10.2	-28.5	$17
308 Light Mag.*	150	2980	2703	2442	2195	1964	2959	2433	1986	1606	1285	+1.6	0.0	-7.5	-22.2	NA
308 Light Mag.	165	2870	2658	2456	2263	2078	3019	2589	2211	1877	1583	+1.7	0.0	-7.5	-21.8	NA
308 High Energy	165	2870	2600	2350	2120	1890	3020	2485	2030	1640	1310	+1.8	0.0	-8.2	-24.0	NA
308 Light Mag.	168	2870	2658	2456	2263	2078	3019	2589	2211	1877	1583	+1.7	0.0	-7.5	-21.8	NA
308 High Energy	180	2740	2550	2370	2200	2030	3000	2600	2245	1925	1645	+1.9	0.0	-8.2	-23.5	NA
30-06 Spfd.	150	2910	2617	2342	2083	1853	2820	2281	1827	1445	1135	+2.5	+0.8	-7.2	-23.4	$17
30-06 Spfd.	152	2910	2654	2413	2184	1968	2858	2378	1965	1610	1307	+2.5	+1.0	-6.6	-21.3	$23
30-06 Spfd.*	165	2800	2534	2283	2047	1825	2872	2352	1909	1534	1220	+2.5	+0.4	-8.4	-25.5	$17
30-06 Spfd.	168	2710	2522	2346	2169	2003	2739	2372	2045	1754	1497	+2.5	+0.4	-8.0	-23.5	$18
30-06 Spfd. (Fed.)	170	2000	1740	1510	NA	NA	1510	1145	860	NA	NA	0.0	0.0	0.0	0.0	NA
30-06 Spfd.	178	2720	2511	2311	2121	1939	2924	2491	2111	1777	1486	+2.5	+0.4	-8.2	-24.6	$23
30-06 Spfd.*	180	2700	2469	2250	2042	1846	2913	2436	2023	1666	1362	-2.5	0.0	-9.3	-27.0	$17
30-06 Spfd.	220	2410	2130	1870	1632	1422	2837	2216	1708	1301	988	+2.5	-1.7	-18.0	0.0	$17
30-06 Light Mag.	150	3100	2815	2548	2295	2058	3200	2639	2161	1755	1410	+1.4	0.0	-6.8	-20.3	NA
30-06 Light Mag.	180	2880	2676	2480	2293	2114	3316	2862	2459	2102	1786	+1.7	0.0	-7.3	-21.3	NA
30-06 High Energy	180	2880	2690	2500	2320	2150	3315	2880	2495	2150	1845	+1.7	0.0	-7.2	-21.0	NA
300 REM SA UM	150	3200	2901	2622	2359	2112	3410	2803	2290	1854	1485	1.3	0.0	-6.4	-19.1	NA
300 REM SA UM	165	3075	2792	2527	2276	2040	3464	2856	2339	1898	1525	1.5	0.0	-7	-20.7	NA
300 REM SA UM	180	2960	2761	2571	2389	2214	3501	3047	2642	2280	1959	2.6	2.2	-3.6	-15.4	NA
300 WSM	150	3300	3061	2834	2619	2414	3628	3121	2676	2285	1941	1.1	0.0	-5.4	-15.9	NA
300 WSM	180	2970	2741	2524	2317	2120	3526	3005	2547	2147	1797	1.6	0.0	-7.0	-20.5	NA
300 WSM	180	3010	2923	2734	2554	2380	3242	2845	2490	2172	1886	1.3	0	-5.9	-17.2	NA
308 Norma Mag.	180	3020	2820	2630	2440	2270	3645	3175	2755	2385	2050	+2.5	+2.0	-3.5	-14.8	NA
300 H&H Magnum*	180	2880	2640	2412	2196	1990	3315	2785	2325	1927	1583	+2.5	+0.8	-6.8	-21.7	$24
300 Win. Mag.	150	3290	2951	2636	2342	2068	3605	2900	2314	1827	1424	+2.5	+1.9	-3.8	-15.8	$22
300 Win. Mag.	165	3100	2877	2665	2462	2269	3522	3033	2603	2221	1897	+2.5	+2.4	-3.0	-16.9	$24
300 Win. Mag.	178	2900	2760	2568	2375	2191	3509	3030	2606	2230	1897	+2.5	+1.4	-5.0	-17.6	$29
300 Win. Mag.*	180	2960	2745	2540	2344	2157	3501	3011	2578	2196	1859	+2.5	+1.2	-5.5	-18.5	$22

Cartridge	Bullet Weight	VELOCITY (fps)					ENERGY (ft. lbs.)					TRAJ. (in.)				Price
		Muzzle	100 yds.	200 yds.	300 yds.	400 yds.	Muzzle	100 yds.	200 yds.	300 yds.	400 yds.	100 yds.	200 yds.	300 yds.	400 yds.	
300 W.M. High Energy	180	3100	2830	2580	2340	2110	3840	3205	2660	2190	1790	+1.4	0.0	-6.6	-19.7	NA
300 W.M. Light Mag.	180	3100	2879	2668	2467	2275	3840	3313	2845	2431	2068	+1.39	0.0	-6.45	-18.7	NA
300 Rem. Ultra Mag.	150	3450	3208	2980	2762	2556	3964	3427	2956	2541	2175	1.7	1.5	-2.6	-11.2	NA
300 Rem. Ultra Mag.	180	3250	3037	2834	2640	2454	4221	3686	3201	2786	2407	2.4	0.0	-3.0	-12.7	NA
300 Wea. Mag.	150	3600	3307	3033	2776	2533	4316	3642	3064	2566	2137	+2.5	+3.2	0.0	-8.1	$32
300 Wea. Mag.	165	3450	3210	3000	2792	2593	4360	3796	3297	2855	2464	+2.5	+3.2	0.0	-7.8	NA
300 Wea. Mag.	178	3120	2902	2695	2497	2308	3847	3329	2870	2464	2104	+2.5	-1.7	-3.6	-14.7	$43
300 Wea. Mag.	180	3330	3110	2910	2710	2520	4430	3875	3375	2935	2540	+1.0	0.0	-5.2	-15.1	NA
303 British	150	2685	2441	2210	1992	1787	2401	1984	1627	1321	1064	+2.5	+0.6	-8.4	-26.2	$18
303 British	180	2460	2124	1817	1542	1311	2418	1803	1319	950	687	+2.5	-1.8	-16.8	0.0	$18
303 Light Mag.	150	2830	2570	2325	2094	1884	2667	2199	1800	1461	1185	+2.0	0.0	-8.4	-24.6	NA
7.62x54mm Rus.	180	2580	2370	2180	2000	1820	2650	2250	1900	1590	1100	+2.5	0.0	-9.8	-28.5	NA
32 Win. Special	170	2250	1921	1626	1372	1175	1911	1393	998	710	521	+2.5	-3.5	-22.9	0.0	$14
8mm Mauser	170	2360	1969	1622	1333	1123	2102	1464	993	671	476	+2.5	-3.1	-22.2	0.0	$18
8mm Rem. Mag.	185	3080	2761	2464	2186	1927	3896	3131	2494	1963	1525	+2.5	+1.4	-5.5	-19.7	$30
338 Win. Mag.	200	2960	2658	2375	2110	1862	3890	3137	2505	1977	1539	+2.5	+1.0	-6.7	-22.3	$27
338 Win. Mag.*	210	2830	2590	2370	2150	1940	3735	3130	2610	2155	1760	+2.5	+1.4	-6.0	-20.9	$33
340 Wea. Mag.*	210	3250	2991	2746	2515	2295	4924	4170	3516	2948	2455	+2.5	+1.9	-1.8	-11.8	$56
340 Wea. Mag.*	250	3000	2806	2621	2443	2272	4995	4371	3812	3311	2864	+2.5	+2.0	-3.5	-14.8	$56
357 Magnum	158	1830	1427	1138	980	883	1175	715	454	337	274	0.0	-16.2	-33.1	0.0	$25**
35 Remington	150	2300	1874	1506	1218	1039	1762	1169	755	494	359	+2.5	-4.1	-26.3	0.0	$16
35 Remington	200	2080	1698	1376	1140	1001	1921	1280	841	577	445	+2.5	-6.3	-17.1	-33.6	$16
356 Winchester	200	2460	2114	1797	1517	1284	2688	1985	1434	1022	732	+2.5	-1.8	-15.1	0.0	$31
356 Winchester	250	2160	1911	1682	1476	1299	2591	2028	1571	1210	937	+2.5	-3.7	-22.2	0.0	$31
358 Winchester	200	2490	2171	1876	1619	1379	2753	2093	1563	1151	844	+2.5	-1.6	-15.6	0.0	$31
350 Rem. Mag.	200	2710	2410	2130	1870	1631	3261	2579	2014	1553	1181	+2.5	-0.2	-10.0	-30.1	$33
35 Whelen	200	2675	2378	2100	1842	1606	3177	2510	1958	1506	1145	+2.5	-0.2	-10.3	-31.1	$20
35 Whelen	225	2500	2300	2110	1930	1770	3120	2650	2235	1870	1560	+2.6	0.0	-10.2	-29.9	NA
35 Whelen	250	2400	2197	2005	1823	1652	3197	2680	2230	1844	1515	+2.5	-1.2	-13.7	0.0	$20
358 Norma Mag.	250	2800	2510	2230	1970	1730	4350	3480	2750	2145	1655	+2.5	+1.0	-7.6	-25.2	NA
38-55 Win.	255	1320	1190	1091	1018	963	987	802	674	587	525	0.0	-23.	0.0	0.0	$25
375 Winchester	200	2200	1841	1526	1268	1089	2150	1506	1034	714	527	+2.5	-4.0	-26.2	0.0	$27
375 Winchester	250	1900	1647	1424	1239	1103	2005	1506	1126	852	676	+2.5	-6.9	-33.3	0.0	$27
376 Steyr	225	2600	2331	2078	1842	1625	3377	2714	2157	1694	1319	2.5	0.0	-10.6	-31.4	NA
38-40 Win.	180	1160	999	901	827	764	538	399	324	273	233	0.0	-33.9	0.0	0.0	$42**
405 WIN	300	2200	1851	1545	1296	3224	2282	1589	1119	4.6	0.0	-19.5	0.0	NA		
44-40 Win.	200	1190	1006	900	822	756	629	449	360	300	254	0.0	-33.3	0.0	0.0	$36**
44 Rem. Mag.	210	1920	1477	1155	982	880	1719	1017	622	450	361	0.0	-17.6	0.0	0.0	$14
44 Rem. Mag.	240	1760	1380	1114	970	878	1650	1015	661	501	411	0.0	-17.6	0.0	0.0	$13
444 Marlin	240	2350	1815	1377	1087	941	2942	1753	1001	630	472	+2.5	-15.1	-31.0	0.0	$22
444 Marlin	265	2120	1733	1405	1160	1012	2644	1768	1162	791	603	+2.5	-6.0	-32.2	0.0	Disc.
444 Marlin Light Mag	265	2335	1913	1551	1266	3208	2153	1415	943	2.0	-4.90	-26.5	0.0	NA		
45-70 Govt.	300	1810	1497	1244	1073	969	2182	1492	1031	767	625	0.0	-14.8	0.0	0.0	$21
45-70 Govt. Supreme	300	1880	1558	1292	1103	988	2355	1616	1112	811	651	0.0	-12.9	-46.0	-105.0	NA
45-70 Govt. CorBon	350	1800	1526	1296	2519	1810	1307	0.0	-14.6	0.0	0.0	NA				
45-70 Govt.	405	1330	1168	1055	977	918	1590	1227	1001	858	758	0.0	-24.6	$21		
45-70 Govt. Garrett	415	1850	3150	3.0	-7.0	NA										
45-70 Govt. Garrett	530	1550	1343	1178	1062	982	2828	2123	1633	1327	1135	0.0	-17.8	NA		
450 Marlin	350	2100	1774	1488	1254	1089	3427	2446	1720	1222	922	0.0	-9.7	-35.2	NA	
458 Win. Magnum	350	2470	1990	1570	1250	1060	4740	3065	1915	1205	870	+2.5	-2.5	-21.6		$43

Notes: Blanks are available in 32 S&W, 38 S&W and 38 Special. "V" after barrel length indicates test barrel was vented to produce ballistics similar to a revolver with a normal barrel-to-cylinder gap. Ammo prices are per 50 rounds except when marked with an ** which signifies a 20 round box; *** signifies a 25-round box. Not all loads are available from all ammo manufacturers. Listed loads are those made by Remington, Winchester, Federal, and others. DISC. is a discontinued load. Prices are rounded to nearest whole dollar and will vary with brand and retail outlet. † = new bullet weight this year; "c" indicates a change in data. MRT= mid-range trajectory. FPE= foot-pounds energy.

Cartridge	Bullet Wgt.	VELOCITY (fps)			ENERGY (ft. lbs.)			Mid-Range Traj. (in.)		Bbl. Lgth. (in).	Est. Price/ box
		Muzzle	50 yds.	100 yds.	Muzzle	50 yds.	100 yds.	50 yds.	100 yds.		
357 (Med.Vel.)	125	1220	1075	985	415	315	270	0.8	3.7	4"V	$25
357 Magnum	125	1450	1240	1090	585	425	330	0.6	2.8	4"V	$25
357 Magnum	140	1360	1195	1075	575	445	360	0.7	3.0	4"V	$25
357 Magnum	145	1290	1155	1060	535	430	360	0.8	3.5	4"V	$26
357 Magnum	150/158	1235	1105	1015	535	430	360	0.8	3.5	4"V	$25
357 Magnum	165	1290	1189	1108	610	518	450	0.7	3.1	8-3/8"	NA
357 Magnum	180	1145	1055	985	525	445	390	0.9	3.9	4"V	$25
357 Magnum	180	1180	1088	1020	557	473	416	0.8	3.6	8"V	NA
357 Mag. CorBon	180	1650	1512	1386	1088	913	767	1.66	0.0	NA	
357 Mag. CorBon	200	1200	1123	1061	640	560	500	3.19	0.0	NA	
357 Rem. Max.	158	1825	1590	1380	1170	885	670	0.4	1.7	10.5"	$14**
41 Rem. Magnum	170	1420	1165	1015	760	515	390	0.7	3.2	4"V	$33
41 Rem. Magnum	175	1250	1120	1030	605	490	410	0.8	3.4	4"V	$14**
41 (Med. Vel.)	210	965	900	840	435	375	330	1.3	5.4	4"V	$30
41 Rem. Magnum	210	1300	1160	1060	790	630	535	0.7	3.2	4"V	$33
41 Rem. Magnum	240	1250	1151	1075	833	706	616	0.8	3.3	6.5V	NA
44 S&W Special	180	980	NA	NA	383	NA	NA	NA	NA	6.5"	NA
44 S&W Special	180	1000	935	882	400	350	311	NA	NA	7.5"V	NA
44 S&W Special	200†	875	825	780	340	302	270	1.2	6.0	6"	$13**
44 S&W Special	200	1035	940	865	475	390	335	1.1	4.9	6.5"	$13**
44 S&W Special	240/246	755	725	695	310	285	265	2.0	8.3	6.5"	$26
44-40 Win. CB	225	750	723	695	281	261	242	NA			
44 Rem. Magnum	180	1610	1365	1175	1035	745	550	0.5	2.3	4"V	$18**
44 Rem. Magnum	200	1400	1192	1053	870	630	492	0.6	NA	6.5"	$20
44 Rem. Magnum	210	1495	1310	1165	1040	805	635	0.6	2.5	6.5"	$18**
44 (Med. Vel.)	240	1000	945	900	535	475	435	1.1	4.8	6.5"	$17
44 R.M. (Jckt)	240	1180	1080	1010	740	625	545	0.9	3.7	4"V	$18**
44 R.M. (Lead)	240	1350	1185	1070	970	750	610	0.7	3.1	4"V	$29
44 Rem. Magnum	250	1180	1100	1040	775	670	600	0.8	3.6	6.5"V	$21
44 Rem. Magnum	250	1250	1148	1070	867	732	635	0.8	3.3	6.5"V	NA
44 Rem. Magnum	275	1235	1142	1070	931	797	699	0.8	3.3	6.5"	NA
44 Rem. Magnum	300	1200	1100	1026	959	806	702	NA	NA	7.5"	$17
44 Rem. Magnum	330	1385	1297	1220	1406	1234	1090	1.83	0.00	NA	NA
45 Colt	200	1000	938	889	444	391	351	1.3	4.8	5.5"	$21
45 Colt	225	960	890	830	460	395	345	1.3	5.5	5.5"	$22
45 Colt+PCorBon	265	1350	1225	1126	1073	884	746	2.65	0.0	NA	
45 Colt+PCorBon	300	1300	1197	1114	1126	956	827	2.78	0.0	NA	
45 Colt	250/255	860	820	780	410	375	340	1.6	6.6	5.5"	$27
454 Casull	250	1300	1151	1047	938	735	608	0.7	3.2	7.5"V	NA
454 Casull	260	1800	1577	1381	1871	1436	1101	0.4	1.8	7.5"V	NA
454 Casull	300	1625	1451	1308	1759	1413	1141	0.5	2.0	7.5"V	NA
454 Cas. CorBon	360	1500	1387	1286	1800	1640	1323	2.01	0.0	NA	
475 Linebaugh	400	1350	1217	1119	1618	1315	1112	NA	NA	NA	NA
480 Ruger	325	1350	1191	1076	1315	1023	835	2.6	0.0	7.5"	NA
50 Action Exp.	325	1400	1209	1075	1414	1055	835	0.2	2.3	6"	$24**
500 S&W	275	1665	1392	1183	1693	1184	854	1.5	NA	8.375	NA
500 S&W	400	1675	1472	1299	2493	1926	1499	1.3	NA	8.375	NA
500 S&W	440	1625	1367	1169	2581	1825	1337	1.6	NA	8.375	NA

NOTES: * = 10 rounds per box. ** = 5 rounds per box. Pricing variations and number of rounds per box can occur with type and brand of ammunition. Listed pricing is the average nominal cost for load style and box quantity shown. Not every brand is available in all shot size variations. Some manufacturers do not provide suggested list prices. All prices rounded to nearest whole dollar. The price you pay will vary dependent upon outlet of purchase. # = new load spec this year; "C" indicates a change in data. PROJ = Projectile.

DRAM EQUIV.	SLUG/ SHOT	LOAD	STYLE	BRANDS	AVG. PRICE/BOX	VELOCITY (fps)
10 Gauge 3-1/2" Magnum						
Max	1-3/4	slug, rifled	slug	Fed.	NA	1280
Max	24 pellets	Buckshot	1 Buck	Fed.	NA	1100
Max	54 pellets	Super-X	4 Buck	Win.	NA.	1150
12 Gauge 3-1/2" Magnum						
Max	18 pellets	premium	00 buck	Fed., Win., Rem.	$7**	1100
Max	24 pellets	premium	1 Buck	Fed.	NA	1100
Max	54 pellets	Super-X	4 Buck	Win.	NA	1050
12 Gauge 3" Magnum						
4	24 pellets	buffered	1 buck	Win., Fed., Rem.	$5**	1040
4	15 pellets	buffered	00 buck	Win., Fed., Rem.	$6**	1210
4	10 pellets	buffered	000 buck	Win., Fed., Rem.	$6**	1225
4	41 pellets	buffered	4 buck	Win., Fed., Rem.	$6**	1210
Max	1-3/8	slug	slug	Bren.	NA	1476
Max	1-1/4	slug, rifled	slug	Fed.	NA	1600
Max	1-3/16	saboted slug	copper slug	Rem.	NA	1500
Max	7/8	slug, rifled	slug	Rem.	NA	1875
Max	1-3/8	buckhammer	slug	Rem.	NA	1500
Max	1	slug, rifled	slug, magnum	Win., Rem.	$5**	1760
Max	1	saboted slug	slug	Rem., Win., Fed.	$10**	1550
Max	385 grs.	partition gold	slug	Win.	NA	2000
12 Gauge 2-3/4"						
4	12 pellets	premium	00 buck	Win., Fed., Rem.	$5**	1290
3-3/4	9 pellets	buffered	00 buck	Win., Fed., Rem., Fio.	$19	1325
Max	9 pellets	Hevi. Shot	00 buck	Rem.	NA	1325
3-3/4	12 pellets	buffered	0 buck	Win., Fed., Rem.	$4**	1275
4	20 pellets	buffered	1 buck	Win., Fed., Rem.	$4**	1075
3-3/4	16 pellets	buffered	1 buck	Win., Fed., Rem.	$4**	1250
4	34 pellets	premium	4 buck	Fed., Rem.	$5**	1250
3-3/4	27 pellets	buffered	4 buck	Win., Fed., Rem., Fio.	$4**	1325
Max	1	saboted slug	slug	Win., Fed., Rem.	$10**	1450
Max	1-1/4	slug, rifled	slug	Fed.	NA	1520
Max	1-1/4	slug	slug	Lightfield	1440	

DRAM EQUIV.	SLUG/ SHOT	LOAD	STYLE	BRANDS	AVG. PRICE/BOX	VELOCITY (fps)
12 Gauge 2-3/4" *(cont.)*						
Max	1-1/4	saboted slug	attached sabot	Rem.	NA	1550
Max	1	slug, rifled	slug, magnum	Rem., Fio.	$5**	1680
Max	1	slug, rifled	slug	Win., Fed., Rem.	$4**	1610
Max	1	sabot slug	slug	Sauvestre	1640	
Max	7/8	slug, rifled	slug	Rem.	NA	1800
Max	400	plat. tip	sabot slug	Win.	NA	1700
Max	385 grains	Part. Gold Slug	slug	Win.	NA	1900
Max	385 grains	Core-Lokt bonded	sabot slug	Rem.	NA	1900
Max	325 grains	Barnes Sabot	slug	Fed.	NA	1900
16 Gauge 2-3/4"						
3	12 pellets	buffered	1 buck	Win., Fed., Rem.	$4**	1225
Max	4/5 oz.	slug, rifled	slug	Win., Fed., Rem.	$4**	1570
Max	.92 oz.	sabot slug	slug	Sauvestre	NA	1560
20 Gauge 3" Magnum						
Max	18 pellets	buck shot	2 buck	Fed.	NA	1200
Max	24 pellets	buffered	3 buck	Win.	$5**	1150
2-3/4	20 pellets	buck	3 buck	Rem.	$4**	1200
Mag	5/8 oz.	saboted slug	275 gr.	Fed.	NA	1900
20 Gauge 2-3/4"						
Max	1 oz.	buckhammer	slug	Rem.	NA	1500
Max	5/8 oz.	saboted slug	copper slug	Rem.	NA	1500
Max	20 pellets	buffered	3 buck	Win., Fed.	$4	1200
Max	5/8 oz.	slug, saboted	slug	Win.,	$9**	1400
2-3/4	5/8 oz.	slug, rifled	slug	Rem.	$4**	1580
Max	3/4 oz.	saboted slug	copper slug	Fed., Rem.	NA	1450
Max	3/4 oz.	slug, rifled	slug	Win., Fed., Rem., Fio.	$4**	1570
Max	.9 oz.	sabot slug	slug	Sauvestre	1480	
Max	260 grains	Part. Gold Slug	slug	Win.	NA	1900
Max	260 grains	Core-Lokt Ultra	slug	Rem.	NA	1900
Max	260 gr.	saboted slug	platinum tip	Win.	NA	1700
Max	1/2 oz.	rifled, slug	slug	Rem.	NA	1800
410 Bore 2-1/2"						
Max	1/5 oz.	slug, rifled	slug	Win., Fed., Rem.	$4**	1815

Browning Mark II Safari

Remington Model 7400

Ruger Deerfield 99/44 Carbine

BENELLI RI RIFLE

Caliber: 300 Win. Mag., 30-06 Springfield. **Barrel:** 20", 22", 24". **Weight:** 7.1 lbs. **Length:** 43.75" **Stock:** Select satin walnut. **Sights:** None. **Features:** Auto-regulating gas-operated system, three-lugged rotary bolt, interchangeable barrels. Introduced 2003. Imported from Italy by Benelli USA.

Price: . . . . **$1065.00 to $1,080.00**

BROWNING BAR MARK II SAFARI SEMI-AUTO RIFLE

Caliber: 243, 25-06, 270, 30-06, 308, 270 WSM, 7mm WSM. **Barrel:** 22" round tapered. **Weight:** 7-3/8 lbs. **Length:** 43" overall. **Stock:** French walnut pistol grip stock and forend, hand checkered. **Sights:** Gold bead on hooded ramp front, click adjustable rear, or no sights. **Features:** Has new bolt release lever; removable trigger assembly with larger trigger guard; redesigned gas and buffer systems. Detachable 4-round box magazine. Scroll-engraved receiver is tapped for scope mounting. BOSS barrel vibration modulator and muzzle brake system available only on models without sights. Mark II Safari introduced 1993. Imported from Belgium by Browning.

Price: Safari, with sights **$833.00**
Price: Safari, no sights **$815.00**
Price: Safari, 270 and 30-06, no sights, BOSS **$891.00**

Browning BAR Mark II Safari Rifle (Magnum)

Same as the standard caliber model, except weighs 8-3/8 lbs., 45" overall, 24" bbl., 3-round mag. Cals. 7mm Mag., 300 Win. Mag., 338 Win. Mag. BOSS barrel vibration modulator and muzzle brake system available only on models without sights. Introduced 1993.

Price: Safari, no sights **$908.00**
Price: Safari, no sights, BOSS **$1,007.00**

BROWNING BAR SHORT TRAC/LONG TRAC AUTO RIFLES

NEW! **Caliber:** (Short Trac models): 270 WSM, 7mm WSM, 300 WSM, 243 Win., 308 WIn.; (Long Trac models): 270 Win., 30-06 Sprfld., 7mm Rem. Mag., 300 Win. Mag. **Barrel:** 23". **Weight:** 6 lbs., 10 oz. to 7 lbs., 4 oz. **Length:** 41-1/2" to 44". **Stock:** Satin-finish walnut, pistol grip, fluted forend. **Sights:** Adj. rear, bead front standard, no sights on BOSS models (optional). **Features:** Designed to handle new WSM chamberings. Gas-operated, blued finish, rotary bolt design (Long Trac models)

Price: Short Trac, WSM calibers **$902.00**
Price: Short Trac, 243, 308 . . . . **$827.00**
Price: Long Trac calibers . . . . **$827.00 to 902.00**

BROWNING BAR STALKER AUTO RIFLES

Caliber: 243, 308, 270, 30-06, 7mm Rem. Mag., 300 Win. Mag., 338 Win. Mag., 270 WSM, 7mm WSM. **Barrel:** 20", 22" and 24". **Weight:** 6 lbs., 12 oz. (243) to 8 lbs., 2 oz. (magnum cals.) **Length:** 41" to 45" overall. **Stock:** Black composite stock and forearm. **Sights:** Hooded front and adjustable rear or none. **Features:** Optional BOSS (no sights); gas-operated action with seven-lug rotary bolt; dual action bars; 3- or 4-shot magazine (depending on caliber). Introduced 2001. Imported by Browning.

Price: BAR Stalker, open sights (243, 308, 270, 30-06) **$825.00**
Price: BAR Stalker, open sights (7mm, 300 Win. Mag., 338 Win. Mag.) **$901.00**

REMINGTON MODEL 7400 AUTO RIFLE

Caliber: 243 Win., 270 Win., 308 Win., 30-06, 4-shot magazine. **Barrel:** 22" round tapered. **Weight:** 7-1/2 lbs. **Length:** 42-5/8" overall. **Stock:** Walnut, deluxe cut checkered pistol grip and forend. Satin or high-gloss finish. **Sights:** Gold bead front sight on ramp; step rear sight with windage adjustable. **Features:** Re-designed and improved version of the Model 742. Positive crossbolt safety. Receiver tapped for scope mount. Introduced 1981.

Price: **$624.00**
Price: Carbine (18-1/2" bbl., 30-06 only) **$624.00**
Price: With black synthetic stock, matte black metal, rifle or carbine **$520.00**
Price: Weathermaster, nickel-plated w/synthetic stock and forend, 270, 30-06 . . . . **$624.00**

RUGER DEERFIELD 99/44 CARBINE

Caliber: 44 Mag., 4-shot rotary magazine. **Barrel:** 18-1/2". **Weight:** 6-1/4 lbs. **Length:** 36-7/8" overall. **Stock:** Hardwood. **Sights:** Gold bead front, folding adjustable aperture rear. **Features:** Semi-automatic action; dual front-locking lugs lock directly into receiver; integral scope mount; push button safety; includes 1" rings and gun lock. Introduced 2000. Made in U.S.A. by Sturm, Ruger & Co.

Price: **$675.00**

RUGER MINI-THIRTY AUTOLOADING RIFLE

Caliber: 7.62X39, 5-shot detachable box magazine. **Barrel:** 18-1/2". Rifling twist 1:10". **Weight:** 6.8 lbs. **Length:** 37-1/4" overall. **Stock:** American hardwood, steel reinforced. **Sights:** Ramp front, fully adjustable rear, folding peepsight. **Features:** Fixed piston gas-operated, positive primary extraction. New buffer system, redesigned ejector system. Ruger S100RM scope rings included on Ranch Rifle.

Price: Blued, scope rings.. . . . . **$695.00**

Browning Lightning

Marlin 336C

Marlin 336 Cowboy

Marlin 336Y Spikehorn

BROWNING MODEL '81 LIGHTNING LEVER-ACTION RIFLE

Caliber: 22-250, 243, 7mm-08, 308 Win., 270 WSM, 7mm WSM, 300 WSM, 358 Win., 450 Marlin, 270 Win., 30-06 Sprg., 7mm Rem. Mag., 300 Win. Mag. 4-shot detachable magazine. **Barrel:** 20" round tapered. **Weight:** 6 lbs., 8 oz. **Length:** 39-1/2" overall. **Stock:** Walnut. Checkered grip and forend, high-gloss finish. **Sights:** Gold bead on ramp front; low profile square notch adjustable rear. **Features:** Wide, grooved trigger; half-cock hammer safety; fold-down hammer. Receiver tapped for scope mount. Recoil pad installed. Introduced 1996. Imported from Japan by Browning.
Price: **$710.00**

BROWNING MODEL '81 LIGHTNING LONG ACTION

Similar to the standard Lightning BLR except has long action to accept 30-06, 270, 7mm Rem. Mag. and 300 Win. Mag. Barrel lengths are 22" for 30-06 and 270, 24" for 7mm Rem. Mag. and 300 Win. Mag. Has six-lug rotary bolt; bolt and receiver are full-length fluted. Fold-down hammer at half-cock. Weighs about 7 lbs., overall length 42-7/8" (22" barrel). Introduced 1996.
Price: **$686.00**

MARLIN MODEL 336C LEVER-ACTION CARBINE

Caliber: 30-30 or 35 Rem., 6-shot tubular magazine. **Barrel:** 20" Micro Groove®. **Weight:** 7 lbs. **Length:** 38-1/2" overall. **Stock:** Checkered American black walnut, capped pistol grip. MarShield® finish; rubber butt pad; swivel studs. **Sights:** Ramp front with WideScan hood, semibuckhorn folding rear adjustable for windage and elevation. **Features:** Hammerblock safety. Receiver tapped for scope mount, offset hammer spur; top of receiver sandblasted to prevent glare. Includes safety lock.
Price: **$529.00**

Marlin Model 336 Cowboy

Similar to the Model 336C except chambered for 38-55 Win., 24" tapered octagon barrel with deep-cut Ballard-type rifling; straight grip walnut stock with hard rubber buttplate; blued steel forend cap; weighs 7-1/2 lbs.; 42-1/2" overall. Introduced 1999. Includes safety lock. Made in U.S.A. by Marlin.
Price: **$735.00**

Marlin Model 336A Lever-Action Carbine

Same as the Marlin 336C except has cut-checkered, walnut-finished hardwood pistol grip stock with swivel studs, 30-30 only, 6-shot. Hammer block safety. Adjustable rear sight, brass bead front. Includes safety lock.
Price: **$451.00**
Price: With 4x scope and mount **$501.00**

Marlin Model 336CC Lever-Action Carbine

Same as the Marlin 336A except has Mossy Oak® BreakUp camouflage stock and forearm. 30-30 only, 6-shot; receiver tapped for scope mount or receiver sight. Introduced 2001. Includes safety lock. Made in U.S.A. by Marlin.
Price: **$503.00**

Marlin Model 336SS Lever-Action Carbine

Same as the 336C except receiver, barrel and other major parts are machined from stainless steel. 30-30 only, 6-shot; receiver tapped for scope. Includes safety lock.
Price: **$640.00**

Marlin Model 336W Lever-Action Rifle

Similar to the Model 336CS except has walnut-finished, cut-checkered Maine birch stock; blued steel barrel band has integral sling swivel; no front sight hood; comes with padded nylon sling; hard rubber butt plate. Introduced 1998. Includes safety lock. Made in U.S.A. by Marlin.
Price: **$457.00**
Price: With 4x scope and mount **$506.00**

Marlin Model 336 Y "Spikehorn"

Similar to the Models in the 336 series except in a compact format with 16-1/2" barrel measuring only 34" in overall length. Weight is 6-1/2 lbs., length of pull 12-1/2". Blued steel barrel and receiver. Chambered for 30/30 cartridge. Introduced 2003.
Price: **$536.00**

MARLIN MODEL 444 LEVER-ACTION SPORTER

Caliber: 444 Marlin, 5-shot tubular magazine. **Barrel:** 22" deep cut Ballard rifling. **Weight:** 7-1/2 lbs. **Length:** 40-1/2" overall. **Stock:** Checkered American black walnut, capped pistol grip, rubber butt pad. MarShield® finish; swivel studs. **Sights:** Hooded ramp front, folding semibuckhorn rear adjustable for windage and elevation. **Features:** Hammer block safety. Receiver tapped for scope mount; offset hammer spur. Includes safety lock.
Price: **$618.00**

Marlin 444P Outfitter

Marlin 1894PG

Marlin 1894 Cowboy

Marlin 1894SS

Marlin 1895

Marlin Model 444P Outfitter Lever-Action
Similar to the 444SS with deep-cut Ballard-type rifling; weighs 6-3/4 lbs.; overall length 37". Available only in 444 Marlin. Introduced 1999. Includes safety lock. Made in U.S.A. by Marlin.
Price: $631.00

MARLIN MODEL 1894 LEVER-ACTION CARBINE
Caliber: 44 Spec./44 Mag., 10-shot tubular magazine. **Barrel:** 20" Ballard-type rifling. **Weight:** 6 lbs. **Length:** 37-1/2" overall. **Stock:** Checkered American black walnut, straight grip and forend. MarShield® finish. Rubber rifle butt pad; swivel studs. **Sights:** Wide Scan hooded ramp front, semi-buckhorn folding rear adjustable for windage and elevation. **Features:** Hammerblock safety. Receiver tapped for scope mount, offset hammer spur, solid top receiver sand blasted to prevent glare. Includes safety lock.
Price: $544.00

Marlin Model 1894PG/1894FG
Pistol-gripped versions of the Model 1894. Model 1894PG is chambered for .44 Magnum; Model 1894FG is chambered for .41 Magnum.
Price: (Model 1894PG) $610.00
Price: (Model 1894FG) $610.00

Marlin Model 1894C Carbine
Similar to the standard Model 1894S except chambered for 38 Spec./357 Mag. with full-length 9-shot magazine, 18-1/2" barrel, hammerblock safety, hooded front sight. Introduced 1983. Includes safety lock.
Price: $556.00

Marlin Model 1894SS
Similar to Model 1894 except has stainless steel barrel, receiver, lever, guard plate, magazine tube and loading plate. Nickel-plated swivel studs.
Price: $680.00

MARLIN MODEL 1895 LEVER-ACTION RIFLE
Caliber: 45-70, 4-shot tubular magazine. **Barrel:** 22" round. **Weight:** 7-1/2 lbs. **Length:** 40-1/2" overall. **Stock:** Checkered American black walnut, full pistol grip. MarShield® finish; rubber butt pad; quick detachable swivel studs. **Sights:** Bead front with WideScan hood, semi-buckhorn folding rear adjustable for windage and elevation. **Features:** Hammer block safety. Solid receiver tapped for scope mounts or receiver sights; offset hammer spur. Includes safety lock.
Price: $631.00

Marlin Model 1895G Guide Gun Lever-Action Rifle
Similar to Model 1895 with deep-cut Ballard-type rifling; straight-grip walnut stock. Overall length is 37", weighs 7 lbs. Introduced 1998. Includes safety lock. Made in U.S.A. by Marlin.
Price: $646.00

Marlin Model 1895GS Guide Gun
Similar to Model 1895G except receiver, barrel and most metal parts are machined from stainless steel. Chambered for 45-70, 4-shot, 18-1/2" barrel. Overall length is 37", weighs 7 lbs. Introduced 2001. Includes safety lock. Made in U.S.A. by Marlin.
Price: $760.00

Marlin 1895M

Remington 7600 Rifle

Ruger Model 96/44

Winchester 94 Traditional

Winchester Model 94 Trapper

Marlin Model 1895M Lever-Action Rifle

Similar to Model 1895 except has an 18-1/2" barrel with Ballard-type cut rifling. New Model 1895MR variant has 22" barrel, pistol grip. Chambered for 450 Marlin. Includes safety lock.
Price: (Model 1895M) **$695.00**
Price: (Model 1895MR) **$761.00**

REMINGTON MODEL 7600 PUMP ACTION

Caliber: 243, 270, 30-06, 308. **Barrel:** 22" round tapered. **Weight:** 7-1/2 lbs. **Length:** 42-5/8" overall. **Stock:** Cut-checkered walnut pistol grip and forend, Monte Carlo with full cheekpiece. Satin or high-gloss finish. **Sights:** Gold bead front sight on matted ramp, open step adjustable sporting rear. **Features:** Redesigned and improved version of the Model 760. Detachable 4-shot clip. Cross bolt safety. Receiver tapped for scope mount. Introduced 1981.
Price: **$588.00**
Price: Carbine (18-1/2" bbl., 30-06 only) **$588.00**
Price: With black synthetic stock, matte black metal,
rifle or carbine **$484.00**

RUGER MODEL 96/44 LEVER-ACTION RIFLE

Caliber: 44 Mag., 4-shot rotary magazine. **Barrel:** 18-1/2". **Weight:** 5-7/8 lbs. **Length:** 37-5/16" overall. **Stock:** American hardwood. **Sights:** Gold bead front, folding leaf rear. **Features:** Solid chrome-moly steel receiver. Manual crossbolt safety, visible cocking indicator; short-throw lever action; integral scope mount; blued finish; color casehardened lever. Introduced 1996. Made In U.S. by Sturm, Ruger & Co.
Price: 96/44M, 44 Mag **$525.00**

WINCHESTER TIMBER CARBINE

Caliber: Chambered for 450 Marlin. **Barrel:** 18" barrel, ported. **Weight:** 6 lbs. **Length:** 36-1/4" overall. **Stock:** Half-pistol grip stock with butt pad; checkered grip and forend. **Sights:** XS ghost-ring sight. **Features:** Introduced 1999. Made in U.S.A. by U.S. Repeating Arms Co., Inc.
Price: **$610.00**

WINCHESTER MODEL 94 TRADITIONAL CW

Caliber: 30-30 Win., 6-shot; 44 Mag., 11-shot tubular magazine. **Barrel:** 20". **Weight:** 6-1/2 lbs. **Length:** 37-3/4" overall. **Stock:** Straight grip checkered walnut stock and forend. **Sights:** Hooded blade front, semi-buckhorn rear. Drilled and tapped for scope mount. Post front sight on Trapper model. **Features:** Solid frame, forged steel receiver; side ejection, exposed rebounding hammer with automatic trigger-activated transfer bar. Introduced 1984.
Price: 30-30 . . . . **$469.00**
Price: 44 Mag. **$492.00**
Price: Traditional (no checkering, 30-30 only) **$435.00**

Winchester Model 94 Trapper

Similar to Model 94 Traditional except has 16" barrel, 5-shot magazine in 30-30, 9-shot in 357 Mag., 44 Magnum/44 Special, 45 Colt. Has stainless steel claw extractor, saddle ring, hammer spur extension, smooth walnut wood.
Price: 30-30 . . . . **$459.00**
Price: 44 Mag., 357 Mag., 45 Colt **$459.00**

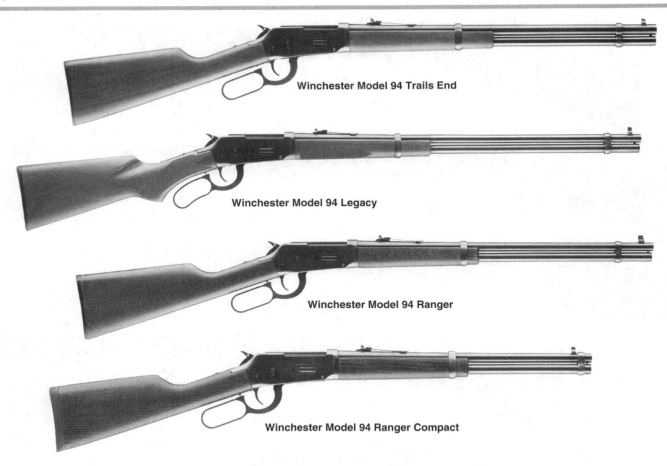

Winchester Model 94 Trails End

Winchester Model 94 Legacy

Winchester Model 94 Ranger

Winchester Model 94 Ranger Compact

Winchester Model 94 Trails End
Similar to the Model 94 Walnut except octagon-barrel version available, chambered only for 357 Mag., 4440, 44 Mag., 45 Colt; 11-shot magazine. Available with standard lever loop. Introduced 1997. From U.S. Repeating Arms Co., Inc.
Price: With standard lever loop. $474.00

Winchester Model 94 Legacy
Similar to the Model 94 Traditional CW except has half-pistol grip walnut stock, checkered grip and forend. Chambered for 30-30, 357 Mag., 44 Mag., 45 Colt; 24" barrel. Introduced 1995. Made in U.S.A. by U.S. Repeating Arms Co., Inc.
Price: With 24" barrel $487.00

Winchester Model 94 Ranger
Similar to the Model 94 Traditional except has a hardwood stock, post style front sight and hammer-spur extension.

Price: (20" barrel) $379.00
Price: Trail's End octagon. $757.00
Price: Trail's End octagon, case color $815.00

Winchester Model 94 Ranger Compact
Similar to the Model 94 Ranger except 357, 30-30 calibers, has 16" barrel and 12-1/2" length of pull, rubber recoil pad, post front sight. Introduced 1998. Made in U.S.A. by U.S. Repeating Arms Co., Inc.
Price: $402.00

WINCHESTER MODEL 1895 LEVER-ACTION RIFLE
Caliber: 405 Win, 4-shot magazine. **Barrel:** 24", round. **Weight:** 8 lbs. **Length:** 42" overall. **Stock:** American walnut. **Sights:** Gold bead front, buckhorn rear adjustable for elevation. **Features:** Recreation of the original Model 1895. Polished blue finish. Two-piece cocking lever, Schnabel forend, straight-grip stock. Introduced 1995. From U.S. Repeating Arms Co., Inc.
Price: Grade I $1,116.00

Includes models for a wide variety of sporting and competitive purposes and uses.

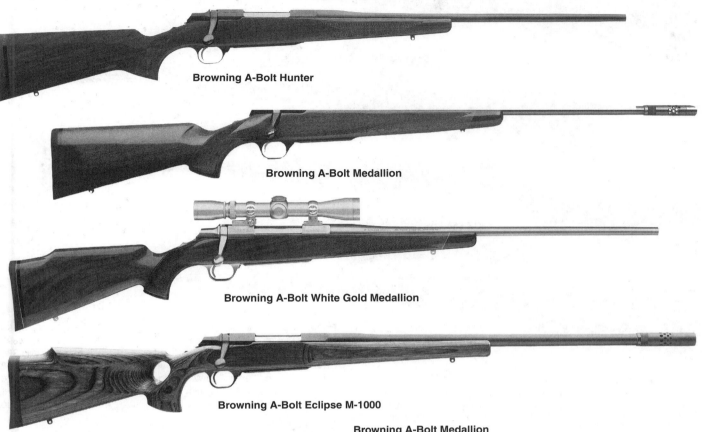

Browning A-Bolt Hunter

Browning A-Bolt Medallion

Browning A-Bolt White Gold Medallion

Browning A-Bolt Eclipse M-1000

BRNO 98 BOLT-ACTION RIFLE

Caliber: 7x64, 243, 270, 308, 30-06, 300 Win. Mag., 9.3x62. **Barrel:** 23.6". **Weight:** 7.2 lbs. **Length:** 40.9" overall. **Stock:** European walnut. **Sights:** Blade on ramp front, open adjustable rear. **Features:** Uses Mauser 98-type action; polished blue. Announced 1998. Imported from the Czech Republic by EuroImports.

Price: Standard calibers	**$507.00**
Price: Magnum calibers	**$547.00**
Price: With set trigger, standard calibers	**$615.00**
Price: As above, magnum calibers	**$655.00**
Price: With full stock, set trigger, standard calibers	**$703.00**
Price: As above, magnum calibers	**$743.00**
Price: 300 Win. Mag., with BOSS	**$933.00**

BROWNING A-BOLT RIFLES

Caliber: 223, 22-250, 243, 7mm-08, 308, 25-06, 260, 270, 30-06, 260 Rem., 7mm Rem. Mag., 300 Win. Short Mag., 300 Win. Mag., 338 Win. Mag., 375 H&H Mag, 223 WSSM, 243 WSSM, 270 WSM, 7mm WSM, 300 WSM. **Barrel:** 22" medium sporter weight with recessed muzzle; 26" on mag. cals. **Weight:** 6-1/2 to 7-1/2 lbs. **Length:** 44-3/4" overall (magnum and standard); 41-3/4" (short action). **Stock:** Classic style American walnut; recoil pad standard on magnum calibers. **Features:** Short-throw (60") fluted bolt, three locking lugs, plunger-type ejector; adjustable trigger is grooved and gold-plated. Hinged floorplate, detachable box magazine (4 rounds std. cals., 3 for magnums). Slide tang safety. BOSS barrel vibration modulator and muzzle brake system not available in 375 H&H. Introduced 1985. Imported from Japan by Browning.

Price: Hunter, no sights	**$672.00**
Price: Hunter, no sights, magnum calibers	**$698.00**
Price: For BOSS	add **$80.00**

Browning A-Bolt Medallion

Similar to standard A-Bolt except has glossy stock finish, rosewood grip and forend caps, engraved receiver, high-polish blue, no sights. New calibers include 223 WSSM, 243 WSSM, 270 WSM, 7mm WSM.

Price: Short-action calibers	**$782.00**
Price: Long-action calibers	**$782.00**
Price: Medallion, 375 H&H Mag., open sights	**$811.00**
Price: 300 Win. Short Magnum	**$811.00**
Price: For BOSS	add **$80.00**

Browning A-Bolt Medallion Left-Hand

Same as the Medallion model A-Bolt except has left-hand action and is available in 270, 30-06, 7mm Rem. Mag., 300 Win. Mag. Introduced 1987.

Price: 270, 30-06 (no sights)	**$813.00**
Price: 7mm Mag., 300 Win. Mag. (no sights)	**$840.00**
Price: For BOSS	add **$80.00**

Browning A-Bolt White Gold Medallion

Similar to the standard A-Bolt except has select walnut stock with brass spacers between rubber recoil pad and between the rosewood gripcap and forend tip; gold-filled barrel inscription; palm-swell pistol grip, Monte Carlo comb, 22 lpi checkering with double borders; engraved receiver flats. In 270, 30-06, 7mm Rem. Mag. and 300 Win. Mag. Introduced 1988.

Price: 270, 30-06	**$1,121.00**
Price: 7mm Rem. Mag, 300 Win. Mag.	**$1,149.00**
Price: For BOSS	add **$80.00**

BROWNING A-BOLT WHITE GOLD RMEF

Caliber: 7mm Rem. Mag. Similar to the A-Bolt Medallion except has select walnut stock with rosewood forend cap, RMEF-engraved grip cap: continental cheekpiece; gold engraved, stainless receiver and bbl. Introduced 2004. Imported from Japan by Browning.

Price:	**$1,224.00**

Browning A-Bolt Stalker

CZ 527 Lux

CZ 550 Lux

CZ 550 American Classic

Browning A-Bolt Eclipse Hunter
Similar to the A-Bolt II except has gray/black laminated, thumbhole stock, BOSS barrel vibration modulator and muzzle brake. Available in long and short action with heavy barrel. In 270 Win., 30-06, 7mm Rem. Mag. Introduced 1996. Imported from Japan by Browning.
Price: 270, 30-06, with BOSS. $1,101.00
Price: 7mm Rem. Mag, with BOSS $1,128.00

Browning A-Bolt Eclipse M1000
Similar to the A-Bolt II Eclipse except has long action and heavy target barrel. Chambered only for 300 Win. Mag. Adjustable trigger, bench-style forend, 3-shot magazine; laminated thumbhole stock; BOSS system standard. Introduced 1997. Imported for Japan by Browning.
Price: $1,134.00

Browning A-Bolt Micro Hunter
Similar to the A-Bolt II Hunter except has 13-5/16" length of pull, 20" barrel, and comes in 260 Rem., 243, 308, 7mm-08, 223, 22 250, 22 Hornet, 270 WSM, 7mm WSM, 300 WSM. Weighs 6 lbs., 1 oz. Introduced 1999. Imported by Browning. Also available in left-hand version.
Price: (no sights). $664.00

Browning A-Bolt Classic Hunter
Similar to the A-Bolt Hunter except has low-luster bluing and walnut stock with Monte Carlo comb, pistol grip palm swell, double-border checkering. Available in 223 WSSM, 243 WSSM. Introduced 1999. Imported by Browning.
Price: WSM. $784.00
Price: WSSM $805.00

Browning A-Bolt Stainless Stalker
Similar to the Hunter model A-Bolt except receiver and barrel are made of stainless steel; the rest of the exposed metal surfaces are finished with a durable matte silver-gray. Graphite-fiberglass composite textured stock. No sights are furnished. Available in 260, 243, 308, 7mm-08, 270, 280, 30-06, 7mm Rem. Mag., 300 WSM, 300 Rem. Ultra Mag., 338 Win. Mag., 338 Rem. Ultra Mag., 375 H&H, 223 WSSM, 243 WSSM, 270 WSM, 7mm WSM. Introduced 1987.

Price: Short-action calibers $871.00
Price: Magnum calibers $899.00
Price: 300 Win. Short Magnum $899.00
Price: For BOSS. . . . . add $80.00
Price: Left-hand, 270, 30-06 . . . . $898.00
Price: Left-hand, 7mm, 300 Win. Mag., 338 Win. Mag. $926.00
Price: Left-hand, 375 H&H, with sights $926.00
Price: Left-hand, for BOSS. . . . . add $80.00

Browning A-Bolt Composite Stalker
Similar to the A-Bolt Hunter except has black graphite-fiberglass stock with textured finish. Matte blue finish on all exposed metal surfaces. Available in 223, 22-250, 243, 7mm-08, 308, 30-06, 270, 280, 25-06, 7mm Rem. Mag., 300 WSM, 300 Win. Mag., 338 Win. Mag., 223 WSSM, 243 WSSM, 270 WSM, 7mm WSM. BOSS barrel vibration modulator and muzzle brake system offered in all calibers. Introduced 1994.
Price: Standard calibers, no sights. $684.00
Price: Magnum calibers, no sights $713.00
Price: For BOSS. . . . . add $80.00

CZ 550 LUX BOLT-ACTION RIFLE
Caliber: 22-250, 243, 6.5x55, 7x57, 7x64, 308 Win., 9.3x62, 270 Win., 30 06. Barrel: 20.47". Weight: 7.5 lbs. Length: 44.68" overall. Stock: Turkish walnut in Bavarian style or FS (Mannlicher). Sights: Hooded front, adjustable rear. Features: Improved Mauser-style action with claw extractor, fixed ejector, square bridge dovetailed receiver; single set trigger. Imported from the Czech Republic by CZ-USA.
Price: Lux. . . . . $566.00 to $609.00
Price: FS (full stock) $706.00

CZ 527 American Classic Bolt-Action Rifle
Similar to the CZ 527 Lux except has classic-style stock with 18 lpi checkering; free-floating barrel; recessed target crown on barrel. No sights furnished. Introduced 1999. Imported from the Czech Republic by CZ-USA.
Price: 22 Hornet, 222 Rem., 223 Rem. . . . . $586.00 to $609.00

CZ 550 American Classic Bolt-Action Rifle
Similar to CZ 550 Lux except has American classic-style stock with 18 lpi checkering; free-floating barrel; recessed target crown. Has 25.6" barrel; weighs 7.48 lbs. No sights furnished. Introduced 1999. Imported from the Czech Republic by CZ-USA.
Price: . . . . $586.00 to $609.00

CZ 550 Magnum

Remington 700 Classic

Remington 700 ADL Synthetic

Remington 700 BDL

Remington 700 BDL Left Hand

CZ 550 Medium Magnum Bolt-Action Rifle
Similar to the CZ 550 Lux except chambered for the 300 Win. Mag. and 7mm Rem. Mag.; 5-shot magazine. Adjustable iron sights, hammer forged barrel, single-set trigger, Turkish walnut stock. Weighs 7.5 lbs. Introduced 2001. Imported from the Czech Republic by CZ-USA.
Price: **$621.00**

CZ 550 Magnum Bolt-Action Rifle
Similar to CZ 550 Lux except has long action for 300 Win. Mag., 375 H&H, 416 Rigby, 458 Win. Mag. Overall length is 46.45"; barrel length 25"; weighs 9.24 lbs. Hooded front sight, express rear with one standing, two folding leaves. Imported from the Czech Republic by CZ-USA.
Price: 300 Win. Mag. **$717.00**
Price: 375 H&H **$756.00**
Price: 416 Rigby **$809.00**
Price: 458 Win. Mag. **$744.00**

REMINGTON MODEL 700 CLASSIC RIFLE
Caliber: 300 Savage. **Barrel:** 24". **Weight:** About 7-1/4 lbs. **Length:** 44-1/2" overall. **Stock:** American walnut, 20 lpi checkering on pistol grip and forend. Classic styling. Satin finish. **Sights:** None furnished. Receiver drilled and tapped for scope mounting. **Features:** A "classic" version of the BDL with straight comb stock. Fitted with rubber recoil pad. Sling swivel studs installed. Hinged floorplate. Limited production in 2003 only.
Price: **$683.00**

REMINGTON MODEL 700 ADL DELUXE RIFLE
Caliber: 270, 30-06. **Barrel:** 22" round tapered. **Weight:** 7-1/4 lbs. **Length:** 41-5/8" overall. **Stock:** Walnut. Satin-finished pistol grip stock with fine line cut checkering, Monte Carlo. **Sights:** Gold bead ramp front; removable, step-adjustable rear with windage screw. **Features:** Side safety, receiver tapped for scope mounts.
Price: **$580.00**

Remington Model 700 ADL Synthetic
Similar to the 700 ADL except has a fiberglass-reinforced synthetic stock with straight comb, raised cheekpiece, positive checkering, and black rubber butt pad. Metal has matte finish. Available in 22-250, 223, 243, 270, 308, 30-06 with 22" barrel, 300 Win. Mag., 7mm Rem. Mag. with 24" barrel. Introduced 1996.
Price: From . . . . **$500.00** to **$527.00**

Remington Model 700 ADL Synthetic Youth
Similar to the Model 700 ADL Synthetic except has 1" shorter stock, 20" barrel. Chambered for 243, 308. Introduced 1998.
Price: **$500.00**

Remington Model 700 BDL Custom Deluxe Rifle
Same as 700 ADL except chambered for 222, 223 (short action, 24" barrel), 7mm-08, 280, 22-250, 25-06, (short action, 22" barrel), 243, 270, 30-06, skipline checkering, black forend tip and gripcap with white line spacers. Matted receiver top, quick-release floorplate. Hooded ramp front sight, quick detachable swivels.
Price: **$683.00**
Also available in 17 Rem., 7mm Rem. Mag., 7mm Rem. Ultra Mag., 300 Win. Mag. (long action, 24" barrel); 300 Rem. Ultra Mag. (26" barrel). Overall length 44-1/2", weight about 7-1/2 lbs.
Price: . . . . **$709.00** to **$723.00**

Remington Model 700 BDL Left-Hand Custom Deluxe
Same as 700 BDL except mirror-image left-hand action, stock. Available in 270, 30-06, 7mm Rem. Mag., 300 Rem. Ultra Mag, 338 Rem. Ultra Mag., 7mm Rem. Ultra Mag.
Price: . . . . **$709.00** to **$749.00**

Remington 700 BDL SS

Remington 700 BDL SS DM

Remington 700 Titanium

Remington 700 VS SF

Remington 700 Sendero SF

Remington Model 700 BDL DM Rifle

Same as 700 BDL except detachable box magazine (4-shot, standard calibers, 3-shot for magnums). Glossy stock finish, open sights, recoil pad, sling swivels. Available in 270, 30-06, 7mm Rem. Mag., 300 Win. Mag. Introduced 1995.
Price: From . . . . **$749.00** to **$776.00**

Remington Model 700 BDL SS Rifle

Similar to 700 BDL rifle except hinged floorplate, 24" standard weight barrel in all calibers; magnum calibers have magnum-contour barrel. No sights supplied, but comes drilled and tapped. Corrosion-resistant follower and fire control, stainless BDL-style barreled action with fine matte finish. Synthetic stock has straight comb and cheekpiece, textured finish, positive checkering, plated swivel studs. Calibers: 270, 30-06; magnums: 7mm Rem. Mag., 7mm Rem. Ultra Mag., 300 Rem. Ultra Mag. (26" barrel) 300 Win. Mag., 338 Rem. Ultra Mag., 7mm Rem. SAUM, 300 Rem. SAUM. Weighs 7-3/8 to 7-1/2 lbs. Introduced 1993.
Price: From . . . . **$735.00** to **$775.00**

Remington Model 700 BDL SS DM Rifle

Same as 700 BDL SS except detachable box magazine. Barrel, receiver and bolt made of #416 stainless steel; black synthetic stock, fineline engraving. Available in 270, 30-06, 7mm Rem. Mag., 300 Win. Mag. Introduced 1995.
Price: From . . . . **$801.00** to **$828.00**

Remington Model 700 LSS Rifle

Similar to 700 BDL except stainless steel barreled action, gray laminated wood stock with Monte Carlo comb and cheekpiece. No sights furnished. Available in (RH) 7mm Rem. Mag., 300 Win. Mag., 300 RUM, 338 RUM, 7mm Rem. Ultra Mag., 375 Rem. Ultra Mag., (LH) 7mm Rem. Ultra Mag., 300 Rem. Ultra Mag., and 338 Rem. RUM. Introduced 1996.
Price: From . . . . (Right-Hand) **$820.00** to **$840.00**; (LH) **$867.00**

Remington Model 700 Titanium

Similar to 700 BDL except has titanium receiver, spiral-cut fluted bolt, skeletonized bolt handle and carbon-fiber and aramid-fiber reinforced stock with sling swivel studs. Barrel 22"; weighs 5-1/4 lbs. (short action) or 5-1/2 lbs. (long action). Satin stainless finish. 260 Rem., 270 Win., 7mm-08, 30-06, 308 Win. Introduced 2001.
Price: **$1,239.00**

Remington Model 700 EtronX VSSF Rifle

Similar to Model 700 VS SF except features battery-powered ignition system for near-zero lock time and electronic trigger mechanism. Requires ammunition with EtronX electrically fired primers. Aluminum-bedded 26" heavy, stainless steel, fluted barrel; overall length 45-7/8"; weight 8 lbs., 14 oz. Black, Kevlar-reinforced composite stock. Light-emitting diode display on grip top indicates fire or safe mode, loaded or unloaded chamber, battery condition. Introduced 2000.
Price: 220 Swift, 22-250 or 243 Win. **$1,332.00**

Remington Model 700 Sendero SF Rifle

Similar to 700 Sendero except stainless steel action and 26" fluted stainless barrel. Weighs 8-1/2 lbs. Chambered for 7mm Rem. SAUM, 300 Rem. SAUM, 7mm Rem. Mag., 7mm STW, 300 Rem. Ultra Mag., 338 Rem. Ultra Mag., 300 Win. Mag., 7mm Rem. Ultra Mag. Introduced 1996.
Price: . . . . **$1,003.00** to **$1,016.00**

Remington Seven LS

Remington Model Seven LS Mag

Remington Model Seven SS Mag

Remington Model Seven Custom MS

Remington Seven Custom KS

REMINGTON MODEL 710 BOLT-ACTION RIFLE
Caliber: 270 Win., 30-06. **Barrel:** 22". **Weight:** 7-1/8 lbs. **Length:** 42-1/2" overall. **Stock:** Gray synthetic. **Sights:** Bushnell Sharpshooter 39x scope mounted and bore-sighted. **Features:** Unique action locks bolt directly into barrel; 60-degree bolt throw; 4-shot dual-stack magazine; key-operated Integrated Security System locks bolt open. Introduced 2001. Made in U.S.A. by Remington Arms Co.
Price: **$425.00**

REMINGTON MODEL SEVEN LS
Caliber: 223 Rem., 243 Win., 7mm-08 Rem., 308 Win. **Barrel:** 20". **Weight:** 6-1/2 lbs. **Length:** 39-1/4" overall. **Stock:** Brown laminated, satin finished. **Features:** Satin finished carbon steel barrel and action, 4-round magazine, hinged magazine floorplate. Furnished with iron sights and sling swivel studs, drilled and tapped for scope mounts.
Price: **$701.00**
Price: 7mm RSAUM, 300 RSAUM, LS Magnum, 22" bbl. **$741.00**

Remington Model Seven SS
Similar to Model Seven LS except stainless steel barreled action and black synthetic stock, 20" barrel. Chambered for 243, 260 Rem., 7mm-08, 308. Introduced 1994.

Price: **$729.00**
Price: 7mm RSAUM, 300 RSAUM, Model Seven SS
Magnum, 22" bbl. **$769.00**

Remington Model Seven Custom MS Rifle
Similar to Model Seven LS except full-length Mannlicher-style stock of laminated wood with straight comb, solid black recoil pad, black steel forend tip, cut checkering, gloss finish. Barrel length 20", weighs 6-3/4 lbs. Available in 222 Rem., 223, 22-250, 243, 6mm Rem., 260 Rem., 7mm-08 Rem., 308, 350 Rem. Mag. Calibers 250 Savage, 257 Roberts, 35 Rem. Polished blue finish. Introduced 1993. From Remington Custom Shop.
Price: From. **$1,332.00**

Remington Model Seven Youth Rifle
Similar to Model Seven LS except hardwood stock, 1" shorter length of pull, chambered for 223, 243, 260 Rem., 7mm-08. Introduced 1993.
Price: **$547.00**

Remington Model Seven Custom KS
Similar to Model Seven LS except gray aramid-fiber reinforced stock with 1" black rubber recoil pad and swivel studs. Blued satin carbon steel barreled action. No sights on 223, 260 Rem., 7mm-08, 308; 35 Rem. and 350 Rem. have iron sights.
Price: **$1,314.00**

Ruger M77 Mark II

Ruger KM77RLFP MKII

Ruger KM77RSFP MKII

Ruger KM77RFP MKII

Ruger 77/44

RUGER M77 MARK II RIFLE

Caliber: 223, 220 Swift, 22-250, 243, 6mm Rem., 257 Roberts, 25-06, 6.5x55 Swedish, 270, 7x57mm, 260 Rem., 280 Rem., 308, 30-06, 7mm Rem. Mag., 7mm Rem. Short Ultra Mag., 300 Rem. Short Ultra Mag., 300 WSM, 300 Win. Mag., 338 Win. Mag., 4-shot magazine. **Barrel:** 20", 22"; 24" (magnums). **Weight:** About 7 lbs. **Length:** 39-3/4" overall. **Stock:** Synthetic American walnut; swivel studs, rubber butt pad. **Sights:** None furnished. Receiver has Ruger integral scope mount base, Ruger 1" rings. Some with iron sights. **Features:** Short action with new trigger, 3-position safety. Steel trigger guard. Left-hand available. Introduced 1989.
Price: M77RMKII (no sights). $675.00
Price: M77RSMKII (open sights) $759.00
Price: M77LRMKII (left-hand, 270, 30-06, 7mm Rem. Mag., 300 Win. Mag.) $675.00
Price: KM77REPMKII (Shorts) $675.00

Ruger M77RSI International Carbine

Same as standard Model 77 except 18" barrel, full-length International-style stock, steel forend cap, loop-type steel sling swivels. Integral-base receiver, open sights, Ruger 1" steel rings. Improved front sight. Available in 243, 270, 308, 30-06. Weighs 7 lbs. Length overall is 38-3/8".
Price: M77RSIMKII $769.00

Ruger M77 Mark II All-Weather and Sporter Model Stainless Rifle

Similar to wood-stock M77 Mark II except all metal parts are stainless steel, has an injection-moulded, glass-fiber-reinforced polymer stock. Laminated wood stock. Chambered for 223, 243, 270, 308, 30-06, 7mm Rem. Mag., 300 Win. Mag., 338 Win. Mag. Fixed blade-type ejector, 3-position safety, new trigger guard with patented floorplate latch. Integral Scope Base Receiver, 1" Ruger scope rings, built-in sling swivel loops. Introduced 1990.

Price: K77RFPMKII $675.00
Price: K77RLFPMKII UltraLight, synthetic stock, rings, no sights $675.00
Price: K77LRBBZMKII, left-hand bolt, rings, no sights, laminated stock $729.00
Price: K77RSFPMKII, synthetic stock, open sights $759.00
Price: K77RBZMKII, no sights, laminated wood stock, 223, 22-250, 243, 270, 280 Rem., 7mm Rem. Mag., 30-06, 308, 300 Win. Mag., 338 Win. Mag. $729.00
Price: K77RSBZMKII, open sights, laminated wood stock, 243, 270, 7mm Rem. Mag., 30-06, 300 Win. Mag., 338 Win. Mag. . $799.00
Price: KM77RFPMKII (Shorts), M77RMKII $675.00

Ruger M77RL Ultra Light

Similar to standard M77 except weighs 6 lbs., chambered for 223, 243, 308, 270, 30-06, 257 Roberts, barrel tapped for target scope blocks, 20" Ultra Light barrel. Overall length 40". Ruger's steel 1" scope rings supplied. Introduced 1983.
Price: M77RLMKII $729.00

Ruger M77 Mark II Compact Rifles

Similar to standard M77 except reduced 16-1/2" barrel, weighs 5-3/4 lbs. Chambered for 223, 243, 260 Rem., 308, and 7mm-08.
Price: M77CR MKII (blued finish, walnut stock) $675.00
Price: KM77CRBBZ MKII (stainless finish, black laminated stock) $729.00

RUGER 77/44 BOLT-ACTION RIFLE

Caliber: 44 Magnum, 4-shot magazine. **Barrel:** 18-1/2". **Weight:** 6 lbs. **Length:** 38-1/4" overall. **Stock:** American walnut with rubber butt pad and swivel studs or black polymer (stainless only). **Sights:** Gold bead front, folding leaf rear. Comes with Ruger 1" scope rings. **Features:** Uses same action as the Ruger 77/22. Short bolt stroke; rotary magazine; three-position safety. Introduced 1997. Made in U.S.A. by Sturm, Ruger & Co.
Price: Blue, walnut, 77/44RS $605.00
Price: Stainless, polymer, stock, K77/44RS $605.00

Sako 75 Hunter

Savage 110GXP3

Savage 11FXP3

Savage 111FCXP3

SAKO 75 HUNTER BOLT-ACTION RIFLE

Caliber: 17 Rem., 222, 223, 22-250, 243, 7mm-08, 308 Win., 25-06, 270, 280, 30-06; 270 Wea. Mag., 7mm Rem. Mag., 7mm STW, 7mm Wea. Mag., 300 Win. Mag., 300 Wea. Mag., 338 Win. Mag., 340 Wea. Mag., 375 H&H, 416 Rem. Mag. **Barrel:** 22", standard calibers; 24", 26" magnum calibers. **Weight:** About 6 lbs. **Length:** NA. **Stock:** European walnut with matte lacquer finish. **Sights:** None furnished; dovetail scope mount rails. **Features:** New design with three locking lugs and a mechanical ejector, key locks firing pin and bolt, cold hammer-forged barrel is free-floating, 2-position safety, hinged floorplate or detachable magazine that can be loaded from the top, short 70 degree bolt lift. Five action lengths. Introduced 1997. Imported from Finland by Beretta USA.
Price: Standard calibers **$1,129.00**
Price: Magnum Calibers **$1,163.00**

SAVAGE MODEL 10GXP3, 110GXP3 PACKAGE GUNS

Caliber: 223 Rem., 22-250 Rem., 243 Win., 7mm-08 Rem., 308 Win., 300 WSM (10GXP3). 2506 Rem., 270 Win., 30-06 Spfld., 7mm Rem. Mag., 300 Win. Mag., 300 Rem. Ultra Mag. (110GXP3). **Barrel:** 22" 24", 26". **Weight:** 7.5 lbs. average. **Length:** 43"-47". **Stock:** Walnut Monte Carlo with checkering. **Sights:** 39X40mm scope, mounted & bore sighted. **Features:** Blued, free-floating and button rifled, internal box magazines, swivel studs, leather sling. Left-hand available.
Price: **$495.00**

SAVAGE MODEL 11FXP3, 111FXP3, 111FCXP3, 11FYXP3 (Youth) PACKAGE GUNS

Caliber: 223 Rem., 22-250 Rem., 243 Win., 308 Win., 300 WSM (11FXP3). 270 Win., 30-06 Spfld., 25-06 Rem., 7mm Rem. Mag., 300 Win. Mag., 338 Win. Mag., 300 Rem. Ultra Mag. (11FCXPE & 111FXP3). **Barrel:** 22"-26". **Weight:** 6.5 lbs. **Length:** 41"-47". **Stock:** Synthetic checkering, dual pillar bed. **Sights:** 39X40mm scope, mounted & bore sighted. **Features:** Blued, free-floating and button rifled, Top loading internal box mag (except 111FXCP3 has detachable box mag.). Nylon sling and swivel studs. Some left-hand available.
Price: Model 11FXP3 . . . . **$505.00**
Price: Model 111FCXP3 . . . . **$425.00**
Price: Model 11FYXP3, 243 Win., 12.5" pull (youth) **$471.00**

SAVAGE MODEL 16FXP3, 116FXP3 SS ACTION PACKAGE GUNS

Caliber: 223 Rem., 243 Win., 308 Win., 300 WSM, 270 Win., 30-06 Spfld., 7mm Rem. Mag., 300 Win. Mag., 338 Win. Mag., 375 H&H, 7mm S&W, 7mm Rem. Ultra Mag., 300 Rem. Ultra Mag. **Barrel:** 22", 24", 26". **Weight:** 6.75 lbs. average. **Length:** 41"-46". **Stock:** Synthetic checkering, dual pillar bed. **Sights:** 39X40mm scope, mounted & bore sighted. **Features:** Free-floating and button rifled. Internal box mag., nylon sling and swivel studs.
Price: **$556.00**

Savage 10FCM Scout Ultra Light

Savage Model 10FP

Savage Model 111F

Savage Model 11G

Savage Model 10GY

SAVAGE MODEL 10FM SIERRA ULTRA LIGHT RIFLE

Caliber: 223, 243, 308. **Barrel:** 20". **Weight:** 6 lbs. **Length:** 41-1/2". **Stock:** "Dual Pillar" bedding in black synthetic stock with silver medallion in grip-cap. **Sights:** None furnished; drilled and tapped for scope mounting. **Features:** True short action. Comes with sling and quick-detachable swivels. Introduced 1998. Made in U.S.A. by Savage Arms, Inc.

Price: **$495.00**

SAVAGE MODEL 10FCM SCOUT ULTRA LIGHT RIFLE

Caliber: 7mm-08 Rem., 308 Win. **Barrel:** 20", 4-shot. **Weight:** 6.25 lbs. **Length:** 39.75" overall. **Stock:** Synthetic checkering, dual pillar bed. **Sights:** Ghost ring rear, gold bead front. **Features:** Blued, detachable box magazine, Savage shooting sling/carry strap. Quick detach swivels.

Price: **$581.00**

SAVAGE MODEL 10/110FP LONG RANGE RIFLE

Caliber: 223, 25-06, 308, 30-06, 300 Win. Mag., 7mm Rem. Mag., 4-shot magazine. **Barrel:** 24", heavy; recessed target muzzle. **Weight:** 8-1/2 lbs. **Length:** 45.5" overall. **Stock:** Black graphite/fiberglass composition; positive checkering. **Sights:** None furnished. Receiver drilled and tapped for scope mounting. **Features:** Pillar-bedded stock. Black matte finish on all metal parts. Double swivel studs on the forend for sling and/or bipod mount. Right- or left-hand. Introduced 1990. From Savage Arms, Inc.

Price: Right- or left-hand. **$558.00**

SAVAGE MODEL 111 CLASSIC HUNTER RIFLES

Caliber: 25-06 Rem., 270 Win., 30-06 Spfld., 7mm Rem. Mag, 300 Win. Mag., 7mm RUM, 300 RUM. **Barrel:** 22", 24", 26" (magnum calibers). **Weight:** 6.5 to 7.5 lbs. **Length:** 42.75" to 47.25". **Stock:** Walnut-finished hardwood (M111G, GC); graphite/fiberglass filled composite. **Sights:** Ramp front, open fully adjustable rear; drilled and tapped for scope mounting. **Features:** Three-position top tang safety, double front locking lugs, free-floated button-rifled barrel. Comes with trigger lock, target, ear puffs. Introduced 1994. Made in U.S.A. by Savage Arms, Inc.

Price: Model 111F (270 Win., 30-06 Spfld., 7mm Rem. Mag.,
300 win. Mag.) **$411.00**

Price: Model 111F (25-06 Rem., 338 Win. Mag., 7mm Rem. Ultra Mag, 300 Rem. Ultra Mag.) **$461.00**

Price: Model 111G
(wood stock, toploading magazine, right- or left-hand) **$436.00**

Price: Model 111GNS (wood stock,
toploading magazine, no sights, right-hand only) **$428.00**

Savage Model 11 Classic Hunter Rifles, Short Action

Similar to the Model 111F except has true short action, chambered for 22 250, Rem., 243 Win., 7mm-08 Rem., 308 Win.; black synthetic stock with "Dual Pillar" bedding, positive checkering. Introduced 1998. Made in U.S.A. by Savage Arms, Inc.

Price: Model 11F **$461.00**
Price: Model 11FL (left-hand) **$461.00**
Price: Model 11FNS (right-hand, no sights) **$453.00**
Price: Model 11G (wood stock) $436.00
Price: Model 11GL (as above, left-hand) **$436.00**
Price: Model 11FC (right-hand, open sights) **$487.00**

Savage Model 10GY

Similar to the Model 111G except weighs 6.3 lbs., is 42-1/2" overall, and the stock is scaled for ladies, small-framed adults and youths. Chambered for 223, 243, 308. Ramp front sight, open adjustable rear; drilled and tapped for scope mounts. Made in U.S.A. by Savage Arms, Inc.

Price: Model 10GY (short action, calibers 223, 243, 308) **$436.00**

Savage Model 114U

Savage Model 116FSAK

Sigarms SHR 970

Steyr Mannlicher SBS

Steyr SBS Forester

SAVAGE MODEL 114U ULTRA RIFLE

Caliber: 270 Win., 30-06 Spfld., 7mm Rem. Mag., 7mm STW, 300 Win. Mag. **Barrel:** 22"-24". **Weight:** 77.5 lbs. **Length:** 43.25"-45.25" overall. **Stock:** Ultra high gloss American walnut with black tip and custom cut checkering. **Sights:** None furnished; drilled and tapped for scope mounting. **Features:** High luster blued barrel action, internal box magazine.
Price: **$552.00**

SAVAGE MODEL 116 WEATHER WARRIORS

Caliber: 375 H&H, 300 Rem. Ultra Mag., 308 Win., 300 Rem. Ultra Mag., 300 WSM, 7mm Rem. Ultra Mag., 7mm Rem. Short Ultra Mag., 7mm S&W, 7mm-08 Rem. **Barrel:** 22", 24" for 7mm Rem. Mag., 300 Win. Mag., 338 Win. Mag. (M116FSS only). **Weight:** 6.25 to 6.5 lbs. **Length:** 41"-47". **Stock:** Graphite/fiberglass filled composite. **Sights:** None furnished; drilled and tapped for scope mounting. **Features:** Stainless steel with matte finish; free-floated barrel; quick-detachable swivel studs; laser etched bolt; scope bases and rings. Left-hand models available in all models, calibers at same price. Model 116FSS introduced 1991; 116FSAK introduced 1994. Made in U.S.A. by Savage Arms, Inc.
Price: Model 116FSS (top-loading magazine) **$520.00**
Price: Model 116FSAK (top-loading magazine,
Savage Adjustable Muzzle Brake system) **$601.00**

SIGARMS SHR 970 SYNTHETIC RIFLE

Caliber: 270, 30-06. **Barrel:** 22". **Weight:** 7.2 lbs. **Length:** 41.9" overall. **Stock:** Textured black fiberglass or walnut. **Sights:** None furnished; drilled and tapped for scope mounting. **Features:** Quick takedown; interchangeable barrels; removable box magazine; cocking indicator; three-position safety. Introduced 1998. Imported by Sigarms, Inc.
Price: Synthetic stock **$499.00**
Price: Walnut stock **$550.00**

STEYR CLASSIC MANNLICHER SBS RIFLE

Caliber: 243, 25-06, 308, 6.5x55, 6.5x57, 270, 7x64 Brenneke, 7mm-08, 7.5x55, 30-06, 9.3x62, 6.5x68, 7mm Rem. Mag., 300 Win. Mag., 8x685, 4-shot magazine. **Barrel:** 23.6" standard; 26" magnum; 20" full stock standard calibers. **Weight:** 7 lbs. **Length:** 40.1" overall. **Stock:** Hand-checkered fancy European oiled walnut with standard forend. **Sights:** Ramp front adjustable for elevation, V notch rear adjustable for windage. **Features:** Single adjustable trigger; 3-position roller safety with "safebolt" setting; drilled and tapped for Steyr factory scope mounts. Introduced 1997. Imported from Austria by GSI, Inc.
Price: Full-stock, standard calibers **$1,749.00**

STEYR SBS FORESTER RIFLE

Caliber: 243, 25-06, 270, 7mm-08, 308 Win., 30-06, 7mm Rem. Mag., 300 Win. Mag. Detachable 4-shot magazine. **Barrel:** 23.6", standard calibers; 25.6", magnum calibers. **Weight:** 7.5 lbs. **Length:** 44.5" overall (23.6" barrel). **Stock:** Oil-finished American walnut with Monte Carlo cheekpiece. Pachmayr 1" swivels. **Sights:** None furnished. Drilled and tapped for Browning A-Bolt mounts. **Features:** Steyr Safe Bolt systems, three-position ambidextrous roller tang safety, for Safe, Loading Fire. Matte finish on barrel and receiver; adjustable trigger. Rotary cold-hammer forged barrel. Introduced 1997. Imported by GSI, Inc.
Price: Standard calibers **$799.00**
Price: Magnum calibers **$829.00**

WEATHERBY MARK V DELUXE BOLT-ACTION RIFLE

Caliber: All Weatherby calibers plus 22-250, 243, 25-06, 270 Win., 280 Rem., 7mm-08, 30-06, 308 Win. **Barrel:** 24" barrel on standard calibers. **Weight:** 8-1/2 to 10-1/2 lbs. **Length:** 46-5/8" to 46-3/4" overall. **Stock:** Walnut, Monte Carlo with cheekpiece; high luster finish; checkered pistol grip and forend; recoil pad. **Sights:** None furnished. **Features:** Cocking indicator; adjustable trigger; hinged floorplate, thumb safety; quick detachable sling swivels. Made in U.S.A. From Weatherby.
Price: 257, 270, 7mm. 300, 340 Wea. Mags., 26" barrel **$1,767.00**
Price: 416 Wea. Mag. with Accubrake, 28" barrel **$2,079.00**
Price: 460 Wea. Mag. with Accubrake, 28" barrel **$2,443.00**
Price: 24" barrel **$1,715.00**

Weatherby Mark V Lazermark

Weatherby Mark V Sporter

Weatherby Mark V Stainless

Weatherby Mark V Synthetic

Weatherby Mark V Lazermark Rifle

Same as Mark V Deluxe except stock has extensive oak leaf pattern laser carving on pistol grip and forend. Introduced 1981.

Price: 257, 270, 7mm Wea. Mag., 300, 340, 26" **$1,923.00**
Price: 378 Wea. Mag., 28" **$2,266.00**
Price: 416 Wea. Mag., 28", Accubrake **$2,266.00**
Price: 460 Wea. Mag., 28", Accubrake **$2,661.00**

Weatherby Mark V Sporter Rifle

Same as the Mark V Deluxe without the embellishments. Metal has low luster blue, stock is Claro walnut with matte finish, Monte Carlo comb, recoil pad. Introduced 1993. From Weatherby.

Price: 22-250, 243, 240 Wea. Mag., 25-06, 7mm-08, 270 WCF, 280, 30-06, 308; 24" **$1,091.00**
Price: 257 Wea., 270, 7mm Wea., 7mm Rem., 300 Wea., 300 Win., 340 Wea., 338 Win. Mag., 26" barrel for Wea. Calibers; 24" for non-Wea. Calibers **$1,143.00**

Weatherby Mark V Stainless Rifle

Similar to the Mark V Deluxe except made of 410-series stainless steel. Also available in 30-378 Wea. Mag. Has lightweight injection moulded synthetic stock with raised Monte Carlo comb, checkered grip and forend, custom floorplate release. Right-hand only. Introduced 1995. Made in U.S.A. From Weatherby.

Price: 22-250, 243 Win., 240 Wby. Mag., 25-06 Rem., 270 Win., 280 Rem., 7mm-08 Rem., 30-06 Spfld., 308 Win., 24" barrel . **$1,018.00**

Price: 257, 270, 7mm, 300, 340 Wby. Mag., 26" barrel **$1,070.00**
Price: 7mm Rem. Mag., 300 Win. Mag., 338 Win. Mag., 375 H&H Mag., 24" barrel **$1,070.00**

Weatherby Mark V Synthetic

Similar to the Mark V Stainless except made of matte finished blued steel. Injection moulded synthetic stock. Weighs 6-1/2 lbs., 24" barrel. Available in 22-250, 240 Wea. Mag., 243, 25-06, 270, 7mm-08, 280, 30-06, 308. Introduced 1997. Made in U.S.A. From Weatherby.

Price: **$923.00**
Price: 257, 270, 7mm, 300, 340 Wea. Mags., 26" barrel **$975.00**
Price: 7mm STW, 7mm Rem. Mag., 300, 338 Win. Mags **$975.00**
Price: 375 H&H, 24" barrel **$975.00**
Price: 30-378 Wea. Mag., 338-378 Wea 28" barrel **$1,151.00**

WEATHERBY MARK V ACCUMARK RIFLE

Caliber: 257, 270, 7mm, 300, 340 Wea. Mags., 338-378 Wea. Mag., 30-378 Wea. Mag., 7mm STW, 7mm Rem. Mag., 300 Win. Mag. **Barrel:** 26", 28". **Weight:** 8-1/2 lbs. **Length:** 46-5/8" overall. **Stock:** Bell & Carlson with full length aluminum bedding block. **Sights:** None furnished. Drilled and tapped for scope mounting. **Features:** Uses Mark V action with heavy contour stainless barrel with black oxidized flutes, muzzle diameter of .705". Introduced 1996. Made in U.S.A. From Weatherby.

Price: 26" **$1,507.00**
Price: 30-378 Wea. Mag., 338-378 Wea. Mag., 28", Accubrake **$1,724.00**
Price: 223, 22-250, 243, 240 Wea. Mag., 25-06, 270, 280 Rem., 7mm-08, 30-06, 308; 24" **$1,455.00**
Price: Accumark Left-hand 257, 270, 7mm, 300, 340 Wea. Mag., 7mm Rem. Mag., 7mm STW, 300 Win. Mag. **$1,559.00**
Price: Accumark Left-hand 30-378, 333-378 Wea. Mags. **$1,788.00**

CENTERFIRE RIFLES — BOLT ACTION

Weatherby Mark V Accumark

Weatherby Mark V Fibermark

Winchester Model 70 Classic

Winchester Model 70 Classic Stainless

Weatherby Mark V Accumark Ultra Lightweight Rifles

Similar to the Mark V Accumark except weighs 5-3/4 lbs., 6-3/4 lbs. in Mag. calibers.; 24", 26" fluted barrel with recessed target crown; hand laminated stock with CNC-machined aluminum bedding plate and faint gray "spider web" finish. Available in 257, 270, 7mm, 300 Wea. Mags., (26"); 243, 240 Wea. Mag., 25-06, 270 Win., 280 Rem., 7mm-08, 7mm Rem. Mag., 30-06, 338-06 A-Square, 308, 300 Win. Mag. (24"). Introduced 1998. Made in U.S.A. by Weatherby.

Price: .... $1,459.00 to $1,517.00
Price: Left-hand models $1,559.00

Weatherby Mark V SVM/SPM Rifles

Similar to the Mark V Accumark except has 26" fluted (SVM) or 24" fluted Krieger barrel, spiderweb-pattern tan laminated synthetic stock. SVM has a fully adjustable trigger. Chambered for 223, 22-250, 220 Swift (SVM only), 243, 7mm-08 and 308. Made in U.S.A. by Weatherby.

Price: SVM (Super Varmint-Master), repeater or single-shot... $1,517.00
New! Price: SPM (Super Predator-Master) $1,459.00

Weatherby Mark V Fibermark Rifles

Similar to other Mark V models except has black Kevlar® and fiberglass composite stock and beadblast blue or stainless finish. Chambered for 19 standard and magnum calibers. Introduced 1983; reintroduced 2001. Made in U.S.A. by Weatherby.

Price: Fibermark .... $1,070.00 to $1,347.00
Price: Fibermark Stainless .... $1,165.00 to $1,390.00

WEATHERBY MARK V SUPER BIG GAMEMASTER DEER RIFLE

Caliber: 240 Wby. Mag., 25-06 Rem., 270 Win., 280 Rem., 30-06 Spfld., 257 Wby. Mag., 270 Wby. Mag., 7mm Rem., Mag., 7mm Wby. Mag., 338-06 A-Square, 300 Win. Mag., 300 Wby. Mag. **Barrel:** 26", target crown.

Weight: 5-3/4 lbs., (6-3/4 lbs. Magnum). **Stock:** Raised comb Monte Carlo composite. **Features:** Fluted barrel, aluminum bedding block, Pachmayr decelerator, 54-degree bolt lift, adj. trigger.

Price: $1,459.00
Price: Magnum $1,517.00

WINCHESTER MODEL 70 CLASSIC SPORTER LT

Caliber: 25-06, 270 Win., 30-06, 7mm STW, 7mm Rem. Mag., 300 Win. Mag., 338 Win. Mag., 3-shot magazine; 5-shot for 25-06, 270 Win., 30-06. **Barrel:** 24", 26" for magnums. **Weight:** 7-3/4 to 8 lbs. **Length:** 46-3/4" overall (26" bbl.). **Stock:** American walnut with cut checkering and satin finish. Classic style with straight comb. **Sights:** None furnished. Drilled and tapped for scope mounting. **Features:** Uses pre-64-type action with controlled round feeding. Three-position safety, stainless steel magazine follower; rubber butt pad; epoxy bedded receiver recoil lug. From U.S. Repeating Arms Co.

Price: 25-06, 270, 30-06.............................. $727.00
Price: Other calibers $756.00
Price: Left-hand, 270 or 30-06 .... $762.00
Price: Left-hand, 7mm Rem. Mag or 300 Win. Mag. $793.00

Winchester Model 70 Classic Stainless Rifle

Same as Model 70 Classic Sporter except stainless steel barrel and pre-64-style action with controlled round feeding and matte gray finish, black composite stock impregnated with fiberglass and graphite, contoured rubber recoil pad. No sights (except 375 H&H). Available in 270 Win., 30-06, 7mm STW, 7mm Rem. Mag., 300 Win. Mag., 300 Ultra Mag., 338 Win. Mag., 375 H&H Mag. (24" barrel), 3- or 5-shot magazine. Weighs 7-1/2 lbs. Introduced 1994.

Price: 270, 30-06 .... $800.00
Price: 375 H&H Mag., with sights $924.00
Price: Other calibers $829.00

Winchester Model 70 Classic Featherweight

Winchester Model 70 Classic Super Grade

Winchester Model 70 WSM

Winchester Model 70 Classic Featherweight

Same as Model 70 Classic except action bedded in standard-grade walnut stock. Available in 22-250, 243, 6.5x55, 308, 7mm-08, 270 Win., 30 06. Drilled and tapped for scope mounts. Weighs 7 lbs. Introduced 1992.

Price: **$726.00**

Winchester Model 70 Classic Compact

Similar to Classic Featherweight except scaled down for smaller shooters. 20" barrel, 12-1/2" length of pull. Pre-64-type action. Available in 243, 308 or 7mm-08. Introduced 1998. Made in U.S.A. by U.S. Repeating Arms Co.

Price: **$740.00**

WINCHESTER MODEL 70 CLASSIC SUPER GRADE

Caliber: 25-06, 270, 30-06, 5-shot magazine; 7mm Rem. Mag., 300 Win. Mag., 338 Win. Mag., 3-shot magazine. **Barrel:** 24", 26" for magnums. **Weight:** 7-3/4 lbs. to 8 lbs. **Length:** 44-1/2" overall (24" bbl.) **Stock:** Walnut with straight comb, sculptured cheekpiece, wraparound cut checkering, tapered forend, solid rubber butt pad. **Sights:** None furnished; comes with scope bases and rings. **Features:** Controlled round feeding with stainless steel claw extractor, bolt guide rail, three-position safety; all steel bottom metal, hinged floorplate, stainless magazine follower. Introduced 1994. From U.S. Repeating Arms Co.

Price: 25-06, 270, 30-06 .... **$995.00**
Price: Other calibers **$1,024.00**

WINCHESTER MODEL 70 WSM RIFLES

Caliber: 300 WSM, 3-shot magazine. **Barrel:** 24". **Weight:** 7-1/4 to 7-3/4 lbs. **Length:** 44" overall. **Stock:** Checkered walnut, black synthetic or laminated wood. **Sights:** None. **Features:** Model 70 designed for the new 300 Winchester Short Magnum cartridge. Short-action receiver, three-position safety, knurled bolt handle. Introduced 2001. From U.S. Repeating Arms Co.

Price: Classic Featherweight WSM (checkered walnut stock and forearm) **$769.00**
Price: Classic Stainless WSM (black syn. stock, stainless steel bbl.) **$829.00**
Price: Classic Laminated WSM (laminated wood stock) **$793.00**

H&R Ultra Hunter

New England Firearms Handi-Rifle

New England Firearms Super Light

BROWNING MODEL 1885 HIGH WALL SINGLE SHOT RIFLE
Caliber: 22-250, 30-06, 270, 7mm Rem. Mag., 454 Casull, 45-70. **Barrel:** 28". **Weight:** 8 lbs., 12 oz. **Length:** 43-1/2" overall. **Stock:** Walnut with straight grip, Schnabel forend. **Sights:** None furnished; drilled and tapped for scope mounting. **Features:** Replica of J.M. Browning's highwall falling block rifle. Octagon barrel with recessed muzzle. Imported from Japan by Browning. Introduced 1985.
Price: **$1,027.00**

HARRINGTON & RICHARDSON ULTRA HUNTER RIFLE
Caliber: 25-06, 308, 450 Marlin. **Barrel:** 22", 26". **Weight:** About 7.5 lbs. **Stock:** Cinnamon laminate. **Sights:** None furnished. Drilled and tapped for scope mounting. **Features:** Break-open action with side-lever release, positive ejection. Scope mount. Blued receiver and barrel. Swivel studs. Introduced 1993. From H&R 1871, Inc.
Price: **$332.00**

MOSSBERG SSi-ONE SINGLE SHOT RIFLE
Caliber: 223 Rem., 22-250 Rem., 243 Win., 270 Win., 308 Rem., 30-06. **Barrel:** 24". **Weight:** 8 lbs. **Length:** 40". **Stock:** Satin-finished walnut, fluted and checkered; sling-swivel studs. **Sights:** None (scope base furnished). **Features:** Frame accepts interchangeable barrels, including 12 gauge, fully rifled slug barrel and 12 ga., 3-1/2" chambered barrel with Ulti-Full Turkey choke tube. Lever-opening, break-action design; single-stage trigger; ambidextrous, top-tang safety; internal eject/extract selector. Introduced 2000. From Mossberg.
Price: SSi-One Sporter (standard barrel) or 12 ga.,
3-1/2" chamber **$459.00**
Price: SSi-One 12 gauge Slug (fully rifled barrel, no sights,
scope base) **$480.00**

NEW ENGLAND FIREARMS HANDI-RIFLE
Caliber: 22 Hornet, 223, 243, 30-30, 270, 280 Rem., 308, 30-06, 357 Mag., 44 Mag., 4570. **Barrel:** 22", 24"; 26" for 280 Rem. **Weight:** 7 lbs. **Stock:**
Walnut-finished hardwood; black rubber recoil pad. **Sights:** Ramp front, folding rear (22 Hornet, 30-30, 45-70). Drilled and tapped for scope mount; 223, 243, 270, 280, 30-06 have no open sights, come with scope mounts. **Features:** Break-open action with side-lever release. The 223, 243, 270 and 30-06 have recoil pad and Monte Carlo stock for shooting with scope. Swivel studs on all models. Blue finish. Introduced 1989. From New England Firearms.
Price: **$270.00**
Price: 280 Rem., 26" barrel **$270.00**
Price: Synthetic Handi-Rifle (black polymer stock and forend, swivels,
recoil pad) **$281.00**
Price: Handi-Rifle Youth (223, 243) **$270.00**
Price: Stainless Handi-Rifle (223 Rem., 243 Rem.) **$337.00**

New England Firearms Super Light Rifle
Similar to Handi-Rifle except new barrel taper, shorter 20" barrel with recessed muzzle, special lightweight synthetic stock and forend. No sights furnished on 223 and 243 versions, but have factory-mounted scope base and offset hammer spur; Monte Carlo stock; 22 Hornet has ramp front, fully adjustable open rear. Overall length 36", weight is 5.5 lbs. Introduced 1997. Made in U.S.A. by New England Firearms.
Price: 22 Hornet, 223 Rem. or 243 Win. **$281.00**

ROSSI CENTERFIRE/SHOTGUN "MATCHED PAIRS"
Caliber: 12 ga./223 Rem., full size, 20 ga./223 Rem. full & youth, 12 ga./342 Win. full, 20 ga./243 Win. full & youth, 12 ga./308 Win. full, 20 ga./308 Win. full & youth, 12 ga./30-06 Spfld. full, 20 ga./30-06 Spfld. full, 12 ga./270 Win. full, 20 ga./270 Win. full. **Barrel:** 28"/23" full, 22"/22" youth. **Weight:** 57 lbs. **Stock:** Straight, exotic woods, walnut finish and swivels with white line space and recoil pad. **Sights:** Bead front shotgun, fully adjustable rifle, drilled and tapped. **Features:** Break Open, positive ejection, internal transfer bar mechanism and manual external safety. Trigger block system included.
Price: **350.00**

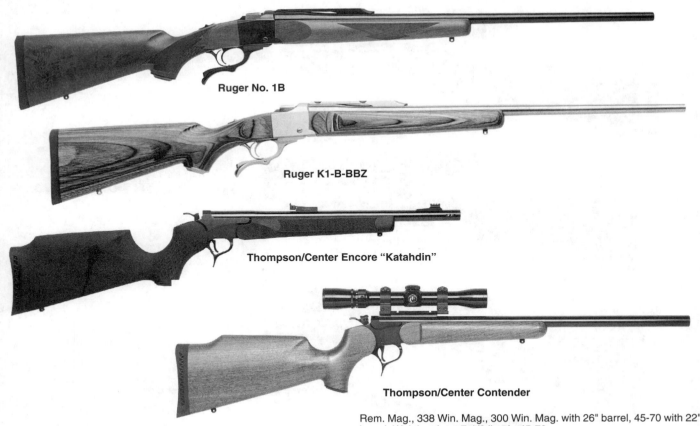

Ruger No. 1B

Ruger K1-B-BBZ

Thompson/Center Encore "Katahdin"

Thompson/Center Contender

RUGER NO. 1B SINGLE SHOT

Caliber: 218 Bee, 22 Hornet, 220 Swift, 22-250, 223, 243, 6mm Rem., 25 06, 257 Roberts, 270, 280, 30-06, 7mm Rem. Mag., 300 Win. Mag., 308 Win., 338 Win. Mag., 270 Wea., 300 Wea. **Barrel:** 26" round tapered with quarter-rib; with Ruger 1" rings. **Weight:** 8 lbs. **Length:** 42-1/4" overall. **Stock:** Walnut, two-piece, checkered pistol grip and semi-beavertail forend. **Sights:** None, 1" scope rings supplied for integral mounts. **Features:** Underlever, hammerless falling block design has auto ejector, top tang safety.

Price: 1B	$875.00
Price: Barreled action	$600.00
Price: K1BBBZ Stainless steel, laminated stock 25-06, 7mm mag, 7mm STW, 300 Win Mag., 243 Win., 30-06, 308 Win.	$910.00

Ruger No. 1A Light Sporter

Similar to the No. 1B Standard Rifle except has lightweight 22" barrel, Alexander Henry-style forend, adjustable folding leaf rear sight on quarter-rib, dovetailed ramp front with gold bead. Calibers 243, 30-06, 270 and 7x57. Weighs about 7-1/4 lbs.

Price: No. 1A	$875.00
Price: Barreled action	$600.00

Ruger No. 1 RSI International

Similar to the No. 1B Standard Rifle except has lightweight 20" barrel, full length International-style forend with loop sling swivel, adjustable folding leaf rear sight on quarter-rib, ramp front with gold bead. Calibers 243, 30-06, 270 and 7x57. Weight is about 7-1/4 lbs.

Price: No. 1 RSI	$890.00
Price: Barreled action	$600.00

Ruger No. 1S Medium Sporter

Similar to the No. 1B Standard Rifle except has Alexander Henry-style forend, adjustable folding leaf rear sight on quarter-rib, ramp front sight base and dovetail-type gold bead front sight. Calibers: 218 Bee, 7mm Rem. Mag., 338 Win. Mag., 300 Win. Mag. with 26" barrel, 45-70 with 22" barrel. Weighs about 7-1/2 lbs. In 45-70.

Price: No. 1S	$875.00
Price: Barreled action	$600.00
Price: K1SBBZ, S/S, 45-70	$910.00

THOMPSON/CENTER ENCORE RIFLE

Caliber: 22-250, 223, 243, 25-06, 270, 7mm-08, 308, 30-06, 7mm Rem. Mag., 300 Win. Mag. **Barrel:** 24", 26". **Weight:** 6 lbs., 12 oz. (24" barrel). **Length:** 38-1/2" (24" barrel). **Stock:** American walnut. Monte Carlo-style; Schnabel forend or black composite. **Sights:** Ramp-style white bead front, fully adjustable leaf-type rear. **Features:** Interchangeable barrels; action opens by squeezing trigger guard; drilled and tapped for T/C scope mounts; polished blue finish. Introduced 1996. Made in U.S.A. by Thompson/Center Arms.

Price:	$599 to $632.00
Price: Extra barrels	$270.00

Thompson/Center Stainless Encore Rifle

Similar to blued Encore except stainless steel with blued sights, black composite stock and forend. Available in 22-250, 223, 7mm 08, 30-06, 308. Introduced 1999. Made in U.S.A. by Thompson/Center Arms.

Price:	$670.00 to $676.00

THOMPSON/CENTER ENCORE "KATAHDIN" CARBINE

Caliber: 45-70 Gov't., 444 Marlin, 450 Marlin. **Barrel:** 18" with muzzle tamer. **Stock:** Composite.

Price:	$619.00

Thompson/Center G2 Contender Rifle

Similar to the G2 Contender pistol, but in a compact rifle format. **Features:** Interchangeable 23" barrels, chambered for 17 HMR, 22LR, 223 Rem., 30-30 Win. and 45-70 Gov't; plus a 45 Cal. Muzzleloading barrel. All of the 16-1/4" and 21" barrels made for the old style Contender will fit. **Weight:** 5-1/2 lbs. Introduced 2003. Made in U.S.A. by Thompson/Center Arms.

Price:	$592.40 to $607.00

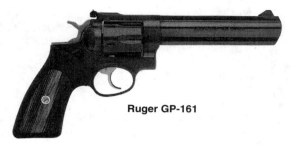

Ruger GP-161

Ruger KGP-141

Ruger Redhawk

Ruger Super Redhawk

COLT ANACONDA

Caliber: 44 Mag., 6-shot. **Barrel:** 4", 6", 8". **Weight:** 53 oz. (8"). **Length:** 11-1/2" overall (4" bbl.) **Grips:** Rubber combat. **Sights:** Red ramp front, white outline rear adjustable for windage and elevation. **Features:** Avail-Target trigger; drilled and tapped for scope mounts.
Price: 44 Mag., 4", 6", 8" . . . . Contact Mfr.

COLT PYTHON ELITE

Caliber: 357 Mag., 6-shot. **Barrel:** 4", 6". **Weight:** 53 oz. (8"). **Length:** 13-5/8" overall (6" bbl.) **Grips:** Walnut. **Sights:** Red ramp front, white outline rear adjustable for windage and elevation. **Features:** Blued or stainless finish.
Price: 357 Mag., 4", 6" . . . . Contact Mfr.

DAN WESSON FIREARMS MODEL 41/741, 44/744 and 45/745 REVOLVERS

Caliber: 41 Mag., 44 Mag., 45 Colt, 6-shot. **Barrel:** 4", 6", 8", 10"; interchangeable; 4", 6", 8" Compensated. **Weight:** 48 oz. (4"). **Length:** 12" overall (6" bbl.) **Grips:** Smooth. **Sights:** 1/8" serrated front, white outline rear adjustable for windage and elevation. **Features:** Available in blue or stainless steel. Smooth, wide trigger with adjustable overtravel, wide hammer spur. Available in Pistol Pac set also. Reintroduced 1997. Contact Dan Wesson Firearms for complete price list.
Price: 41 Mag., 4", vent heavy (blue or stainless) $643.00
Price: 44 Mag., 6", vent heavy (blue or stainless) $689.00
Price: 45 Colt, 8", vent heavy (blue or stainless) $766.00
Price: Compensated models (all calibers) . . . . $812.00 to $934.00

DAN WESSON FIREARMS LARGE FRAME SERIES REVOLVERS

Caliber: 41, 741-41 Magnum; 44, 744-44 Magnum; 45, 745-45 Long Colt; 360, 7360-357; 460, 7460-45. **Barrel:** 2"-10". **Weight:** 49 oz.-69 oz. **Grips:** Standard, Hogue rubber Gripper Grips. **Sights:** Standard front, serrated ramp with color insert. Standard rear, adjustable wide notch. Other sight options available. **Features:** Available in blue or stainless steel. Smooth, wide trigger with overtravel, wide hammer spur. Double and single action.
Price: . . . . $769.00 to $889.00

RUGER GP100 REVOLVERS

Caliber: 38 Spec., 357 Mag., 6-shot. **Barrel:** 3", 3" full shroud, 4", 4" full shroud, 6", 6" full shroud. **Weight:** 3" barrel-35 oz., 3" full shroud-36 oz., 4" barrel-37 oz., 4" full shroud-38 oz. **Sights:** Fixed; adjustable on 4" full shroud, all 6" barrels. **Grips:** Ruger Santoprene Cushioned Grip with Goncalo Alves inserts. **Features:** Uses action, frame incorporating improvements and features of both the Security-Six and Redhawk revolvers. Full length, short ejector shroud. Satin blue and stainless steel.

Price: GP141 (357, 4" full shroud, adj. sights, blue). $499.00
Price: GP160 (357, 6", adj. sights, blue) $499.00
Price: GP161 (357, 6" full shroud, adj. sights, blue), 46 oz. $499.00
Price: GPF340 (357, 4") $495.00
Price: GPF341 (357, 4" full shroud) $495.00
Price: KGP141 (357, 4" full shroud, adj. sights, stainless) $555.00
Price: KGP160 (357, 6", adj. sights, stainless), 43 oz. $555.00
Price: KGP161 (357, 6" full shroud, adj. sights, stainless) 46 oz. $555.00
Price: KGPF340 (357, 4", stainless), KGPF840 (38 Special) . . . $555.00
Price: KGPF341 (357, 4" full shroud, stainless) $555.00
Price: KGPF840 (38 Special, 4", stainless) $555.00

RUGER REDHAWK

Caliber: 44 Rem. Mag., 45 Colt, 6-shot. **Barrel:** 5-1/2", 7-1/2". **Weight:** About 54 oz. (7-1/2" bbl.). **Length:** 13" overall (7-1/2" barrel). **Grips:** Square butt cushioned grip panels. **Sights:** Interchangeable Patridge type front, rear adjustable for windage and elevation. **Features:** Stainless steel, brushed satin finish, blued ordnance steel. 9-1/2" sight radius. Introduced 1979.
Price: Blued, 44 Mag., 5-1/2" RH445, 7-1/2" RH44 . . . . $585.00
Price: Blued, 44 Mag., 7-1/2" RH44R, with scope mount, rings . $625.00
Price: Stainless, 44 Mag., KRH445, 5-1/2", 7-1/2" KRH44 . . . . . $645.00
Price: Stainless, 44 Mag., 7-1/2", with scope mount, rings
KRH44R $685.00
Price: Stainless, 45 Colt, KRH455, 5-1/2", 7-1/2" KRH45 . . . . . . $645.00
Price: Stainless, 45 Colt, 7-1/2", with scope mount and rings
KRH45R $685.00

Ruger Super Redhawk Revolver

Similar to standard Redhawk except has heavy extended frame with Ruger Integral Scope Mounting System on wide topstrap. Also available 454 Casull and 480 Ruger. Wide hammer spur lowered for better scope clearance. Incorporates mechanical design features and improvements of GP 100. Choice of 7-1/2" or 9-1/2" barrel, both ramp front sight base with Redhawk-style Interchangeable Insert sight blades, adjustable rear sight. Comes with Ruger "Cushioned Grip" panels with wood panels. Target gray stainless steel. Introduced 1987.
Price: KSRH7 (7-1/2"), KSRH9 (9-1/2"), 44 Mag $685.00
Price: KSRH7454 (7-1/2") 454 Casull, 9-1/2 KSRH9454 . . . . . . $775.00
Price: KSRH7480 (7-1/2") 480 Ruger $775.00
Price: KSRH9480 (9-1/2") 480 Ruger $775.00

Smith & Wesson Model 629 Classic DX

Smith & Wesson Model 500

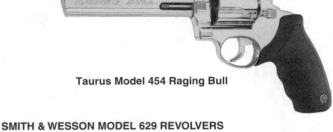

Taurus Model 454 Raging Bull

Taurus Raging Bull Model 416

SMITH & WESSON MODEL 629 REVOLVERS

Caliber: 44 Magnum, 44 S&W Special, 6-shot. **Barrel:** 5", 6", 8-3/8". **Weight:** 47 oz. (6" bbl.). **Length:** 11-3/8" overall (6" bbl.). **Grips:** Soft rubber; wood optional. **Sights:** 1/8" red ramp front, white outline rear, internal lock, adjustable for windage and elevation.

Price: Model 629, 4" $717.00
Price: Model 629, 6" $739.00
Price: Model 629, 8-3/8" barrel $756.00

Smith & Wesson Model 629 Classic Revolver

Similar to standard Model 629, full lug 5", 6-1/2" or 8-3/8" barrel, chamfered front of cylinder, interchangeable red ramp front sight with adjustable white outline rear, Hogue grips with S&W monogram, frame is drilled and tapped for scope mounting. Factory accurizing and endurance packages. Overall length with 5" barrel is 10-1/2"; weighs 51 oz. Introduced 1990.

Price: Model 629 Classic (stainless), 5", 6-1/2" $768.00
Price: As above, 8-3/8" $793.00
Price: Model 629 with HiViz front sight $814.00

Smith & Wesson Model 629 Classic DX Revolver

Similar to Model 629 Classic, offered only with 6-1/2" or 8-3/8" full-lug barrel, five front sights: red ramp, black Patridge, black Patridge with gold bead, black ramp, black Patridge with white dot, white outline rear sight, adjustable sight, internal lock. Hogue combat-style and wood round butt grip. Introduced 1991.

Price: Model 629 Classic DX, 6-1/2" $986.00
Price: As above, 8-3/8" $1,018.00

SMITH & WESSON MODEL 66 STAINLESS COMBAT MAGNUM

Caliber: 357 Mag. and 38 Spec. +P, 6-shot. **Barrel:** 2-1/2", 4", 6". **Weight:** 36 oz. (4" barrel). **Length:** 9-9/16" overall. **Grips:** Soft rubber. **Sights:** Red ramp front, micro-click rear adjustable for windage and elevation. **Features:** Satin finish stainless steel. Internal lock.

Price: 4" $579.00; 6" $608.00

Smith & Wesson Model 686 Magnum PLUS Revolver

Similar to the Model 66 except has 7-shot cylinder, 2-1/2", 4" or 6" barrel. Weighs 34-1/2 oz., overall length 7-1/2" (2-1/2" barrel). Hogue rubber grips. Internal lock. Introduced 1996. Made in U.S.A. by Smith & Wesson.

Price: 4" barrel $653.00; 6" barrel $663.00

SMITH & WESSON MODEL 610 CLASSIC HUNTER REVOLVER

Caliber: 10mm, 40 S&W, 6-shot cylinder. **Barrel:** 6-1/2" full lug. **Weight:** 52 oz. **Length:** 12" overall. **Grips:** Hogue rubber combat. **Sights:** Interchangeable blade front, micro-click rear adjustable for windage and

elevation. **Features:** Stainless steel construction; target hammer, target trigger; unfluted cylinder; drilled and tapped for scope mounting. Introduced 1998.

Price: $785.00

SMITH & WESSON MODEL 657 REVOLVER

Caliber: 41 Mag., 6-shot. **Barrel:** 7-1/2" full lug. **Weight:** 48 oz. **Grips:** Soft rubber. **Sights:** Pinned 1/8" red ramp front, micro-click rear adjustable for windage and elevation. Target hammer, drilled and tapped, unfluted cylinder. **Features:** Stainless steel construction.

Price: $706.00

SMITH & WESSON MODEL 500

Caliber: 50. **Barrel:** 4 and 8-3/8". **Weight:** 72.5 oz. **Length:** NA. **Grips:** Rubber. **Sights:** Interchangeable blade, front, adjustable rear. **Features:** Built on the massive, new XFrame, recoil compensator, ball detent cylinder latch. Made in U.S.A. by Smith & Wesson.

Price: $1,150.00

TAURUS MODEL 425/627 TRACKER REVOLVERS

Caliber: 357 Mag., 7-shot; 41 Mag., 5-shot. **Barrel:** 4" and 6". **Weight:** 28.840 oz. (titanium) 24.328. (6"). **Grips:** Rubber. **Sights:** Fixed front, adjustable rear. **Features:** Double action stainless steel, Shadow Gray or Total Titanium; vent rib (steel models only); integral keylock action. Imported by Taurus International.

Price: . . . . $508.00 to $516.00
Price: Total Titanium $688.00

TAURUS MODEL 460 "TRACKER"

Caliber: 45 Colt, 5-shot. **Barrel:** 4" or 6". **Weight:** 33/38.4 oz. **Grips:** Rubber. **Sights:** Adjustable. **Features:** Double action, ventilated rib, matte stainless steel, comes with five "Stellar" fullmoon clips.

Price: $516.00
Price: (Shadow gray, Total Titanium) $688.00

TAURUS MODEL 444/454/480 RAGING BULL REVOLVERS

Caliber: 44 Mag., 45 LC, 454 Casull, 480 Ruger, 5-shot. **Barrel:** 5", 6-1/2", 8-3/8". **Weight:** 53-63 oz. **Length:** 12" overall (6-1/2" barrel). **Grips:** Soft black rubber. **Sights:** Patridge front, adjustable rear. **Features:** Double action, ventilated rib, ported, integral key lock. Introduced 1997. Imported by Taurus International.

Price: Blue . . . . $578.00 to $797.00; matte stainless $641.00 to $859.00

TAURUS RAGING BULL MODEL 416

Caliber: 41 Magnum, 6-shot. **Barrel:** 6-1/2". **Weight:** 61.9 oz. **Grips:** Rubber. **Sights:** Adjustable. **Features:** Double action, ported, ventilated rib, matte stainless, integral keylock.

Price: $641.00

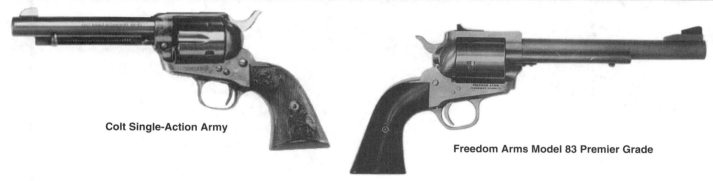

Colt Single-Action Army

Freedom Arms Model 83 Premier Grade

Freedom Arms Model 83 Field Grade

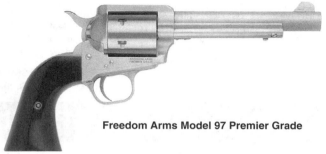

Freedom Arms Model 97 Premier Grade

COLT SINGLE-ACTION ARMY REVOLVER
Caliber: 357 Mag., 38 Special, .32-20, 44-40, 45 Colt, 6-shot. **Barrel:** 4-3/4", 5-1/2", 7-1/2". **Weight:** 40 oz. (4-3/4" barrel). **Length:** 10-1/4" overall (4-3/4" barrel). **Grips:** Black Eagle composite. **Sights:** Blade front, notch rear. **Features:** Available in full nickel finish with nickel grip medallions, or Royal Blue with color casehardened frame. Reintroduced 1992.
Price: $1,380.00

FREEDOM ARMS MODEL 83 PREMIER GRADE REVOLVER
Caliber: 357 Mag., 41 Mag., 44 Mag., 454 Casull, 475 Linebaugh, 50 AE, 5-shot. **Barrel:** 4-3/4", 6", 7-1/2", 9" (357 Mag. only), 10". **Weight:** 52.8 oz. **Length:** 13" (7-1/2" bbl.). **Grips:** Impregnated hardwood. **Sights:** Blade front, notch or adjustable rear. **Features:** All stainless steel construction; sliding bar safety system. Lifetime warranty. Made in U.S.A. by Freedom Arms, Inc.
Price: 454 Casull, 475 Linebaugh, 50 AE. $2,058.00
Price: 454 Casull, fixed sight $1,979.00
Price: 357 Mag., 41 Mag., 44 Mag. $1,976.00
Price: 44 Mag., fixed sight $1,911.00

Freedom Arms Model 83 Field Grade Revolver
Model 83 frame. Weighs 52-56 oz. Adjustable rear sight, replaceable front blade, matte finish, Pachmayr grips. All stainless steel. Introduced 1988. Made in U.S.A. by Freedom Arms Inc.
Price: 454 Casull, 475 Linebaugh, 50 AE, adj. sights. $1,591.00
Price: 454 Casull, fixed sights $1,553.00
Price: 357 Mag., 41 Mag., 44 Mag. $1,527.00

FREEDOM ARMS MODEL 97 PREMIER GRADE REVOLVER
Caliber: 22 LR, 357 Mag., 41 Mag., 44 Special, 45 Colt, 5-shot. **Barrel:** 4-1/2", 5-1/2", 7-1/2", 10". **Weight:** 37 oz. (45 Colt 5-1/2"). **Length:** 10-3/4" (5-1/2" bbl.). **Grips:** Impregnated hardwood. **Sights:** Adjustable rear, replaceable blade front. **Features:** Stainless steel, brushed finish, automatic transfer bar safety system. Introduced in 1997. Made in U.S.A. by Freedom Arms.
Price: 357 Mag., 41 Mag., 45 Colt $1,668.00
Price: 357 Mag., 45 Colt, fixed sight $1,576.00

RUGER NEW MODEL BLACKHAWK AND BLACKHAWK CONVERTIBLE
Caliber: 30 Carbine, 357 Mag./38 Spec., 41 Mag., 45 Colt, 6-shot. **Barrel:** 4-5/8" or 5-1/2", either caliber; 7-1/2" (30 Carbine and 45 Colt). **Weight:**

Ruger Blackhawk

42 oz. (6-1/2" bbl.). **Length:** 12-1/4" overall (5-1/2" bbl.). **Grips:** American walnut. **Sights:** 1/8" ramp front, micro-click rear adjustable for windage and elevation. **Features:** Ruger transfer bar safety system, independent firing pin, hardened chrome moly steel frame, music wire springs throughout. Case and lock included.
Price: Blue, 357 Mag., 4-5/8", 6-1/2" (BN34, BN36) $435.00
Price: As above, stainless (KBN34, KBN36) $530.00
Price: Blue, 357 Mag./9mm Convertible, 4-5/8", 6-1/2" (BN34X, BN36X) includes extra cylinder $489.00
Price: Blue, 41 Mag., 4-5/8", 6-1/2" (BN41, BN42) $435.00
Price: Blue, 45 Colt, 4-5/8", 5-1/2", 7-1/2" (BN44, BN455, BN45) $435.00
Price: Stainless, 45 Colt, 4-5/8", 7-1/2" (KBN44, KBN45) $530.00
Price: Blue, 45 Colt/45 ACP Convertible, 4-5/8", 5-1/2" (BN44X, BN455X) includes extra cylinder $489.00

Ruger Bisley Single-Action Revolver
Similar to standard Blackhawk, hammer is lower with smoothly curved, deeply checkered wide spur. The trigger is strongly curved with wide smooth surface. Longer grip frame has handfilling shape. Adjustable rear sight, rampstyle front. Unfluted cylinder and roll engraving, adjustable sights. Chambered for 357, 44 Mags. and 45 Colt; 7-1/2" barrel; overall length of 13"; weighs 48 oz. Plastic lockable case. Introduced 1985.
Price: RB35W, 357Mag, RBD44W, 44Mag, RB45W, 45 Colt . . . $535.00

SINGLE ACTION REVOLVERS

Ruger Bisley Single-Action

Ruger Super Blackhawk Hunter

RUGER NEW MODEL SUPER BLACKHAWK
Caliber: 44 Mag., 6-shot. Also fires 44 Spec. **Barrel:** 4-5/8", 5-1/2", 7-1/2", 10-1/2" bull. **Weight:** 48 oz. (7-1/2" bbl.), 51 oz. (10-1/2" bbl.). **Length:** 13-3/8" overall (7-1/2" bbl.). **Grips:** American walnut. **Sights:** 1/8" ramp front, microclick rear adjustable for windage and elevation. **Features:** Ruger transfer bar safety system, fluted or unfluted cylinder, steel grip and cylinder frame, round or square back trigger guard, wide serrated trigger, wide spur hammer. With case and lock.
Price: Blue, 4-5/8", 5-1/2", 7-1/2" (S458N, S45N, S47N) **$519.00**
Price: Blue, 10-1/2" bull barrel (S411N) **$529.00**

Price: Stainless, 4-5/8", 5-1/2", 7-1/2" (KS458N, KS45N, KS47N) **$535.00**
Price: Stainless, 10-1/2" bull barrel (KS411N) **$545.00**

RUGER NEW MODEL SUPER BLACKHAWK HUNTER
Caliber: 44 Mag., 6-shot. **Barrel:** 7-1/2", full-length solid rib, unfluted cylinder. **Weight:** 52 oz. **Length:** 13-5/8". **Grips:** Black laminated wood. **Sights:** Adjustable rear, replaceable front blade. **Features:** Reintroduced Ultimate SA revolver. Includes instruction manual, high-impact case, set 1" medium scope rings, gun lock, ejector rod as standard.
Price: **$639.00**

SINGLE-SHOT PISTOLS

Maximum Single Shot

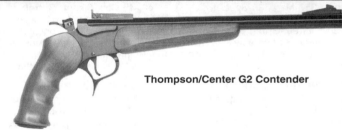

Thompson/Center G2 Contender

MAXIMUM SINGLE-SHOT PISTOL
Caliber: 22 LR, 22 Hornet, 22 BR, 22 PPC, 223 Rem., 22-250, 6mm BR, 6mm PPC, 243, 250 Savage, 6.5mm-35M, 270 MAX, 270 Win., 7mm TCU, 7mm BR, 7mm-35, 7mm INTR, 7mm-08, 7mm Rocket, 7mm Super-Mag., 30 Herrett, 30 Carbine, 30-30, 308 Win., 30x39, 32-20, 350 Rem. Mag., 357 Mag., 357 Maximum, 358 Win., 375 H&H, 44 Mag., 454 Casull. **Barrel:** 8-3/4", 10-1/2", 14". **Weight:** 61 oz. (10-1/2" bbl.); 78 oz. (14" bbl.). **Length:** 15", 18-1/2" overall (with 10-1/2" and 14" bbl., respectively). **Grips:** Smooth walnut stocks and forend. Also available with 17" finger groove grip. **Sights:** Ramp front, fully adjustable open rear. **Features:** Falling block action; drilled and tapped for M.O.A. scope mounts; integral grip frame/receiver; adjustable trigger; Douglas barrel (interchangeable). Introduced 1983. Made in U.S.A. by M.O.A. Corp.
Price: Stainless receiver, blue barrel **$799.00**
Price: Stainless receiver, stainless barrel **$883.00**
Price: Extra blued barrel **$254.00**
Price: Extra stainless barrel **$317.00**
Price: Scope mount **$60.00**

SAVAGE STRIKER BOLT-ACTION HUNTING HANDGUN
Caliber: 223, 243, 7mm-08, 308, 300 WSM 2-shot mag. **Barrel:** 14". **Weight:** About 5 lbs. **Length:** 22-1/2" overall. **Stock:** Black composite ambidextrous midgrip; grooved forend; "Dual Pillar" bedding. **Sights:** None furnished; drilled and tapped for scope mounting. **Features:** Short left-hand bolt with right-hand ejection; free-floated barrel; uses Savage Model 110 rifle scope rings/bases. Introduced 1998. Made in U.S.A. by Savage Arms, Inc.

Price: Model 503 (blued barrel and action) **$285.00**
Price: Model 503 R17FSS (stainless barrel and action) **$281.00**
Price: Model 516FSAK black stock (ss, aMB, 300WSM) **$260.00**

THOMPSON/CENTER ENCORE PISTOL
Caliber: 22-250, 223, 260 Rem., 7mm-08, 243, 308, 270, 30-06, 375 JDJ, 204 Ruger, 44 Mag., 454 Casull, 480 Ruger, 444 Marlin single shot, 450 Marlin with muzzle tamer, no sights. **Barrel:** 12", 15", tapered round. **Weight:** NA. **Length:** 21" overall with 12" barrel. **Grips:** American walnut with finger grooves, walnut forend. **Sights:** Blade on ramp front, adjustable rear, or none. **Features:** Interchangeable barrels; action opens by squeezing the trigger guard; drilled and tapped for scope mounting; blue finish. Announced 1996. Made in U.S.A. by Thompson/Center Arms.
Price: .... **$578.00** to **$641.00**

Thompson/Center Stainless Encore Pistol
Similar to blued Encore, made of stainless steel, available with 15" barrel in 223, 22-250, 243 Win., 7mm-08, 308, 30-06 Sprgfld., 45-70 Gov't., 45-410 VR. With black rubber grip and forend. Made in U.S.A. by Thompson/Center Arms.
Price: .... **$633.00** to **$670.00**

Thompson/Center G2 Contender Pistol
A second generation Contender pistol maintaining the same barrel interchangeability with older Contender barrels and their corresponding forends (except Herrett forend). The G2 frame will not accept oldstyle grips due to the change in grip angle. Incorporates an automatic hammer block safety with builtin interlock. Features include trigger adjustable for overtravel, adjustable rear sight; ramp front sight blade, blued steel finish.
Price: **$566.75**

Benelli M1 Field Camouflage

Benelli Super Black Eagle

Browning Gold Deer Hunter

Remington Model 1187 Premier

Remington Model 1187 SPS Deer

BENELLI M1 FIELD SHOTGUN
Gauge: 12, 20 ga. **Barrel:** 24" rifled barrel. **Weight:** 7 lbs., 4 oz. **Stock:** High impact polymer. **Sights:** Iron sights. **Features:** Sporting version of the military & police gun. Uses the rotating Montefeltro bolt system. Imported from Italy by Benelli U.S.A.
Price: . . . (Synthetic) **$985.00**; (Wood) **$1,000.00**; (Timber HD) **$1,085.00**
Price: 24" rifled barrel (Synthetic) **$1,060.00**; Timber HD **$1,165.00**
Price: Synthetic stock, left-hand version (24", 26", 28" brls.) . . **$1,005.00**
Price: Timber HD camo left-hand, 21", 24" barrel **$1,105.00**
Price: MI Field Steady-grip **$1,175.00**

BENELLI SUPER BLACK EAGLE SLUG GUN
Gauge: 12, 3" chamber. **Barrel:** 24" rifled barrel, drilled and tapped for scope. **Weight:** 7 lbs., 8 oz. **Length:** 45.5" overall. **Stock:** Polymer. **Sights:** Iron. **Features:** Matte finish receiver; uses Montefeltro inertia recoil bolt system. Introduced 1991. Imported from Italy by Benelli U.S.A.
Price: **$1,345.00**

BROWNING GOLD RIFLED DEER HUNTER AUTO SHOTGUN
Gauge: 12, 3" or 20, 3" chamber. **Barrel:** 22. **Weight:** 7 lbs., 12 oz. **Length:** 42-1/2"). **Stock:** 14"x1-1/2"x2-1/3"; select walnut with gloss finish; palm swell grip. **Features:** Self-regulating, self-cleaning gas system shoots all loads; lightweight receiver with special nonglare deep black finish; large reversible safety button; large rounded trigger guard, gold trigger. Cantilever scope mount; sling swivel studs. Imported by Browning.

Price: 12 gauge **$887.00**
Price: With Mossy Oak Breakup camouflage **$1,046.00**
Price: 20 ga. (satin-finish walnut stock, 3" chamber) **$987.00**

Browning Gold Deer Stalker
Similar to the Gold Deer Hunter except has black composite stock and forend, fully rifled barrel, cantilever scope mount. Introduced 1999. Imported by Browning.
Price: 12 gauge **$967.00**

REMINGTON MODEL 11-87 PREMIER SLUG GUN
Gauge: 12, 20, 3" chamber. **Barrel:** 21" rifled. **Weight:** About 7-3/4 lbs. **Length:** 41" overall. **Stock:** Walnut with satin or high-gloss finish; cut checkering; solid brown buttpad; no white spacers. **Sights:** Cantilever scope mounts. **Features:** Pressure compensating gas system allows shooting 2-3/4" or 3" loads interchangeably with no adjustments. Stainless magazine tube; redesigned feed latch, barrel support ring on operating bars; pinned forend. Introduced 1987.
Price: Premier cantilever deer barrel, fully-rifled, 21" sling, swivels, Monte Carlo stock **$859.00**

Remington Model 11-87 SPS Deer Shotgun
Similar to the 11-87 Premier except has fully-rifled 21" barrel with rifle sights, black nonreflective, synthetic stock and forend, black carrying sling. Introduced 1993.
Price: **$824.00**
Price: With wood stock (Model 1187 SP Deer Gun) Rem choke, 21" barrel w/rifle sights **$756.00**

Remington Model 11-87 SPS Cantilever

Remington 1100 LT-20 Deer

Traditions ALS 2100

Weatherby SAS Slug

Remington Model 11-87 SPS Cantilever Shotgun

Similar to the 11-87 SPS except has fully rifled barrel; synthetic stock with Monte Carlo comb; cantilever scope mount deer barrel. Comes with sling and swivels. Introduced 1994.

Price: **$872.00**

REMINGTON MODEL 1100 LT-20 SYNTHETIC DEER SHOTGUN

Gauge: 20. **Barrel:** 21" fully rifled. **Weight:** 6-3/4 lbs. **Stock:** Rifle sights, 2-3/4" chamber, and fiberglass-reinforced synthetic stock. Introduced 1997. Made in U.S. A.

Price: **$583.00**

Remington Model 1100 Synthetic Deer Shotgun

Similar to Model 1100 LT20 except 12 gauge, 21" fully rifled barrel with cantilever scope mount and fiberglass-reinforced synthetic stock with Monte Carlo comb. Introduced 1997. Made in U.S. by Remington.

Price: **$629.00**

TRADITIONS ALS 2100 SLUG HUNTER

Gauge: 12, 3" chamber. **Barrel:** 24" fully rifled. **Weight:** 6 lbs., 4 oz. **Length:** 44". **Stock:** Walnut or black composite. **Features:** Gas operated. Adjustable fiber optic sights. Introduced 2001 by Traditions.

Price: Walnut, rifle barrel **$529.00**

Price: Synthetic, rifle barrel **$499.00**

Price: Walnut, cantilever **$549.00**

Price: Synthetic, cantilever **$529.00**

WEATHERBY SAS SLUG GUN

Gauge: 12 ga. **Barrel:** 22". **Stock:** Synthetic. **Sights:** Cantilever scope base. **Features:** Matte blue finish. Easy to shoot, load, clean, lightweight, lessened recoil.

Price: . . . . **$699.00 to 849.00**

Benelli Nova Pump Slug

Browning BPS 10 gauge

Browning BPS 10 gauge
Mossy Oak® Shadow Grass

Ithaca Model 37 Deerslayer II

BENELLI NOVA PUMP SHOTGUN

Gauge: 12, 20. **Barrel:** 18.5". **Stock:** Black synthetic. **Sights:** Adjustable rifle type or ghost ring. **Weight:** 7.2 lbs. **Features:** 2-3/4", 3" chamber (32/1" 12 ga. only). Montefeltro rotating bolt design with dual action bars, magazine cutoff, synthetic trigger assembly, 4-shot magazine. Introduced 1999. Imported from Italy by Benelli USA.
Price: With rifle sights **$355.00**
Price: With ghostring sights **$395.00**

Benelli Nova Pump Rifled Slug Gun

Similar to Nova Pump Slug Gun except has 24" barrel and rifled bore; open rifle sights; synthetic stock; weighs 8.1 pounds.
Price: . . . . (Synthetic) **$500.00**; Timber HD **$575.00**

BROWNING BPS PUMP SHOTGUN

Gauge: 12, 3" chamber. **Barrel:** 22" rifled Buck Special. **Weight:** 7 lbs., 10 oz. **Length:** 42-3/4" overall (28" barrel). **Stock:** 14-1/4"x1-1/2"x2-1/2". Select walnut, semi-beavertail forend, full pistol grip stock. **Features:** Bottom feeding and ejection, receiver top safety, high post vent. rib. Double action bars eliminate binding. Introduced 1977. Imported from Japan by Browning.
Price: 12 ga. Deer Hunter (22" rifled bbl., cantilever mount) **$606.00**

Browning BPS Game Gun Deer Hunter

Similar to the standard BPS except has newly designed receiver/magazine tube/barrel mounting system to eliminate play, heavy 20.5" barrel with rifle type sights with adjustable rear, solid receiver scope mount, "rifle" stock dimensions for scope or open sights, sling swivel studs. Gloss or matte finished wood with checkering, polished blue metal. Introduced 1992.
Price: **$568.00**

ITHACA MODEL 37 DEERSLAYER II PUMP SHOTGUN

Gauge: 12, 16, 20; 3" chamber. **Barrel:** 24", 26", fully rifled. **Weight:** 11 lbs. **Stock:** Cut-checkered American walnut with Monte Carlo comb. **Sights:** Rifle-type. **Features:** Integral barrel and receiver. Bottom ejection. Brushed blue finish. Reintroduced 1997. Made in U.S. by Ithaca Gun Co. Storm models have synthetic stock.
Price: **$633.00**
Price: Smooth Bore Deluxe **$582.00**
Price: Rifled Deluxe **$582.00**
Price: Storm **$399.00**

ITHACA MODEL 37 DEERSLAYER III PUMP SHOTGUN

Gauge: 12, 20, 2-3/4" and 3" chambers. **Barrel:** 26" free floated. **Weight:** 9 lbs. **Stock:** Monte Carlo laminate. **Sights:** Rifled. **Features:** Barrel length gives increased velocity. Trigger and sear set hand filed and stoned for creep free operation. Weaver-style scope base. Swivel studs. Matte blue.
Price: . . . . **Custom order only**

MARLIN 410 LEVER ACTION SHOTGUN

Gauge: 410 caliber, 2-1/2 chamber. **Barrel:** 22" cylinder bore. **Weight:** 7-1/4 lbs. **Length:** 40-1/2" overall. **Stock:** 14"x1-1/2"x2-1/2". Dual Comb. **Sights:** Open rear, brass bead front. **Features:** American black walnut pistol grip stock with fluted comb; cut checkering; rubber rifle butt pad; tough Mar-Shield® finish; blued steel forend cap. Shoots 2-3/4", 3" or 3-1/2" shells. Back bored and ported barrel to reduce recoil, improve patterns. Ambidextrous thumb safety, twin extractors, dual slide bars. Mossberg Cablelock included. Introduced 1988.
Price: . . . . **See dealer**

Winchester 1300 Deer Black Shadow Gun

Winchester 9410

MOSSBERG MODEL 835 ULTIMAG DEER COMBO

Gauge: 12, 3-1/2" chamber. **Barrel:** Ported 24" rifled bore, 24" vent rib. **Weight:** 7-3/4 lbs. **Length:** 48-1/2" overall. **Stock:** 14"x1-1/2"x2-1/2". Dual Comb. **Sights:** White bead front, brass midbead; rifle sights. **Features:** Shoots 2-3/4", 3" or 3-1/2" shells. Back bored and ported barrel to reduce recoil, improve patterns. Ambidextrous thumb safety, twin extractors, dual slide bars. Mossberg Cablelock included. Introduced 1988.
Price: Combos, 24" rifled or smooth bore, rifle sights, 24" vent. rib .. **NA**
Price: AccuMag UltiFull choke tube, Mossy Oak camo finish. **$556.00**

MOSSBERG MODEL 500 SLUGSTER

Gauge: 12, 20, 3" chamber. **Barrel:** 24", ported rifled bore. Integral scope mount. **Weight:** 7-1/4 lbs. **Length:** 44" overall. **Stock:** 14" pull, 1-3/8" drop at heel. Walnut; Dual Comb design for proper eye positioning with or without scoped barrels. Recoil pad and swivel studs. **Features:** Ambidextrous thumb safety, twin extractors, dual slide bars. Comes with scope mount. Mossberg Cablelock included. Introduced 1988.
Price: Rifled bore, integral scope mount, 12 or 20 ga. **$361.00**
Price: Fiber Optic, rifle sights **$361.00**
Price: Rifled bore, rifle sights **$338.00**
Price: 20 ga., Standard or Bantam, from **$338.00**

REMINGTON MODEL 870 EXPRESS SLUG GUNS

Gauge: 12, 20, 3". **Barrel:** 20". **Weight:** 6.25 to 7-1/4 lbs. **Stock:** Hardwood, synthetic. **Sights:** Rifle sights or cantilever scope mounts. **Features:** Balistically balanced performance, milder recoil. Double action bars, crossbolt safety, blue finish.
Price: Express Combo, 12 ga., 26" vent rib with mod. Rem choke and 20" fully rifled barrel with rifle sights, or Rem. choke ... **$443.00** to **$476.00**
Price: Express Combo (20 ga.) with extra Deer rifled barrel, fully rifled or Rem. choke .... **$443.00** to **$476.00**
Price: 20 ga. Youth Deer 20" FR/RS **$365.00**

Remington Model 870 Express Rifle-Sighted Deer Gun

Same as Model 870 Express except 20" barrel with fixed imp. cyl. choke, open iron sights, Monte Carlo stock. Introduced 1991.
Price: **$332.00**
Price: With fully rifled barrel **$365.00**
Price: Express Synthetic Deer (black synthetic stock, black matte metal) **$372.00**

Remington Model 870 SPS Super Slug Deer Gun

Similar to the Model 870 Express Synthetic except has 23" rifled, modified contour barrel with cantilever scope mount. Comes with black synthetic stock and forend with swivel studs, black Cordura nylon sling. Introduced 1999. Fully rifled centilever barrel.
Price: **$580.00**

WINCHESTER MODEL 1300 PUMP SLUG GUN

Gauge: 12, 20, 3" chamber, 5-shot capacity. **Barrel:** 22" rifled, 28" smoothbore combo. **Weight:** 6-3/8 lbs. **Length:** 42-5/8" overall. **Features:** Introduced 1984. From U.S. Repeating Arms Co., Inc.
Price: .... **NA**

Winchester Model 1300 Deer Black Shadow Shotgun

Similar to Model 1300 Black Shadow Turkey Gun except ramp-type front sight, fully adjustable rear, drilled and tapped for scope mounting. Black composite stock and forend, matte black metal. Smoothbore 22" barrel with one imp. cyl. WinChoke tube; 12 gauge only, 3" chamber. Weighs 6-3/4 lbs. Introduced 1994. From U.S. Repeating Arms Co., Inc.
Price: With rifled barrel **$377.00**
Price: With cantilever scope mount **$422.00**
Price: Combo (22" rifled and 28" smoothbore bbls.) **$455.00**
Price: Wood stock (20 ga., 22" rifled barrel) **$377.00**
Price: Compact Ranger deer model, 12 & 20 ga.............. **$392.00**

WINCHESTER MODEL 9410 LEVERACTION SHOTGUN

Gauge: .410, 2-1/2" chamber. **Barrel:** 24" cyl. bore, also Invector choke system. **Weight:** 6-3/4 lbs. **Length:** 42-1/8" overall. **Stock:** Checkered walnut straightgrip; checkered walnut forearm. **Sights:** Adjustable "V" rear, TruGlo® front. **Features:** Model 94 rifle action (smoothbore) chambered for .410 shotgun. Angle Controlled Eject extractor/ejector; choke tubes; 9-shot tubular magazine; 13-1/2" length of pull. Introduced 2001. From U.S. Repeating Arms Co.
Price: 9410 fixed choke **$579.00**
Price: 9410 Packer w/chokes **$600.00**
Price: 9410 w/Invector, traditional model **$645.00**
Price: 9410 w/Invector, Packer model **$667.00**
Price: 9410 w/Invector, semifancy traditional **$789.00**

H&R 928 Ultra Slug Hunter Deluxe

Mossberg SSi One

New England Firearms Tracker II

Savage 210F Master Shot Slug Warrior

HARRINGTON & RICHARDSON SB2-980 ULTRA SLUG

Gauge: 12, 20, 3" chamber. **Barrel:** 22" (20 ga. Youth) 24", fully rifled. **Weight:** 9 lbs. **Length:** NA. **Stock:** Walnut-stained hardwood. **Sights:** None furnished; comes with scope mount. **Features:** Uses the H&R 10 gauge action with heavywall barrel. Monte Carlo stock has sling swivels; comes with black nylon sling. Introduced 1995. Made in U.S. by H&R 1871, LLC.
Price: **$259.00**

Harrington & Richardson Model 928 Ultra Slug Hunter Deluxe

Similar to the SB2980 Ultra Slug except uses 12 gauge action and 12 gauge barrel blank bored to 20 gauge, then fully rifled with 1:28" twist. Has hand-checkered camo laminate Monte Carlo stock and forend. Comes with Weaver-style scope base, offset hammer extension, ventilated recoil pad, sling swivels and nylon sling. Introduced 1997. Made in U.S. by H&R 1871 LLC.
Price: **$315.00**

MOSSBERG SSi-ONE 12 GAUGE SLUG SHOTGUN

Gauge: 12, 3" chamber. **Barrel:** 24", fully rifled. **Weight:** 8 pounds. **Length:** 40" overall. **Stock:** Walnut, fluted and cut checkered; sling-swivel studs; drilled and tapped for scope base. **Sights:** None (scope base supplied). **Features:** Frame accepts interchangeable rifle barrels (see Mossberg SSi-One rifle listing); lever-opening, break-action design; ambidextrous, top-tang safety; internal eject/extract selector. Introduced 2000. From Mossberg.
Price: **$480.00**

NEW ENGLAND FIREARMS TRACKER II SLUG GUN

Gauge: 12, 20, 3" chamber. **Barrel:** 24" (Cyl.), rifle bore. **Weight:** 5-1/4 lbs. **Length:** 40" overall. **Stock:** Walnut-finished hardwood with full pistol grip, recoil pad. **Sights:** Blade front, fully adjustable rifle-type rear. **Features:** Break-open action with sidelever release; blued barrel, color casehardened frame. Introduced 1992. From New England Firearms.
Price: Tracker II **$187.00**

SAVAGE MODEL 210F SLUG WARRIOR

Gauge: 12, 3" chamber; 2-shot magazine. **Barrel:** 24" 1:35" rifling twist. **Weight:** 7-1/2 lbs. **Length:** 43.5" overall. **Stock:** Glass-filled polymer with positive checkering. **Features:** Based on the Savage Model 110 action; 60 bolt lift; controlled round feed; comes with scope mount. Introduced 1996. Made in U.S. by Savage Arms.
Price: **$458.00**
Price: (Camo) **$495.00**

TARHUNT RSG12 PROFESSIONAL RIFLED SLUG GUN

Gauge: 12, 16 & 20, 2-3/4" or 3" chamber, 1-shot magazine. **Barrel:** 23", fully rifled with muzzle brake. **Weight:** 7-3/4 lbs. **Length:** 41-1/2" overall. **Stock:** Matte black McMillan fiberglass with Pachmayr Decelerator pad. **Sights:** None furnished; comes with Leupold windage or Weaver bases. **Features:** Uses rifle-style action with two locking lugs; two-position safety; Shaw barrel; single stage, trigger; muzzle brake. Many options available. Right- and left-hand models at same prices. Introduced 1991. Made in U.S. by TarHunt Custom Rifles, Inc.
Price: 12 ga. Professional model, right- or left-hand;
Elite 16 ga. **$2,395.00**
Price: Millennium/10th Anniversary models (limited to 25 guns) ..... **NA**
Price: NP3 nickel/Teflon metal finish, black McMillan
Fibergrain stock, Jewell adj. trigger **$2,300.00**

TarHunt RSG20 Mountaineer Slug Gun

Similar to the RSG12 Professional except chambered for 20 gauge (3" shells); 23" Shaw rifled barrel, with muzzle brake; two-lug bolt; one-shot blind magazine; matte black finish; McMillan fiberglass stock with Pachmayr Decelerator pad; receiver drilled and tapped for Rem. 700 bases. Weighs 6-1/2 lbs. Introduced 1997. Made in U.S. by TarHunt Custom Rifles, Inc.
Price: **$2,395.00**

THOMPSON/CENTER ENCORE RIFLED SLUG GUN

Gauge: 20, 3" chamber. **Barrel:** 26", fully rifled. **Weight:** About 7 pounds. **Length:** 40-1/2" overall. **Stock:** Walnut with walnut forearm. **Sights:** Steel, click-adjustable rear and ramp-style front, both with fiber optics. **Features:** Encore system features a variety of rifle, shotgun and muzzle-loading rifle barrels interchangeable with the same frame. Break-open design operates by pulling up and back on trigger guard spur. Composite stock and forearm available. Introduced 2000.
Price: **$665.00**

THE WEB DIRECTORY

Compiled by Holt Bodinson

This deer gun-specific web directory is a distillation of the extensive Web Directory found in *Gun Digest 2005*. If you've surfed the web for very long, you know that websites come and go, often literally overnight. Those listed below have shown some staying power, but unfortunately we can guarantee neither the completeness of the list nor the functionality of the web addresses cited.

If the web site you desire is not listed, or if the web address is no longer valid, try a search engine such as Microsoft Internet Explorer, Metacrawler, GoTo.com, Yahoo, HotBot, AltaVista, Lycos, Excite, InfoSeek, Looksmart, Google, or WebCrawler. Type in a key word such as gun, firearm, rifle, pistol, blackpowder, shooting, hunting– frankly, any word that relates to the sport–and hit Enter. Each search engine seems to comb through the World Wide Web in a different fashion and produces different results. We find Google to be among the best.

Accessing the various search engines is simple. Just type www.google.com for example, and you're on your way.

Welcome to the digital world of firearms!

Ammunition and Components

Accurate Arms Co. Inc www.accuratepowder.com
ADCO/Nobel Sport Powder www.adcosales.com
Alliant Powder www.alliantpowder.com
Ballistic Products, Inc. www.ballisticproducts.com
Barnes Bullets www.barnesbullets.com
Beartooth Bullets www.beartoothbullets.com
Berger Bullets, Ltd. www.bergerbullets.com
Black Hills Ammunition, Inc. www.black-hills.com
Brenneke of America Ltd. www.brennekeusa.com
Buffalo Arms www.buffaloarms.com
Cheaper Than Dirt www.cheaperthandirt.com
Cheddite France www.cheddite.com
Clean Shot Powder www.cleanshot.com
Dillon Precision www.dillonprecision.com
Federal Cartridge Co. www.federalpremium.com
Fiocchi of America www.fiocchiusa.com
Garrett Cartridges www.garrettcartridges.com
GOEX Inc. www.goexpowder.com
Hodgdon Powder www.hodgdon.com
Hornady www.hornady.com
IMR Smokeless Powders www.imrpowder.com
Lapua www.lapua.com
Lightfield Ammunition Corp www.lightfield-ammo.com
Lomont Precision Bullets www.klomont.com/kent
Lyman www.lymanproducts.com
Midway USA www.midwayusa.com
National Bullet Co. www.nationalbullet.com
Norma www.norma.cc
Nosler Bullets Inc www.nosler.com
PowerBelt Bullets www.powerbeltbullets.com
Precision Ammunition www.precisionammo.com
Precision Reloading www.precisionreloading.com
Remington www.remington.com
Sellier & Bellot USA inc. www.sb-usa.com
Sierra www.sierrabullets.com
Speer Bullets www.speer-bullets.com
Vihtavuori Lapua www.lapua.com
Western Powders Inc. www.westernpowders.com
Widener's Reloading & Shooters Supply
www.wideners.com
Winchester Ammunition www.winchester.com

Cleaning Products

Accupro www.accupro.com
Ballistol USA www.ballistol.com
Birchwood Casey www.birchwoodcasey.com
Bore Tech www.boretech.com
Break-Free, Inc. www.break-free.com
Bruno Shooters Supply www.brunoshooters.com
Butch's Bore Shine www.lymanproducts.com
C.J. Weapons Accessories www.cjweapons.com
Clenzoil www.clenzoil.com
Corrosion Technologies www.corrosionx.com

Dewey Mfg. www.deweyrods.com
Eezox Inc. www.xmission.com
G 96 www.g96.com
Hollands Shooters Supply www.hollandgun.com
Hoppes www.hoppes.com
Hydrosorbent Products www.dehumidify.com
Inhibitor VCI Products www.inhibitor.com
Iosso Products www.iosso.com
KG Industries www.kgcoatings.com
Kleen-Bore Inc. www.kleen-bore.com
L&R Mfg. www.lrultrasonics.com
Militec-1 www.militec-1.com
Mpro7 Gun Care www.mp7.com
Otis Technology, Inc. www.otisgun.com
Outers www.outers-guncare.com
Ox-Yoke Originals Inc. www.oxyoke.com
Parker-Hale Ltd. www.parker-hale.com
Prolix Lubricant www.prolixlubricant.com
ProShot Products www.proshotproducts.com
ProTec Lubricants www.proteclubricants.com
Rusteprufe Labs www.rusteprufe.com
Sagebrush Products www.sagebrushproducts.com
Sentry Solutions Ltd. www.sentrysolutions.com
Shooters Choice Gun Care www.shooters-choice.com
Silencio www.silencio.com
Slip 2000 www.slip2000.com
Stony Point Products www.stoneypoint.com
Tetra Gun www.tetraproducts.com
World's Fastest Gun Bore Cleaner
www.michaels-oregon.com

Firearm Manufacturers and Importers

Austin & Halleck www.austinhalleck.com
Beretta U.S.A. Corp. www.berettausa.com
Bernardelli www.bernardelli.com
Bowen Classic Arms www.bowenclassicarms.com
Briley Mfg. www.briley.com
BRNO Arms www.zbrojovka.com
Browning www.browning.com
Cape Outfitters www.doublegun.com
Casull Arms Corp. www.casullarms.com
Chadick's Ltd. www.chadicks-ltd.com
Champlin Firearms www.champlinarms.com
Chapuis Arms www.doubleguns.com/chapuis.htm
Colt Mfg Co. www.colt.com
Connecticut Valley Arms www.cva.com
Cooper Firearms www.cooperfirearms.com
Dan Wesson Firearms www.danwessonfirearms.com
Dixie Gun Works www.dixiegun.com
FN Herstal www.fnherstal.com
Franchi www.franchiusa.com
Freedom Arms www.freedomarms.com

Gary Reeder Custom Guns
www.reeder-customguns.com
Gibbs Rifle Company www.gibbsrifle.com
Griffin & Howe www.griffinhowe.com
Heckler and Koch www.hecklerkoch-usa.com
Henry Repeating Arms Co. www.henryrepeating.com
Ithaca Gun Co. www.ithacagun.com
Knight Rifles www.knightrifles.com
Korth www.korthwaffen.de
Lone Star Rifle Co. www.lonestarrifle.com
Magnum Research www.magnumresearch.com
Markesbery Muzzleloaders www.markesbery.com
Marlin www.marlinfirearms.com
Mauser www.mauserwaffen.de
McMillan Bros Rifle Co. www.mcfamily.com
New England Arms Corp. www.newenglandarms.com
New England Firearms www.hr1871.com
New Ultra Light Arms www.newultralight.com
O.F. Mossberg & Sons www.mossberg.com
Pedersoli Davide & Co. www.davide-pedersoli.com
Remington www.remingtonmndco.com
Savage Arms Inc. www.savagearms.com
Scattergun Technologies Inc. www.wilsoncombat.com
Smith & Wesson www.smith-wesson.com
Steyr Mannlicher www.gsifirearms.com
Sturm, Ruger & Company www.ruger-firearms.com
Tar-Hunt Slug Guns, Inc. www.tar-hunt.com
Taurus www.taurususa.com
Thompson Center Arms www.tcarms.com
U.S. Repeating Arms Co. www.winchester-guns.com
Weatherby www.weatherby.com
Winchester Firearms www.winchester-guns.com

Gun Parts, Barrels, After-Market Accessories

300 Below www.300below.com
Accuracy International of North America
www.accuracyinternational.org
Accuracy Speaks, Inc. www.accuracyspeaks.com
Advanced Barrel Systems www.carbonbarrels.com
AK-USA www.ak-103.com
American Spirit Arms Corp. www.gunkits.com
AMT Gun Parts www.amt-gunparts.com
Badger Barrels, Inc. www.badgerbarrels.com
Bar-Sto Precision Machine www.barsto.com
Battenfeld Technologies
www.battenfeldtechnologies.com
Belt Mountain Enterprises www.beltmountain.com
Brownells www.brownells.com
Buffer Technologies www.buffertech.com
Bullberry Barrel Works www.bullberry.com
Bushmaster Firearms/Quality Parts
www.bushmaster.com
Butler Creek Corp www.butler-creek.com

THE WEB DIRECTORY

Cape Outfitters Inc. www.capeoutfitters.com
Caspian Arms Ltd. www.caspianarmsltd.8m.com
Cheaper Than Dirt www.cheaperthandirt.com
Chesnut Ridge www.chestnutridge.com/
Chip McCormick Corp www.chipmccormickcorp.com
Colonial Arms www.colonialarms.com
Digi-Twist www.fmtcorp.com
Dixie Gun Works www.dixiegun.com
Douglas Barrels www.benchrest.com/douglas/
DPMS www.dpmsinc.com
D.S. Arms, Inc. www.dsarms.com
Ed Brown Products www.edbrown.com
Forrest Inc. www.gunmags.com
Fulton Armory www.fulton-armory.com
Galazan www.connecticutshotgun.com
Gemtech www.gem-tech.com
Gentry, David www.gentrycustom.com
GG&G www.gggaz.com
Green Mountain Rifle Barrels www.gmriflebarrel.com
Gun Parts Corp. www.e-gunparts.com
Harris Barrels wwharris@msn.com
Hart Rifle Barrels www.hartbarrels.com
Hastings Barrels www.hastingsbarrels.com
Heinie Specialty Products www.heinie.com
Holland Shooters Supply www.hollandgun.com
100 Straight Products www.100straight.com
I.M.A. www.ima-usa.com
Jarvis, Inc. www.jarvis-custom.com
J&T Distributing www.jtdistributing.com
King's Gunworks www.kingsgunworks.com
Krieger Barrels www.kriegerbarrels.com
Les Baer Custom, Inc. www.lesbaer.com
Lone Wolf Dist. www.lonewolfdist.com
Lothar Walther Precision Tools Inc.
    www.lothar-walther.de
M&A Parts, Inc. www.m-aparts.com
MAB Barrels www.mab.com.au
Marvel Products, Inc. www.marvelprod.com
Michaels of Oregon Co. www.michaels-oregon.com
North Mfg. Co. www.rifle-barrels.com
Numrich Gun Parts Corp. www.e-gunparts.com
Pachmayr www.pachmayr.com
Pac-Nor Barrels www.pac-nor.com
Scattergun Technologies Inc. www.wilsoncombat.com
Western Gun Parts www.westerngunparts.com

Gunsmithing Supplies and Instruction

American Gunsmithing Institute
    www.americangunsmith.com
Battenfeld Technologies
    www.battenfeldtechnologies.com
Brownells, Inc. www.brownells.com
B-Square Co. www.b-square.com
Clymer Mfg. Co. www.clymertool.com
Craftguard Metal Finishing crftgrd@aol.com
Dem-Bart www.dembartco.com
Doug Turnbull Restoration
    www.turnbullrestoration.com
Du-Lite Corp. www.dulite.com
Dvorak Instruments www.dvorakinstruments.com
Gradient Lens Corp. www.gradientlens.com
Gunline Tools www.gunline.com
JGS Precision Tool Mfg. LLC www.jgstools.com
Mag-Na-Port International www.magnaport.com
Manson Precision Reamers www.mansonreamers.com
Midway www.midwayusa.com
Olympus America Inc. www.olympus.com
Trinidad State Junior College www.trinidadstate.edu

Handgun Grips

Ajax Custom Grips, Inc. www.ajaxgrips.com
Altamont Co. www.altamontco.com
Badger Grips www.pistolgrips.com
Blu Magnum Grips www.blumagnum.com
Buffalo Brothers www.buffalobrothers.com
Crimson Trace Corp. www.crimsontrace.com
Eagle Grips www.eaglegrips.com
Falcon Industries www.ergogrips.net
Hogue Grips www.getgrip.com
Kirk Ratajesak www.kgratajesak.com
Lett Custom Grips www.lettgrips.com
N.C. Ordnance www.gungrip.com
Nill-Grips USA www.nill-grips.com
Pachmayr www.pachmayr.com
Pearce Grips www.pearcegrip.com
Trausch Grips Int.Co. www.trausch.com
Uncle Mike's: www.uncle-mikes.com

Miscellaneous Shooting Products

10X Products Group www.10Xwear.com
Aero Peltor www.aearo.com
Beartooth www.beartoothproducts.com
Dalloz Safety www.cdalloz.com
Deben Group Industries Inc. www.deben.com
Decot Hy-Wyd Sport Glasses www.sportyglasses.com
E.A.R., Inc. www.earinc.com
First Choice Armor www.firstchoicearmor.com
Gunstands www.gunstands.com
Howard Leight Hearing Protectors
    www.howardleight.com
Hunters Specialties www.hunterspec.com
Johnny Stewart Wildlife Calls www.hunterspec.com
North Safety Products www.northsafety-brea.com
Pro-Ears www.pro-ears.com
Silencio www.silencio.com
Smart Lock Technologies www.smartlock.com
Surefire www.surefire.com
Walker's Game Ear Inc. www.walkersgameear.com

Muzzleloading Firearms and Products

American Pioneer Powder
    www.americanpioneerpowder.com
Austin & Halleck, Inc. www.austinhalleck.com
CVA www.cva.com
Davis, Vernon C. & Co. www.mygunroom/vcdavis&co/
Dixie Gun Works, Inc. www.dixiegun.com
Elephant/Swiss Black Powder
    www.elephantblackpowder.com
Goex Black Powder www.goexpowder.com
Jedediah Starr Trading Co. www.jedediah-starr.com
Jim Chambers Flintlocks www.flintlocks.com
Kahnke Gunworks www.powderandbow.com/kahnke/
Knight Rifles www.knightrifles.com
Log Cabin Shop www.logcabinshop.com
Lyman www.lymanproducts.com
Millennium Designed Muzzleloaders
    www.mdm-muzzleloaders.com
Mountain State Muzzleloading
    www.mtnstatemuzzleloading.com
MSM, Inc. www.msmfg.com
Muzzleload Magnum Products www.mmpsabots.com
Muzzleloading Technologies, Inc.
    www.mtimuzzleloading.com
Navy Arms www.navyarms.com
October Country Muzzleloading www.oct-country.com
Ox-Yoke Originals Inc. www.oxyoke.com
Palmetto Arms www.palmetto.it

Rightnour Mfg. Co. Inc. www.rmcsports.com
The Rifle Shop trshoppe@aol.com
Thompson Center Arms www.tcarms.com
Traditions Performance Muzzleloading
    www.traditionsfirearms.com

Publications, Videos, and CDs

American Firearms Industry www.amfire.com
American Handgunner www.americanhandgunner.com
American Hunter www.nrapublications.org
American Rifleman www.nrapublications.org
American Shooting Magazine
    www.americanshooting.com
Blackpowder Hunting www.blackpowderhunting.org
Black Powder Journal www.blackpowderjournal.com
Blue Book Publications www.bluebookinc.com
DBI Books/Krause Publications www.krause.com
Gun List www.gunlist.com
Gun Video www.gunvideo.com
GUNS Magazine www.gunsmagazine.com
Guns & Ammo www.gunsandammomag.com
Gunweb Magazine WWW Links www.imags.com
Gun Week www.gunweek.com
Gun World www.gunworld.com
Harris Publications www.harrispublications.com
Heritage Gun Books www.gunbooks.com
Krause Publications www.krause.com
Moose Lake Publishing MooselakeP@aol.com
Munden Enterprises Inc. www.bob-munden.com
Outdoor Videos www.outdoorvideos.com
Precision Shooting www.precisionshooting.com
Ray Riling Arms Books www.rayrilingarmsbooks.com
Rifle and Handloader Magazines
    www.riflemagazine.com
Safari Press Inc. www.safaripress.com
Shoot! Magazine www.shootmagazine.com
Shooters News www.shootersnews.com
Shooting Illustrated www.nrapublications.org
Shooting Industry www.shootingindustry.com
Shooting Sports Retailer ssretailer@ad.com
Shooting Sports USA www.nrapublications.org
Shotgun News www.shotgunnews.com
Shotgun Report www.shotgunreport.com
Shotgun Sports Magazine www.shotgun-sports.com
Small Arms Review www.smallarmsreview.com
Sports Afield www.sportsafield.comm
Sports Trend www.sportstrend.com
Sportsmen on Film www.sportsmenonfilm.com
The Gun Journal www.shooters.com
The Shootin Iron www.off-road.com/4x4web/si/si.html
The Single Shot Exchange Magazine
    singleshot@earthlink.net
The Sixgunner www.sskindustries.com
Voyageur Press www.voyageurpress.com
VSP Publications www.gunbooks.com
Vulcan Outdoors Inc. www.vulcanpub.com

Reloading Tools and Supplies

Ballisti-Cast Mfg. www.ballisti-cast.com
Bruno Shooters Supply www.brunoshooters.com
CH Tool & Die www.cdhd.com
Colorado Shooters Supply www.hochmoulds.com
Corbin Mfg & Supply Co. www.corbins.com
Dillon Precision www.dillonprecision.com
Forster Precision Products www.forsterproducts.com
Hanned Line www.hanned.com
Harrell's Precision www.harrellsprec.com
Holland's Shooting Supplies www.hollandgun.com
Hornady www.hornady.com

THE WEB DIRECTORY

Huntington Reloading Products
www.huntingtons.com
J & J Products Co. www.jandjproducts.com
Lead Bullet Technology LBTisaccuracy@lmbris.net
Lee Precision, Inc. www.leeprecision.com
Littleton Shotmaker www.leadshotmaker.com
Load Data www.loaddata.com
Lyman www.lymanproducts.com
Magma Engineering www.magmaengr.com
Mayville Engineering Co. (MEC)
www.mecreloaders.com
Midway www.midwayusa.com
Moly-Bore www.molybore.com
MTM Case-Guard www.mtmcase-guard.com
NECO www.neconos.com
NEI www.neihandtools.com
Neil Jones Custom Products www.neiljones.com
Ponsness/Warren www.reloaders.com
Ranger Products
www.pages.prodigy.com/rangerproducts.home.htm
Rapine Bullet Mold Mfg Co.
www.customloads.com/rapine.html
RCBS www.rcbs.com
Redding Reloading Equipment
www.redding-reloading.com
Russ Haydon's Shooting Supplies
www.shooters-supply.com
Sinclair Int'l Inc. www.sinclairintl.com
Stoney Point Products Inc www.stoneypoint.com
Thompson Bullet Lube Co.
www.thompsonbulletlube.com
Vickerman Seating Die www.castingstuff.com
Wilson (L.E. Wilson) www.lewilson.com

Scopes, Sights, Mounts and Accessories

Accusight www.accusight.com
ADCO www.shooters.com/adco/index/htm
Adirondack Optics www.adkoptics.com
Aimpoint www.aimpoint.com
Aim Shot, Inc. www.miniosprey.com
Aimtech Mount Systems www.aimtech-mounts.com
Alpec Team, Inc. www.alpec.com
Alpen Outdoor Corp. www.alpenoutdoor.com
American Technologies Network, Corp.
www.atncorp.com
AmeriGlo, LLC www.ameriglo.net
AO Sight Systems Inc. www.aosights.com
Ashley Outdoors, Inc. www.ashleyoutdoors.com
ATN www.atncorp.com
BSA Optics www.bsaoptics.com
B-Square Company, Inc. www.b-square.com
Burris www.burrisoptics.com
Bushnell Performance Optics www.bushnell.com
Carl Zeiss Optical Inc. www.zeiss.com
Carson Optical www.carson-optical.com
C-More Systems www.cmore.com
Conetrol Scope Mounts www.conetrol.com
Crimson Trace Corp. www.crimsontrace.com
Crossfire L.L.C. www.amfire.com/hesco/html
DCG Supply Inc. www.dcgsupply.com
D&L Sports www.dlsports.com
EasyHit, Inc. www.easyhit.com
EAW www.eaw.de
Electro-Optics Technologies
www.eotechmdc.com/holosight
Europtik Ltd. www.europtik.com
Fujinon, Inc. www.fujinon.com
Gilmore Sports www.gilmoresports.com
Hakko Co. Ltd. www.hakko-japan.co.jp

Hesco www.hescosights.com
Hitek Industries www.nightsight.com
HIVIZ www.hivizsights.com
Horus Vision www.horusvision.com
Hunter Co. www.huntercompany.com
Innovative Weaponry,Inc. www.ptnightsights.com
Ironsighter Co. www.ironsighter.com
ITT Night Vision www.ittnightvision.com
Kahles www.kahlesoptik.com
Kowa Optimed Inc. www.kowascope.com
Laser Bore Sight www.laserboresight.com
Laser Devices Inc. www.laserdevices.com
LaserLyte www.laserlyte.com
LaserMax Inc. www.lasermax-inc.com
Laser Products www.surefire.com
Leapers, Inc. www.leapers.com
Leatherwood www.leatherwoodoptics.com
Leica Camera Inc. www.leica-camera.com/usa
Leupold www.leupold.com
Lyman www.lymanproducts.com
Lynx www.b-square.com
Marble's Outdoors www.marblesoutdoors.com
MDS, Inc. www.mdsincorporated.com
Meprolight www.kimberamerica.com
Micro Sight Co. www.microsight.com
Millett www.millettsights.com
Miniature Machine Corp. www.mmcsight.com
Montana Vintage Arms www.montanavintagearms.com
Mounting Solutions Plus www.mountsplus.com
NAIT www.nait.com
Newcon International Ltd.
newconsales@newcon-optik.com
Nikon Inc. www.nikonusa.com
North American Integrated Technologies
www.nait.com
O.K. Weber, Inc. www.okweber.com
Pentax Corp. www.pentaxlightseeker.com
Premier Reticle www.premierreticles.com
Redfield www.redfieldoptics.com
R&R Int'l Trade www.nightoptic.com
Schmidt & Bender www.schmidt-bender.com
Scopecoat www.scopecoat.com
Scopelevel www.scopelevel.com
Segway Industries www.segway-industries.com
Shepherd Scope Ltd. www.shepherdscopes.com
Sightron www.sightron.com
Simmons www.simmonsoptics.com
S&K www.scopemounts.com
Springfield Armory www.springfield-armory.com
Sure-Fire www.surefire.com
Swarovski/Kahles www.swarovskioptik.com
Swift Instruments Inc. www.swift-optics.com
Talley Mfg. Co. www.talleyrings.com
Tasco www.tascosales.com
Trijicon Inc. www.trijicon-inc.com
Truglo Inc. www.truglo.com
US Night Vision www.usnightvision.com
U.S. Optics Technologies Inc. www.usoptics.com
Valdada-IOR Optics www.valdada.com
Warne www.warnescopemounts.com
Weaver Scopes www.weaveroptics.com
Wilcox Industries Corp www.wilcoxind.com
Williams Gun Sight Co. www.williamsgunsight.com
Zeiss www.zeiss.com

Stocks

Advanced Technology www.atigunstocks.com
Bell & Carlson, Inc. www.bellandcarlson.com
Boyd's Gunstock Industries, Inc. www.boydboys.com
Butler Creek Corp www.butler-creek.com

Calico Hardwoods, Inc. www.calicohardwoods.com
Choate Machine www.riflestock.com
Elk Ridge Stocks www.reamerrentals.com/elk_ridge.htm
Fajen www.battenfeldtechnologies.com
Great American Gunstocks www.gunstocks.com
Herrett's Stocks www.herrettstocks.com
High Tech Specialties www.bansnersrifle.com/hightech
Holland's Shooting Supplies www.hollandgun.com
Lone Wolf www.lonewolfriflestocks.com
McMillan Fiberglass Stocks www.mcmfamily.com
MPI Stocks www.mpistocks.com
Precision Gun Works www.precisiongunstocks.com
Ram-Line www.outers-guncare.com
Rimrock Rifle Stock www.rimrockstocks.com
Royal Arms Gunstocks www.imt.net/~royalarms
Speedfeed, Inc. www.speedfeedinc.com
Tiger-Hunt Curly Maple Gunstocks
www.gunstockwood.com
Wenig Custom Gunstocks Inc. www.wenig.com

Major Shooting Web Sites and Links

24 Hour Campfire www.24hourcampfire.com
Alphabetic Index of Links www.gunsgunsguns.com
Auction Arms www.auctionarms.com
Benchrest Central www.benchrest.com
Bullseye Pistol www.bullseyepistol.com
Dave Kopel Articles
www.davekoppel.org/DavePage.htm
Firearms History www.researchpress.co.uk/firearms
Firearm News www.firearmnews.com
For The Hunt www.forthehunt.com
Gun Broker Auctions www.gunbroker.com
Gun Index www.gunindex.com
Gun Industry www.gunindustry.com
Gun Blast www.gunblast.com
Gun Boards www.gunboards.com
Gun Law www.gunlaw.com
GunLinks www.gunlinks.com
Gun Manuals www.gunmanuals.ch/manuals.htm
Gun Nuts www.gunuts.com
Guns For Sale www.gunsamerica.com
Gun Show Auction www.gunshowauction.com
GunXchange www.gunxchange.com
Hunting Digest www.huntingdigest.com
Hunting Information (NSSF) www.huntinfo.org
Hunting Net www.hunting.net
Hunting Network www.huntingnetwork.com
John Lott Articles www.tsra.com/LottPage.htm
Keep and Bear Arms www.keepandbeararms.com
Leverguns www.leverguns.com
Outdoor Yellow Pages www.outdoorsyp.com
Real Guns www.realguns.com/links/glinks.htm
Rec.Guns www.recguns.com
Shooters' Gun Calendar
www.guncalendar.com/index.cfm
Shooter's Online Services www.shooters.com
Shooters Search www.shooterssearch.com
Shotgun Sports Resource Guide
www.shotgunsports.com
Sixgunner www.sixgunner.com
Sportsman's Web www.sportsmansweb.com
Surplus Rifles www.surplusrifle.com
Surplus Pistols www.surpluspistol.com
Where To Shoot www.wheretoshoot.com

SOURCES FOR DEER HUNTING REGULATIONS

Alabama Department of Conservation and Natural Resources
64 North Union Street
Montgomery, AL 36130
(334) 242-3465
www.dcnr.state.al.us/agfd

Division of Wildlife Conservation
P.O. Box 25526
Juneau, AK 99802-6197
(907) 465-6197
www.state.ak.us/local/akpages/fish.game/
wildlife

Arizona Game and Fish Department
2221 West Greenway Road
Phoenix, AZ 85023-4312
(602) 942-3000
www.gfd.state.az.us

Arkansas Game & Fish Commission
#2 Natural Resources Drive
Little Rock, AR 72205
(800) 354-4263
www.agfc.state.ar.us

California Department Fish & Game
1416 9th Street
Sacramento, CA 95818
(916) 227-2244
www.cfg.state.ca.us

Colorado Division of Wildlife
1313 Sherman Room #718
Denver, CO 80203
(303) 297-1192
http://wildlife.state.co.us/

Connecticut Department of Environmental Protection
Wildlife Division
79 Elm Street
Hartford, CT 06106-5127
(800) 424-3105
http://dep.state.ct.us/pao/

Delaware Division of Fish and Wildlife
89 Kings Highway
Dover, DE 19901
(302) 739-4431
dep.state.ct.us/burnatr/wildlife

Florida Department of Game and Freshwater Fish
620 South Meridian Street
Tallahassee, FL 32399-1600
(850) 488-4676
www.state.fl.us/gfc

Georgia Department of Natural Resources
Wildlife Management Division
2111 Highway 278
Social Circle, GA 30025
(770) 918-6416
www.ganet.org/dnr/

Idaho Department of Fish and Game
P.O. Box 25
Boise, ID 83707
(208) 334-3700
www.state.id.us/fishgame

Illinois Department of Natural Resources
524 South Second Street, Room 210
Springfield, IL 62701
(217) 782-2965
www.dnr.state.il.us/ildnr/

Indiana Department of Natural Resources
402 West Washington Street
Indianapolis, IN 46204
(317) 232-4080
www.dnr.state.in.us

Iowa Department of Natural Resources
Wallace State Office Building
Des Moines, IA 50319-0034
(515) 281-5145
www.dnr.state.ia.us

Kansas Parks and Wildlife
900 SW Jackson Street, Suite 502
Topeka, KS 66612-1233
(785) 273-6740
www.kdwp.state.ks.us

Kentucky Department of Wildlife Resources
#1 Game Farm Road
Frankfort, KY 40601
(502) 564-4336
www.state.ky.us/agencies/fw/kdfwr.htm

Louisiana Wildlife & fisheries
P.O. Box 98000
Baton Rouge, LA 70898
(504) 765-2980
www.wlf.state.la.us

Maine Department of Inland Fisheries & Wildlife
285 State Street
41 State House Station
Augusta, ME 04333-0041
(207) 287-2571
webmaster_ifw@state.me.us

Maryland Department of Natural Resources
Wildlife Division
580 Taylor Avenue, E-1
Annapolis, MD 21401
(401) 260-8540
www.dnr.state.md.us/huntersguide

Massachusetts Department Fisheries and Wildlife
Field Headquarters
Westboro, MA 01581
(508) 792-7270, ext. 110
www.state.ma.us/dfwele/

Michigan Department of Natural Resources
4590 118th Avenue, Route 3
Allegan, MI 49010
(517) 373-1230
www.dnr.state.mi.us

Minnesota Department of Natural Resources
500 Lafayette Road
St. Paul, MN 55155-4026
(651) 296-4506
www.dnr.state.mn.us

Mississippi Department of Wildlife
2906 North State Street
Jackson, MS 39205
(800) 546-4868
www.mdfo.state.ms.us

Missouri Department of Conservation
P.O. Box 180
Jefferson City, MO 65102
(573) 751-4115
www.dnr.state.mo.us

Montana Department of Fish, Wildlife, and Parks
1420 East 6th Avenue
Helena, MT 59620
(406) 444-2535
http://fwp.state.mt.us/

Nebraska Game and Parks
2200 North 33rd Street
Lincoln, NE 68503
(402) 471-5003
www.ngpc.state.ne.us

Nevada Division of Wildlife
P.O. Box 10678
Reno, NV 89520
(702) 688-1500
www.ndw.state.nv.us

SOURCES FOR DEER HUNTING REGULATIONS

New Hampshire Fish and Game Department
2 Hazen Drive
Concord, NH 03301
(603) 271-3211
www.wildlife.state.nh.us

New Jersey Division of Fish, Game, and Wildlife
P.O. Box 400
Trenton, NJ 08625-0400
(609) 292-2965
www.state.nj.us/dep/fgw

New Mexico Department of Game and Fish
P.O. Box 25112
Sante Fe, NM 87504
(505) 827-7911
www.gmfs.state.nm.us

New York Department of Environment Conservation
Wildlife Division
50 Wolfe Road
Albany, NY 12233
(518) 457-3521
www.dec.state.ny.us/

North Carolina Wildlife Resources Commission
512 North Salisbury Street
Raleigh, NC 27640
(919) 662-4370
www.ncwildlife.org/

North Dakota Game and Fish Department
100 N. Bismarck Expressway
Bismarck, ND 58501-5095
(701) 328-6300
www.state.nd.us/gnf/hunting

Ohio Division of Wildlife
1840 Belcher Drive
Columbus, OH 43224
(614) 265-6300
www.dnr.state.oh.us/odnr/wildlife/hunting

Oklahoma Division of Wildlife
1801 North Lincoln Boulevard
Oklahoma City, OK 73152
(405) 521-3853
www.odr.state.ok.us

Oregon Department of Fish and Game
P.O. Box 59
Portland, OR 97207
(503) 872-5270
www.odfg.state.or.us

Pennsylvania Game Commission
2001 Elmerton Avenue
Harrisburg, PA 17110
(717) 787-4250
www.pgc.state.pa.us

Rhode Island Fish and Wildlife
Oliver Steadman Government Center
480 Tower Hill Road
Wake Field, RI 02879
(401) 789-3094
www.state.ri.us

South Carolina Department of Natural Resources
Wildlife Division
P.O. Box 167
Columbia, SC 29202
(803) 734-3843
www.dnr.state.sc.us

South Dakota Department of Game, Fish, and Parks
523 East Capitol
Pierre, SD 57501
(605) 773-3485
www.state.sd.us

Tennessee Wildlife Resource Agency
Ellington Agricultural Center
Nashville, TN 37302
(615) 781-6580
www.state.tn.us

Texas Parks and Wildlife
4200 Smith School Road
Austin, TX 78744
(512) 389-4820
www.tpwd.state.tx.us/hunt

Utah Wildlife Resources
1594 West, North Temple, Suite 2110
Salt Lake City, UT 84114-6301
(801) 538-4700
www.nr.state.ut.us

Vermont Department of Fish and Wildlife
103 South Main Street, 10 South Building
Waterbury, VT 05671-0501
(802) 241-3700
www.dnr.state.vt.us/fw/fwhome

Virginia Department of Game and Inland Fisheries
P.O. Box 11104
Richmond, VA 23230-1104
(804) 367-1000
www.dgif.state.va.us

Washington Department of Fish and Wildlife
600 Capitol Way North
Olympia, WA 98501-1091
(360) 902-2464
www.wa.gov/wfdw

West Virginia Department of Natural Resources
Wildlife Division
1900 Kanawha Boulevard East
Capital Complex, Building 3
Charleston WV 25305
(304) 558-3380
www.wvdnr.state.wv.us

Wisconsin Department of Natural Resources
Box 7921
Madison, WI 53707
(608) 266-2621
www.dnr.state.wi.us/

Wyoming Game and Fish Department
5400 Bishop Boulevard
Cheyenne, WY 82006
(307) 777-4600
http://gf.state.wy.us/

The Accurate Rifle
Precisions Shooting, Inc., 222 Mckee Street, Manchester CT 06040. $37 yr.
Dedicated to the rifle accuracy enthusiast.

American Gunsmith
Belvoir Publications, Inc., 75 Holly Hill Lane, Greenwich, CT 06836-2626/203-661-6111. $49.00 (12 issues).
Technical journal of firearms repair and maintenance.

American Handgunner*
Publisher's Development Corp., 591 Camino de la Reina, Suite 200, San Diego, CA 92108/800-537-3006 $16.95 yr.
Articles for handgun enthusiasts, competitors, police and hunters.

American Hunter (M)
National Rifle Assn., 11250 Waples Mill Rd., Fairfax, VA 22030 (Same address for both.) Publications Div. $35.00 yr.
Wide scope of hunting articles.

American Rifleman (M)
National Rifle Assn., 11250 Waples Mill Rd., Fairfax, VA 22030 (Same address for both). Publications Div. $35.00 yr.
Firearms articles of all kinds.

Blackpowder Hunting (M)
Intl. Blackpowder Hunting Assn., P.O. Box 1180Z, Glenrock, WY 82637/307-436-9817. $20.00 1 yr., $36.00 2 yrs.
How-to and where-to features by experts on hunting; shooting; ballistics; traditional and modern blackpowder rifles, shotguns, pistols and cartridges.

Black Powder Times
P.O. Box 234, Lake Stevens, WA 98258. $20.00 yr.; add $5 per year for Canada, $10 per year other foreign.
Tabloid newspaper for blackpowder activities; test reports.

Blade Magazine
Krause Publications, 700 East State St., Iola, WI 54990-0001. $25.98 for 12 issues. Foreign price (including Canada-Mexico) $50.00.
A magazine for all enthusiasts of handmade, factory and antique knives.

Deer & Deer Hunting Magazine
Krause Publications, 700 E. State St., Iola, WI 54990-0001. $19.95 yr. (9 issues). Website: www.krause.com
For the serious deer hunter.

Field & Stream
Time4 Media, Two Park Ave., New York, NY 10016/212-779-5000. 12 issues/$19.97.
Monthly shooting column. Articles on hunting and fishing.

Fur-Fish-Game
A.R. Harding Pub. Co., 2878 E. Main St., Columbus, OH 43209. $15.95 yr.
Practical guidance regarding trapping, fishing and hunting.

Gun List†
700 E. State St., Iola, WI 54990. $37.98 yr. (26 issues); $66.98 2 yrs. (52 issues).
Indexed market publication for firearms collectors and active shooters; guns, supplies and services. Website: www.krause.com

Gun News Digest (Q)
Second Amendment Fdn., P.O. Box 488, Station C, Buffalo, NY 14209/716-885-6408; Fax:716-884-4471. $10 U.S.; $20 foreign.

Gun World
Y-Visionary Publishing, LP 265 South Anita Drive, Ste. 120, Orange, CA 92868. $21.97 yr.; $34.97 2 yrs.
For the hunting, reloading and shooting enthusiast.

Guns & Ammo
Primedia, 6420 Wilshire Blvd., Los Angeles, CA 90048/213-782-2780. $23.94 yr.
Guns, shooting, and technical articles.

Guns
Publishers Development Corporation, P.O. Box 85201, San Diego, CA 92138/800-537-3006. $19.95 yr.
In-depth articles on a wide range of guns, shooting equipment and related accessories for gun collectors, hunters and shooters.

Knife World
Knife World Publications, P.O. Box 3395, Knoxville, TN 37927. $15.00 yr.; $25.00 2 yrs.
Published monthly for knife enthusiasts and collectors. Articles on custom and factory knives; other knife-related interests, monthly column on knife identification, military knives.

Muzzle Blasts (M)
National Muzzle Loading Rifle Assn., P.O. Box 67, Friendship, IN 47021/812-667-5131. $35.00 yr. annual membership.
For the blackpowder shooter.

Muzzleloader Magazine*
Scurlock Publishing Co., Inc., Dept. Gun, Route 5, Box 347-M, Texarkana, TX 75501. $18.00 U.S.; $22.50 U.S./yr. for foreign subscribers.
The publication for blackpowder shooters.

National Knife Magazine (M)
Natl. Knife Coll. Assn., 7201 Shallowford Rd., P.O. Box 21070, Chattanooga, TN 37424-0070. Membership $35 yr.; $65.00 International yr.

North American Hunter* (M)
P.O. Box 3401, Minnetonka, MN 55343/612-936-9333; e-mail: huntingclub@pclink.com. $18.00 yr. (7 issues).
Articles on all types of North American hunting.

Outdoor Life
Time4 Media, Two Park Ave., New York, NY 10016. $14.97/10 issues.
Extensive coverage of hunting and shooting. Shooting column by Jim Carmichel.

Petersen's HUNTING Magazine
Primedia, 6420 Wilshire Blvd., Los Angeles, CA 90048. $19.94 yr.; Canada $29.34 yr.; foreign countries $29.94 yr.
Hunting articles for all game; test reports.

Rifle*
Wolfe Publishing Co., 2626 Stearman Road, Ste. A, Prescott, AZ 86301/520-445-7810; Fax: 520-778-5124. $19.00 yr.
The sporting firearms journal.

Rifle's Hunting Annual
Wolfe Publishing Co., 2626 Stearman Road, Ste. A, Prescott, AZ 86301/520-445-7810; Fax: 520-778-5124. $4.99 Annual.
Dedicated to the finest pursuit of the hunt.

The Shotgun News‡
Primedia, 2 News Plaza, P.O. Box 1790, Peoria, IL 61656/800-495-8362. 36 issues/ yr. @ $28.95; 12 issues/yr. @ $19.95. Foreign subscription call for rates. Sample copy $4.00.
Gun ads of all kinds.

Sports Afield
15621 Chemical Lane, Huntington Beach CA 92648. U.S./800-234-3537. International/714-894-9080. Nine issues for $29.97. Website: www.sportsafield.com.
America's oldest outdoor publication is now devoted to high-end sporting pursuits, especially in North America and Africa.

Wisconsin Outdoor Journal
Krause Publications, 700 E. State St., Iola, WI 54990-0001. $17.97 yr. (8 issues).
For Wisconsin's avid hunters and fishermen, with features from all over that state with regional reports, legislative.

---

*Published bi-monthly
† Published weekly
‡Published three times per month. All others are published monthly.

M=Membership requirements; write for details.
Q=Published Quarterly.

THE ARMS LIBRARY

FOR COLLECTOR ◆ HUNTER ◆ SHOOTER ◆ OUTDOORSMAN

IMPORTANT NOTICE TO BOOK BUYERS

Books listed here may be bought from Ray Riling Arms Books Co., 6844 Gorsten St., Philadelphia, PA 19119, Phone 215-438-2456; FAX: 215-438-5395. E-Mail: sales@rayrilingarmsbooks.com. Larry Riling is the researcher and compiler of "The Arms Library" and a seller of gun books for over 32 years. The Riling stock includes books classic and modern, many hard-to-find items, and many not obtainable elsewhere. These pages list a portion of the current stock. They offer prompt, complete service, with delayed shipments occurring only on out-of-print or out-of-stock books.

Visit our web site at **www.rayrilingarmsbooks.com** and order all of your favorite titles on line from our secure site.

NOTICE FOR ALL CUSTOMERS: Remittance in U.S. funds must accompany all orders. For your convenience we accept VISA, MasterCard, Discover Card & American Express. For shipments in the U.S. add $7.00 for the 1st book and $2.00 for each additional book for postage and insurance.

Minimum order $10.00. International Orders add $13.00 for the 1st book and $5.00 for each additional book. All International orders are shipped at the buyer's risk unless an additional $5 for insurance is included. USPS does not offer insurance to all countries unless shipped Air-Mail please e-mail or call for pricing.

Payments in excess of order or for "Backorders" are credited or fully refunded at request. Books "As-Ordered" are not returnable except by permission and a handling charge on these of 10% or $2.00 per book which ever is greater is deducted from refund or credit. Only Pennsylvania customers must include current sales tax.

A full variety of arms books also available from Rutgers Book Center, 127 Raritan Ave., Highland Park, NJ 08904/908-545-4344; FAX: 908-545-6686 or I.D.S.A. Books, 1324 Stratford Drive, Piqua, OH 45356/937-773-4203; FAX: 937-778-1922.

BALLISTICS AND HANDLOADING

ABC's of Reloading, 6th Edition, by C. Rodney James and the editors of Handloader's Digest, DBI Books, a division of Krause Publications, Iola, WI, 1997. 288 pp., illus. Paper covers. $21.95
　The definitive guide to every facet of cartridge and shotshell reloading.

Blackpowder Loading Manual, 3rd Edition, by Sam Fadala, DBI Books, a division of Krause Publications, Iola, WI, 1995. 368 pp., illus. Paper covers. $20.95
　Revised and expanded edition of this landmark blackpowder loading book. Covers hundreds of loads for most of the popular blackpowder rifles, handguns and shotguns.

Cartridges of the World, 10th Edition, by Frank Barnes, Krause Publications, Iola, WI, 2003. 512 pp., illus. Paper covers. $27.99
　Completely revised edition of the general purpose reference work for which collectors, police, scientists and laymen reach first for answers to cartridge identification questions.

Complete Blackpowder Handbook, 4th Edition, by Sam Fadala, DBI Books, a division of Krause Publications, Iola, WI, 2001. 400 pp., illus. Paper covers. $22.95
　Expanded and completely rewritten edition of the definitive book on the subject of blackpowder.

Why Not Load Your Own?, by Col. T. Whelen, Gun Room Press, Highland Park, NJ 1996, 4th ed., rev. 237 pp., illus. $20.00
　A basic reference on handloading, describing each step, materials and equipment. Includes loads for popular cartridges.

Wildcat Cartridges Volumes 1 & 2 Combination, by the editors of Handloaders magazine, Wolfe Publishing Co., Prescott, AZ, 1997. 350 pp., illus. Paper covers. $39.95
　A profile of the most popular information on wildcat cartridges that appeared in the Handloader magazine.

COLLECTORS

Blue Book of Gun Values, 25th Edition, edited by S.P. Fjestad, Blue Book Publications, Inc. Minneapolis, MN 2004. $39.95
　This new 25th Edition simply contains more firearms values and information than any other single publication. Expanded to over 1,600 pages featuring over 100,000 firearms prices, the new Blue Book of Gun Values also contains over Ω million words of text – no other book is even close! Most of the information contained in this publication is simply not available anywhere else, for any price!

Blue Book of Modern Black Powder Values, 3rd Edtion by Dennis Adler, Blue Book Publications, Inc. Minneapolis, MN 2003. 271 pp., illustrated. 41 color photos. Softcover. $24.95
　This new title contains more up-to-date black powder values and related information than any other single publication. This new book will keep you up to date on modern black powder models and prices, including most makes & models introduced this year!

Browning Sporting Firearms: Dates Of Manufacture, by D. R. Morse. Phoenix, AZ: Firing Pin Enterprizes, 2003. 37 pages. Softcover. New. $6.95
　Covers their pistols, revolvers, rifles, shotguns and commemoratives. Plus, Models & Serial Numbers.

Flayderman's Guide to Antique American Firearms and Their Values, 8th Edition, edited by Norm Flayderman, Krause Publications, Iola, WI, 2001. 692 pp., illus. Paper covers. $34.95
　A completely updated and new edition with more than 3,600 models and variants extensively described with all marks and specifications necessary for quick identification.

The Guns of Remington: Historic Firearms Spanning Two Centuries, compiled by Howard M. Madaus, Biplane Productions, Publisher, in cooperation with Buffalo Bill Historical Center, Cody, WY, 1998. 352 pp., illustrated with over 800 color photos. $79.95
　A complete catalog of the firearms in the exhibition, "It Never Failed Me: The Arms & Art of Remington Arms Company" at the Buffalo Bill Historical Center, Cody, Wyoming.

The Hawken Rifle: Its Place in History, by Charles E. Hanson, Jr., The Fur Press, Chadron, NE, 1979. 104 pp., illus. Paper covers. $15.00
　A definitive work on this famous rifle.

The History Of Smith & Wesson Firearms, by Dean Boorman, Lyons Press, New York, NY, 2002. 44 pages, illustrated in full color. Hardcover. New in new dust jacket. $29.95
　The definitive guide to one of the world's best-known firearms makers. Takes the story through the years of the Military & Police .38 & of the Magnum cartridge, to today's wide range of products for law-enforcement customers.

The History of Winchester Rifles, by Dean Boorman, Lyons Press, New York, NY, 2001. 144 pp., illus. 150 full-color photos. $29.95
　A captivating and wonderfully photographed history of one of the most legendary names in gun lore.

Legendary Sporting Guns, by Eric Joly, Abbeville Press, New York, N.Y., 1999. 228 pp., illustrated. $65.00
　A survey of hunting through the ages and relates how many different types of firearms were created and refined for use afield.

Longrifles of Pennsylvania, Volume 1, Jefferson, Clarion & Elk Counties, by Russel H. Harringer, George Shumway Publisher, York, PA, 1984. 200 pp., illus. $50.00
　First in series that will treat in great detail the longrifles and gunsmiths of Pennsylvania.

Marlin Firearms: A History of the Guns and the Company That Made Them, by Lt. Col. William S. Brophy, USAR, Ret., Stackpole Books, Harrisburg, PA, 1989. 672 pp., illus. $80.00
　The definitive book on the Marlin Firearms Co. and their products.

Modern Beretta Firearms, by Gene Gangarosa, Jr., Stoeger Publishing Co., So. Hackensack, NJ, 1994. 288 pp., illus. Paper covers. $16.95
　Traces all models of modern Beretta pistols, rifles, machine guns and combat shotguns. Greatly updated and expanded edition describing and valuing over 7,000 firearms manufactured from 1900 to 1996. The standard for valuing modern firearms.

Modern Gun Identification & Value Guide, 13th Edition, by Russell and Steve Quertermous, Collector Books, Paducah, KY, 1998. 504 pp., illus. Paper covers. $14.95
Features current values for over 2,500 models of rifles, shotguns and handguns, with over 1,800 illustrations.

Remington 'America's Oldest Gunmaker', The Official Authorized History Of The Remington Arms Company, by Roy Marcot. Madison, NC: Remington Arms Company, 1999. 1st edition. 312 pages, with 167 b&w illustrations, plus 291 color plates. $79.95
This is without a doubt the finest history of that firm ever to have been compiled. Based on firsthand research in the Remington companies archives, it is extremely well written.

Remington Sporting Firearms: Dates of Manufacture, by Morse, D. R. Phoenix, AZ: Firing Pin Enterprizes, 2003. 43 pages. Softcover. New. $6.95
Covers their pistols, revolvers, rifles, shotguns and commemoratives. Plus models & serial numbers. Search has proven that these weapons either functioned properly or were inadequate relative to the design and ingenuity of the proprietary cartridges.

Ruger and his Guns, by R.L. Wilson, Simon & Schuster, New York, NY, 1996. 358 pp., illus. $65.00
A history of the man, the company and their firearms.

Savage Sporting Firearms: Dates of Manufacture 1907-1997, by D. R. Morse. Phoenix, AZ: Firing Pin Enterprizes, 2003. 22 pages. Softcover. New. $6.95
Covers their pistols, revolvers, rifles, shotguns and commemoratives. Plus models & serial numbers.

Smith & Wesson Sporting Firearms: Dates Of Manufacture, by D. R. Morse. Phoenix, AZ: Firing Pin Enterprizes, 2003. 76 pages. Softcover. New. $6.95
Covers their pistols, revolvers, rifles, shotguns and commemoratives. Plus models & serial numbers.

Winchester Bolt Action Military & Sporting Rifles 1877 to 1937, by Herbert G. Houze, Andrew Mowbray Publishing, Lincoln, RI, 1998. 295 pp., illus. $45.00
Winchester was the first American arms maker to commercially manufacture a bolt action repeating rifle, and this book tells the exciting story of these Winchester bolt actions.

The Winchester Book, by George Madis, David Madis Gun Book Distributor, Dallas, TX, 2000. 650 pp., illus. $54.50
A new, revised 25th anniversary edition of this classic book on Winchester firearms. Complete serial ranges have been added.

Winchester Dates of Manufacture 1849-1984, by George Madis, Art & Reference House, Brownsboro, TX, 1984. 59 pp. $9.50
A most useful work, compiled from records of the Winchester factory.

The Winchester Lever Legacy, by Clyde "Snooky" Williamson, Buffalo Press, Zachary, LA, 1988. 664 pp., illustrated. $75.00
A book on reloading for the different calibers of the Winchester lever action rifle.

Winchester Sporting Firearms: Dates Of Manufacture, by Morse, D. R. Phoenix, AZ: Firing Pin Enterprizes, 2003.
Covers their pistols, revolvers, rifles.

GENERAL

2004 Standard Catalog of Firearms, 14th Edition, The Collector's Price & Reference Guide, by Ned Schwing, Iola, WI: Krause Publishing, 2003. 14th edition. 1,384 Pages, illustrated. 6,000+ b&w photos plus a 16-page color section. Softcover. $34.95
This is the largest, most comprehensive and best-selling firearm book of all time! And this year's edition is a blockbuster for both shooters and firearm collectors. More than 25,000 firearms are listed and priced in up to six grades of condition. That's almost 110,000 prices! Gun enthusiasts will love the new full-color section of photos highlighting the finest firearms sold at auction this past year.

Advanced Muzzleloader's Guide, by Toby Bridges, Stoeger Publishing Co., So. Hackensack, NJ, 1985. 256 pp., illus. Paper covers. $14.95
The complete guide to muzzle-loading rifles, pistols and shotguns—flintlock and percussion.

Bolt Action Rifles, 4th Edition, by Frank de Haas, DBI Books, a division of Krause Publications, Iola, WI, 2004. 628 pp., illus. Paper covers. $27.95
A revised edition of the most definitive work on all major bolt-action rifle designs.

Firearms Assembly Disassembly; Part 4 : Centerfire Rifles (2nd Edition), by J. B. Wood, Iola, WI: Krause Publications, 2004. 2nd edition. 576 pages, 1,750 b&w photos. Softcover. $24.95
The increasing cost of gunsmithing services has caused enthusiasts to perform minor repairs, refinishing, and deep cleaning on their own firearms. This updated edition shows how to easily disassemble and reassemble centerfire rifles and the correct tools

needed. Sixty-six popular guns are taken apart and individually photographed. The cross-reference index identifies more than 400 similar or identical rifle patterns that also follow these disassembly and reassembly directions. Covers the Argentine Mauser to Marlin Model 9 to Russian AK-47 to U.S. M-1 Garand to Winchester Model 1894.

Gun Digest 2004, 58th Edition, edited by Ken Ramage, DBI Books a division of Krause Publications, Iola, WI, 2002. 544 pp., illustrated. Paper covers. $27.95
This all new 58th edition continues the editorial excellence, quality, content and comprehensive cataloging that firearms enthusiasts have come to know and expect. The most read gun book in the world for the last half century.

Gun Talk, edited by Dave Moreton, Winchester Press, Piscataway, NJ, 1973. 256 pp., illus. $9.95
A treasury of original writing by the top gun writers and editors in America. Practical advice about every aspect of the shooting sports.

Gun Trader's Guide (2005 - 26th Edition), by Jarrett (ed.). Pocomoke, MD: Stoeger Publishing, 2004. 26th edition. Softcover. $21.99
The Gun Trader's Guide has been the standard reference for collectors, dealers, shooters and gun enthusiasts since 1953. This 592 page edition provides complete updated specifications, dates of manufacture and current market average values for over 6,000 handguns, rifles and shotguns, both foreign and domestic. A complete index is provided for easy reference to all guns plus handy thumb tabs help readers find, identify and price firearms with ease.

Guns Illustrated 2004, 24th Edition, edited by Ken Ramage, DBI Books a division of Krause Publications, Iola, WI, 2003. 388 pp., illustrated. Softcovers. $24.95
Highly informative, technical articles on a wide range of shooting topics by some of the top writers in the industry. A catalog section lists more than 3,000 firearms currently manufactured in or imported to the U.S.

Guns & Shooting: A Selected Bibliography, by Ray Riling, Ray Riling Arms Books Co., Phila., PA, 1982. 434 pp., illus. Limited, numbered edition. $75.00.

The Hunter's Guide to Accurate Shooting, by Wayne Van Zwoll, Guilford, CT: Lyons Press, 2002. 1st edition. 288 pp. Hardcover. $29.95
Firearms expert Van Zwoll explains exactly how to shoot the big-game rifle accurately. Taking into consideration every pertinent factor, he shows a step-by-step analysis of shooting and hunting with the big-game rifle.

The Hunting Time: Adventures In Pursuit Of North American Big Game: A Forty-Year Chronicle, by John E. Howard, Deforest, WI: Saint Huberts Press, 2002. 1st edition. 537 pages, illustrated with drawings. Hardcover. $29.95
From a novice's first hunt for whitetailed deer in his native Wisconsin, to a seasoned hunter's pursuit of a Boone and Crockett Club record book caribou in the

Jack O'Connor - The Legendary Life Of America's Greatest Gunwriter, by R. Anderson. Long Beach, CA: Safari Press, 2002. 1st edition. 240pp, profuse photos. Hardcover. $29.95
This is the book all hunters in North America have been waiting for--the long-awaited biography on Jack O'Connor! Jack O'Connor was the preeminent North American big-game hunter and gunwriter of the twentieth century, and Robert Anderson's masterfully written new work is a blockbuster filled with fascinating facts and stories about this controversial character. With the full cooperation of the O'Connor children, Anderson spent three years interviewing O'Connor's family and friends as well as delving into JOC's papers, photos, and letters, including the extensive correspondence between O'Connor and Bob Householder, and the O'Connor papers from Washington State University. O'Connor's lifelong friend Buck Buckner has contributed two chapters on his experiences with the master of North American hunting.

Modern Gun Values: 12th Edition, edited by Ken Ramage, Krause Publications, Iola, WI 2003. 608 Pages, 3,000+ b&w photos. Softcover. $21.95
Back by popular demand, this all-new expanded edition helps collectors identify the firearm, evaluate condition and determine value. Detailed specifications—and current values from specialized experts—are provided for domestic and imported handguns, rifles, shotguns and commemorative firearms. Heavily illustrated. Over 7,500 arms described and valued, in three grades of condition, according to the NRA's Modern standards.

The Quotable Hunter, edited by Jay Cassell and Peter Fiduccia, The Lyons Press, N.Y., 1999. 224 pp., illustrated. $20.00
This collection of more than three hundred memorable quotes from hunters through the ages captures the essence of the sport, with all its joys idiosyncrasies, and this classic reprint explores the *first* expanding bullet; service rifles; shooting positions; trajectories; recoil; external ballistics; and other valuable information.

THE ARMS LIBRARY

The Shooter's Bible 2004, No. 95, edited by William S. Jarrett, Stoeger Publishing Co., Wayne, NJ, 2003. 576 pp., illustrated. Paper covers. $23.95
Over 3,000 firearms currently offered by major American and foreign gunmakers. Represented are handguns, rifles, shotguns and black powder arms with complete specifications and retail prices.

The Shooter's Bible 2003, No. 94, edited by William S. Jarrett, Stoeger Publishing Co., Wayne, NJ, 2002. 576 pp., illustrated. Paper covers. $23.95
Over 3,000 firearms currently offered by major American and foreign gunmakers. Represented are handguns, rifles, shotguns and black powder arms with complete specifications and retail prices.

Weatherby: The Man, The Gun, The Legend, by Grits and Tom Gresham, Cane River Publishing Co., Natchitoches, LA, 1992. 290 pp., illus. $24.95
A fascinating look at the life of the man who changed the course of firearms development in America.

The Winchester Era, by David Madis, Art & Reference House, Brownsville, TX, 1984. 100 pp., illus. $19.95

GUNSMITHING

Accurizing the Factory Rifle, by M.L. McPhereson, Precision Shooting, Inc., Manchester, CT, 1999. 335 pp., illustrated. Paper covers. $44.95
A long-awaiting book, which bridges the gap between the rudimentary (mounting sling swivels, scope blocks and that general level of accomplishment) and the advanced (precision chambering, barrel fluting, and that general level of accomplishment) books that are currently available today.

The Art of Engraving, by James B. Meek, F. Brownell & Son, Montezuma, IA, 1973. 196 pp., illus. $42.95
A complete, authoritative, imaginative and detailed study in training for gun engraving. The first book of its kind—and a great one.

Checkering and Carving of Gun Stocks, by Monte Kennedy, Stackpole Books, Harrisburg, PA, 1962. 175 pp., illus. $39.95
Revised, enlarged cloth-bound edition of a much sought-after, dependable work.

Firearms Assembly/Disassembly Part II: Revolvers, Revised Edition, The Gun Digest Book of, by J.B. Wood, DBI Books, a division of Krause Publications, Iola, WI, 1997. 480 pp., illus. Paper covers. $27.95
Covers 49 popular revolvers plus 130 variants. The most comprehensive and professional presentation available to either hobbyist or gunsmith.

Firearms Assembly/Disassembly Part IV: Centerfire Rifles, 3rd Revised Edition, The Gun Digest Book of, by J.B. Wood, Krause Publications, Iola, WI, 2004. 480 pp., illus. Paper covers. $24.95
Covers 54 popular centerfire rifles plus 300 variants. The most comprehensive and professional presentation available to either hobbyist or gunsmith.

Firearms Assembly/Disassembly, Part V: Shotguns, Revised Edition, The Gun Digest Book of, by J.B. Wood, Krause Publications, Iola, WI, 2002. 480 pp., illus. Paper covers. $24.95
Covers 46 popular shotguns plus over 250 variants with step-by-step instructions on how to dismantle and reassemble each. The most comprehensive and professional presentation available to either hobbyist or gunsmith.

Firearms Assembly 3: The NRA Guide to Rifle and Shotguns, NRA Books, Wash., DC, 1980. 264 pp., illus. Paper covers. $14.95
Text and illustrations explaining the takedown of 125 rifles and shotguns, domestic and foreign.

Firearms Assembly 4: The NRA Guide to Pistols and Revolvers, NRA Books, Wash., DC, 1980. 253 pp., illus. Paper covers. $13.95
Text and illustrations explaining the takedown of 124 pistol and revolver models, domestic and foreign.

Firearms Bluing and Browning, by R.H. Angier, Stackpole Books, Harrisburg, PA. 151 pp., illus. $19.95
A world master gunsmith reveals his secrets of building, repairing and renewing a gun, quite literally, lock, stock and barrel. A useful, concise text on chemical

Gunsmithing: Pistols & Revolvers, by Patrick Sweeney, DBI Books, a division of Krause Publications, Iola, WI, 1998. 352 pp., illus. Paper covers. $24.95
Do-it-Yourself projects, diagnosis and repair for pistols and revolvers.

Gunsmithing: Rifles, by Patrick Sweeney, Krause Publications, Iola, WI, 1999. 352 pp., illustrated. Paper covers. $24.95
Tips for lever-action rifles. Building a custom Ruger 10/22. Building a better hunting rifle.

Gunsmithing Tips and Projects, a collection of the best articles from the *Handloader* and *Rifle* magazines, by various authors, Wolfe Publishing Co., Prescott, AZ, 1992. 443 pp., illus. Paper covers. $25.00
Includes such subjects as shop, stocks, actions, tuning, triggers, barrels, customizing, etc.

Gunsmith Kinks, by F.R. (Bob) Brownell, F. Brownell & Son, Montezuma, IA, 1st ed., 1969. 496 pp., well illus. $22.98
A widely useful accumulation of shop kinks, short cuts, techniques and pertinent comments by practicing gunsmiths from all over the world.

Gunsmith Kinks 2, by Bob Brownell, F. Brownell & Son, Publishers, Montezuma, IA, 1983. 496 pp., illus. $22.95
A collection of gunsmithing knowledge, shop kinks, new and old techniques, shortcuts and general know-how straight from those who do them best—the gunsmiths.

Gunsmith Kinks 3, edited by Frank Brownell, Brownells Inc., Montezuma, IA, 1993. 504 pp., illus. $24.95
Tricks, knacks and "kinks" by professional gunsmiths and gun tinkerers. Hundreds of valuable ideas are given in this volume.

Gunsmith Kinks 4, edited by Frank Brownell, Brownells Inc., Montezuma, IA, 2001. 564 pp., illus. $27.75
332 detailed illustrations. 560+ pages with 706 separate subject headings and over 5000 cross-indexed entries. An incredible gold mine of information.

How to Convert Military Rifles, Williams Gun Sight Co., Davision, MI, new and enlarged seventh edition, 1997. 76 pp., illus. Paper covers. $13.95
This latest edition updated the changes that have occured over the past thirty years. Tips, instructions and illustratons on how to convert popular military rifles as the Enfield, Mauser 96 nad SKS just to name a few are presented.

Mauser M98 & M96, by R.A. Walsh, Wolfe Publishing Co., Prescott, AR, 1998. 123 pp., illustrated. Paper covers. $32.50
How to build your own favorite custom Mauser rifle from two of the best bolt action rifle designs ever produced—the military Mauser Model 1898 and Model 1896 bolt

RIFLES, HANDGUNS & SHOTGUNS

The Accurate Rifle, by Warren Page, Claymore Publishing, Ohio, 1997. 254 pages, illustrated. Revised edition. Paper Covers. $17.95
Provides hunters & shooter alike with detailed practical information on the whole range of subjects affecting rifle accuracy, he explains techniques in ammo, sights

Big Bore Handguns, by John Taffin, Krause Publishing, Iola, WI: 2002. 1st edition. 352 pages, 320 b&w photos with a 16-page color section. Hardcover. $39.95
Gives honest reviews and an inside look at shooting, hunting, and competing with the biggest handguns around. Covers handguns from major gunmakers, as well as handgun customizing, accessories, reloading, and cowboy activities. Significant coverage is also given to handgun customizing, accessories, reloading, and popular shooting hobbies including hunting and cowboy activities. Accessories consist of stocks, handgun holster rigs, and much more. Firearms include single-shot pistols, revolvers, and semi-automatics.

Big Bore Sixguns, by John Taffin, Krause Publications, Iola, WI, 1997. 336 pp., illus. $39.95
The author takes aim on the entire range of big bores from .357 Magnums to .500 Maximums, single actions and cap-and-ball sixguns to custom touches for big bores.

The Great Remington 8 And Model 81 Autoloading Rifles, by John Henwood. Canada: Collector Grade Publications, 2003. 1st edition. 304 pages, 291 illustrations, 31 in color. Hardcover. $59.95
This first Collector Grade edition includes chapters on the genesis of the Remington Arms Company; Browning's five long recoil patents; the history of the Modèle 1900, the nearly identical clone produced by FN in Belgium, and the use of Browning, Remington and Winchester autoloading rifles by the French Air Service during World War I; the "cosmetic revamping" of the Model 8 which resulted in the Model 81; in-depth histories of production changes, markings, shipping dates, codes, and costs; deluxe-grade (engraved) and special models (factory experimentals, military, police and F.B.I. variants); contemporary autoloaders from around the world; notes on collecting the 8 and 81; how the long recoil autoloader works; disassembly, troubleshooting, and Model 8 and 81 component interchangeability; ammunition, ballistics, and reloading; factory options and aftermarket accessories (charger clips, magazine conversions, iron sights, scopes and mounts). The last chapter, titled "The Legend", is a fascinating study of Remington advertisements, posters and sporting art, which have become increasingly popular collectibles in recent times.

The Ithaca Featherlight Repeater; the Best Gun Going, by Walter C. Snyder, Southern Pines, NC, 1998. 300 pp., illus. $89.95.

Know Your Ruger Single Actions: The Second Decade 1963-1973, by John C. Dougan. Blacksmith Corp., North Hampton, OH, 1994. 143 pp., illus. Paper covers. $19.95

Know Your Ruger S/A Revolvers 1953-1963 (revised edition), by John C. Dougan. Blacksmith Corp., North Hampton, OH, 2002. 191 pp., illus. Paper covers. $19.95.

THE ARMS LIBRARY

Remington Autoloading And Pump Action Rifles, by Eugene Myszkowski, Tucson, AZ: Excalibur Publications, 2002. 132 pages, with 162 photographs, 6 illustrations and 18 charts. Softcover. $20.95

An illustrated history of Remington's centerfire Models 760, 740, 742, 7400 and 7600. The book is thoroughly researed and features many previously unpublished photos of the rifles, their accessories and accoutrements. Also covers high grade, unusual and experimental rifles. Contains information on collecting, serial numbers and barrel codes.

The Remington 700, by John F. Lacy, Taylor Publishing Co., Dallas, TX, 2002. 208 pp., illus. $49.95

Covers the different models, limited editions, chamberings, proofmarks, serial numbers, military models, and much more.

Rifles of the World, 2nd Edition, by John Walter, DBI Books, a division of Krause Publications, Iola, WI, 1998. 384 pp., illus. $24.95

The definitive guide to the world's centerfire and rimfire rifles.

Sixgun Cartridges and Loads, by Elmer Keith, reprint edition by The Gun Room Press, Highland Park, NJ, 1984. 151 pp., illus. $24.95

A manual covering the selection, use and loading of the most suitable and popular revolver cartridges.

Sixguns, by Elmer Keith, Wolfe Publishing Company, Prescott, AZ, 1992. 336 pp. Paper covers. $29.95. Hardcover $35.00

The history, selection, repair, care, loading, and use of this historic frontiersman's friend—the one-hand firearm.

Standard Catalog Of Smith & Wesson; 2nd Edition, by Jim Supica and Richard Nahas. Krause Publications, Iola, WI: 2001. 2nd edition. 272 Pages, 350 b&w photos, with 16 page color section. Pictorial hardcover. $34.95

Clearly details 775 Smith & Wesson models, knives, holsters, ammunition and police items with complete pricing information, illustrated glossary and index.

The Thompson/Center Contender Pistol, by Charles Tephens, Paladin Press, Boulder, CO, 1997. 58 pp., illus. Paper covers. $14.00

How to tune and time, load and shoot accurately with the Contender pistol.

The .380 Enfield No. 2 Revolver, by Mark Stamps and Ian Skennerton, I.D.S.A. Books, Piqua, OH, 1993. 124 pp., 80 illus. Paper covers. $19.95

HUNTING

Advanced Black Powder Hunting, by Toby Bridges, Stoeger Publishing Co., Wayne, NJ, 1998. 288 pp., illus. Paper covers. $21.95

The first modern day publication to be filled from cover to cover with guns, loads, projectiles, accessories and the techniques to get the most from today's front loading guns.

Advanced Strategies for Trophy Whitetails, by David Morris, Safari Press, Inc., Huntington Beach, CA, 1999. 399 pp., illustrated. $29.95

Aggressive Whitetail Hunting, by Greg Miller, Krause Publications, Iola, WI, 1995. 208 pp., illus. Paper covers. $14.95

Learn how to hunt trophy bucks in public forests, private farmlands and exclusive hunting grounds from one of America's foremost hunters.

Blacktail Trophy Tactics, by Boyd Iverson, Stoneydale Press, Stevensville, MI, 1992. 166 pp., illus. Paper covers. $14.95

A comprehensive analysis of blacktail deer habits, describing a deer's and man's use of scents, still hunting, tree techniques, etc.

The Complete Book of Mule Deer Hunting, by Walt Prothero, The Lyons Press, New York, NY, 2000. 192 pp., illustrated. Paper covers. $24.95

Field-tested practical advice on how to bag the trophy buck of a lifetime.

Deer & Deer Hunting, by Al Hofacker, Krause Publications, Iola, WI, 1993. 208 pp., illus. $34.95

Coffee-table volume packed full of how-to-information that will guide hunts for years to come.

Deer and Deer Hunting: The Serious Hunter's Guide, by Dr. Robert Wegner, Stackpole Books, Harrisburg, PA, 1984. 384 pp., illus. Paper covers. $18.95

In-depth information from the editor of "Deer & Deer Hunting" magazine. Major bibliography of English language books on deer and deer hunting from 1838-1984.

Deer and Deer Hunting Book 2, by Dr. Robert Wegner, Stackpole Books, Harrisburg, PA, 1987. 400 pp., illus. Paper covers. $18.95

Strategies and tactics for the advanced hunter.

Deer and Deer Hunting, Book 3, by Dr. Robert Wegner, Stackpole Books, Harrisburg, PA, 1990. 368 pp., illus. $18.95

This comprehensive volume covers natural history, deer hunting lore, profiles of deer hunters, and discussion of important issues facing deer hunters today.

The Deer Hunters: The Tactics, Lore, Legacy and Allure of American Deer Hunting, Edited by Patrick Durkin, Krause Publications, Iola, WI, 1997. 208 pp., illus. $29.95

More than twenty years of research from America's top whitetail hunters, researchers, and photographers have gone in to the making of this book.

Deer Hunting, by R. Smith, Stackpole Books, Harrisburg, PA, 1978. 224 pp., illus. Paper covers. $14.95

Hunting Mature Bucks, by Larry L. Weishuhn, Krause Publications, Iola, WI, 1995. 256 pp., illus. Paper covers. $14.95

One of North America's top white-tailed deer authorities shares his expertise on hunting those big, smart and elusive bucks.

Hunting Open-Country Mule Deer, by Dwight Schuh, Sage Press, Nampa, ID, 1989. 180 pp., illus. $18.95

Hunting Trophy Deer, by John Wootters, The Lyons Press, New York, NY, 1997. 272 pp., illus. $24.95

A revised edition of the definitive manual for identifying, scouting, and successfully hunting a deer of a lifetime.

Hunting Trophy Whitetails, by David Morris, Stoneydale Press, Stevensville, MT, 1993. 483 pp., illus. $29.95

This is one of the best whitetail books published in the last two decades. The author is the former editor of *North American Whitetail* magazine.

Hunting Western Deer, by Jim and Wes Brown, Stoneydale Press, Stevensville, MT, 1994. 174 pp., illus. Paper covers. $14.95

A pair of expert Oregon hunters provide insight into hunting mule deer and blacktail deer in the western states.

Mule Deer: Hunting Today's Trophies, by Tom Carpenter and Jim Van Norman, Krause Publications, Iola, WI, 1998. 256 pp., illustrated. Paper covers. $19.95

A tribute to both the deer and the people who hunt them. Includes info on where to look for big deer, prime mule deer habitat and effective weapons for the hunt.

My Health is Better in November, by Havilah Babcock, University of S. Carolina Press, Columbia, SC, 1985. 284 pp., illus. $24.95

Adventures in the field set in the plantation country and backwater streams of SC.

Proven Whitetail Tactics, by Greg Miller, Krause Publications, Iola, WI, 1997. 224 pp., illus. Paper covers. $19.95

Proven tactics for scouting, calling and still-hunting whitetail.

Records of North American Big Game 11th Edition, with hunting chapters by Craig Boddington, Tom McIntyre and Jim Zumbo, The Boone and Crockett Club, Missoula, MT, 1999. 700 pp., featuring a 32 page color section. $49.95

Listing over 17,150, of the top trophy big game animals ever recorded. Over 4,000 new listings are featured in this latest edition.

Records of North American Elk and Mule Deer, 2nd Edition, edited by Jack and Susan Reneau, Boone & Crockett Club, Missoula, MT, 1996. 360 pp., illus. Paper cover, $18.95; hardcover, $24.95

Updated and expanded edition featuring more than 150 trophy, field and historical photos of the finest elk and mule deer trophies ever recorded.

Southern Deer & Deer Hunting, by Larry Weishuhn and Bill Bynum, Krause Publications, Iola, WI, 1995. 256 pp., illus. Paper covers. $14.95

Mount a trophy southern whitetail on your wall with this firsthand account of stalking big bucks below the Mason-Dixon line.

Stand Hunting for Whitetails, by Richard P. Smith, Krause Publications, Iola, WI, 1996. 256 pp., illus. Paper covers. $14.95

The author explains the tricks and strategies for successful stand hunting.

Taking Big Bucks, by Ed Wolff, Stoneydale Press, Stevensville, MT, 1987. 169 pp., illus. $18.95

Solving the whitetail riddle.

Whitetail: Behavior Through the Seasons, by Charles J. Alsheimer, Krause Publications, Iola, WI, 1996. 208 pp., illus. $34.95

In-depth coverage of whitetail behavior presented through striking portraits of the whitetail in every season.

Whitetail: The Ultimate Challenge, by Charles J. Alsheimer, Krause Publications, Iola, WI, 1995. 228 pp., illus. Paper covers. $14.95

Learn deer hunting's most intriguing secrets—fooling deer using decoys, scents and calls— from America's premier authority.

Whitetails by the Moon, by Charles J. Alsheimer, edited by Patrick Durkin, Krause Publications, Iola, WI, 1999. 208 pp., illustrated. Paper covers. $19.95

Predict peak times to hunt whitetails. Learn what triggers the rut.

A

A Zone Bullets, 2039 Walter Rd., Billings, MT 59105 / 800-252-3111; FAX: 406-248-1961

A.G. Russell Knives, Inc., 1920 North 26th Street, Springdale, AR 72764 / 479-751-7341; FAX: 479-751-4520 ag@agrussell.com agrussell.com

A.W. Peterson Gun Shop, Inc., 4255 W. Old U.S. 441, Mt. Dora, FL 32757-3299 / 352-383-4258; FAX: 352-735-1001

AC Dyna-tite Corp., 155 Kelly St., P.O. Box 0984, Elk Grove Village, IL 60007 / 847-593-5566; FAX: 847-593-1304

Acadian Ballistic Specialties, P.O. Box 787, Folsom, LA 70437 / 504-796-0078 gunsmith@neasolft.com

Acra-Bond Laminates, 134 Zimmerman Rd., Kalispell, MT 59901 / 406-257-9003; FAX: 406-257-9003 merlins@digisys.net www.acrabondlaminates.com

Action Bullets & Alloy Inc., RR 1, P.O. Box 189, Quinter, KS 67752 / 785-754-3609; FAX: 785-754-3629 bullets@ruraltel.net

Action Direct, Inc., P.O. Box 770400, Miami, FL 33177 / 305-969-0056; FAX: 305-256-3541 www.action-direct.com

Action Products, Inc., 22 N. Mulberry St., Hagerstown, MD 21740 / 301-797-1414; FAX: 301-733-2073

Action Target, Inc., PO Box 636, Provo, UT 84603 / 801-377-8033; FAX: 801-377-8096

Actions by "T" Teddy Jacobson, 16315 Redwood Forest Ct., Sugar Land, TX 77478 / 281-277-4008; FAX: 281-277-9112 tjacobson@houston.rr.com www.actionsbyt.us

AcuSport Corporation, 1 Hunter Place, Bellefontaine, OH 43311-3001 / 513-593-7010; FAX: 513-592-5625

AFSCO Ammunition, 731 W. Third St., P.O. Box L, Owen, WI 54460 / 715-229-2516 sailers@webtv.net

Ahlman Guns, 9525 W. 230th St., Morristown, MN 55052 / 507-685-4243; FAX: 507-685-4280 www.ahlmans.com

Aimtech Mount Systems, P.O. Box 223, Thomasville, GA 31799 / 229-226-4313; FAX: 229-227-0222 mail@aimtech-mounts.com www.aimtech-mounts.com

Ajax Custom Grips, Inc., 9130 Viscount Row, Dallas, TX 75247 / 214-630-8893; FAX: 214-630-4942

Alana Cupp Custom Engraver, P.O. Box 207, Annabella, UT 84711 / 801-896-4834

Alaska Bullet Works, Inc., 9978 Crazy Horse Drive, Juneau, AK 99801 / 907-789-3834; FAX: 907-789-3433

Alessi Holsters, Inc., 2465 Niagara Falls Blvd., Amherst, NY 14228-3527 / 716-691-5615

Allard, Gary/Creek Side Metal & Woodcrafters, Fishers Hill, VA 22626 / 703-465-3903

Allen Co., Inc., 525 Burbank St., Broomfield, CO 80020 / 303-469-1857; or 800-876-8600; FAX: 303-466-7437

Allen Firearm Engraving, P.O. Box 155, Camp Verde, AZ 86322 / 928-567-6711 rosebudmkco@netzero.com

Allen Mfg., 6449 Hodgson Rd., Circle Pines, MN 55014 / 612-429-8231

Alley Supply Co., PO Box 848, Gardnerville, NV 89410 / 775-782-3800; FAX: 775-782-3827 jetalley@aol.com www.alleysupplyco.com

Alliant Techsystems Smokeless Powder Group, P.O. Box 6, Rt. 114, Bldg. 229, Radford, VA 24141-0096 www.alliantpowder.com

Allred Bullet Co., 932 Evergreen Drive, Logan UT 84321 / 435-752-6983; FAX: 435-752-6983

Alumna Sport by Dee Zee, 1572 NE 58th Ave., P.O. Box 3090, Des Moines, IA 50316 / 800-798-9899

Amadeo Rossi S.A., Rua: Amadeo Rossi, 143, Sao Leopoldo, RS 93030-220 BRAZIL / 051-592-5566

American Ammunition, 3545 NW 71st St., Miami, FL 33147 / 305-835-7400; FAX: 305-694-0037

American Gripcraft, 3230 S Dodge 2, Tucson, AZ 85713 / 602-790-1222

American Gunsmithing Institute, 1325 Imola Ave #504, Napa, CA 94559 / 707-253-0462; FAX: 707-253-7149

Ammo Load, Inc., 1560 E. Edinger, Suite G, Santa Ana, CA 92705 / 714-558-8858; FAX: 714-569-0319

Andela Tool & Machine, Inc., RD3, Box 246, Richfield Springs, NY 13439

Anderson Manufacturing Co., Inc., 22602 53rd Ave. SE, Bothell, WA 98021 / 206-481-1858; FAX: 206-481-7839

Angelo & Little Custom Gun Stock Blanks, P.O. Box 240046, Dell, MT 59724-0046

AO Sight Systems, 2401 Ludelle St., Fort Worth, TX 76105 / 888-744-4880; or 817-536-0136; FAX: 817-536-3517

Aplan Antiques & Art, James O., James O., HC 80, Box 793-25, Piedmont, SD 57769 / 605-347-5016

AR-7 Industries, LLC, 998 N. Colony Rd., Meriden, CT 06450 / 203-630-3536; FAX: 203-630-3637

Arizona Ammunition, Inc., 21421 No. 14th Ave., Suite E, Phoenix, AZ 85027 / 623-516-9004; FAX: 623-516-9012 www.azammo.com

Armfield Custom Bullets, 10584 County Road 100, Carthage, MO 64836 / 417-359-8480; FAX: 417-359-8497

Armoloy Co. of Ft. Worth, 204 E. Daggett St., Fort Worth, TX 76104 / 817-332-5604; FAX: 817-335-6517

Armor (See Buck Stop Lure Co., Inc.)

Armor Metal Products, P.O. Box 4609, Helena, MT 59604 / 406-442-5560; FAX: 406-442-5650

Ashley Outdoors, Inc., 2401 Ludelle St., Fort Worth, TX 76105 / 888-744-4880; FAX: 800-734-7939

Aspen Outfitting Co., Jon Hollinger, 9 Dean St., Aspen, CO 81611 / 970-925-3406

A-Square Co., 205 Fairfield Ave., Jeffersonville, IN 47130 / 812-283-0577; FAX: 812-283-0375

Austin & Halleck, Inc., 2150 South 950 East, Provo, UT 84606-6285 / 877-543-3256; or 801-374-9990; FAX: 801-374-9998 www.austinhallek.com

Axtell Rifle Co., 353 Mill Creek Road, Sheridan, MT 59749 / 406-842-5814

B

Badger Shooters Supply, Inc., P.O. Box 397, Owen, WI 54460 / 800-424-9069; FAX: 715-229-2332

Baekgaard Ltd., 1855 Janke Dr., Northbrook, IL 60062 / 708-498-3040; FAX: 708-493-3106

Baelder, Harry, Alte Goennebeker Strasse 5, 24635, Rickling, GERMANY / 04328-722732; FAX: 04328-722733

Baer's Hollows, P.O. Box 284, Eads, CO 81036 / 719-438-5718

Bagmaster Mfg., Inc., 2731 Sutton Ave., St. Louis, MO 63143 / 314-781-8002; FAX: 314-781-3363 sales@bagmaster.com www.bagmaster.com

Ballard Rifle & Cartridge Co., LLC, 113 W. Yellowstone Ave., Cody, WY 82414 / 307-587-4914; FAX: 307-527-6097 ballard@wyoming.com www.ballardrifles.com

Ballistic Products, Inc., 20015 75th Ave. North, Corcoran, MN 55340-9456 / 763-494-9237; FAX: 763-494-9236 info@ballisticproducts.com www.ballisticproducts.com

Ballistic Research, 1108 W. May Ave., McHenry, IL 60050 / 815-385-0037

Ballisti-Cast, Inc., P.O. Box 1057, Minot, ND 58702-1057 / 701-497-3333; FAX: 701-497-3335

Bandcor Industries, Div. of Man-Sew Corp., 6108 Sherwin Dr., Port Richey, FL 34668 / 813-848-0432

Barnes, 4347 Tweed Dr., Eau Claire, WI 54703-6302

Barnes Bullets, Inc., P.O. Box 215, American Fork, UT 84003 / 801-756-4222; or 800-574-9200; FAX: 801-756-2465 email@barnesbullets.com www.barnesbullets.com

Bear Arms, 374-A Carson Road, St. Mathews, SC 29135

Bear Mountain Gun & Tool, 120 N. Plymouth, New Plymouth, ID 83655 / 208-278-5221; FAX: 208-278-5221

Beartooth Bullets, PO Box 491, Dept. HLD, Dover, ID 83825-0491 / 208-448-1865 bullets@beartoothbullets.com beartoothbullets.com

Belding's Custom Gun Shop, 10691 Sayers Rd., Munith, MI 49259 / 517-596-2388

Bell & Carlson, Inc., Dodge City Industrial Park, 101 Allen Rd., Dodge City, KS 67801 / 800-634-8586; or 620-225-6688; FAX: 620-225-6688 email@belландcarlson.com www.belландcarlson.com

Bell Reloading, Inc., 1725 Harlin Lane Rd., Villa Rica, GA 30180

Bell's Gun & Sport Shop, 3309-19 Mannheim Rd, Franklin Park, IL 60131

Bell's Legendary Country Wear, 22 Circle Dr., Bellmore, NY 11710 / 516-679-1158

Benchmark Knives (See Gerber Legendary Blades)

Benelli Armi S.P.A., Via della Stazione, 61029, Urbino, ITALY / 39-722-307-1; FAX: 39-722-327427

Benelli USA Corp, 17603 Indian Head Hwy, Accokeek, MD 20607 / 301-283-6981; FAX: 301-283-6988 benelliusa.com

Beretta S.P.A., Pietro, Via Beretta, 18, 25063, Gardone Vae Trompia, ITALY / 39-30-8341-1 info@benetta.com www.benetta.com

Beretta U.S.A. Corp., 17601 Beretta Drive, Accokeek, MD 20607 / 301-283-2191; FAX: 301-283-0435

Berger Bullets Ltd., 5443 W. Westwind Dr., Glendale, AZ 85310 / 602-842-4001; FAX: 602-934-9083

Bianchi International, Inc., 100 Calle Cortez, Temecula, CA 92590 / 909-676-5621; FAX: 909-676-6777

Big Bear Arms & Sporting Goods, Inc., 1112 Milam Way, Carrollton, TX 75006 / 972-416-8051; or 800-400-BEAR; FAX: 972-416-0771

Big Bore Bullets of Alaska, PO Box 521455, Big Lake, AK 99652 / 907-373-2673; FAX: 907-373-2673 doug@mtaonline.net www.awloo.com/bbb/index.

Big Bore Express, 16345 Midway Rd., Nampa, ID 83651 / 208-466-9975; FAX: 208-466-6927 bigbore.com

Big Spring Enterprises "Bore Stores", P.O. Box 1115, Big Spring Rd., Yellville, AR 72687 / 870-449-5297; FAX: 870-449-4446

Bill Russ Trading Post, William A. Russ, 25 William St., Addison, NY 14801-1326 / 607-359-3896

Billingsley & Brownell, P.O. Box 25, Dayton, WY 82836 / 307-655-9344

Bill's Gun Repair, 1007 Burlington St., Mendota, IL 61342 / 815-539-5786

Billy Bates Engraving, 2302 Winthrop Dr. SW, Decatur, AL 35603 / 256-355-3690 bbrn@aol.com

Birchwood Casey, 7900 Fuller Rd., Eden Prairie, MN 55344 / 800-328-6156; or 612-937-7933; FAX: 612-937-7979

Bison Studios, 1409 South Commerce St., Las Vegas, NV 89102 / 702-388-2891; FAX: 702-383-9967

Bitterroot Bullet Co., 2001 Cedar Ave., Lewiston, ID 83501-0412 / 208-743-5635 brootbil@lewiston.com

Black Belt Bullets (See Big Bore Express)

Black Hills Ammunition, Inc., P.O. Box 3090, Rapid City, SD 57709-3090 / 605-348-5150; FAX: 605-348-9827

Black Hills Shooters Supply, P.O. Box 4220, Rapid City, SD 57709 / 800-289-2506

Black Powder Products, 67 Township Rd. 1411, Chesapeake, OH 45619 / 614-867-8047

Black Sheep Brand, 3220 W. Gentry Parkway, Tyler, TX 75702 / 903-592-3853; FAX: 903-592-0527

Blacksmith Corp., P.O. Box 280, North Hampton, OH 45349 / 937-969-8389; FAX: 937-969-8399 sales@blacksmithcorp.com www.blacksmithcorp.com

Blaser Jagdwaffen GmbH, D-88316, Isny Im Allgau, GERMANY

Blount, Inc., Sporting Equipment Div., 2299 Snake River Ave., P.O. Box 856, Lewiston, ID 83501 / 800-627-3640; or 208-746-2351; FAX: 208-799-3904

Blue Mountain Bullets, 64146 Quail Ln., Box 231, John Day, OR 97845 / 541-820-4594; FAX: 541-820-4594

Blue Ridge Machinery & Tools, Inc., P.O. Box 536-GD, Hurricane, WV 25526 / 800-872-6500; FAX: 304-562-5311 blueridgemachine@worldnet.att.net www.blueridgemachinery.com

BMC Supply, Inc., 26051 - 179th Ave. S.E., Kent, WA 98042

Bob Allen Co., P.O. Box 477, 214 SW Jackson, Des Moines, IA 50315 / 800-685-7020; FAX: 515-283-0779

MANUFACTURER'S DIRECTORY

Bob Allen Sportswear, 220 S. Main St., Osceola, IA
50213 / 210-344-8531; FAX: 210-342-2703
sales@bob-allen.com www.bob-allen.com

Boker USA, Inc., 1550 Balsam Street, Lakewood, CO
80214 / 303-462-0662; FAX: 303-462-0668
sales@bokerusa.com bokerusa.com

Boltin, John M., P.O. Box 644, Estill, SC 29918 /
803-625-2185

Bo-Mar Tool & Mfg. Co., 6136 State Hwy. 300, Longview,
TX 75604 / 903-759-4784; FAX: 903-759-9141
marykor@earthlink.net bo-mar.com

Bonanza (See Forster Products), 310 E. Lanark Ave.,
Lanark, IL 61046 / 815-493-6360; FAX:
815-493-2371

Boonie Packer Products, P.O. Box 12517, Salem, OR
97309-0517 / 800-477-3244; or 503-581-3244; FAX:
503-581-3191 booniepacker@aol.com
www.booniepacker.com

Borden Ridges Rimrock Stocks, RR 1 Box 250 BC,
Springville, PA 18844 / 570-965-2505; FAX:
570-965-2328

Borden Rifles Inc., RD 1, Box 250BC, Springville, PA
18844 / 717-965-2505; FAX: 717-965-2328

Border Barrels Ltd., Riccarton Farm, Newcastleton,
SCOTLAND UK

Bowen Classic Arms Corp., P.O. Box 67, Louisville, TN
37777 / 865-984-3583 www.bowenclassicarms.com

Bowen Knife Co., Inc., P.O. Box 590, Blackshear, GA
31516 / 912-449-4794

Bowerly, Kent, 710 Golden Pheasant Dr., Redmond, OR
97756 / 541-923-3501 jkbowerly@aol.com

Boyds' Gunstock Industries, Inc., 25376 403 Rd. Ave.,
Mitchell, SD 57301 / 605-996-5011; FAX:
605-996-9878

Brace, Larry D., 771 Blackfoot Ave., Eugene, OR 97404
/ 541-688-1278; FAX: 541-607-5833

Brass Eagle, Inc., 7050A Bramalea Rd., Unit 19,
Mississauga,, ON L4Z 1C7 CANADA /
416-848-4844

Brauer Bros., 1520 Washington Avenue., St. Louis, MO
63103 / 314-231-2864; FAX: 314-249-4952
www.brauerbros.com

Break-Free, Inc., 13386 International Parkway,
Jacksonville, FL 32218 / 800-428-0588; FAX:
904-741-5407 contactus@armorholdings.com
www.break-free.com

Brenneke GmbH, P.O. Box 1646, 30837 Langenhagen,
Langenhagen, GERMANY / +49-511-97262-0; FAX:
+49-511-97262-62 info@brenneke.de brenneke.com

Briese Bullet Co., Inc., 3442 42nd Ave. SE, Tappen, ND
58487 / 701-327-4578; FAX: 701-327-4579

Briley Mfg. Inc., 1230 Lumpkin, Houston, TX 77043 /
800-331-5718; or 713-932-6995; FAX: 713-932-1043

Broad Creek Rifle Works, Ltd., 120 Horsey Ave., Laurel,
DE 19956 / 302-875-5446; FAX: 302-875-1448
bcrw4guns@aol.com

Brockman's Custom Gunsmithing, P.O. Box 357,
Gooding, ID 83330 / 208-934-5050

Brocock Ltd., 43 River Street, Digbeth, Birmingham, B5
5SA ENGLAND / 011-021-773-1200; FAX:
011-021-773-1211 sales@brocock.co.un
www.brocock.co.uk

Broken Gun Ranch, 10739 126 Rd., Spearville, KS
67876 / 316-385-2587; FAX: 316-385-2597
nbowlin@ucom.net www.brokengunranch

Brown Precision, Inc., 7786 Molinos Ave., Los Molinos,
CA 96055 / 530-384-2506; FAX: 916-384-1638
www.brownprecision.com

Brown Products, Inc., Ed, 43825 Muldrow Trail, Perry,
MO 63462 / 573-565-3261; FAX: 573-565-2791
edbrown@edbrown.com www.edbrown.com

Brownells, Inc., 200 S. Front St., Montezuma, IA 50171 /
800-741-0015; FAX: 800-264-3068
orderdesk@brownells.com www.brownells.com

Browning Arms Co., One Browning Place, Morgan, UT
84050 / 801-876-2711; FAX: 801-876-3331
www.browning.com

Browning Arms Co. (Parts & Service), 3005 Arnold
Tenbrook Rd., Arnold, MO 63010 / 617-287-6800;
FAX: 617-287-9751

BRP, Inc. High Performance Cast Bullets, 1210
Alexander Rd., Colorado Springs, CO 80909 /
719-633-0658

BSA Guns Ltd., Armoury Rd. Small Heath, Birmingham
B11 2PP, ENGLAND / 011-021-772-8543; FAX:
011-021-773-0845 sales@bsagun.com
www.bsagun.com

BSA Optics, 3911 SW 47th Ave., Ste. 914, Ft.
Lauderdale, FL 33314 / 954-581-2144; FAX:
954-581-3165 4info@basaoptics.com
www.bsaoptics.com

B-Square Company, Inc., P.O. Box 11281, 2708 St.
Louis Ave., Ft. Worth, TX 76110 / 817-923-0964 or
800-433-2909; FAX: 817-926-7012

Knives, Inc., 1900 Weld Blvd., P.O. Box 1267, El Cajon,
CA 92020 / 619-449-1100; or 800-326-2825; FAX:
619-562-5774

Buck Stix-SOS Products Co., Box 3, Neenah, WI 54956

Buck Stop Lure Co., Inc., 3600 Grow Rd. NW, P.O. Box
636, Stanton, MI 48888 / 989-762-5091; FAX:
989-762-5124 buckstop@nethawk.com
www.buckstopscents.com

Buckeye Custom Bullets, 6490 Stewart Rd., Elida, OH
45807 / 419-641-4463

Buckhorn Gun Works, 8109 Woodland Dr., Black Hawk,
SD 57718 / 605-787-6472

Buckskin Bullet Co., P.O. Box 1893, Cedar City, UT
84721 / 435-586-3286

Buffalo Arms Co., 660 Vermeer Ct., Ponderay, ID 83852
/ 208-263-6953; FAX: 208-265-2096
www.buffaloarms.com

Buffalo Bullet Co., Inc., 12637 Los Nietos Rd., Unit A,
Santa Fe Springs, CA 90670 / 800-423-8069; FAX:
562-944-5054

Buffalo Gun Center, 3385 Harlem Rd., Buffalo, NY 14225
/ 716-833-2581; FAX: 716-833-2265
www.buffaloguncenter.com

Buffalo Rock Shooters Supply, R.R. 1, Ottawa, IL 61350
/ 815-433-2471

Bull Mountain Rifle Co., 6327 Golden West Terrace,
Billings, MT 59106 / 406-656-0778

Bullberry Barrel Works, Ltd., 2430 W. Bullberry Ln.,
Hurricane, UT 84737 / 435-635-9866; FAX:
435-635-0348 fred@bullberry.com
www.bullberry.com

Bullet Metals, Bill Ferguson, P.O. Box 1238, Sierra Vista,
AZ 85636 / 520-458-5321; FAX: 520-458-1421
info@theantimonyman.com www.bullet-metals.com

Bullet N Press, 1210 Jones St., Gastonia, NC 28052 /
704-853-0265 bnpress@quik.com
www.clt.quik.com/bnpress

Bullet Swaging Supply, Inc., P.O. Box 1056, 303
McMillan Rd., West Monroe, LA 71291 /
318-387-3266; FAX: 318-387-7779
leblackmon@colla.com

Bull-X, Inc., 411 E. Water St., Farmer City, IL 61842-1556
/ 309-928-2574 or 800-248-3845; FAX:
309-928-2130

Burkhart Gunsmithing, Don, P.O. Box 852, Rawlins, WY
82301 / 307-324-6007

Burnham Bros., P.O. Box 1148, Menard, TX 78659 /
915-396-4572; FAX: 915-396-4574

Burris Co., Inc., PO Box 1747, 331 E. 8th St., Greeley,
CO 80631 / 970-356-1670; FAX: 970-356-8702

Bushmaster Hunting & Fishing, 451 Alliance Ave.,
Toronto, ON M6N 2J1 CANADA / 416-763-4040;
FAX: 416-763-0623

Bushnell Sports Optics Worldwide, 9200 Cody, Overland
Park, KS 66214 / 913-752-3400 or 800-423-3537;
FAX: 913-752-3550

Buster's Custom Knives, P.O. Box 214, Richfield, UT
84701 / 435-896-5319; FAX: 435-896-8333
www.warenskiknives.com

Butler Creek Corp., 2100 S. Silverstone Way, Meridian,
ID 83642-8151 / 800-423-8327 or 406-388-1356;
FAX: 406-388-7204

Butler Enterprises, 834 Oberting Rd., Lawrenceburg, IN
47025 / 812-537-3584

Buzz Fletcher Custom Stockmaker, 117 Silver Road,
P.O. Box 189, Taos, NM 87571 / 505-758-3486

C

Cabela's, One Cabela Drive, Sidney, NE 69160 /
308-254-5505; FAX: 308-254-8420

Cabinet Mtn. Outfitters Scents & Lures, P.O. Box 766,
Plains, MT 59859 / 406-826-3970

Cache La Poudre Rifleworks, 140 N. College, Ft. Collins,
CO 80524 / 920-482-6913

California Sights (See Fautheree, Andy)

Camdex, Inc., 2330 Alger, Troy, MI 48083 /
810-528-2300; FAX: 810-528-0989

Cameron's, 16690 W. 11th Ave., Golden, CO 80401 /
303-279-7365; FAX: 303-628-5413
ncnoremac@aol.com

Camillus Cutlery Co., 54 Main St., Camillus, NY 13031 /
315-672-8111; FAX: 315-672-8832

Cannon Safe, Inc., 216 S. 2nd Ave. #BLD-932, San
Bernardino, CA 92400 / 310-692-0636; or
800-242-1055; FAX: 310-692-7252

Canons Delcour, Rue J.B. Cools, B-4040, Herstal,
BELGIUM / 32.(0)42.40.61.40; FAX:
32(0)42.40.22.88

Canyon Cartridge Corp., P.O. Box 152, Albertson, NY
11507 / 516-294-8946

Cape Outfitters, 599 County Rd. 206, Cape Girardeau,
MO 63701 / 573-335-4103; FAX: 573-335-1555

Caraville Manufacturing, P.O. Box 4545, Thousand
Oaks, CA 91359 / 805-499-1234

Carbide Checkering Tools (See J&R Engineering)

Carhartt, Inc., P.O. Box 600, 3 Parklane Blvd., Dearborn,
MI 48121 / 800-358-3825; or 313-271-8460; FAX:
313-271-3455

Carl Zeiss Inc., 13005 N. Kingston Ave., Chester, VA
23836 / 800-441-3005; FAX: 804-530-8481

Carlson, Douglas R, Antique American Firearms, P.O.
Box 71035, Dept GD, Des Moines, IA 50325 /
515-224-6552

Carolina Precision Rifles, 1200 Old Jackson Hwy.,
Jackson, SC 29831 / 803-827-2069

Carrell, William. See: CARRELL'S PRECISION
FIREARMS

Carrell's Precision Firearms, William Carrell, 1952
W.Silver Falls Ct., Meridian, ID 83642-3837

Carry-Lite, Inc., P.O. Box 1587, Fort Smith, AR 72902 /
479-782-8971; FAX: 479-783-0234

Carter's Gun Shop, 225 G St., Penrose, CO 81240 /
719-372-6240

Cascade Bullet Co., Inc., 2355 South 6th St., Klamath
Falls, OR 97601 / 503-884-9316

Cascade Shooters, 2155 N.W. 12th St., Redwood, OR
97756

Case & Sons Cutlery Co., W R, Owens Way, Bradford,
PA 16701 / 814-368-4123; or 800-523-6350; FAX:
814-768-5369

Case Sorting System, 12695 Cobblestone Creek Rd.,
Poway, CA 92064 / 619-486-9340

Cash Mfg. Co., Inc., P.O. Box 130, 201 S. Klein Dr.,
Waunakee, WI 53597-0130 / 608-849-5664; FAX:
608-849-5664

Cast Performance Bullet Company, P.O. Box 153,
Riverton, WY 82501 / 307-857-2940; FAX:
307-857-3132 castperform@wyoming.com
castperformance.com

Casull Arms Corp., P.O. Box 1629, Afton, WY 83110 /
307-886-0200

Caywood Gunmakers, 18 Kings Hill Estates, Berryville,
AR 72616 / 870-423-4741 www.caywoodguns.com

CCI/Speer Div of ATK, P.O. Box 856, 2299 Snake River
Ave., Lewiston, ID 83501 / 800-627-3640 or
208-746-2351

CCL Security Products, 199 Whiting St, New Britain, CT
06051 / 800-733-8588

Cedar Hill Game Calls, Inc., 238 Vic Allen Rd,
Downsville, LA 71234 / 318-982-5632; FAX:
318-368-2245

Centaur Systems, Inc., 1602 Foothill Rd., Kalispell, MT
59901 / 406-755-8609; FAX: 406-755-8609

Center Lock Scope Rings, 9901 France Ct., Lakeville,
MN 55044 / 952-461-2114; FAX: 952-461-2194
marklee55044@usfamily.net

CH Tool & Die Co. (See 4-D Custom Die Co.), 711 N Sandusky St., P.O. Box 889, Mt. Vernon, OH 43050-0889 / 740-397-7214; FAX: 740-397-6600

Chace Leather Products, 507 Alden St., Fall River, MA 02722 / 508-678-7556; FAX: 508-675-9666 chacelea@aol.com www.chaceleather.com

Chambers Flintlocks Ltd., Jim, 116 Sams Branch Rd., Candler, NC 28715 / 828-667-8361; FAX: 828-665-0852 www.flintlocks.com

Champion Shooters' Supply, P.O. Box 303, New Albany, OH 43054 / 614-855-1603; FAX: 614-855-1209

Champion Target Co., 232 Industrial Parkway, Richmond, IN 47374 / 800-441-4971

Champion's Choice, Inc., 201 International Blvd., LaVergne, TN 37086 / 615-793-4066; FAX: 615-793-4070 champ.choice@earthlink.net www.champchoice.com

Champlin Firearms, Inc., P.O. Box 3191, Woodring Airport, Enid, OK 73701 / 580-237-7388; FAX: 580-242-6922 info@champlinarms.com www.champlinarms.com

Chapuis Armes, 21 La Gravoux, BP15, 42380, St. Bonnet-le-Chatea, FRANCE / (33)77.50.06.96

Cheddite, France S.A., 99 Route de Lyon, F-26501, Bourg-les-Valence, FRANCE / 33-75-56-4545; FAX: 33-75-56-3587 export@cheddite.com

Chelsea Gun Club of New York City Inc., 237 Ovington Ave., Apt. D53, Brooklyn, NY 11209 / 718-836-9422; or 718-833-2704

Cherry Creek State Park Shooting Center, 12500 E. Belleview Ave., Englewood, CO 80111 / 303-693-1765

CheVron Bullets, RR1, Ottawa, IL 61350 / 815-433-2471

Cheyenne Pioneer Products, PO Box 28425, Kansas City, MO 64188 / 816-413-9196; FAX: 816-455-2859 cheyennepp@aol.com www.cartridgeboxes.com

Chicago Cutlery Co., 1536 Beech St., Terre Haute, IN 47804 / 800-457-2665

Choate Machine & Tool Co., Inc., P.O. Box 218, 116 Lovers Ln., Bald Knob, AR 72010 / 501-724-6193; or 800-972-6390; FAX: 501-724-5873

Churchill Glove Co., James, PO Box 298, Centralia, WA 98531 / 360-736-2816; FAX: 360-330-0151

Cimarron F.A. Co., P.O. Box 906, Fredericksburg, TX 78624-0906 / 830-997-9090; FAX: 830-997-0802 cimgraph@koc.com www.cimarron-firearms.com

Cincinnati Swaging, 2605 Marlington Ave., Cincinnati, OH 45208

Clark Custom Guns, Inc., 336 Shootout Lane, Princeton, LA 71067 / 318-949-9884; FAX: 318-949-9829

Clark Firearms Engraving, P.O. Box 80746, San Marino, CA 91118 / 818-287-1652

Clarkfield Enterprises, Inc., 1032 10th Ave., Clarkfield, MN 56223 / 612-669-7140

Claro Walnut Gunstock Co., 1235 Stanley Ave., Chico, CA 95928 / 530-342-5188; FAX: 530-342-5199 wally@clarowalnutgunstocks.com www.clarowalnutgunstocks.com

Clean Shot Technologies, 21218 St. Andrews Blvd. Ste 504, Boca Raton, FL 33433 / 888-866-2532

Clearview Mfg. Co., Inc., 413 S. Oakley St., Fordyce, AR 71742 / 501-352-8557; FAX: 501-352-7120

Clearview Products, 3021 N. Portland, Oklahoma City, OK 73107

Cleland's Outdoor World, Inc, 10306 Airport Hwy., Swanton, OH 43558 / 419-865-4713; FAX: 419-865-5865

Clements' Custom Leathercraft, Chas, 1741 Dallas St., Aurora, CO 80010-2018 / 303-364-0403; FAX: 303-739-9824 gryphons@home.com kuntaoslcat.com

Clenzoil Worldwide Corp, Jack Fitzgerald, 25670 1st St., Westlake, OH 44145-1430 / 440-899-0482; FAX: 440-899-0483

Clymer Mfg. Co., 1645 W. Hamlin Rd., Rochester Hills, MI 48309-3312 / 248-853-5555; FAX: 248-853-1530

Cold Steel Inc., 3036 Seaborg Ave. Ste. A, Ventura, CA 93003 / 800-255-4716; or 800-624-2363; FAX: 805-642-9727

Cole-Grip, 16135 Cohasset St., Van Nuys, CA 91406 / 818-782-4424

Coleman Co., Inc., 250 N. St. Francis, Wichita, KS 67201

Cole's Gun Works, Old Bank Building, Rt. 4 Box 250, Moyock, NC 27958 / 919-435-2345

Colt's Mfg. Co., Inc., PO Box 1868, Hartford, CT 06144-1868 / 800-962-COLT; or 860-236-6311; FAX: 860-244-1449

Compass Industries, Inc., 104 East 25th St., New York, NY 10010 / 212-473-2614 or 800-221-9904; FAX: 212-353-0826

Compasseco, Ltd., 151 Atkinson Hill Ave., Bardtown, KY 40004 / 502-349-0910

Competition Electronics, Inc., 3469 Precision Dr., Rockford, IL 61109 / 815-874-8001; FAX: 815-874-8181

Competitor Corp., Inc., 26 Knight St. Unit 3, Jaffrey, NH 03452 / 603-532-9483; FAX: 603-532-8209 competitorcorp@aol.com competitor-pistol.com

Component Concepts, Inc., 530 S. Springbrook Road, Newberg, OR 97132 / 503-554-8095; FAX: 503-554-9370 cci@cybcon.com www.phantomonline.com

Concept Development Corp., 16610 E. Laser Drive, Suite 5, Fountain Hills, AZ 85268-6644

Conetrol Scope Mounts, 10225 Hwy. 123 S., Seguin, TX 78155 / 830-379-3030; or 800-CONETROL; FAX: 830-379-3030 email@conetrol.com www.conetrol.com

Cooper Arms, P.O. Box 114, Stevensville, MT 59870 / 406-777-0373; FAX: 406-777-5228

Cooper-Woodward Perfect Lube, 4120 Oesterle Rd., Helena, MT 59602 / 406-459-2287 cwperfectlube@mt.net cwperfectlube.com

Corbin Mfg. & Supply, Inc., 600 Industrial Circle, P.O. Box 2659, White City, OR 97503 / 541-826-5211; FAX: 541-826-8669 sales@corbins.com www.corbins.com

Cor-Bon Inc./Glaser LLC, P.O. Box 173, 1311 Industry Rd., Sturgis, SD 57785 / 605-347-4544; or 800-221-3489; FAX: 605-347-5055 email@corbon.com www.corbon.com

Corkys Gun Clinic, 4401 Hot Springs Dr., Greeley, CO 80634-9226 / 970-330-0516

CP Bullets, 1310 Industrial Hwy #5-6, South Hampton, PA 18966 / 215-953-7264; FAX: 215-953-7275

Craftguard, 3624 Logan Ave., Waterloo, IA 50703 / 319-232-2959; FAX: 319-234-0804

Crandall Tool & Machine Co., 19163 21 Mile Rd., Tustin, MI 49688 / 616-829-4430

Crit'R Call (See Rocky Mountain Wildlife Products)

Crosman Blades (See Coleman Co., Inc.)

Crouse's Country Cover, P.O. Box 160, Storrs, CT 06268 / 860-423-8736

CRR, Inc./Marble's Inc., 420 Industrial Park, P.O. Box 111, Gladstone, MI 49837 / 906-428-3710; FAX: 906-428-3711

Cullity Restoration, 209 Old Country Rd., East Sandwich, MA 02537 / 508-888-1147

Cumberland Arms, 514 Shafer Road, Manchester, TN 37355 / 800-797-8414

Cumberland Mountain Arms, P.O. Box 710, Winchester, TN 37398 / 615-967-8414; FAX: 615-967-9199

Cummings Bullets, 1417 Esperanza Way, Escondido, CA 92027

Curly Maple Stock Blanks (See Tiger-Hunt)

Curtis Cast Bullets, 527 W. Babcock St., Bozeman, MT 59715 / 406-587-8117; FAX: 406-587-8117

Curtis Gun Shop (See Curtis Cast Bullets)

Custom Bullets by Hoffman, 2604 Peconic Ave., Seaford, NY 11783

Custom Chronograph, Inc., 5305 Reese Hill Rd., Sumas, WA 98295 / 360-988-7801

Custom Riflestocks, Inc., Michael M. Kokolus, 7005 Herber Rd., New Tripoli, PA 18066 / 610-298-3013; FAX: 610-298-2431 mkokolus@prodigy.net

Custom Single Shot Rifles, 9651 Meadows Lane, Guthrie, OK 73044 / 405-282-3634

Custom Tackle and Ammo, P.O. Box 1886, Farmington, NM 87499 / 505-632-3539

Cutco Cutlery, P.O. Box 810, Olean, NY 14760 / 716-372-3111

CVA, 5988 Peachtree Corners East, Norcross, GA 30071 / 770-449-4687; FAX: 770-242-8546 info@cva.com www.cva.com

CZ USA, PO Box 171073, Kansas City, KS 66117 / 913-321-1811; FAX: 913-321-4901

D

D.L. Unmussig Bullets, 7862 Brentford Dr., Richmond, VA 23225 / 804-320-1165; FAX: 804-320-4587

Dade Screw Machine Products, 2319 NW 7th Ave., Miami, FL 33127 / 305-573-5050

Dakota Arms, Inc., 130 Industry Road, Sturgis, SD 57785 / 605-347-4686; FAX: 605-347-4459 info@dakotaarms.com www.dakotaarms.com

Dakota Corp., 77 Wales St., P.O. Box 543, Rutland, VT 05701 / 802-775-6062; or 800-451-4167; FAX: 802-773-3919

Daly, Charles/KBI, P.O. Box 6625, Harrisburg, PA 17112 / 866-DALY GUN

Dan Wesson Firearms, 5169 Rt. 12 South, Norwich, NY 13815 / 607-336-1174; FAX: 607-336-2730 danwessonfirearms@citlink.net danwessonfirearms.com

Danner Shoe Mfg. Co., 12722 NE Airport Way, Portland, OR 97230 / 503-251-1100; or 800-345-0430; FAX: 503-251-1119

Dan's Whetstone Co., Inc., 130 Timbs Place, Hot Springs, AR 71913 / 501-767-1616; FAX: 501-767-9598 questions@danswhetstone.com www.danswhetstone.com

Danuser Machine Co., 550 E. Third St., P.O. Box 368, Fulton, MO 65251 / 573-642-2246; FAX: 573-642-2240 sales@danuser.com www.danuser.com

Dara-Nes, Inc. (See Nesci Enterprises, Inc.)

Darlington Gun Works, Inc., P.O. Box 698, 516 S. 52 Bypass, Darlington, SC 29532 / 803-393-3931

Darwin Hensley Gunmaker, P.O. Box 329, Brightwood, OR 97011 / 503-622-5411

David W. Schwartz Custom Guns, 2505 Waller St., Eau Claire, WI 54703 / 715-832-1735

Davide Pedersoli and Co., Via Artigiani 57, Gardone VT, Brescia 25063, ITALY / 030-8915000; FAX: 030-8911019 info@davidepedersoli.com www.davide_pedersoli.com

DBI Books Division of Krause Publications, 700 E. State St., Iola, WI 54990-0001 / 715-445-2214

D-Boone Ent., Inc., 5900 Colwyn Dr., Harrisburg, PA 17109

Dead Eye's Sport Center, 76 Baer Rd., Shickshinny, PA 18655 / 570-256-7432 deadeyeprizz@aol.com

Dem-Bart Checkering Tools, Inc., 1825 Bickford Ave., Snohomish, WA 98290 / 360-568-7356 walt@dembartco.com www.dembartco.com

Denver Instrument Co., 6542 Fig St., Arvada, CO 80004 / 800-321-1135; or 303-431-7255; FAX: 303-423-4831

DeSantis Holster & Leather Goods, Inc., P.O. Box 2039, 149 Denton Ave., New Hyde Park, NY 11040-0701 / 516-354-8000; FAX: 516-354-7501

Desert Mountain Mfg., P.O. Box 130184, Coram, MT 59913 / 800-477-0762; or 406-387-5361; FAX: 406-387-5361

Dietz Gun Shop & Range, Inc., 421 Range Rd., New Braunfels, TX 78132 / 210-885-4662

Dilliott Gunsmithing, Inc., 657 Scarlett Rd., Dandridge, TN 37725 / 865-397-9204 gunsmithd@aol.com dilliottgunsmithing.com

Dillon Precision Products, Inc., 8009 East Dillon's Way, Scottsdale, AZ 85260 / 480-948-8009; or 800-762-3845; FAX: 480-998-2786 sales@dillonprecision.com www.dillonprecision.com

Dixie Gun Works, P.O. Box 130, Union City, TN 38281 / 731-885-0700; FAX: 731-885-0440 info@dixiegunworks.com www.dixiegunworks.com

Dixon Muzzleloading Shop, Inc., 9952 Kunkels Mill Rd., Kempton, PA 19529 / 610-756-6271 dixonmuzzleloading.com

DKT, Inc., 14623 Vera Drive, Union, MI 49130-9744 / 800-741-7083 orders; FAX: 616-641-2015

DLO Mfg., 10807 SE Foster Ave., Arcadia, FL 33821-7304

DMT--Diamond Machining Technology Inc., 85 Hayes Memorial Dr., Marlborough, MA 01752 FAX: 508-485-3924

Dohring Bullets, 100 W. 8 Mile Rd., Ferndale, MI 48220

Domino, P.O. Box 108, 20019 Settimo Milanese, Milano, ITALY / 1-39-2-33512040; FAX: 1-39-2-33511587

Don Klein Custom Guns, 433 Murray Park Dr., Ripon, WI 54971 / 920-748-2931 daklein@charter.net www.donkleincustomguns.com

Donnelly, C. P., 405 Kubli Rd., Grants Pass, OR 97527 / 541-846-6604

Doskocil Mfg. Co., Inc., P.O. Box 1246, 4209 Barnett, Arlington, TX 76017 / 817-467-5116; FAX: 817-472-9810

Douglas Barrels, Inc., 5504 Big Tyler Rd., Charleston, WV 25313-1398 / 304-776-1341; FAX: 304-776-8560 www.benchrest.com/douglas

Dr. O's Products Ltd., P.O. Box 111, Niverville, NY 12130 / 518-784-3333; FAX: 518-784-2800

Drain, Mark, SE 3211 Kamilche Point Rd., Shelton, WA 98584 / 206-426-5452

Dremel Mfg. Co., 4915-21st St., Racine, WI 53406

Dri-Slide, Inc., 411 N. Darling, Fremont, MI 49412 / 616-924-3950

Dropkick, 1460 Washington Blvd., Williamsport, PA 17701 / 717-326-6561; FAX: 717-326-4950

DS Arms, Inc., P.O. Box 370, 27 West 990 Industrial Ave., Barrington, IL 60010 / 847-277-7258; FAX: 847-277-7259 www.dsarms.com

Duncan's Gun Works, Inc., 1619 Grand Ave., San Marcos, CA 92069 / 760-727-0515

DunLyon R&D, Inc., 52151 E. US Hwy. 60, Miami, AZ 85539 / 928-473-9027

Duofold, Inc., RD 3 Rt. 309, Valley Square Mall, Tamaqua, PA 18252 / 717-386-2666; FAX: 717-386-3652

Dutchman's Firearms, Inc., 4143 Taylor Blvd., Louisville, KY 40215 / 502-366-0555

Dybala Gun Shop, P.O. Box 1024, FM 3156, Bay City, TX 77414 / 409-245-0866

Dynamit Nobel-RWS, Inc., 81 Ruckman Rd., Closter, NJ 07624 / 201-767-7971; FAX: 201-767-1589

E

E&L Mfg., Inc., 4177 Riddle Bypass Rd., Riddle, OR 97469 / 541-874-2137; FAX: 541-874-3107

E. Arthur Brown Co., 3404 Pawnee Dr., Alexandria, MN 56308 / 320-762-8847

Eagle Grips, Eagle Business Center, 460 Randy Rd., Carol Stream, IL 60188 / 800-323-6144; or 708-260-0400; FAX: 708-260-0486

Eclectic Technologies, Inc., 45 Grandview Dr., Suite A, Farmington, CT 06034

Ed Brown Products, Inc., P.O. Box 492, Perry, MO 63462 / 573-565-3261; FAX: 573-565-2791 edbrown@edbrown.com www.edbrown.com

Edenpine, Inc. c/o Six Enterprises, Inc., 320 D Turtle Creek Ct., San Jose, CA 95125 / 408-999-0201; FAX: 408-999-0216

EdgeCraft Corp., S. Weiner, 825 Southwood Road, Avondale, PA 19311 / 610-268-0500; or 800-342-3255; FAX: 610-268-3545 www.edgecraft.com

Eichelberger Bullets, Wm., 158 Crossfield Rd., King Of Prussia, PA 19406

Ekol Leather Care, P.O. Box 2652, West Lafayette, IN 47906 / 317-463-2250; FAX: 317-463-7004

El Paso Saddlery Co., P.O. Box 27194, El Paso, TX 79926 / 915-544-2233; FAX: 915-544-2535 epsaddlery.com www.epsaddlery.com

Electro Prismatic Collimators, Inc., 1441 Manatt St., Lincoln, NE 68521

Electronic Shooters Protection, Inc., 15290 Gadsden Ct., Brighton, CO 80603 / 800-797-7791; FAX: 303-659-8668 esp@usa.net espamerican.com

Electronic Trigger Systems, Inc., P.O. Box 645, Park Rapids, MN 56470 / 218-732-5333

Eley Ltd., P.O. Box 705, Witton, Birmingham, B6 7UT ENGLAND / 021-356-8899; FAX: 021-331-4173

Elite Ammunition, P.O. Box 3251, Oakbrook, IL 60522 / 708-366-9006

Ellett Bros., 267 Columbia Ave., P.O. Box 128, Chapin, SC 29036 / 803-345-3751; or 800-845-3711; FAX: 803-345-1820

Ellicott Arms, Inc. / Woods Pistolsmithing, 8390 Sunset Dr., Ellicott City, MD 21043 / 410-465-7979

Elliott, Inc., G. W., 514 Burnside Ave., East Hartford, CT 06108 / 203-289-5741; FAX: 203-289-3137

EMAP USA, 6420 Wilshire Blvd., Los Angeles, CA 90048 / 213-782-2000; FAX: 213-782-2867

Emerging Technologies, Inc. (See Laseraim Technologies, Inc.)

EMF Co., Inc., 1900 E. Warner Ave., Suite 1-D, Santa Ana, CA 92705 / 949-261-6611; FAX: 949-756-0133

Empire Cutlery Corp., 12 Kruger Ct., Clifton, NJ 07013 / 201-472-5155; FAX: 201-779-0759

English, Inc., A.G., 708 S. 12th St., Broken Arrow, OK 74012 / 918-251-3399 agenglish@wedzone.net www.agenglish.com

Estate Cartridge, Inc., 900 Bob Ehlen Dr., Anoka, MN 55303-7502 / 409-856-7277; FAX: 409-856-5486

Euber Bullets, No. Orwell Rd., Orwell, VT 05760 / 802-948-2621

Euroarms of America, Inc., P.O. Box 3277, Winchester, VA 22604 / 540-662-1863; FAX: 540-662-4464 www.euroarms.net

Evolution Gun Works, Inc., 4050 B-8 Skyron Dr., Doylestown, PA 18901 / 215-348-9892; FAX: 215-348-1056 egw@pil.net www.egw-guns.com

Eze-Lap Diamond Prods., P.O. Box 2229, 15164 West State St., Westminster, CA 92683 / 714-847-1555; FAX: 714-897-0280

E-Z-Way Systems, P.O. Box 4310, Newark, OH 43058-4310 / 614-345-6645; or 800-848-2072; FAX: 614-345-6600

F

Federal Cartridge Co., 900 Ehlen Dr., Anoka, MN 55303 / 612-323-2300; FAX: 612-323-2506

Fiocchi Munizioni S.P.A. (See U.S. Importer-Fiocch

Fiocchi of America, Inc., 5030 Fremont Rd., Ozark, MO 65721 / 417-725-4118; or 800-721-2666; FAX: 417-725-1039

Flambeau, Inc., 15981 Valplast Rd., Middlefield, OH 44062 / 216-632-1631; FAX: 216-632-1581 www.flambeau.com

Flayderman & Co., Inc., P.O. Box 2446, Ft. Lauderdale, FL 33303 / 954-761-8855

Flintlocks, Etc., 160 Rossiter Rd., P.O. Box 181, Richmond, MA 01254 / 413-698-3822; FAX: 413-698-3866 flintetc@berkshire.rr.com

Flitz International Ltd., 821 Mohr Ave., Waterford, WI 53185 / 414-534-5898; FAX: 414-534-2991

FN Manufacturing, P.O. Box 24257, Columbia, SC 29224 / 803-736-0522

Forrest Tool Co., P.O. Box 768, 44380 Gordon Lane, Mendocino, CA 95460 / 707-937-2141; FAX: 717-937-1817

Forster, Kathy (See Custom Checkering)

Forster, Larry L., Box 212, 216 Highway 13 E., Gwinner, ND 58040-0212 / 701-678-2475

Forster Products, 310 E. Lanark Ave., Lanark, IL 61046 / 815-493-6360; FAX: 815-493-2371

Fort Hill Gunstocks, 12807 Fort Hill Rd., Hillsboro, OH 45133 / 513-466-2763

Fort Knox Security Products, 1051 N. Industrial Park Rd., Orem, UT 84057 / 801-224-7233; or 800-821-5216; FAX: 801-226-5493

4-D Custom Die Co., 711 N. Sandusky St., PO Box 889, Mt. Vernon, OH 43050-0889 / 740-397-7214; FAX: 740-397-6600 info@ch4d.com ch4d.com

Fowler Bullets, 806 Dogwood Dr., Gastonia, NC 28054 / 704-867-3259

Frank Knives, 13868 NW Keleka Pl., Seal Rock, OR 97376 / 541-563-3041; FAX: 541-563-3041

Freedom Arms, Inc., P.O. Box 150, Freedom, WY 83120 / 307-883-2468; FAX: 307-883-2005

Frontier, 2910 San Bernardo, Laredo, TX 78040 / 956-723-5409; FAX: 956-723-1774

Frontier Arms Co., Inc., 401 W. Rio Santa Cruz, Green Valley, AZ 85614-3932

Frontier Products Co., 2401 Walker Rd., Roswell, NM 88201-8950 / 614-262-9357

Frontier Safe Co., 3201 S. Clinton St., Fort Wayne, IN 46806 / 219-744-7233; FAX: 219-744-6678

Frost Cutlery Co., P.O. Box 22636, Chattanooga, TN 37422 / 615-894-6079; FAX: 615-894-9576

G

G.C. Bullet Co., Inc., 40 Mokelumne River Dr., Lodi, CA 95240

Gain Twist Barrel Co., Rifle Works and Armory, 707 12th St., Cody, WY 82414 / 307-587-4919; FAX: 307-527-6097

Galati International, P.O. Box 10, 616 Burley Ridge Rd., Wesco, MO 65586 / 636-584-0785; FAX: 573-775-4308 support@galatiinternational.com www.galatiinternational.com

Galaxy Imports Ltd., Inc., P.O. Box 3361, Victoria, TX 77903 / 361-573-4867; FAX: 361-576-9622 galaxy@cox-internet.com

GALCO International Ltd., 2019 W. Quail Ave., Phoenix, AZ 85027 / 623-474-7070; FAX: 623-582-6854 customerservice@usgalco.com www.usgalco.com

Game Haven Gunstocks, 13750 Shire Rd., Wolverine, MI 49799 / 616-525-8257

Gamebore Division, Polywad, Inc., P.O. Box 7916, Macon, GA 31209 / 478-477-0669; or 800-998-0669

Gander Mountain, Inc., 12400 Fox River Rd., Wilmont, WI 53192 / 414-862-6848

Garrett Cartridges, Inc., P.O. Box 178, Chehalis, WA 98532 / 360-736-0702 www.garrettcartridges.com

Gary Goudy Classic Stocks, 1512 S. 5th St., Dayton, WA 99328 / 509-382-2726 goudy@innw.net

Gary Reeder Custom Guns, 2601 7th Avenue East, Flagstaff, AZ 86004 / 928-526-3313; FAX: 928-527-0840 gary@reedercustomguns.com www.reedercustomguns.com

Gator Guns & Repair, 7952 Kenai Spur Hwy., Kenai, AK 99611-8311

Genco, P.O. Box 5704, Asheville, NC 28803

Genecco Gun Works, 10512 Lower Sacramento Rd., Stockton, CA 95210 / 209-951-0706; FAX: 209-931-3872

Gene's Custom Guns, P.O. Box 10534, White Bear Lake, MN 55110 / 651-429-5105; FAX: 651-429-7365

Gentex Corp., 5 Tinkham Ave., Derry, NH 03038 / 603-434-0311; FAX: 603-434-3002 sales@derry.gentexcorp.com www.derry.gentexcorp.com

Gentner Bullets, 109 Woodlawn Ave., Upper Darby, PA 19082 / 610-352-9396

George Madis Winchester Consultants, George Madis, P.O. Box 545, Brownsboro, TX 75756 / 903-852-6480; FAX: 903-852-3045 gmadis@earthlink.com www.georgemadis.com

Gerber Legendary Blades, 14200 SW 72nd Ave., Portland, OR 97223 / 503-639-6161; or 800-950-6161; FAX: 503-684-7008

Getz Barrel Company, P.O. Box 88, 426 E. Market St., Beavertown, PA 17813 / 570-658-7263; FAX: 570-658-4110 www.getzbrl.com

Gibbs Rifle Co., Inc., 219 Lawn St., Martinsburg, WV 25401 / 304-262-1651; FAX: 304-262-1658 support@gibbsrifle.com www.gibbsrifle.com

Glacier Glove, 4890 Aircenter Circle, Suite 210, Reno, NV 89502 / 702-825-8225; FAX: 702-825-6544

Glass, Herb, P.O. Box 25, Bullville, NY 10915 / 914-361-3021

Gner's Hard Cast Bullets, 1107 11th St., LaGrande, OR 97850 / 503-963-8796

Goens, Dale W., P.O. Box 224, Cedar Crest, NM 87008 / 505-281-5419

Goergen's Gun Shop, Inc., 17985 538th Ave., Austin, MN 55912 / 507-433-9280

GOEX, Inc., P.O. Box 659, Doyline, LA 71023-0659 / 318-382-9300; FAX: 318-382-9303 mfahringer@goexpowder.com www.goexpowder.com

Golden Bear Bullets, 3065 Fairfax Ave., San Jose, CA 95148 / 408-238-9515

Gonic Arms/North American Arms, Inc., 134 Flagg Rd., Gonic, NH 03839 / 603-332-8456; or 603-332-8457

Gotz Bullets, 11426 Edgemere Ter., Roscoe, IL 61073-8232

Grand Slam Hunting Products, Box 121, 25454 Military Rd., Cascade, MD 21719 / 301-241-4900; FAX: 301-241-4900 rlj6call@aol.com

Graves Co., 1800 Andrews Ave., Pompano Beach, FL 33069 / 800-327-9103; FAX: 305-960-0301

Great American Gunstock Co., 3420 Industrial Drive, Yuba City, CA 95993 / 800-784-4867; FAX: 530-671-3906 gunstox@hotmail.com www.gunstocks.com

Green Mountain Rifle Barrel Co., Inc., P.O. Box 2670, 153 West Main St., Conway, NH 03818 / 603-447-1095; FAX: 603-447-1099 www.gmriflebarrel.com

Greenwood Precision, P.O. Box 407, Rogersville, MO 65742 / 417-725-2330

Grier's Hard Cast Bullets, 1107 11th St., LaGrande, OR 97850 / 503-963-8796

Gruning Precision, Inc., 7101 Jurupa Ave., No. 12, Riverside, CA 92504 / 909-289-4371; FAX: 909-689-7791 gruningprecision@earthlink.net www.gruningprecision.com

GSI, Inc., 7661 Commerce Ln., Trussville, AL 35173 / 205-655-8299

GTB-Custom Bullets, 482 Comerwood Court, S. San Francisco, CA 94080 / 650-583-1550

Guardsman Products, 411 N. Darling, Fremont, MI 49412 / 616-924-3950

Gun City, 212 W. Main Ave., Bismarck, ND 58501 / 701-223-2304

Gun Hunter Books (See Gun Hunter Trading Co.), 5075 Heisig St., Beaumont, TX 77705 / 409-835-3006; FAX: 409-838-2266 gunhuntertrading@hotmail.com

Gun Hunter Trading Co., 5075 Heisig St., Beaumont, TX 77705 / 409-835-3006; FAX: 409-838-2266 gunhuntertrading@hotmail.com

Gun Leather Limited, 116 Lipscomb, Ft. Worth, TX 76104 / 817-334-0225; FAX: 800-247-0609

Gun List (See Krause Publications), 700 E State St., Iola, WI 54990 / 715-445-2214; FAX: 715-445-4087

Gun South, Inc. (See GSI, Inc.)

Gun Vault, 7339 E. Acoma Dr., Ste. 7, Scottsdale, AZ 85260 / 602-951-6855

Gun-Alert, 1010 N. Maclay Ave., San Fernando, CA 91340 / 818-365-0864; FAX: 818-365-1308

Guncraft Books (See Guncraft Sports, Inc.), 10737 Dutchtown Rd., Knoxville, TN 37932 / 865-966-4545; FAX: 865-966-4500 findit@guncraft.com www.guncraft.com

Guncraft Sports, Inc., 10737 Dutchtown Rd., Knoxville, TN 37932 / 865-966-4545; FAX: 865-966-4500 findit@guncraft.com www.usit.net/guncraft

Guncraft Sports, Inc., Marie C. Wiest, 10737 Dutchtown Rd., Knoxville, TN 37932 / 865-966-4545; FAX: 865-966-4500 findit@guncraft.com www.guncraft.com

Guncrafter Industries, 171 Madison 1510, Huntsville, AR 72740 / 479-665-2466 www.guncrafterindustries.com

Gun-Ho Sports Cases, 110 E. 10th St., St. Paul, MN 55101 / 612-224-9491

Gunline Tools, 2950 Saturn St., "O", Brea, CA 92821 / 714-993-5100; FAX: 714-572-4128

GUNS Magazine, 591 Camino de la Reina, Suite 200, San Diego, CA 92108 / 619-297-5350; FAX: 619-297-5353

Gunsmithing Ltd., 57 Unquowa Rd., Fairfield, CT 06824 / 203-254-0436; FAX: 203-254-1535

Gunsmithing, Inc., 30 West Buchanan St., Colorado Springs, CO 80907 / 719-632-3795; FAX: 719-632-3493

H

H&B Forge Co., Rt. 2, Geisinger Rd., Shiloh, OH 44878 / 419-895-1856

H&P Publishing, 7174 Hoffman Rd., San Angelo, TX 76905 / 915-655-5953

H&R 1871.LLC, 60 Industrial Rowe, Gardner, MA 01440 / 508-632-9393; FAX: 508-632-2300 hr1871@hr1871.com www.hr1871.com

Handgun Press, P.O. Box 406, Glenview, IL 60025 / 847-657-6500; FAX: 847-724-8831 handgunpress@earthlink.net

Hank's Gun Shop, Box 370, 50 West 100 South, Monroe, UT 84754 / 801-527-4456

Hanned Precision (See The Hanned Line)

Harper's Custom Stocks, 928 Lombrano St., San Antonio, TX 78207 / 210-732-7174

Harrell's Precision, 5756 Hickory Dr., Salem, VA 24153 / 540-380-2683

Harris Engineering Inc., Dept GD54, Barlow, KY 42024 / 502-334-3633; FAX: 502-334-3000

Harris Enterprises, P.O. Box 105, Bly, OR 97622 / 503-353-2625

Harris Hand Engraving, Paul A., 113 Rusty Ln., Boerne, TX 78006-5746 / 512-391-5121

Harris Publications, 1115 Broadway, New York, NY 10010 / 212-807-7100; FAX: 212-627-4678

Harrison Bullets, 6437 E. Hobart St., Mesa, AZ 85205

Harry Lawson Co., 3328 N. Richey Blvd., Tucson, AZ 85716 / 520-326-1117; FAX: 520-326-1117

Hart & Son, Inc., Robert W., 401 Montgomery St., Nescopeck, PA 18635 / 717-752-3655; FAX: 717-752-1088

Hart Rifle Barrels, Inc., P.O. Box 182, 1690 Apulia Rd., Lafayette, NY 13084 / 315-677-9841; FAX: 315-677-9610 hartrb@aol.com hartbarrels.com

Hastings, P.O. Box 224, Clay Center, KS 67432 / 785-632-3169; FAX: 785-632-6554

Hatfield Gun, 224 N. 4th St., St. Joseph, MO 64501

Hawk, Inc., 849 Hawks Bridge Rd., Salem, NJ 08079 / 609-299-2700; FAX: 609-299-2800 info@hawkbullets.com www.hawkbullets.com

Hawken Shop, The (See Dayton Traister)

Heckler & Koch GmbH, PO Box 1329, 78722 Oberndorf, Neckar, GERMANY / 49-7423179-0; FAX: 49-7423179-2406

Heckler & Koch, Inc., 21480 Pacific Blvd., Sterling, VA 20166-8900 / 703-450-1900; FAX: 703-450-8160 www.hecklerkoch-usa.com

Heidenstrom Bullets, Dalghte 86-3660 Rjukan, 35091818, NORWAY, olau.joh@online.tuo

Henriksen Tool Co., Inc., 8515 Wagner Creek Rd., Talent, OR 97540 / 541-535-2309; FAX: 541-535-2309

Henry Repeating Arms Co., 110 8th St., Brooklyn, NY 11215 / 718-499-5600; FAX: 718-768-8056 info@henryrepeating.com www.henryrepeating.com

Hensley, Gunmaker, Darwin, PO Box 329, Brightwood, OR 97011 / 503-622-5411

Hercules, Inc. (See Alliant Techsystems, Smokeless)

Heritage Manufacturing, Inc., 4600 NW 135th St., Opa Locka, FL 33054 / 305-685-5966; FAX: 305-687-6721 infohmi@heritagemfg.com www.heritagemfg.com

Heritage/VSP Gun Books, P.O. Box 887, McCall, ID 83638 / 208-634-4104; FAX: 208-634-3101 heritage@gunbooks.com www.gunbooks.com

Herrett's Stocks, Inc., P.O. Box 741, Twin Falls, ID 83303 / 208-733-1498

Herter's Manufacturing Inc., 111 E. Burnett St., P.O. Box 518, Beaver Dam, WI 53916-1811 / 414-887-1765; FAX: 414-887-8444

High Bridge Arms, Inc., 3185 Mission St., San Francisco, CA 94110 / 415-282-8358

High North Products, Inc., P.O. Box 2, Antigo, WI 54409 / 715-627-2331; FAX: 715-623-5451

High Performance International, 5734 W. Florist Ave., Milwaukee, WI 53218 / 414-466-9040

High Precision, Bud Welsh, 80 New Road, E. Amherst, NY 14051 / 716-688-6344; FAX: 716-688-0425 welsh5168@aol.com www.high-precision.com

Hinman Outfitters, Bob, 107 N Sanderson Ave., Bartonville, IL 61607-1839 / 309-691-8132

Hi-Performance Ammunition Company, 484 State Route 366, Apollo, PA 15613 / 412-327-8100

Hodgdon Powder Co., 6231 Robinson, Shawnee Mission, KS 66202 / 913-362-9455; FAX: 913-362-1307

Hogue Grips, P.O. Box 1138, Paso Robles, CA 93447 / 800-438-4747 or 805-239-1440; FAX: 805-239-2553

Hoppe's Div. Penguin Industries, Inc., P.O. Box 1690, Oregon City, OR 97045-0690 / 610-384-6000

Horizons Unlimited, P.O. Box 426, Warm Springs, GA 31830 / 706-655-3603; FAX: 706-655-3603

Hornady Mfg. Co., P.O. Box 1848, Grand Island, NE 68802 / 800-338-3220 or 308-382-1390; FAX: 308-382-5761

Horseshoe Leather Products, Andy Arratoonian, The Cottage Sharow, Ripon U.K., ENGLAND U.K. / 44-1765-605858 andy@horseshoe.co.uk www.holsters.org

Howa Machinery, Ltd., Sukaguchi, Shinkawa-cho Nishikasugai-gun, Aichi 452-8601, JAPAN / 81-52-408-1231; FAX: 81-52-401-4999 howa@howa.co.jp http://www.howa.cojpl

Howell Machine, 815 1/2 D St., Lewiston, ID 83501 / 208-743-7418

H-S Precision, Inc., 1301 Turbine Dr., Rapid City, SD 57701 / 605-341-3006; FAX: 605-342-8964

HT Bullets, 244 Belleville Rd., New Bedford, MA 02745 / 508-999-3338

Huey Gun Cases, 820 Indiana St., Lawrence, KS 66044-2645 / 816-444-1637; FAX: 816-444-1637 hueycases@aol.com www.hueycases.com

Hume, Don, P.O. Box 351, Miami, OK 74355 / 800-331-2686; FAX: 918-542-4340 info@donhume.com www.donhume.com

Hunkeler, A. (See Buckskin Machine Works), 3235 S 358th St., Auburn, WA 98001 / 206-927-5412

Hunter Co., Inc., 3300 W. 71st Ave., Westminster, CO 80030 / 303-427-4626; FAX: 303-428-3980 debbiet@huntercompany.com www.huntercompany.com

Hunterjohn, PO Box 771457, St. Louis, MO 63177 / 314-531-7250 www.hunterjohn.com

Hunter's Specialties Inc., 6000 Huntington Ct. NE, Cedar Rapids, IA 52402-1268 / 319-395-0321; FAX: 319-395-0326

Hunters Supply, Inc., P.O. Box 313, Tioga, TX 76271 / 940-437-2458; FAX: 940-437-2228 hunterssupply@hotmail.com www.hunterssupply.net

Huntington Die Specialties, 601 Oro Dam Blvd., Oroville, CA 95965 / 530-534-1210; FAX: 530-534-1212 buy@huntingtons.com www.huntingtons.com

Hydrosorbent Products, PO Box 437, Ashley Falls, MA 01222 / 800-448-7903; FAX: 413-229-8743 orders@dehumidify.com www.dehumidify.com

I

Image Ind. Inc., 382 Balm Court, Wood Dale, IL 60191 / 630-766-2402; FAX: 630-766-7373

Impact Case & Container, Inc., P.O. Box 1129, Rathdrum, ID 83858 / 877-687-2452; FAX: 208-687-0632 bradk@icc-case.com www.icc-case.com

Imperial Schrade Corp., 7 Schrade Ct., Box 7000, Ellenville, NY 12428 / 914-647-7601; FAX: 914-647-8701 csc@schradeknives.com www.schradeknives.com

Import Sports Inc., 1750 Brielle Ave., Unit B1, Wanamassa, NJ 07712 / 732-493-0302; FAX: 732-493-0301 gsodini@aol.com www.bersa-11ama.com

IMR Powder Co., 1080 Military Turnpike, Suite 2, Plattsburgh, NY 12901 / 518-563-2253; FAX: 518-563-6916

Ion Industries, Inc., 3508 E Allerton Ave., Cudahy, WI 53110 / 414-486-2007; FAX: 414-486-2017

Iosso Products, 1485 Lively Blvd., Elk Grove Village, IL 60007 / 847-437-8400; FAX: 847-437-8478

Iron Bench, 12619 Bailey Rd., Redding, CA 96003 / 916-241-4623

Ironside International Publishers, Inc., P.O. Box 1050, Lorton, VA 22199

Ironsighter Co., P.O. Box 85070, Westland, MI 48185 / 734-326-8731; FAX: 734-326-3378 www.ironsighter.com

Irwin, Campbell H., 140 Hartland Blvd., East Hartland, CT 06027 / 203-653-3901

Island Pond Gun Shop, Cross St., Island Pond, VT 05846 / 802-723-4546

Israel Arms Inc., 5625 Star Ln. #B, Houston, TX 77057 / 713-789-0745; FAX: 713-914-9515 www.israelarms.com

Ithaca Gun Company LLC, 901 Rt. 34 B, King Ferry, NY 13081 / 315-364-7171; FAX: 315-364-5134 info@ithacagun.com

J

J&L Superior Bullets (See Huntington Die Special)

J. Dewey Mfg. Co., Inc., P.O. Box 2014, Southbury, CT 06488 / 203-264-3064; FAX: 203-262-6907 deweyrods@worldnet.att.net www.deweyrods.com

J. Korzinek Riflesmith, RD 2, Box 73D, Canton, PA 17724 / 717-673-8512

J.A. Blades, Inc. (See Christopher Firearms Co.)

J.R. Williams Bullet Co., 2008 Tucker Rd., Perry, GA 31069 / 912-987-0274

J.W. Morrison Custom Rifles, 4015 W. Sharon, Phoenix, AZ 85029 / 602-978-3754

J/B Adventures & Safaris Inc., 2275 E. Arapahoe Rd., Ste. 109, Littleton, CO 80122-1521 / 303-771-0977

Jack A. Rosenberg & Sons, 12229 Cox Ln., Dallas, TX 75234 / 214-241-6302

Jack Dever Co., 8520 NW 90th St., Oklahoma City, OK 73132 / 405-721-6393 jbdever1@home.com

James Churchill Glove Co., PO Box 298, Centralia, WA 98531 / 360-736-2816; FAX: 360-330-0151 churchillglove@localaccess.com

Javelina Lube Products, P.O. Box 337, San Bernardino, CA 92402 / 909-350-9556; FAX: 909-429-1211

Jenkins Recoil Pads, 5438 E. Frontage Ln., Olney, IL 62450 / 618-395-3416

Jensen Bullets, RR 1 Box 187, Arco, ID 83213 / 208-785-5590

Jensen's Custom Ammunition, 5146 E. Pima, Tucson, AZ 85712 / 602-325-3346; FAX: 602-322-5704

Jericho Tool & Die Co., Inc., 2917 St. Hwy. 7, Bainbridge, NY 13733 / 607-563-8222; FAX: 607-563-8560 jerichotool.com www.jerichotool.com

Jerry Phillips Optics, P.O. Box L632, Langhorne, PA 19047 / 215-757-5037; FAX: 215-757-7097

Jester Bullets, Rt. 1 Box 27, Orienta, OK 73737

Jewell Triggers, Inc., 3620 Hwy. 123, San Marcos, TX 78666 / 512-353-2999; FAX: 512-392-0543

JGS Precision Tool Mfg., LLC, 60819 Selander Rd., Coos Bay, OR 97420 / 541-267-4331; FAX: 541-267-5996 jgstools@harborside.com www.jgstools.com

Jim Norman Custom Gunstocks, 14281 Cane Rd., Valley Center, CA 92082 / 619-749-6252

Jim's Precision, Jim Ketchum, 1725 Moclips Dr., Petaluma, CA 94952 / 707-762-3014

JLK Bullets, 414 Turner Rd., Dover, AR 72837 / 501-331-4194

John Rigby & Co., 500 Linne Rd. Ste. D, Paso Robles, CA 93446 / 805-227-4236; FAX: 805-227-4723 jribgy@calinet www.johnrigbyandco.com

John's Custom Leather, 523 S. Liberty St., Blairsville, PA 15717 / 724-459-6802; FAX: 724-459-5996

Johnson Wood Products, 34897 Crystal Road, Strawberry Point, IA 52076 / 563-933-6504 johnsonwoodproducts@yahoo.com

Jones Moulds, Paul, 4901 Telegraph Rd., Los Angeles, CA 90022 / 213-262-1510

JP Sales, Box 307, Anderson, TX 77830

JRP Custom Bullets, RR2 2233 Carlton Rd., Whitehall, NY 12887 / 518-282-0084 or 802-438-5548

Justin Phillippi Custom Bullets, P.O. Box 773, Ligonier, PA 15658 / 412-238-9671

K

K&M Industries, Inc., Box 66, 510 S. Main, Troy, ID 83871 / 208-835-2281; FAX: 208-835-5211

K&M Services, 5430 Salmon Run Rd., Dover, PA 17315 / 717-292-3175; FAX: 717-292-3175

K.L. Null Holsters Ltd., 161 School St. NW, Hill City Station, Resaca, GA 30735 / 706-625-5643; FAX: 706-625-9392 ken@klnullholsters.com www.klnullholsters.com

Ka Pu Kapili, P.O. Box 745, Honokaa, HI 96727 / 808-776-1644; FAX: 808-776-1731

KA-BAR Knives, 200 Homer St., Olean, NY 14760 / 800-282-0130; FAX: 716-790-7188 info@ka-bar.com www.ka-bar.com

Kahles A. Swarovski Company, 2 Slater Rd., Cranston, RI 02920 / 401-946-2220; FAX: 401-946-2587

Kailua Custom Guns Inc., 51 N. Dean Street, Coquille, OR 97423 / 541-396-5413 kailuacustom@aol.com www.kailuacustom.com

Kalispel Case Line, P.O. Box 267, Cusick, WA 99119 / 509-445-1121

Kamik Outdoor Footwear, 554 Montee de Liesse, Montreal, PQ H4T 1P1 CANADA / 514-341-3950; FAX: 514-341-1861

Kasenit Co., Inc., 39 Park Ave., Highland Mills, NY 10930 / 845-928-9595; FAX: 845-986-8038

Kaswer Custom, Inc., 13 Surrey Drive, Brookfield, CT 06804 / 203-775-0564; FAX: 203-775-6872

KDF, Inc., 2485 Hwy. 46 N., Seguin, TX 78155 / 830-379-8141; FAX: 830-379-5420

Keith's Bullets, 942 Twisted Oak, Algonquin, IL 60102 / 708-658-3520

Keith's Custom Gunstocks, Keith M. Heppler, 540 Banyan Circle, Walnut Creek, CA 94598 / 925-934-3509; FAX: 925-934-3143 kmheppler@hotmail.com

Kelbly, Inc., 7222 Dalton Fox Lake Rd., North Lawrence, OH 44666 / 216-683-4674; FAX: 216-683-7349

Kelley's, P.O. Box 125, Woburn, MA 01801-0125 / 800-879-7273; FAX: 781-272-7077 kels@star.net www.kelsmilitary.com

Ken Eyster Heritage Gunsmiths, Inc., 6441 Bisop Rd., Centerburg, OH 43011 / 740-625-6131; FAX: 740-625-7811

Ken Starnes Gunmaker, 15940 SW Holly Hill Rd., Hillsboro, OR 97123-9033 / 503-628-0705; FAX: 503-443-2096 kstarnes@kdsa.com

Keng's Firearms Specialty, Inc./US Tactical Systems, 875 Wharton Dr., P.O. Box 44405, Atlanta, GA 30336-1405 / 404-691-7611; FAX: 404-505-8445

Kennedy Firearms, 10 N. Market St., Muncy, PA 17756 / 717-546-6695

Ken's Kustom Kartridges, 331 Jacobs Rd., Hubbard, OH 44425 / 216-534-4595

Kershaw Knives, 25300 SW Parkway Ave., Wilsonville, OR 97070 / 503-682-1966; or 800-325-2891; FAX: 503-682-7168

Kesselring Gun Shop, 4024 Old Hwy. 99N, Burlington, WA 98233 / 360-724-3113; FAX: 360-724-7003 info@kesselrings.com www.kesselrings.com

Kickeez I.N.C., Inc., 301 Industrial Dr., Carl Junction, MO 64834-8806 / 419-649-2100; FAX: 417-649-2200 kickey@ipa.net

Kilham & Co., Main St., P.O. Box 37, Lyme, NH 03768 / 603-795-4112

Kim Ahrends Custom Firearms, Inc., Box 203, Clarion, IA 50525 / 515-532-3449; FAX: 515-532-3926

Kimber of America, Inc., 1 Lawton St., Yonkers, NY 10705 / 800-880-2418; FAX: 914-964-9340

King & Co., P.O. Box 1242, Bloomington, IL 61702 / 309-473-3964; FAX: 309-473-2161

King's Gun Works, 1837 W. Glenoaks Blvd., Glendale, CA 91201 / 818-956-6010; FAX: 818-548-8606

Kirkpatrick Leather Co., PO Box 677, Laredo, TX 78040 / 956-723-6631; FAX: 956-725-0672 mike@kirkpatrickleather.com www.kirkpatrickleather.com

Kleen-Bore, Inc., 16 Industrial Pkwy., Easthampton, MA 01027 / 413-527-0300; FAX: 413-527-2522 info@kleen-bore.com www.kleen-bore.com

Kleinendorst, K. W., RR 1, Box 1500, Hop Bottom, PA 18824 / 717-289-4687

Klingler Woodcarving, P.O. Box 141, Thistle Hill, Cabot, VT 05647 / 802-426-3811

Knifeware, Inc., P.O. Box 3, Greenville, WV 24945 / 304-832-6878

Knight Rifles, 21852 Hwy. J46, P.O. Box 130, Centerville, IA 52544 / 515-856-2626; FAX: 515-856-2628 www.knightrifles.com

Knight Rifles (See Modern Muzzle Loading, Inc.)

Knight's Mfg. Co., 7750 Ninth St. SW, Vero Beach, FL 32968 / 561-562-5697; FAX: 561-569-2955 civiliansales@knightarmco.com

Kolar, 1925 Roosevelt Ave., Racine, WI 53406 / 414-554-0800; FAX: 414-554-9093

Kolpin Outdoors, Inc., P.O. Box 107, 205 Depot St., Fox Lake, WI 53933 / 414-928-3118; FAX: 414-928-3687 cdutton@kolpin.com www.kolpin.com

Korth Germany GmbH, Robert Bosch Strasse, 11, D-23909, 23909 Ratzeburg, GERMANY / 4541-840363; FAX: 4541-84 05 35 info@korthwaffen.de www.korthwaffen.com

Korth USA, 437R Chandler St., Tewksbury, MA 01876 / 978-851-8656; FAX: 978-851-9462 info@kortusa.com www.korthusa.com

Korzinek Riflesmith, J., RD 2 Box 73D, Canton, PA 17724 / 717-673-8512

Koval Knives, 5819 Zarley St., Suite A, New Albany, OH 43054 / 614-855-0777; FAX: 614-855-0945 koval@kovalknives.com www.kovalknives.com

Kowa Optimed, Inc., 20001 S. Vermont Ave., Torrance, CA 90502 / 310-327-1913; FAX: 310-327-4177 scopekowa@kowa.com www.kowascope.com

Kramer Designs, P.O. Box 129, Clancy, MT 59634 / 406-933-8658; FAX: 406-933-8658

Kramer Handgun Leather, P.O. Box 112154, Tacoma, WA 98411 / 800-510-2666; FAX: 253-564-1214 www.kramerleather.com

Krause Publications, Inc., 700 E. State St., Iola, WI 54990 / 715-445-2214; FAX: 715-445-4087

Krieger Barrels, Inc., 2024 Mayfield Rd, Richfield, WI 53076 / 262-628-8558; FAX: 262-628-8748

Kukowski, Ed. See: ED'S GUN HOUSE

Kulis Freeze Dry Taxidermy, 725 Broadway Ave., Bedford, OH 44146 / 216-232-8352; FAX: 216-232-7305 jkulis@kastaway.com kastaway.com

KVH Industries, Inc., 110 Enterprise Center, Middletown, RI 02842 / 401-847-3327; FAX: 401-849-0045

Kwik-Site Co., 5555 Treadwell St., Wayne, MI 48184 / 734-326-1500; FAX: 734-326-4120 kwiksiteco@aol.com

L

L&R Lock Co., 1137 Pocalla Rd., Sumter, SC 29150 / 803-775-6127; FAX: 803-775-5171

L.B.T., Judy Smith, HCR 62, Box 145, Moyie Springs, ID 83845 / 208-267-3588

L.E. Wilson, Inc., Box 324, 404 Pioneer Ave., Cashmere, WA 98815 / 509-782-1328; FAX: 509-782-7200

L.L. Bean, Inc., Freeport, ME 04032 / 207-865-4761; FAX: 207-552-2802

Labanu, Inc., 2201-F Fifth Ave., Ronkonkoma, NY 11779 / 516-467-6197; FAX: 516-981-4112

LaBounty Precision Reboring, Inc, 7968 Silver Lake Rd., PO Box 186, Maple Falls, WA 98266 / 360-599-2047; FAX: 360-599-3018

LaCrosse Footwear, Inc., 18550 NE Riverside Parkway, Portland, OR 97230 / 503-766-1010; or 800-323-2668; FAX: 503-766-1015

LaFrance Specialties, P.O. Box 87933, San Diego, CA 92138 / 619-293-3373; FAX: 619-293-0819 timlafrance@att.net lafrancespecialties.com

Lakefield Arms Ltd. (See Savage Arms, Inc.)

Lakewood Products LLC, 275 June St., Berlin, WI 54923 / 800-872-8458; FAX: 920-361-7719 lakewood@centurytel.net www.lakewoodproducts.com

Lamson & Goodnow Mfg. Co., 45 Conway St., Shelburne Falls, MA 03170 / 413-625-6564; or 800-872-6564; FAX: 413-625-9816 www.lamsonsharp.com

Lansky Levine, Arthur. See: LANSKY SHARPENERS

Lansky Sharpeners, Arthur Lansky Levine, PO Box 50830, Las Vegas, NV 89016 / 702-361-7511; FAX: 702-896-9511

Lapua Ltd., P.O. Box 5, Lapua, FINLAND / 6-310111; FAX: 6-4388991

MANUFACTURER'S DIRECTORY

LaRocca Gun Works, 51 Union Place, Worcester, MA 01608 / 508-754-2887; FAX: 508-754-2887 www.laroccagunworks.com

Larry Lyons Gunworks, 110 Hamilton St., Dowagiac, MI 49047 / 616-782-9478

Laser Devices, Inc., 2 Harris Ct. A-4, Monterey, CA 93940 / 831-373-0701; FAX: 831-373-0903 sales@laserdevices.com www.laserdevices.com

Laseraim Technologies, Inc., P.O. Box 3548, Little Rock, AR 72203 / 501-375-2227

Lawrence Leather Co., P.O. Box 1479, Lillington, NC 27546 / 910-893-2071; FAX: 910-893-4742

Lazzeroni Arms Co., PO Box 26696, Tucson, AZ 85726 / 888-492-7247; FAX: 520-624-4250

Le Clear Industries (See E-Z-Way Systems), P.O. Box 4310, Newark, OH 43058-4310 / 614-345-6645; FAX: 614-345-6600

Leatherman Tool Group, Inc., 12106 NE Ainsworth Cir., P.O. Box 20595, Portland, OR 97294 / 503-253-7826; FAX: 503-253-7830

Lebeau-Courally, Rue St. Gilles, 386 4000, Liege, BELGIUM / 042-52-48-43; FAX: 32-4-252-2008 info@lebeau-courally.com www.lebeau-courally.com

Leckie Professional Gunsmithing, 546 Quarry Rd., Ottsville, PA 18942 / 215-847-8594

Lee Precision, Inc., 4275 Hwy. U, Hartford, WI 53027 / 262-673-3075; FAX: 262-673-9273 info@leeprecision.com www.leeprecision.com

Lee Supplies, Mark, 9901 France Ct., Lakeville, MN 55044 / 612-461-2114

Leica USA, Inc., 156 Ludlow Ave., Northvale, NJ 07647 / 201-767-7500; FAX: 201-767-8666

LEM Gun Specialties, Inc. The Lewis Lead Remover, P.O. Box 2855, Peachtree City, GA 30269-2024 / 770-487-0556

Leonard Day, 6 Linseed Rd Box 1, West Hatfield, MA 01088-7505 / 413-337-8369

Les Baer Custom, Inc., 29601 34th Ave., Hillsdale, IL 61257 / 309-658-2716; FAX: 309-658-2610 www.lesbaer.com

Lett Custom Grips, 672 Currier Rd., Hopkinton, NH 03229-2652 / 800-421-5388; FAX: 603-226-4580 info@lettgrips.com www.lettgrips.com

Leupold & Stevens, Inc., 14400 NW Greenbrier Pky., Beaverton, OR 97006 / 503-646-9171; FAX: 503-526-1455

Lever Arms Service Ltd., 2131 Burrard St., Vancouver, BC V6J 3H7 CANADA / 604-736-2711; FAX: 604-738-3503 leverarms@leverarms.com www.leverarms.com

Lew Horton Dist. Co., Inc., 15 Walkup Dr., Westboro, MA 01581 / 508-366-7400; FAX: 508-366-5332

Liberty Metals, 2233 East 16th St., Los Angeles, CA 90021 / 213-581-9171; FAX: 213-581-9351 libertymfgsolder@hotmail.com

Liberty Safe, 999 W. Utah Ave., Payson, UT 84651-1744 / 800-247-5625; FAX: 801-489-6409

Liberty Shooting Supplies, P.O. Box 357, Hillsboro, OR 97123 / 503-640-5518; FAX: 503-640-5518 info@libertyshootingsupplies.com www.libertyshootingsupplies.com

Lilja Precision Rifle Barrels, P.O. Box 372, Plains, MT 59859 / 406-826-3084; FAX: 406-826-3083 lilja@riflebarrels.com www.riflebarrels.com

Linder Solingen Knives, 4401 Sentry Dr. #B, Tucker, GA 30084 / 770-939-6915; FAX: 770-939-6738

Lindsley Arms Cartridge Co., P.O. Box 757, 20 College Hill Rd., Henniker, NH 03242 / 603-428-3127

Linebaugh Custom Sixguns, P.O. Box 455, Cody, WY 82414 / 307-645-3332 www.sixgunner.com

List Precision Engineering, Unit 1 Ingley Works, 13 River Road, Barking, ENGLAND / 011-081-594-1686

Lithi Bee Bullet Lube, 1728 Carr Rd., Muskegon, MI 49442 / 616-788-4479 lithibee@att.net

"Little John's" Antique Arms, 1740 W. Laveta, Orange, CA 92668

Loch Leven Industries/Convert-A-Pell, P.O. Box 2751, Santa Rosa, CA 95405 / 707-573-8735; FAX: 707-573-0369

Lock's Philadelphia Gun Exchange, 6700 Rowland Ave., Philadelphia, PA 19149 / 215-332-6225; FAX: 215-332-4800 locks.gunshop@verizon.net

Lodewick, Walter H., 2816 NE Halsey St., Portland, OR 97232 / 503-284-2554 wlodewick@aol.com

Lodgewood Mfg., P.O. Box 611, Whitewater, WI 53190 / 262-473-5444; FAX: 262-473-6448 lodgewd@idcnet.com lodgewood.com

Log Cabin Sport Shop, 8010 Lafayette Rd., Lodi, OH 44254 / 330-948-1082; FAX: 330-948-4307 logcabin@logcabinshop.com www.logcabinshop.com

Logan, Harry M., Box 745, Honokaa, HI 96727 / 808-776-1644

Logdewood Mfg., P.O. Box 611, Whitewater, WI 53190 / 262-473-5444; FAX: 262-473-6448 lodgewd@idcnet.com www.lodgewood.com

Lohman Mfg. Co., Inc., 4500 Doniphan Dr., P.O. Box 220, Neosho, MO 64850 / 417-451-4438; FAX: 417-451-2576

Lomont Precision Bullets, 278 Sandy Creek Rd., Salmon, ID 83467 / 208-756-6819; FAX: 208-756-6824 www.klomont.com

London Guns Ltd., Box 3750, Santa Barbara, CA 93130 / 805-683-4141; FAX: 805-683-1712

Lone Star Gunleather, 1301 Brushy Bend Dr., Round Rock, TX 78681 / 512-255-1805

Lone Star Rifle Company, 11231 Rose Road, Conroe, TX 77303 / 936-856-3363; FAX: 936-856-3363 dave@lonestar.com

Long, George F., 1500 Rogue River Hwy., Ste. F, Grants Pass, OR 97527 / 541-476-7552

Lyman Instant Targets, Inc. (See Lyman Products)

Lyman Products Corp., 475 Smith Street, Middletown, CT 06457-1541 / 800-423-9704; FAX: 860-632-1699 lymansales@cshore.com www.lymanproducts.com

M

Madis Books, 2453 West Five Mile Pkwy., Dallas, TX 75233 / 214-330-7168

Magma Engineering Co., P.O. Box 161, 20955 E. Ocotillo Rd., Queen Creek, AZ 85242 / 602-987-9008; FAX: 602-987-0148

Mag-Na-Port International, Inc., 41302 Executive Dr., Harrison Twp., MI 48045-1306 / 586-469-6727; FAX: 586-469-0425 email@magnaport.com www.magnaport.com

Magnum Research, Inc., 7110 University Ave. NE, Minneapolis, MN 55432 / 800-772-6168 or 763-574-1868; FAX: 763-574-0109 info@magnumresearch.com

Magnus Bullets, P.O. Box 239, Toney, AL 35773 / 256-420-8359; FAX: 256-420-8360

Mag-Pack Corp., P.O. Box 846, Chesterland, OH 44026 / 440-285-9480 magpack@aol.com

MagSafe Ammo Co., 4700 S US Highway 17/92, Casselberry, FL 32707-3814 / 407-834-9966; FAX: 407-834-8185 www.magsafeonline.com

Magtech Ammunition Co. Inc., 6845 20th Ave. S., Ste. 120, Centerville, MN 55038

Mahony, Philip Bruce, 67 White Hollow Rd., Lime Rock, CT 06039-2418 / 203-435-9341 filbalony-redbeard@snet.net

Maine Custom Bullets, RFD 1, Box 1755, Brooks, ME 04921

Mandall Shooting Supplies Inc., 3616 N. Scottsdale Rd., Scottsdale, AZ 85251 / 480-945-2553; FAX: 480-949-0734

Marble Arms (See CRR, Inc./Marble's Inc.)

Marchmon Bullets, 6502 Riverdale Rd., Whitmore Lake, MI 48189

Mark Lee Supplies, 9901 France Ct., Lakeville, MN 55044 / 952-461-2114; FAX: 952-461-2194 marklee55044@usfamily.net

Markell, Inc., 422 Larkfield Center 235, Santa Rosa, CA 95403 / 707-573-0792; FAX: 707-573-9867

Markesbery Muzzle Loaders, Inc., 7785 Foundation Dr., Ste. 6, Florence, KY 41042 / 606-342-5553 or 606-342-2380

Marksman Products, 5482 Argosy Dr., Huntington Beach, CA 92649 / 714-898-7535; or 800-822-8005; FAX: 714-891-0782

Marlin Firearms Co., 100 Kenna Dr., North Haven, CT 06473 / 203-239-5621; FAX: 203-234-7991 www.marlinfirearms.com

MarMik, Inc., 2116 S. Woodland Ave., Michigan City, IN 46360 / 219-872-7231; FAX: 219-872-7231

Marshall Enterprises, 792 Canyon Rd., Redwood City, CA 94062

Marshall Fish Mfg. Gunsmith Sptg. Co., Rd. Box 2439, Westport, NY 12993 / 518-962-4897; FAX: 518-962-4897

Martin B. Retting Inc., 11029 Washington, Culver City, CA 90232 / 213-837-2412

Martini & Hagn, 1264 Jimsmith Lake Rd, Cranbrook, BC V1C 6V6 CANADA / 250-417-2926; FAX: 250-417-2928

Martin's Gun Shop, 937 S. Sheridan Blvd., Lakewood, CO 80226 / 303-922-2184

Master Lock Co., 2600 N. 32nd St., Milwaukee, WI 53245 / 414-444-2800

Match Prep-Doyle Gracey, P.O. Box 155, Tehachapi, CA 93581 / 661-822-5383; FAX: 661-823-8680

Mathews Gun Shop & Gunsmithing, Inc., 10224 S. Paramount Blvd., Downey, CA 90241 / 562-928-2129; FAX: 562-928-8629

Matthews Cutlery, 4401 Sentry Dr. #B, Tucker, GA 30084 / 770-939-6915

Mauser Werke Oberndorf Waffensysteme GmbH, Postfach 1349, 78722, Oberndorf/N., GERMANY

Maverick Arms, Inc., 7 Grasso Ave., P.O. Box 497, North Haven, CT 06473 / 203-230-5300; FAX: 203-230-5420

Maxi-Mount Inc., P.O. Box 291, Willoughby Hills, OH 44096-0291 / 440-944-9456; FAX: 440-944-9456 maximount454@yahoo.com

Mayville Engineering Co. (See MEC, Inc.)

McBros Rifle Co., P.O. Box 86549, Phoenix, AZ 85080 / 602-582-3713; FAX: 602-581-3825

McCament, Jay. See: JAY MCCAMENT CUSTOM GUNMAKER

McCann, Tom, 14 Walton Dr., New Hope, PA 18938 / 215-862-2728

McCann Industries, P.O. Box 641, Spanaway, WA 98387 / 253-537-6919; FAX: 253-537-6919 mccann.machine@worldnet.att.net www.mccannindustries.com

McCluskey Precision Rifles, 10502 14th Ave. NW, Seattle, WA 98177 / 206-781-2776

McGowen Rifle Barrels, 5961 Spruce Lane, St. Anne, IL 60964 / 815-937-9816; FAX: 815-937-4024

McKenzie, Lynton, 6940 N. Alvernon Way, Tucson, AZ 85718 / 520-299-5090

McMillan Fiberglass Stocks, Inc., 1638 W. Knudsen Dr. #102, Phoenix, AZ 85027 / 623-582-9635; FAX: 623-581-3825 mfsinc@mcmfamily.com www.mcmfamily.com

McMillan Optical Gunsight Co., 28638 N. 42nd St., Cave Creek, AZ 85331 / 602-585-7868; FAX: 602-585-7872

McMillan Rifle Barrels, P.O. Box 3427, Bryan, TX 77805 / 409-690-3456; FAX: 409-690-0156

McMurdo, Lynn (See Specialty Gunsmithing), PO Box 404, Afton, WY 83110 / 307-886-5535

MCS, Inc., 166 Pocono Rd., Brookfield, CT 06804-2023 / 203-775-1013; FAX: 203-775-9462

McWelco Products, 6730 Santa Fe Ave., Hesperia, CA 92345 / 619-244-8876; FAX: 619-244-9398 products@mcwelco.com www.mawelco.com

MDS, P.O. Box 1441, Brandon, FL 33509-1441 / 813-653-1180; FAX: 813-684-5953

MEC, Inc., 715 South St., Mayville, WI 53050 / 414-387-4500; FAX: 414-387-5802 reloaders@mayul.com www.mayvl.com

Meister Bullets (See Gander Mountain)

Meprolight (See Hesco-Meprolight)

Mercer Custom Guns, 216 S. Whitewater Ave., Jefferson, WI 53549 / 920-674-3839

Metal Merchants, PO Box 186, Walled Lake, MI 48390-0186

Michaels Of Oregon, Co., P.O. Box 1690, Oregon City, OR 97045 www.michaels-oregon.com

Micro Sight Co., 242 Harbor Blvd., Belmont, CA 94002 / 415-591-0769; FAX: 415-591-7531

MANUFACTURER'S DIRECTORY

Mid-America Recreation, Inc., 1328 5th Ave., Moline, IL 61265 / 309-764-5089; FAX: 309-764-5089 fmilcusguns@aol.com www.midamericarecreation.com

Middlebrooks Custom Shop, 7366 Colonial Trail East, Surry, VA 23883 / 757-357-0881; FAX: 757-365-0442

Midway Arms, Inc., 5875 W. Van Horn Tavern Rd., Columbia, MO 65203 / 800-243-3220; or 573-445-6363; FAX: 573-446-1018

Midwest Gun Sport, 1108 Herbert Dr., Zebulon, NC 27597 / 919-269-5570

Midwest Sport Distributors, Box 129, Fayette, MO 65248

Mike Davis Products, 643 Loop Dr., Moses Lake, WA 98837 / 509-765-6178; or 509-766-7281

Mike Yee Custom Stocking, 29927 56 Pl. S., Auburn, WA 98001 / 253-839-3991

Millennium Designed Muzzleloaders, PO Box 536, Routes 11 & 25, Limington, ME 04049 / 207-637-2316

Miller Arms, Inc., P.O. Box 260 Purl St., St. Onge, SD 57779 / 605-642-5160; FAX: 605-642-5160

Miller Custom, 210 E. Julia, Clinton, IL 61727 / 217-935-9362

Miller Single Trigger Mfg. Co., 6680 Rt. 5-20, P.O. Box 471, Bloomfield, NY 14469 / 585-657-6338

Millett Sights, 7275 Murdy Circle, Adm. Office, Huntington Beach, CA 92647 / 714-842-5575 or 800-645-5388; FAX: 714-843-5707

Mirador Optical Corp., P.O. Box 11614, Marina Del Rey, CA 90295-7614 / 310-821-5587; FAX: 310-305-0386

Mitchell, Jack, c/o Geoff Gaebe, Addieville East Farm, 200 Pheasant Dr., Mapleville, RI 02839 / 401-568-3185

Mitchell Bullets, R.F., 430 Walnut St., Westernport, MD 21562

Mitchell Mfg. Corp., P.O. Box 9295, Fountain Valley, CA 92728 / 714-444-2220

Mitchell Optics, Inc., 2072 CR 1100 N, Sidney, IL 61877 / 217-688-2219; or 217-621-3018; FAX: 217-688-2505 mitche1@attglobal.net

Mitchell's Accuracy Shop, 68 Greenridge Dr., Stafford, VA 22554 / 703-659-0165

Mitchell's Mauser, P.O. Box 9295, Fountain Valley, CA 92728 / 714-979-7663; FAX: 714-899-3660

MI-TE Bullets, 1396 Ave. K, Ellsworth, KS 67439 / 785-472-4575; FAX: 785-472-5579

Mittleman, William, P.O. Box 65, Etna, CA 96027

MJK Gunsmithing, Inc., 417 N. Huber Ct., E. Wenatchee, WA 98802 / 509-884-7683

MKS Supply, Inc. (See Hi-Point Firearms)

MMC, 5050 E. Belknap St., Haltom City, TX 76117 / 817-831-9557; FAX: 817-834-5508

MOA Corporation, 2451 Old Camden Pike, Eaton, OH 45320 / 937-456-3669 www.moaguns.com

Modern Gun Repair School, PO Box 846, Saint Albans, VT 05478 / 802-524-2223; FAX: 802-524-2053 jfwp@dlilearn.com www.mgsinfoadlifearn.com

Modern Muzzleloading, Inc., P.O. Box 130, Centerville, IA 52544 / 515-856-2626

Molin Industries, Tru-Nord Division, P.O. Box 365, 204 North 9th St., Brainerd, MN 56401 / 218-829-2870

Monell Custom Guns, 228 Red Mills Rd., Pine Bush, NY 12566 / 914-744-3021

Moneymaker Guncraft Corp., 1420 Military Ave., Omaha, NE 68131 / 402-556-0226

Montana Armory, Inc. (See C. Sharps Arms Co. Inc.), 100 Centennial Dr., P.O. Box 885, Big Timber, MT 59011 / 406-932-4353; FAX: 406-932-4443

Montana Outfitters, Lewis E. Yearout, 308 Riverview Dr. E., Great Falls, MT 59404 / 406-761-0859; or 406-727-4560

Montana Precision Swaging, P.O. Box 4746, Butte, MT 59702 / 406-494-0600; FAX: 406-494-0600

Montana Rifleman, Inc., 2593A Hwy. 2 East, Kalispell, MT 59901 / 406-755-4867

Montana Vintage Arms, 2354 Bear Canyon Rd., Bozeman, MT 59715

Morrison Custom Rifles, J. W., 4015 W Sharon, Phoenix, AZ 85029 / 602-978-3754

Morrison Precision, 6719 Calle Mango, Hereford, AZ 85615 / 520-378-6207 morprec@c2i2.com

Moss Double Tone, Inc., P.O. Box 1112, 2101 S. Kentucky, Sedalia, MO 65301 / 816-827-0827

Mountain Plains Industries, 3720 Otter Place, Lynchburg, VA 24503 / 800-687-3000; FAX: 434-845-6594 mpitargets@cstone.net

Mountain State Muzzleloading Supplies, Inc., Box 154-1, Rt. 2, Williamstown, WV 26187 / 304-375-7842; FAX: 304-375-3737

Mowrey Gun Works, P.O. Box 246, Waldron, IN 46182 / 317-525-6181; FAX: 317-525-9595

Mowrey's Guns & Gunsmithing, 119 Fredericks St., Canajoharie, NY 13317 / 518-673-3483

MPC, P.O. Box 450, McMinnville, TN 37110-0450 / 615-473-5513; FAX: 615-473-5516 thebox@blomand.net www.mpc-thebox.com

MPI Stocks, PO Box 83266, Portland, OR 97283 / 503-226-1215; FAX: 503-226-2661

MSR Targets, P.O. Box 1042, West Covina, CA 91793 / 818-331-7840

MTM Molded Products Co., Inc., 3370 Obco Ct., Dayton, OH 45414 / 937-890-7461; FAX: 937-890-1747

Mullins Ammunition, Rt. 2 Box 304N, Clintwood, VA 24228 / 276-926-6772; FAX: 276-926-6092 mammo@extremeshockusa.com www.extremeshockusa

Mundy, Thomas A., 69 Robbins Road, Somerville, NJ 08876 / 201-722-2199

Murmur Corp., 2823 N. Westmoreland Ave., Dallas, TX 75222 / 214-630-5400

Murphy, R.R. Murphy Co., Inc. See: MURPHY, R.R. CO., INC.

Murphy, R.R. Co., Inc., R.R. Murphy Co., Inc. Murphy, P.O. Box 102, Ripley, TN 38063 / 901-635-4003; FAX: 901-635-2320

Murray State College, 1 Murray Campus St., Tishomingo, OK 73460 / 508-371-2371 darnold@mscok.edu

Muzzleloaders Etcetera, Inc., 9901 Lyndale Ave. S., Bloomington, MN 55420 / 952-884-1161 www.muzzleloaders-etcetera.com

N

N.B.B., Inc., 24 Elliot Rd., Sterling, MA 01564 / 508-422-7538; or 800-942-9444

N.C. Ordnance Co., P.O. Box 3254, Wilson, NC 27895 / 919-237-2440; FAX: 919-243-9845

Nagel's Custom Bullets, 100 Scott St., Baytown, TX 77520-2849

National Bullet Co., 1585 E. 361 St., Eastlake, OH 44095 / 216-951-1854; FAX: 216-951-7761

Navy Arms Co., 219 Lawn St., Martinsburg, WV 25401 / 304-262-9870; FAX: 304-262-1658

Navy Arms Company, Valmore J. Forgett Jr., 815 22nd Street, Union City, NJ 07087 / 201-863-7100; FAX: 201-863-8770 info@navyarms.com www.navyarms.com

NCP Products, Inc., 3500 12th St. N.W., Canton, OH 44708 / 330-456-5130; FAX: 330-456-5234

NEI Handtools, Inc., 10960 Gary Player Dr., El Paso, TX 79935

Neil A. Jones Custom Products, 17217 Brookhouser Road, Saegertown, PA 16433 / 814-763-2769; FAX: 814-763-4228

Nelson, Gary K., 975 Terrace Dr., Oakdale, CA 95361 / 209-847-4590

Nelson, Stephen. See: NELSON'S CUSTOM GUNS, INC.

Nelson's Custom Guns, Inc., Stephen Nelson, 7430 Valley View Dr. N.W., Corvallis, OR 97330 / 541-745-5232 nelsons-custom@attbi.com

Nesci Enterprises Inc., P.O. Box 119, Summit St., East Hampton, CT 06424 / 203-267-2588

Nesika Bay Precision, 22239 Big Valley Rd., Poulsbo, WA 98370 / 206-697-3830

Nettestad Gun Works, 38962 160th Avenue, Pelican Rapids, MN 56572 / 218-863-4301

New England Ammunition Co., 1771 Post Rd. East, Suite 223, Westport, CT 06880 / 203-254-8048

New England Arms Co., Box 278, Lawrence Lane, Kittery Point, ME 03905 / 207-439-0593; FAX: 207-439-0525 info@newenglandarms.com www.newenglandarms.com

New Ultra Light Arms, LLC, P.O. Box 340, Granville, WV 26534

Newark Electronics, 4801 N. Ravenswood Ave., Chicago, IL 60640

Newell, Robert H., 55 Coyote, Los Alamos, NM 87544 / 505-662-7135

Newman Gunshop, 2035 Chester Ave. #411, Ottumwa, IA 52501-3715 / 515-937-5775

Nicholson Custom, 17285 Thornlay Road, Hughesville, MO 65334 / 816-826-8746

Nikon, Inc., 1300 Walt Whitman Rd., Melville, NY 11747 / 516-547-8623; FAX: 516-547-0309

Nitex Gun Shop, P.O. Box 1706, Uvalde, TX 78801 / 830-278-8843

Norincoptics (See BEC, Inc.)

Norma Precision AB (See U.S. Importers-Dynamit)

Normark Corp., 10395 Yellow Circle Dr., Minnetonka, MN 55343-9101 / 612-933-7060; FAX: 612-933-0046

North American Arms, Inc., 2150 South 950 East, Provo, UT 84606-6285 / 800-821-5783; or 801-374-9990; FAX: 801-374-9998

North American Correspondence Schools The Gun Pro, Oak & Pawney St., Scranton, PA 18515 / 717-342-7701

North Star West, P.O. Box 488, Glencoe, CA 95232 / 209-293-7010 northstarwest.com

Northern Precision, 329 S. James St., Carthage, NY 13619 / 315-493-1711

Northlake Outdoor Footwear, P.O. Box 10, Franklin, TN 37065-0010 / 615-794-1556; FAX: 615-790-8005

Northside Gun Shop, 2725 NW 109th, Oklahoma City, OK 73120 / 405-840-2353

Northwest Arms, 26884 Pearl Rd., Parma, ID 83660 / 208-722-6771; FAX: 208-722-1062

No-Sho Mfg. Co., 10727 Glenfield Ct., Houston, TX 77096 / 713-723-5332

Nosler, Inc., P.O. Box 671, Bend, OR 97709 / 800-285-3701; or 541-382-3921; FAX: 541-388-4667 www.nosler.com

Novak's, Inc., 1206 1/2 30th St., P.O. Box 4045, Parkersburg, WV 26101 / 304-485-9295; FAX: 304-428-6722

Nowlin Mfg. Co., 20622 S 4092 Rd., Claremore, OK 74017 / 918-342-0689; FAX: 918-342-0624 nowlinguns@msn.com nowlinguns.com

NRI Gunsmith School, P.O. Box 182968, Columbus, OH 43218-2968

Nu-Line Guns,Inc., 1053 Caulks Hill Rd., Harvester, MO 63304 / 314-441-4500; or 314-447-4501; FAX: 314-447-5018

Null Holsters Ltd. K.L., 161 School St NW, Resaca, GA 30735 / 706-625-5643; FAX: 706-625-9392

Numrich Gun Parts Corporation, 226 Williams Lane, P.O. Box 299, West Hurley, NY 12491 / 866-686-7424; FAX: 877-GUNPART info@gunpartscorp.com www.@-gunparts.com

Nygord Precision Products, Inc., P.O. Box 12578, Prescott, AZ 86304 / 928-717-2315; FAX: 928-717-2198 nygords@northlink.com www.nygordprecision.com

O

O.F. Mossberg & Sons, Inc., 7 Grasso Ave., North Haven, CT 06473 / 203-230-5300; FAX: 203-230-5420

Obermeyer Rifled Barrels, 23122 60th St., Bristol, WI 53104 / 262-843-3537; FAX: 262-843-2129

October Country Muzzleloading, P.O. Box 969, Dept. GD, Hayden, ID 83835 / 208-772-2068; FAX: 208-772-9230 ocinfo@octobercountry.com www.octobercountry.com

Oehler Research, Inc., P.O. Box 9135, Austin, TX 78766 / 512-327-6900; or 800-531-5125; FAX: 512-327-6903 www.oehler-research.com

Oil Rod and Gun Shop, 69 Oak St., East Douglas, MA 01516 / 508-476-3687

OK Weber, Inc., P.O. Box 7485, Eugene, OR 97401 / 541-747-0458; FAX: 541-747-5927 okweber@pacinfo www.okweber.com

Oklahoma Ammunition Co., 3701A S. Harvard Ave., No. 367, Tulsa, OK 74135-2265 / 918-396-3187; FAX: 918-396-4270

Oklahoma Leather Products, Inc., 500 26th NW, Miami, OK 74354 / 918-542-6651; FAX: 918-542-6653

Old Wagon Bullets, 32 Old Wagon Rd., Wilton, CT 06897

Old West Bullet Moulds, J Ken Chapman, P.O. Box 519, Flora Vista, NM 87415 / 505-334-6970

Old Western Scrounger Ammunition Inc., 50 Industrial Parkway, Carson City, NV 89706 / 775-246-2091; FAX: 775-246-2095 www.ows-ammunition.com

Old World Gunsmithing, 2901 SE 122nd St., Portland, OR 97236 / 503-760-7681

Old World Oil Products, 3827 Queen Ave. N., Minneapolis, MN 55412 / 612-522-5037

Ole Frontier Gunsmith Shop, 2617 Hwy. 29 S., Cantonment, FL 32533 / 904-477-8074

Olympic Optical Co., P.O. Box 752377, Memphis, TN 38175-2377 / 901-794-3890; or 800-238-7120; FAX: 901-794-0676 80

One Of A Kind, 15610 Purple Sage, San Antonio, TX 78255 / 512-695-3364

One Ragged Hole, P.O. Box 13624, Tallahassee, FL 32317-3624

Op-Tec, P.O. Box L632, Langhorn, PA 19047 / 215-757-5037; FAX: 215-757-7097

Optical Services Co., P.O. Box 1174, Santa Teresa, NM 88008-1174 / 505-589-3833

Orchard Park Enterprise, P.O. Box 563, Orchard Park, NY 14127 / 616-656-0356

Oregon Arms, Inc. (See Rogue Rifle Co., Inc.)

Oregon Trail Bullet Company, PO Box 529, Dept. P, Baker City, OR 97814 / 800-811-0548; FAX: 514-523-1803

Original Box, Inc., 700 Linden Ave., York, PA 17404 / 717-854-2897; FAX: 717-845-4276

Original Deer Formula Co., The, P.O. Box 1705, Dickson, TN 37056 / 800-874-6965; FAX: 615-446-0646 deerformula1@aol.com www.deerformula

Orion Rifle Barrel Co., RR2, 137 Cobler Village, Kalispell, MT 59901 / 406-257-5649

Otis Technology, Inc., RR 1 Box 84, Boonville, NY 13309 / 315-942-3320

Outa-Site Gun Carriers, 219 Market St., Laredo, TX 78040 / 210-722-4678; or 800-880-9715; FAX: 210-726-4858

Outdoor Edge Cutlery Corp., 4699 Nautilus Ct. S. Ste. 503, Boulder, CO 80301-5310 / 303-652-8212; FAX: 303-652-8238

Outdoor Enthusiast, 3784 W. Woodland, Springfield, MO 65807 / 417-883-9841

Outdoor Sports Headquarters, Inc., 967 Watertower Ln., West Carrollton, OH 45449 / 513-865-5855; FAX: 513-865-5962

Outers Laboratories Div. of ATK, Route 2, P.O. Box 39, Onalaska, WI 54650 / 608-781-5800; FAX: 608-781-0368

Ox-Yoke Originals, Inc., 34 Main St., Milo, ME 04463 / 800-231-8313; or 207-943-7351; FAX: 207-943-2416

Ozark Gun Works, 11830 Cemetery Rd., Rogers, AR 72756 / 479-631-1024; FAX: 479-631-1024 ogw@hotmail.com www.eocities.com/ocarkgunworks

P

P&M Sales & Services, LLC, 4697 Tote Rd. Bldg. H-B, Comins, MI 48619 / 989-848-8364; FAX: 989-848-8364 info@pmsales-online.com

P.A.C.T., Inc., P.O. Box 531525, Grand Prairie, TX 75053 / 214-641-0049

P.S.M.G. Gun Co., 10 Park Ave., Arlington, MA 02174 / 781-646-1699; FAX: 781-643-7212 psmg2@aol.com

Pachmayr Div. Lyman Products, 475 Smith St., Middletown, CT 06457 / 860-632-2020; or 800-225-9626; FAX: 860-632-1699 lymansales@cshore.com www.pachmayr.com

Pacific Rifle Co., P.O. Box 841, Carlton, OR 97111 / 503-852-6276 pacificrifle@aol.com

PAC-NOR Barreling, 99299 Overlook Rd., P.O. Box 6188, Brookings, OR 97415 / 503-469-7330; FAX: 503-469-7331 info@pac-nor.com www.pac-nor.com

Paco's (See Small Custom Mould & Bullet Co.)

Page Custom Bullets, P.O. Box 25, Port Moresby, NEW GUINEA

Palsa Outdoor Products, P.O. Box 81336, Lincoln, NE 68501 / 402-488-5288; FAX: 402-488-2321

Parker & Sons Shooting Supply, 9337 Smoky Row Road, Strawberry Plains, TN 37871 / 865-933-3286; FAX: 865-932-8586

Parker Gun Finishes, 9337 Smokey Row Rd., Strawberry Plains, TN 37871 / 865-933-3286; FAX: 865-932-8586

Parsons Optical Mfg. Co., PO Box 192, Ross, OH 45061 / 513-867-0820; FAX: 513-867-8380 psscopes@concentric.net

Partridge Sales Ltd., John, Trent Meadows, Rugeley, ENGLAND

Pasadena Gun Center, 206 E. Shaw, Pasadena, TX 77506 / 713-472-0417; FAX: 713-472-1322

Passive Bullet Traps, Inc. (See Savage Range Systems, Inc.)

Paterson Gunsmithing, 438 Main St., Paterson, NJ 07502 / 201-345-4100

Pathfinder Sports Leather, 2920 E. Chambers St., Phoenix, AZ 85040 / 602-276-0016

Patrick W. Price Bullets, 16520 Worthley Drive, San Lorenzo, CA 94580 / 510-278-1547

Paul D. Hillmer Custom Gunstocks, 7251 Hudson Heights, Hudson, IA 50643 / 319-988-3941

Paul Jones Moulds, 4901 Telegraph Rd., Los Angeles, CA 90022 / 213-262-1510

Paulsen Gunstocks, Rt. 71, Box 11, Chinook, MT 59523 / 406-357-3403

Payne Photography, Robert, Robert, P.O. Box 141471, Austin, TX 78714 / 512-272-4554

Pease Accuracy, Bob, P.O. Box 310787, New Braunfels, TX 78131 / 210-625-1342

Pecatonica River Longrifle, 5205 Nottingham Dr., Rockford, IL 61111 / 815-968-1995; FAX: 815-968-1996

Pence Precision Barrels, 7567 E. 900 S., S. Whitley, IN 46787 / 219-839-4745

Pendleton Woolen Mills, P.O. Box 3030, 220 N.W. Broadway, Portland, OR 97208 / 503-226-4801

Penn Bullets, P.O. Box 756, Indianola, PA 15051

Pennsylvania Gun Parts Inc., RR 7 Box 150, Mount Pleasant, PA 15666

Pennsylvania Gunsmith School, 812 Ohio River Blvd., Avalon, Pittsburgh, PA 15202 / 412-766-1812; FAX: 412-766-0855 pgs@pagunsmith.com www.pagunsmith.com

Penrod Precision, 312 College Ave., P.O. Box 307, N. Manchester, IN 46962 / 260-982-8385; FAX: 260-982-1819

Pentax Corp., 35 Inverness Dr. E., Englewood, CO 80112 / 303-799-8000; FAX: 303-790-1131

Pete Mazur Restoration, 13083 Drummer Way, Grass Valley, CA 95949 / 530-268-2412; FAX: 530-268-2412

Pete Rickard, Inc., 115 Roy Walsh Rd, Cobleskill, NY 12043 / 518-234-2731; FAX: 518-234-2454 rickard@telenet.net www.peterickard.com

Peter Dyson & Son Ltd., 3 Cuckoo Lane, Honley, Holmfirth, Yorkshire, HD9 6AS ENGLAND / 44-1484-661062; FAX: 44-1484-663709 peter@peterdyson.co.uk www.peterdyson.co.uk

Peter Hale/Engraver, 800 E. Canyon Rd., Spanish Fork, UT 84660 / 801-798-8215

Peters Stahl GmbH, Stettiner Strasse 42, D-33106, Paderborn, GERMANY / 05251-750025; FAX: 05251-75611

PFRB Co., P.O. Box 1242, Bloomington, IL 61702 / 309-473-3964; or 800-914-5464; FAX: 309-473-2161

Philip S. Olt Co., P.O. Box 550, 12662 Fifth St., Pekin, IL 61554 / 309-348-3633; FAX: 309-348-3300

Phillippi Custom Bullets, Justin, P.O. Box 773, Ligonier, PA 15658 / 724-238-2962; FAX: 724-238-9671 jrp@wpa.net http://www.wpa.net~jrphil

Phillips & Rogers, Inc., 100 Hilbig #C, Conroe, TX 77301 / 409-435-0011

Phoenix Arms, 4231 Brickell St., Ontario, CA 91761 / 909-937-6900; FAX: 909-937-0060

Pilgrim Pewter, Inc. (See Bell Originals Inc. Sid)

Pilkington, Scott (See Little Trees Ramble)

Pine Technical College, 1100 4th St., Pine City, MN 55063 / 800-521-7463; FAX: 612-629-6766

Pinetree Bullets, 133 Skeena St., Kitimat, BC V8C 1Z1 CANADA / 604-632-3768; FAX: 604-632-3768

Pioneer Arms Co., 355 Lawrence Rd., Broomall, PA 19008 / 215-356-5203

Plaza Cutlery, Inc., 3333 Bristol, 161 South Coast Plaza, Costa Mesa, CA 92626 / 714-549-3932

Plum City Ballistic Range, N2162 80th St., Plum City, WI 54761 / 715-647-2539

PlumFire Press, Inc., 30-A Grove Ave., Patchogue, NY 11772-4112 / 800-695-7246; FAX: 516-758-4071

PMC/Eldorado Cartridge Corp., P.O. Box 62508, 12801 U.S. Hwy. 95 S., Boulder City, NV 89005 / 702-294-0025; FAX: 702-294-0121 kbauer@pmcammo.com www.pmcammo.com

Ponsness/Warren, 768 Ohio St., Rathdrum, ID 83858 / 800-732-0706; FAX: 208-687-2233

Pony Express Reloaders, 608 E. Co. Rd. D, Suite 3, St. Paul, MN 55117 / 612-483-9406; FAX: 612-483-9884

Pony Express Sport Shop, 23404 Lyons Ave., PMB 448, Newhall, CA 91321-2511 / 818-895-1231

Potts, Wayne E., 912 Poplar St., Denver, CO 80220 / 303-355-5462

Powder Horn Ltd., PO Box 565, Glenview, IL 60025 / 305-565-6060

Precision Airgun Sales, Inc., 5247 Warrensville Ctr Rd., Maple Hts., OH 44137 / 216-587-5005; FAX: 216-587-5005

Precision Cast Bullets, 101 Mud Creek Lane, Ronan, MT 59864 / 406-676-5135

Precision Delta Corp., PO Box 128, Ruleville, MS 38771 / 662-756-2810; FAX: 662-756-2590

Precision Firearm Finishing, 25 N.W. 44th Avenue, Des Moines, IA 50313 / 515-288-8680; FAX: 515-244-3925

Precision Gun Works, 104 Sierra Rd., Dept. GD, Kerrville, TX 78028 / 830-367-4587

Precision Reloading, Inc., P.O. Box 122, Stafford Springs, CT 06076 / 860-684-7979; FAX: 860-684-6788 info@precisionreloading.com www.precisionreloading.com

Precision Sales International, Inc., PO Box 1776, Westfield, MA 01086 / 413-562-5055; FAX: 413-562-5056 precision-sales.com

Precision Shooting, Inc., 222 McKee St., Manchester, CT 06040 / 860-645-8776; FAX: 860-643-8215 www.theaccuraterifle.com

Precision Sport Optics, 15571 Producer Lane, Unit G, Huntington Beach, CA 92649 / 714-891-1309; FAX: 714-892-6920

Premier Reticles, 920 Breckinridge Lane, Winchester, VA 22601-6707 / 540-722-0601; FAX: 540-722-3522

Prescott Projectile Co., 1808 Meadowbrook Road, Prescott, AZ 86303

Preslik's Gunstocks, 4245 Keith Ln., Chico, CA 95926 / 916-891-8236

Price Bullets, Patrick W., 16520 Worthley Dr., San Lorenzo, CA 94580 / 510-278-1547

Prime Reloading, 30 Chiswick End, Meldreth, ROYSTON UK / 0763-260636

Primedia Publishing Co., 6420 Wilshire Blvd., Los Angeles, CA 90048 / 213-782-2000; FAX: 213-782-2867

PRL Bullets, c/o Blackburn Enterprises, 114 Stuart Rd., Ste. 110, Cleveland, TN 37312 / 423-559-0340

Pro Load Ammunition, Inc., 5180 E. Seltice Way, Post Falls, ID 83854 / 208-773-9444; FAX: 208-773-9441

Professional Gunsmiths of America, Rt 1 Box 224, Lexington, MO 64067 / 660-259-2636

Professional Hunter Supplies (See Star Custom Bullets), P.O. Box 608, 468 Main St., Ferndale, CA 95536 / 707-786-9140; FAX: 707-786-9117 wmebride@humboldt.com

PrOlix Lubricants, P.O. Box 1348, Victorville, CA 92393 / 760-243-3129; FAX: 760-241-0148 prolix@accex.net www.prolixlubricant.com

Pro-Mark Div. of Wells Lamont, 6640 W. Touhy, Chicago, IL 60648 / 312-647-8200

MANUFACTURER'S DIRECTORY

Proofmark Corp., P.O. Box 357, Burgess, VA 22432 / 804-453-4337; FAX: 804-453-4337 proofmark@rivnet.net www.proofmarkbullets.com

Pro-Port Ltd., 41302 Executive Dr., Harrison Twp., MI 48045-1306 / 586-469-6727; FAX: 586-469-0425 e-mail@magnaport.com www.magnaport.com

Pro-Shot Products, Inc., P.O. Box 763, Taylorville, IL 62568 / 217-824-9133; FAX: 217-824-8861 www.proshotproducts.com

Protektor Model, 1-11 Bridge St., Galeton, PA 16922 / 814-435-2442 mail@protektormodel.com www.protektormodel.com

Prototech Industries, Inc., 10532 E Road, Delia, KS 66418 / 785-771-3571 prototec@grapevine.net

ProWare, Inc., 15847 NE Hancock St., Portland, OR 97230 / 503-239-0159

PWL Gunleather, P.O. Box 450432, Atlanta, GA 31145 / 800-960-4072; FAX: 770-822-1704 covert@pwlusa.com www.pwlusa.com

Q

Quality Arms, Inc., Box 19477, Dept. GD, Houston, TX 77224 / 281-870-8377 arrieta2@excite.com www.gunshop.com

Quality Cartridge, P.O. Box 445, Hollywood, MD 20636 / 301-373-3719 www.qual-cart.com

Quality Custom Firearms, Stepehn Billeb, 22 Vista View Drive, Cody, WY 82414 / 307-587-4278; FAX: 307-587-4297 stevebilleb@wyoming.com

Quarton Beamshot, 4538 Centerview Dr., Ste. 149, San Antonio, TX 78228 / 800-520-8435; FAX: 210-735-1326 www.beamshot.com

Que Industries, Inc., PO Box 2471, Everett, WA 98203 / 425-303-9088; FAX: 206-514-3266 queinfo@queindustries.com

Queen Cutlery Co., PO Box 500, Franklinville, NY 14737 / 800-222-5233; FAX: 800-299-2618

R

R&C Knives & Such, 2136 CANDY CANE WALK, Manteca, CA 95336-9501 / 209-239-3722; FAX: 209-825-6947

R&D Gun Repair, Kenny Howell, RR1 Box 283, Beloit, WI 53511

R&J Gun Shop, 337 S. Humbolt St., Canyon City, OR 97820 / 541-575-2130 rjgunshop@highdestertnet.com

R&S Industries Corp., 8255 Brentwood Industrial Dr., St. Louis, MO 63144 / 314-781-5169 ron@miraclepolishingcloth.com www.miraclepolishingcloth.com

R. Murphy Co., Inc., 13 Groton-Harvard Rd., P.O. Box 376, Ayer, MA 01432 / 617-772-3481 www.r.murphyknives.com

R.A. Wells Custom Gunsmith, 3452 1st Ave., Racine, WI 53402 / 414-639-5223

R.E. Seebeck Assoc., P.O. Box 59752, Dallas, TX 75229

R.E.I., P.O. Box 88, Tallevast, FL 34270 / 813-755-0085

R.E.T. Enterprises, 2608 S. Chestnut, Broken Arrow, OK 74012 / 918-251-GUNS; FAX: 918-251-0587

R.F. Mitchell Bullets, 430 Walnut St., Westernport, MD 21562

R.I.S. Co., Inc., 718 Timberlake Circle, Richardson, TX 75080 / 214-235-0933

R.T. Eastman Products, P.O. Box 1531, Jackson, WY 83001 / 307-733-3217; or 800-624-4311

Rabeno, Martin, 530 The Eagle Pass, Durango, CO 81301 / 970-382-0353 fancygun@aol.com

Radack Photography, Lauren, 21140 Jib Court L-12, Aventura, FL 33180 / 305-931-3110

Radiator Specialty Co., 1900 Wilkinson Blvd., P.O. Box 34689, Charlotte, NC 28234 / 800-438-6947; FAX: 800-421-9525

Radical Concepts, P.O. Box 1473, Lake Grove, OR 97035 / 503-538-7437

Rainier Ballistics, 4500 15th St. East, Tacoma, WA 98424 / 800-638-8722; FAX: 253-922-7854 sales@rainierballistics.com www.rainierballistics.com

Ralph Bone Engraving, 718 N. Atlanta St., Owasso, OK 74055 / 918-272-9745

Ram-Line ATK, P.O. Box 39, Onalaska, WI 54650

Ramon B. Gonzalez Guns, P.O. Box 370, Monticello, NY 12701 / 914-794-4515; FAX: 914-794-4515

Rampart International, 2781 W. MacArthur Blvd., B-283, Santa Ana, CA 92704 / 800-976-7240 or 714-557-6405

Ranch Products, P.O. Box 145, Malinta, OH 43535 / 313-277-3118; FAX: 313-565-8536

Randall-Made Knives, P.O. Box 1988, Orlando, FL 32802 / 407-855-8075

Randco UK, 286 Gipsy Rd., Welling, DA16 1JJ ENGLAND / 44 81 303 4118

Randolph Engineering, Inc., Ranger Shooting Glasses, 26 Thomas Patten Dr., Randolph, MA 02368 / 800-541-1405; FAX: 781-986-0337 sales@randolphusa.com www.randolphusa.com

Randy Duane Custom Stocks, 7822 Church St., Middletown, VA 22645-9521

Range Brass Products Company, P.O. Box 218, Rockport, TX 78381

Ransom International Corp., 1027 Spire Dr, Prescott, AZ 86302 / 520-778-7899; FAX: 520-778-7993 ransom@primenet.com www.ransom-intl.com

Rapine Bullet Mould Mfg. Co., 9503 Landis Lane, East Greenville, PA 18041 / 215-679-5413; FAX: 215-679-9795

Ravell Ltd., 289 Diputacion St., 08009, Barcelona, SPAIN / 34(3) 4874486; FAX: 34(3) 4881394

Ray Riling Arms Books Co., 6844 Gorsten St., Philadelphia, PA 19119 / 215-438-2456; FAX: 215-438-5395 sales@rayrilingarmsbooks.com www.rayrilingarmsbooks.com

Ray's Gunsmith Shop, 3199 Elm Ave., Grand Junction, CO 81504 / 970-434-6162; FAX: 970-434-6162

Raytech Div. of Lyman Products Corp., 475 Smith Street, Middletown, CT 06457-1541 / 860-632-2020 or 800-225-9626; FAX: 860-632-1699 raysales@cshore.com www.raytech-ind.com

RCBS Operations/ATK, 605 Oro Dam Blvd., Oroville, CA 95965 / 530-533-5191 or 800-533-5000; FAX: 530-533-1647 www.rcbs.com

RCBS/ATK, 605 Oro Dam Blvd., Oroville, CA 95965 / 800-533-5000; FAX: 916-533-1647

Reardon Products, P.O. Box 126, Morrison, IL 61270 / 815-772-3155

Red Diamond Dist. Co., 1304 Snowdon Dr., Knoxville, TN 37912

Redding Reloading Equipment, 1089 Starr Rd., Cortland, NY 13045 / 607-753-3331; FAX: 607-756-8445 techline@redding-reloading.com www.redding-reloading.com

Redfield Media Resource Center, 4607 N.E. Cedar Creek Rd., Woodland, WA 98674 / 360-225-5000; FAX: 360-225-7616

Redman's Rifling & Reboring, 189 Nichols Rd., Omak, WA 98841 / 509-826-5512

Redwood Bullet Works, 3559 Bay Rd., Redwood City, CA 94063 / 415-367-6741

Reed, Dave, Rt. 1, Box 374, Minnesota City, MN 55959 / 507-689-2944

Reimer Johannsen, Inc., 438 Willow Brook Rd., Plainfield, NH 03781 / 603-469-3450; FAX: 603-469-3471

Reloaders Equipment Co., 4680 High St., Ecorse, MI 48229

Reloading Specialties, Inc., Box 1130, Pine Island, MN 55463 / 507-356-8500; FAX: 507-356-8800

Remington Arms Co., Inc., 870 Remington Drive, P.O. Box 700, Madison, NC 27025-0700 / 800-243-9700; FAX: 910-548-8700

Renegade, P.O. Box 31546, Phoenix, AZ 85046 / 602-482-6777; FAX: 602-482-1952

Renfrew Guns & Supplies, R.R. 4, Renfrew, ON K7V 3Z7 CANADA / 613-432-7080

Reno, Wayne, 2808 Stagestop Road, Jefferson, CO 80456

Republic Arms, Inc. (See Cobra Enterprises, Inc.)

Retting, Inc., Martin B., 11029 Washington, Culver City, CA 90232 / 213-837-2412

Rhino, P.O. Box 787, Locust, NC 28097 / 704-753-2198

Rhodeside, Inc., 1704 Commerce Dr., Piqua, OH 45356 / 513-773-5781

Rice, Keith (See White Rock Tool & Die)

Richards Micro-Fit Stocks, 8331 N. San Fernando Ave., Sun Valley, CA 91352 / 818-767-6097; FAX: 818-767-7121

Ridgeline, Inc., Bruce Sheldon, P.O. Box 930, Dewey, AZ 86327-0930 / 800-632-5900; FAX: 520-632-5900

Ridgetop Sporting Goods, P.O. Box 306, 42907 Hilligoss Ln. East, Eatonville, WA 98328 / 360-832-6422; FAX: 360-832-6422

Ries, Chuck, 415 Ridgecrest Dr., Grants Pass, OR 97527 / 503-476-5623

Rifles, Inc., 3580 Leal Rd., Pleasanton, TX 78064 / 830-569-2055; FAX: 830-569-2297

Riggs, Jim, 206 Azalea, Boerne, TX 78006 / 210-249-8567

Riley Ledbetter Airguns, 1804 E. Sprague St., Winston Salem, NC 27107-3521 / 919-784-0676

Rim Pac Sports, Inc., 1034 N. Soldano Ave., Azusa, CA 91702-2135

Ringler Custom Leather Co., 31 Shining Mtn. Rd., Powell, WY 82435 / 307-645-3255

Ripley Rifles, 42 Fletcher Street, Ripley, Derbyshire, DE5 3LP ENGLAND / 011-0773-748353

RMS Custom Gunsmithing, 4120 N. Bitterwell, Prescott Valley, AZ 86314 / 520-772-7626

Robert Evans Engraving, 332 Vine St., Oregon City, OR 97045 / 503-656-5693

Robert Valade Engraving, 931 3rd Ave., Seaside, OR 97138 / 503-738-7672

Robinett, R. G., P.O. Box 72, Madrid, IA 50156 / 515-795-2906

Robinson, Don, Pennsylvania Hse, 36 Fairfax Crescent, W Yorkshire, ENGLAND / 0422-364458 donrobinsonuk@yahoo.co.uk www.guns4u2.co.uk

Robinson Armament Co., PO Box 16776, Salt Lake City, UT 84116 / 801-355-0401; FAX: 801-355-0402 zdf@robarm.com www.robarm.com

Robinson Firearms Mfg. Ltd., 1699 Blondeaux Crescent, Kelowna, BC V1Y 4J8 CANADA / 604-868-9596

Robinson H.V. Bullets, 3145 Church St., Zachary, LA 70791 / 504-654-4029

Rochester Lead Works, 76 Anderson Ave., Rochester, NY 14607 / 716-442-8500; FAX: 716-442-4712

Rock River Arms, 101 Noble St., Cleveland, IL 61241

Rockwood Corp., Speedwell Division, 136 Lincoln Blvd., Middlesex, NJ 08846 / 800-243-8274; FAX: 980-560-7475

Rocky Mountain Armoury, Mr. Felix LesMerises, 610 Main Street, P.O. Box 691, Frisco, CO 80443-0691 / 970-668-0136; FAX: 970-668-4484 felix@rockymountainarmoury.com

Rocky Mountain Arms, Inc., 1813 Sunset Pl, Unit D, Longmont, CO 80501 / 800-375-0846; FAX: 303-678-8766

Rocky Mountain Target Co., 3 Aloe Way, Leesburg, FL 34788 / 352-365-9598

Rocky Mountain Wildlife Products, P.O. Box 999, La Porte, CO 80535 / 970-484-2768; FAX: 970-484-0807 critrcall@earthlink.net www.critrcall.com

Rocky Shoes & Boots, 294 Harper St., Nelsonville, OH 45764 / 800-848-9452; or 614-753-1951; FAX: 614-753-4024

Rogue Rifle Co., Inc., 1140 36th St. N., Ste. B, Lewiston, ID 83501 / 208-743-4355; FAX: 208-743-4163

Rogue River Rifleworks, 500 Linne Road #D, Paso Robles, CA 93446 / 805-227-4706; FAX: 805-227-4723 rrrifles@calinet.com

Rohner, Hans, 1148 Twin Sisters Ranch Rd., Nederland, CO 80466-9600

Rohner, John, 186 Virginia Ave, Asheville, NC 28806 / 303-444-3841

Rohrbaugh, P.O. Box 785, Bayport, NY 11705 / 631-363-2843; FAX: 631-363-2681 API380@aol.com

Romain's Custom Guns, Inc., RD 1, Whetstone Rd., Brockport, PA 15823 / 814-265-1948 romwhetstone@penn.com

MANUFACTURER'S DIRECTORY

Ron Frank Custom Classic Arms, 7131 Richland Rd., Ft. Worth, TX 76118 / 817-284-9300; FAX: 817-284-9300 rfrank3974@aol.com

Rooster Laboratories, P.O. Box 414605, Kansas City, MO 64141 / 816-474-1622; FAX: 816-474-7622

Rorschach Precision Products, 417 Keats Cir., Irving, TX 75061 / 214-790-3487

Rosenberg & Son, Jack A., 12229 Cox Ln., Dallas, TX 75234 / 214-241-6302

Ross, Don, 12813 West 83 Terrace, Lenexa, KS 66215 / 913-492-6982

Rosser, Bob, 2809 Crescent Ave., Suite 20, Homewood, AL 35209 / 205-870-4422; FAX: 205-870-4421 www.hand-engravers.com

Rossi Firearms, Gary Mchalik, 16175 NW 49th Ave., Miami, FL 33014-6314 / 305-474-0401; FAX: 305-623-7506

Rottweil Compe, 1330 Glassell, Orange, CA 92667

Roy Baker's Leather Goods, PO Box 893, Magnolia, AR 71754 / 870-234-0344

Royal Arms Gunstocks, 919 8th Ave. NW, Great Falls, MT 59404 / 406-453-1149 royalarms@lmt.net www.lmt.net/~royalarms

Roy's Custom Grips, 793 Mt. Olivet Church Rd., Lynchburg, VA 24504 / 434-993-3470

Rubright Bullets, 1008 S. Quince Rd., Walnutport, PA 18088 / 215-767-1339

Rucker Dist. Inc., P.O. Box 479, Terrell, TX 75160 / 214-563-2094

Ruger (See Sturm, Ruger & Co., Inc.)

Ruger, Chris. See: RUGER'S CUSTOM GUNS

Ruger's Custom Guns, Chris Ruger, 1050 Morton Blvd., Kingston, NY 12401 / 845-336-7106; FAX: 845-336-7106 rugerscustom@outdrs.net rugergunsmith.com

Rundell's Gun Shop, 6198 Frances Rd., Clio, MI 48420 / 313-687-0559

Rupert's Gun Shop, 2202 Dick Rd., Suite B, Fenwick, MI 48834 / 517-248-3252 17rupert@pathwaynet.com

Russ Haydon's Shooters' Supply, 15018 Goodrich Dr. NW, Gig Harbor, WA 98329 / 877-663-6249; FAX: 253-857-7884 www.shooters-supply.com

Russ, William. See: BILL RUSS TRADING POST

Rusteprufe Laboratories, 1319 Jefferson Ave., Sparta, WI 54656 / 608-269-4144; FAX: 608-366-1972 rusteprufe@centurytel.net www.rusteprufe.com

Rusty Duck Premium Gun Care Products, 7785 Foundation Dr., Suite 6, Florence, KY 41042 / 606-342-5553; FAX: 606-342-5556

RWS (See U.S. Importer-Dynamit Nobel-RWS, Inc.), 81 Ruckman Rd., Closter, NJ 07624 / 201-767-7971; FAX: 201-767-1589

S

S&K Scope Mounts, RD 2 Box 72E, Sugar Grove, PA 16350 / 814-489-3091; or 800-578-9862; FAX: 814-489-5466 comments@scopemounts.com www.scopemounts.com

SAECO (See Redding Reloading Equipment)

Safari Arms/Schuetzen Pistol Works, 620-626 Old Pacific Hwy. SE, Olympia, WA 98513 / 360-459-3471; FAX: 360-491-3447 info@yarms.com www.olyarms.com

Safari Press, Inc., 15621 Chemical Lane B, Huntington Beach, CA 92649 / 714-894-9080; FAX: 714-894-4949 info@safaripress.com www.safaripress.com

Safariland Ltd., Inc., 3120 E. Mission Blvd., P.O. Box 51478, Ontario, CA 91761 / 909-923-7300; FAX: 909-923-7400

Sako Ltd (See U.S. Importer-Stoeger Industries)

Sam Welch Gun Engraving, Sam Welch, HC 64 Box 2110, Moab, UT 84532 / 435-259-8131

Samco Global Arms, Inc., 6995 NW 43rd St., Miami, FL 33166 / 305-593-9782; FAX: 305-593-1014 samco@samcoglobal.com www.samcoglobal.com

Sampson, Roger, 2316 Mahogany St., Mora, MN 55051 / 612-679-4868

San Marco (See U.S. Importers-Cape Outfitters-EMF

Sandia Die & Cartridge Co., 37 Atancacio Rd. NE, Albuquerque, NM 87123 / 505-298-5729

Sarco, Inc., 323 Union St., Stirling, NJ 07980 / 908-647-3800; FAX: 908-647-9413

Saunders Gun & Machine Shop, 145 Delhi Rd, Manchester, IA 52057 / 563-927-4026

Savage Arms (Canada), Inc., 248 Water St., P.O. Box 1240, Lakefield, ON K0L 2H0 CANADA / 705-652-8000; FAX: 705-652-8431 www.savagearms.com

Savage Arms, Inc., 100 Springdale Rd., Westfield, MA 01085 / 413-568-7001; FAX: 413-562-7764

Savage Range Systems, Inc., 100 Springdale Rd., Westfield, MA 01085 / 413-568-7001; FAX: 413-562-1152 snailtraps@savagearms.com www.snailtraps.com

Saville Iron Co. (See Greenwood Precision)

Savino, Barbara J., P.O. Box 51, West Burke, VT 05871-0051

Scansport, Inc., P.O. Box 700, Enfield, NH 03748 / 603-632-7654

Sceery Game Calls, P.O. Box 6520, Sante Fe, NM 87502 / 505-471-9110; FAX: 505-471-3476

Schaefer Shooting Sports, P.O. Box 1515, Melville, NY 11747-0515 / 516-643-5466; FAX: 516-643-2426 robert@robertschaefer.com www.schaefershooting.com

Schmidt & Bender, Inc., P.O. Box 134, Meriden, NH 03770 / 603-469-3565; FAX: 603-469-3471 scopes@cyberportal.net www.schmidtbender.com

Schmidtke Group, 17050 W. Salentine Dr., New Berlin, WI 53151-7349

Schneider Bullets, 3655 West 214th St., Fairview Park, OH 44126

Schneider Rifle Barrels, Inc., 1403 W Red Baron Rd., Payson, AZ 85541 / 602-948-2525

Schroeder Bullets, 1421 Thermal Ave., San Diego, CA 92154 / 619-423-3523; FAX: 619-423-8124

Schulz Industries, 16247 Minnesota Ave., Paramount, CA 90723 / 213-439-5903

Schumakers Gun Shop, 512 Prouty Corner Lp. A, Colville, WA 99114 / 509-684-4848

Scope Control, Inc., 5775 Co. Rd. 23 SE, Alexandria, MN 56308 / 612-762-7295

Score High Gunsmithing, 9812-A, Cochiti SE, Albuquerque, NM 087123 / 800-326-5632 or 505-292-5532; FAX: 505-292-2592

Scot Powder, Rt.1 Box 167, McEwen, TN 37101 / 800-416-3006; FAX: 615-729-4211

Scott Fine Guns Inc., Thad, P.O. Box 412, Indianola, MS 38751 / 601-887-5929

Searcy Enterprises, P.O. Box 584, Boron, CA 93596 / 760-762-6771; FAX: 760-762-0191

Seebeck Assoc., R.E., P. O. Box 59752, Dallas, TX 75229

Seecamp Co. Inc., L. W., PO Box 255, New Haven, CT 06502 / 203-877-3429; FAX: 203-877-3429

Segway Industries, P.O. Box 783, Suffern, NY 10901-0783 / 914-357-5510

Seligman Shooting Products, Box 133, Seligman, AZ 86337 / 602-422-3607 shootssp@yahoo.com

Sellier & Bellot, USA, Inc., P.O. Box 27006, Shawnee Mission, KS 66225 / 913-685-0916; FAX: 913-685-0917

Selsi Co., Inc., P.O. Box 10, Midland Park, NJ 07432-0010 / 201-935-0388; FAX: 201-935-5851

Semmer, Charles (See Remington Double Shotguns), 7885 Cyd Dr, Denver, CO 80221 / 303-429-6947

Sentinel Arms, P.O. Box 57, Detroit, MI 48231 / 313-331-1951; FAX: 313-331-1456

Servus Footwear Co., 1136 2nd St., Rock Island, IL 61204 / 309-786-7741; FAX: 309-786-9808

Shappy Bullets, 76 Milldale Ave., Plantsville, CT 06479 / 203-621-3704

Sharp Shooter Supply, 4970 Lehman Road, Delphos, OH 45833 / 419-695-3179

Shaw, Inc., E. R. (See Small Arms Mfg. Co.)

Shay's Gunsmithing, 931 Marvin Ave., Lebanon, PA 17042

Sheffield Knifemakers Supply, Inc., P.O. Box 741107, Orange City, FL 32774-1107 / 386-775-6453; FAX: 386-774-5754

Sheldon, Bruce. See: RIDGELINE, INC.

Shepherd Enterprises, Inc., Box 189, Waterloo, NE 68069 / 402-779-2424; FAX: 402-779-4010 sshepherd@shepherdscopes.com www.shepherdscopes.com

Sherwood, George, 46 N. River Dr., Roseburg, OR 97470 / 541-672-3159

Shideler, David W., 1202 Timberlake Trail, Ft. Wayne, IN 46804

Shilen, Inc., 205 Metro Park Blvd., Ennis, TX 75119 / 972-875-5318; FAX: 972-875-5402

Shiloh Rifle Mfg., P.O. Box 279, Big Timber, MT 59011

Shockley, Harold H., 204 E. Farmington Rd., Hanna City, IL 61536 / 309-565-4524

Shoot Where You Look, Leon Measures, Dept GD, 408 Fair, Livingston, TX 77351

Shooters Arms Manufacturing, Inc., Rivergate Mall, Gen. Maxilom Ave., Cebu City 6000, PHILIPPINES / 6332-254-8478 www.shootersarms.com.ph

Shooter's Choice Gun Care, 15050 Berkshire Ind. Pky., Middlefield, OH 44062 / 440-834-8888; FAX: 440-834-3388 www.shooterschoice.com

Shooter's Edge Inc., 3313 Creekstone Dr., Fort Collins, CO 80525

Shooters Supply, 1120 Tieton Dr., Yakima, WA 98902 / 509-452-1181

Shooter's World, 3828 N. 28th Ave., Phoenix, AZ 85017 / 602-266-0170

Shooters, Inc., 5139 Stanart St., Norfolk, VA 23502 / 757-461-9152; FAX: 757-461-9155 gflocker@aol.com

Shootin' Shack, 357 Cypress Drive, No. 10, Tequesta, FL 33469 / 561-842-0990; FAX: 561-545-4861

Shooting Specialties (See Titus, Daniel)

Shooting Star, 1715 FM 1626 Ste 105, Manchaca, TX 78652 / 512-462-0009

Shoot-N-C Targets (See Birchwood Casey)

Shotguns Unlimited, 2307 Fon Du Lac Rd., Richmond, VA 23229 / 804-752-7115

Siegrist Gun Shop, 8752 Turtle Road, Whittemore, MI 48770 / 989-873-3929

Sierra Bullets, 1400 W. Henry St., Sedalia, MO 65301 / 816-827-6300; FAX: 816-827-6300

Sierra Specialty Prod. Co., 1344 Oakhurst Ave., Los Altos, CA 94024 / 415-965-1536

Sightron, Inc., 1672B Hwy. 96, Franklinton, NC 27525 / 919-528-8783; FAX: 919-528-0995 info@sightron.com www.sightron.com

Silencio/Safety Direct, 56 Coney Island Dr., Sparks, NV 89431 / 800-648-1812 or 702-354-4451; FAX: 702-359-1074

Silent Hunter, 1100 Newton Ave., W. Collingswood, NJ 08107 / 609-854-3276

Silhouette Leathers, P.O. Box 1161, Gunnison, CO 81230 / 970-641-6630 oldshooter@yahoo.com

Silver Eagle Machining, 18007 N. 69th Ave., Glendale, AZ 85308

Silver Ridge Gun Shop (See Goodwin, Fred)

Simmons, Jerry, 715 Middlebury St., Goshen, IN 46528-2717 / 574-533-8546

Simmons Gun Repair, Inc., 700 S. Rogers Rd., Olathe, KS 66062 / 913-782-3131; FAX: 913-782-4189

Simmons Outdoor Corp., 6001 Oak Canyon, Irvine, CA 92618 / 949-451-1450; FAX: 949-451-1460 www.meade.com

Sinclair International, Inc., 2330 Wayne Haven St., Fort Wayne, IN 46803 / 260-493-1858; FAX: 260-493-2530 sales@sinclairintl.com www.sinclairintl.com

Singletary, Kent, 4538 W Carol Ave., Glendale, AZ 85302 / 602-526-6836 kent@kscustom www.kscustom.com

Siskiyou Gun Works (See Donnelly, C. P.)

Six Enterprises, 320-D Turtle Creek Ct., San Jose, CA 95125 / 408-999-0201; FAX: 408-999-0216

Skeoch, Brian R., P.O. Box 279, Glenrock, WY 82637 / 307-436-9655 brianskeoch@aol.com

Skip's Machine, 364 29 Road, Grand Junction, CO 81501 / 303-245-5417

Sklany's Machine Shop, 566 Birch Grove Dr., Kalispell, MT 59901 / 406-755-4257

Slezak, Jerome F., 1290 Marlowe, Lakewood (Cleveland), OH 44107 / 216-221-1668

Slug Site, Ozark Wilds, 21300 Hwy. 5, Versailles, MO 65084 / 573-378-6430 john@ebeling.com john.ebeling.com

Small Custom Mould & Bullet Co., Box 17211, Tucson, AZ 85731

Smart Parts, 1203 Spring St., Latrobe, PA 15650 / 412-539-2660; FAX: 412-539-2298

Smires, C. L., 5222 Windmill Lane, Columbia, MD 21044-1328

Smith & Wesson, 2100 Roosevelt Ave., Springfield, MA 01104 / 413-781-8300; FAX: 413-731-8980

Smith, Judy. See: L.B.T.

Smith Saddlery, Jesse W., 0499 County Road J, Pritchett, CO 81064 / 509-325-0622

Smokey Valley Rifles, E1976 Smokey Valley Rd., Scandinavia, WI 54977 / 715-467-2674

Snapp's Gunshop, 6911 E. Washington Rd., Clare, MI 48617 / 989-386-9226 snapp@glccomputers.com

Sno-Seal, Inc. (See Atsko/Sno-Seal, Inc.)

Sound Tech Silencers, Box 391, Pelham, AL 35124 / 205-664-5860 silenceio@wmconnect.com www.soundtechsilencers.com

Southeastern Community College, 1015 S. Gear Ave., West Burlington, IA 52655 / 319-752-2731

Southern Ammunition Co., Inc., 4232 Meadow St., Loris, SC 29569-3124 / 803-756-3262; FAX: 803-756-3583

Spartan-Realtree Products, Inc., 1390 Box Circle, Columbus, GA 31907 / 706-569-9101; FAX: 706-569-0042

Specialty Gunsmithing, Lynn McMurdo, P.O. Box 404, Afton, WY 83110 / 307-886-5535

Specialty Shooters Supply, Inc., 3325 Griffin Rd., Suite 9mm, Fort Lauderdale, FL 33317

Speer Bullets, P.O. Box 856, Lewiston, ID 83501 / 208-746-2351; www.speer-bullets.com

Spegel, Craig, P.O. Box 387, Nehalem, OR 97131 / 503-368-5653

Speiser, Fred D., 2229 Dearborn, Missoula, MT 59801 / 406-549-8133

Spencer Reblue Service, 1820 Tupelo Trail, Holt, MI 48842 / 517-694-7474

Spencer's Rifle Barrels, Inc., 4107 Jacobs Creek Dr., Scottsville, VA 24590 / 804-293-6836; FAX: 804-293-6836 www.spencerriflebarrels.com

Spolar Power Load, Inc., 17376 Filbert, Fontana, CA 92335 / 800-227-9667

Sport Flite Manufacturing Co., P.O. Box 1082, Bloomfield Hills, MI 48303 / 248-647-3747

Sports Afield Magazine, 15621 Chemical Lane B, Huntington Beach, CA 92649 / 714-894-9080; FAX: 714-894-4949 info@sportsafield.com www.sportsafield.com

Sports Innovations, Inc., P.O. Box 5181, 8505 Jacksboro Hwy., Wichita Falls, TX 76307 / 817-723-6015

Sportsman Safe Mfg. Co., 6309-6311 Paramount Blvd., Long Beach, CA 90805 / 800-266-7150; or 310-984-5445

Sportsman's Communicators, 588 Radcliffe Ave., Pacific Palisades, CA 90272 / 800-538-3752

Sportsmatch U.K. Ltd., 16 Summer St. Leighton,, Buzzard Beds, Bedfordshire, LU7 8HT ENGLAND / 4401525-381638; FAX: 4401525-851236 info@sportsmatch-uk.com www.sportsmatch-uk.com

Sportsmen's Exchange & Western Gun Traders, Inc., 560 S. C St., Oxnard, CA 93030 / 805-483-1917

Spyderco, Inc., 820 Spyderco Way, Golden, CO 80403 / 800-525-7770; or 800-525-7770; FAX: 303-278-2229 sales@spyderco.com www.spyderco.com

Stackpole Books, 5067 Ritter Rd., Mechanicsburg, PA 17055-6921 / 717-796-0411; or 800-732-3669; FAX: 717-796-0412 tmanney@stackpolebooks.com www.stackpolebooks.com

Stalker, Inc., P.O. Box 21, Fishermans Wharf Rd., Malakoff, TX 75148 / 903-489-1010

Stalwart Corporation, P.O. Box 46, Evanston, WY 82931 / 307-789-7687; FAX: 307-789-7688

Stan Baker Sports, Stan Baker, 10000 Lake City Way, Seattle, WA 98125 / 206-522-4575

Stan De Treville & Co., 4129 Normal St., San Diego, CA 92103 / 619-298-3393

Stanley Bullets, 2085 Heatheridge Ln., Reno, NV 89509

Star Ammunition, Inc., 5520 Rock Hampton Ct., Indianapolis, IN 46268 / 800-221-5927; FAX: 317-872-5847

Star Custom Bullets, P.O. Box 608, 468 Main St., Ferndale, CA 95536 / 707-786-9140; FAX: 707-786-9117 wmebridge@humboldt.com

Star Machine Works, P.O. Box 1872, Pioneer, CA 95666 / 209-295-5000

Starke Bullet Company, P.O. Box 400, 605 6th St. NW, Cooperstown, ND 58425 / 888-797-3431

Starkey Labs, 6700 Washington Ave. S., Eden Prairie, MN 55344

Starkey's Gun Shop, 9430 McCombs, El Paso, TX 79924 / 915-751-3030

Starlight Training Center, Inc., Rt. 1, P.O. Box 88, Bronaugh, MO 64728 / 417-843-3555

Starline, Inc., 1300 W. Henry St., Sedalia, MO 65301 / 660-827-6640; FAX: 660-827-6650 info@starlinebrass.com http://www.starlinebrass.com

Starr Trading Co., Jedediah, P.O. Box 2007, Farmington Hills, MI 48333 / 810-683-4343; FAX: 810-683-3282

Starrett Co., L. S., 121 Crescent St., Athol, MA 01331 / 978-249-3551; FAX: 978-249-8495

Steelman's Gun Shop, 10465 Beers Rd., Swartz Creek, MI 48473 / 810-735-4884

Steve Henigson & Associates, P.O. Box 2726, Culver City, CA 90231 / 310-305-8288; FAX: 310-305-1905

Steve Kamyk Engraver, 9 Grandview Dr., Westfield, MA 01085-1810 / 413-568-0457 stevek201@attbi

Steven Dodd Hughes, P.O. Box 545, Livingston, MT 59047 / 406-222-9377; FAX: 406-222-9377

Steves House of Guns, Rt. 1, Minnesota City, MN 55959 / 507-689-2573

Stewart Game Calls, Inc., Johnny, P.O. Box 7954, 5100 Fort Ave., Waco, TX 76714 / 817-772-3261; FAX: 817-772-3670

Stewart's Gunsmithing, P.O. Box 5854, Pietersburg North 0750, Transvaal, SOUTH AFRICA / 01521-89401

Steyr Mannlicher GmbH & Co KG, Mannlicherstrasse 1, 4400 Steyr, Steyr, AUSTRIA / 0043-7252-896-0; FAX: 0043-7252-78620 office@steyr-mannlicher.com www.steyr-mannlicher.com

STI International, 114 Halmar Cove, Georgetown, TX 78628 / 800-959-8201; FAX: 512-819-0465 www.stiguns.com

Stiles Custom Guns, 76 Cherry Run Rd., Box 1605, Homer City, PA 15748 / 712-479-9945

Stoeger Industries, 17603 Indian Head Hwy., Suite 200, Accokeek, MD 20607-2501 / 301-283-6300; FAX: 301-283-6986 www.stoegerindustries.com

Stoeger Publishing Co. (See Stoeger Industries)

Stone Enterprises Ltd., 426 Harveys Neck Rd., P.O. Box 335, Wicomico Church, VA 22579 / 804-580-5114; FAX: 804-580-8421

Stone Mountain Arms, 5988 Peachtree Corners E., Norcross, GA 30071 / 800-251-9412

Stoney Point Products, Inc., P.O. Box 234, 1822 N Minnesota St., New Ulm, MN 56073-0234 / 507-354-3360; FAX: 507-354-7236 stoney@newulmtel.net www.stoneypoint.com

Storm, Gary, P.O. Box 5211, Richardson, TX 75083 / 214-385-0862

Stott's Creek Armory, Inc., 2526 S. 475W, Morgantown, IN 46160 / 317-878-5489; FAX: 317-878-9489 sccalendar@aol.com www.Sccalendar.aol.com

Stratco, Inc., P.O. Box 2270, Kalispell, MT 59901 / 406-755-1221; FAX: 406-755-1226

Strayer, Sandy. See: STRAYER-VOIGT, INC.

Strayer-Voigt, Inc., Sandy Strayer, 3435 Ray Orr Blvd, Grand Prairie, TX 75050 / 972-513-0575

Strong Holster Co., 39 Grove St., Gloucester, MA 01930 / 508-281-3300; FAX: 508-281-6321

Strutz Rifle Barrels, Inc., W. C., P.O. Box 611, Eagle River, WI 54521 / 715-479-4766

Stuart, V. Pat, Rt.1, Box 447-S, Greenville, VA 24440 / 804-556-3845

Sturgeon Valley Sporters, Ken Ide, P.O. Box 283, Vanderbilt, MI 49795 / 517-983-4338 k.ide@mail.com

Sturm Ruger & Co. Inc., 200 Ruger Rd., Prescott, AZ 86301 / 928-541-8820; FAX: 520-541-8850 www.ruger.com

"Su-Press-On", Inc., P.O. Box 09161, Detroit, MI 48209 / 313-842-4222

Sullivan, David S. (See Westwind Rifles, Inc.)

Sun Welding Safe Co., 290 Easy St. No.3, Simi Valley, CA 93065 / 805-584-6678; or 800-729-SAFE; FAX: 805-584-6169 sunwelding.com

Sunny Hill Enterprises, Inc., W1790 Cty. HHH, Malone, WI 53049 / 920-795-4722; FAX: 920-795-4822

Super 6 LLC, Gary Knopp, 3806 W. Lisbon Ave., Milwaukee, WI 53208 / 414-344-3343; FAX: 414-344-0304

Sure-Shot Game Calls, Inc., P.O. Box 816, 6835 Capitol, Groves, TX 77619 / 409-962-1636; FAX: 409-962-5465

Svon Corp., 2107 W. Blue Heron Blvd., Riviera Beach, FL 33404 / 508-881-8852

Swann, D. J., 5 Orsova Close, Eltham North Vic., 3095 AUSTRALIA / 03-431-0323

Swanndri New Zealand, 152 Elm Ave., Burlingame, CA 94010 / 415-347-6158

Swanson, Mark, 975 Heap Avenue, Prescott, AZ 86301 / 928-778-4423

Swarovski Optik North America Ltd., 2 Slater Rd., Cranston, RI 02920 / 401-946-2220; or 800-426-3089; FAX: 401-946-2587

Sweet Home, Inc., P.O. Box 900, Orrville, OH 44667-0900

Swenson's 45 Shop, A. D., 3839 Ladera Vista Rd, Fallbrook, CA 92028-9431

Swift Bullet Co., P.O. Box 27, 201 Main St., Quinter, KS 67752 / 913-754-3959; FAX: 913-754-2359

Swift Instruments, Inc., 952 Dorchester Ave., Boston, MA 02125 / 617-436-2960; FAX: 617-436-3232

Swift River Gunworks, 450 State St., Belchertown, MA 01007 / 413-323-4052

Szweda, Robert (See RMS Custom Gunsmithing)

T

T&S Industries, Inc., 1027 Skyview Dr., W. Carrollton, OH 45449 / 513-859-8414

T.G. Faust, Inc., 544 Minor St., Reading, PA 19602 / 610-375-8549; FAX: 610-375-4488

T.K. Lee Co., 1282 Branchwater Ln., Birmingham, AL 35216 / 205-913-5222 odonmich@aol.com www.scopedot.com

T.W. Menck Gunsmith, Inc., 5703 S. 77th St., Ralston, NE 68127 guntools@cox.net http://llwww.members.cox.net/guntools

Tabler Marketing, 2554 Lincoln Blvd., Suite 555, Marina Del Rey, CA 90291 / 818-755-4565; FAX: 818-755-0972

Taconic Firearms Ltd., Perry Lane, P.O. Box 553, Cambridge, NY 12816 / 518-677-2704; FAX: 518-677-5974

Talley, Dave, P.O. Box 821, Glenrock, WY 82637 / 307-436-8724; or 307-436-9315

Talon Industries Inc. (See Cobra Enterprises, Inc.)

Tamarack Products, Inc., P.O. Box 625, Wauconda, IL 60084 / 708-526-9333; FAX: 708-526-9353

Tanglefree Industries, 1261 Heavenly Dr., Martinez, CA 94553 / 800-982-4868; FAX: 510-825-3874

Tank's Rifle Shop, P.O. Box 474, Fremont, NE 68026-0474 / 402-727-1317 jtank@tanksrifleshop.com www.tanksrifleshop.com

Taracorp Industries, Inc., 1200 Sixteenth St., Granite City, IL 62040 / 618-451-4400

Target Shooting, Inc., P.O. Box 773, Watertown, SD 57201 / 605-882-6955; FAX: 605-882-8840

Tar-Hunt Custom Rifles, Inc., 101 Dogtown Rd., Bloomsburg, PA 17815 / 570-784-6368; FAX: 570-389-9150 www.tar-hunt.com

Tarnhelm Supply Co., Inc., 431 High St., Boscawen, NH 03303 / 603-796-2551; FAX: 603-796-2918 info@tarnhelm.com www.tarnhelm.com

Tasco Sales, Inc., 2889 Commerce Pky., Miramar, FL 33025

Taurus Firearms, Inc., 16175 NW 49th Ave., Miami, FL 33014 / 305-624-1115; FAX: 305-623-7506

MANUFACTURER'S DIRECTORY

Taurus International Firearms (See U.S. Importer)

Taurus S.A. Forjas, Avenida Do Forte 511, Porto Alegre, RS BRAZIL 91360 / 55-51-347-4050; FAX: 55-51-347-3065

Taylor & Robbins, P.O. Box 164, Rixford, PA 16745 / 814-966-3233

Taylor's & Co., Inc., 304 Lenoir Dr., Winchester, VA 22603 / 540-722-2017; FAX: 540-722-2018

TCCI, P.O. Box 302, Phoenix, AZ 85001 / 602-237-3823; FAX: 602-237-3858

TCSR, 3998 Hoffman Rd., White Bear Lake, MN 55110-4626 / 800-328-5323; FAX: 612-429-0526

TDP Industries, Inc., P.O. Box 249, Ottsville, PA 18942-0249 / 215-345-8687; FAX: 215-345-6057

Techno Arms (See U.S. Importer- Auto-Ordnance Corp

Tecnolegno S.p.A., Via A. Locatelli, 6 10, 24019 Zogno, I ITALY / 0345-55111; FAX: 0345-55155

Ted Blocker Holsters, Inc., 9396 S.W. Tigard St., Tigard, OR 97223 / 800-650-9742; FAX: 503-670-9692 www.tedblocker.com

Tele-Optics, 630 E. Rockland Rd., P.O. Box 6313, Libertyville, IL 60048 / 847-362-7757; FAX: 847-362-7757

Tennessee Valley Mfg., 14 County Road 521, Corinth, MS 38834 / 601-286-5014 tvm@avsia.com www.avsia.com/tvm

Ten-Ring Precision, Inc., Alex B. Hamilton, 1449 Blue Crest Lane, San Antonio, TX 78232 / 210-494-3063; FAX: 210-494-3066

TEN-X Products Group, 1905 N Main St, Suite 133, Cleburne, TX 76031-1305 / 972-243-4016; or 800-433-2225; FAX: 972-243-4112

Tepeco, P.O. Box 342, Friendswood, TX 77546 / 713-482-2702

Terry K. Kopp Professional Gunsmithing, Rt 1 Box 224, Lexington, MO 64067 / 816-259-2636

Testing Systems, Inc., 220 Pegasus Ave., Northvale, NJ 07647

Tetra Gun Care, 8 Vreeland Rd., Florham Park, NJ 07932 / 973-443-0004; FAX: 973-443-0263

Tex Shoemaker & Sons, Inc., 714 W. Cienega Ave., San Dimas, CA 91773 / 909-592-2071; FAX: 909-592-2378 texshoemaker@texshoemaker.com www.texshoemaker.com

Texas Platers Supply Co., 2453 W. Five Mile Parkway, Dallas, TX 75233 / 214-330-7168

Thad Rybka Custom Leather Equipment, 2050 Canoe Creek Rd., Springvale, AL 35146-6709

Thad Scott Fine Guns, Inc., P.O. Box 412, Indianola, MS 38751 / 601-887-5929

The A.W. Peterson Gun Shop, Inc., 4255 West Old U.S. 441, Mount Dora, FL 32757-3299 / 352-383-4258

The Accuracy Den, 25 Bitterbrush Rd., Reno, NV 89523 / 702-345-0225

The Ballistic Program Co., Inc., 2417 N. Patterson St., Thomasville, GA 31792 / 912-228-5739 or 800-368-0835

The Competitive Pistol Shop, 5233 Palmer Dr., Ft. Worth, TX 76117-2433 / 817-834-8479

The Concealment Shop, Inc., 3550 E. Hwy. 80, Mesquite, TX 75149 / 972-289-8997; or 800-444-7090; FAX: 972-289-4410 info@theconcealmentshop.com www.theconcealmentshop.com

The Country Armourer, P.O. Box 308, Ashby, MA 01431-0308 / 508-827-6797; FAX: 508-827-4845

The Creative Craftsman, Inc., 95 Highway 29 North, P.O. Box 331, Lawrenceville, GA 30246 / 404-963-2112; FAX: 404-513-9488

The Custom Shop, 890 Cochrane Crescent, Peterborough, ON K9H 5N3 CANADA / 705-742-6693

The Ensign-Bickford Co., 660 Hopmeadow St., Simsbury, CT 06070

The Firearm Training Center, 9555 Blandville Rd., West Paducah, KY 42086 / 502-554-5886

The Fouling Shot, 6465 Parfet St., Arvada, CO 80004

The Gun Doctor, 435 East Maple, Roselle, IL 60172 / 708-894-0668

The Gun Room, 1121 Burlington, Muncie, IN 47302 / 765-282-9073; FAX: 765-282-5270 bshstleguns@aol.com

The Gun Room Press, 127 Raritan Ave., Highland Park, NJ 08904 / 732-545-4344; FAX: 732-545-6686 gunbooks@rutgersgunbooks.com www.rutgersgunbooks.com

The Gun Shop, 62778 Spring Creek Rd., Montrose, CO 81401

The Gun Shop, 5550 S. 900 East, Salt Lake City, UT 84117 / 801-263-3633

The Gun Works, 247 S. 2nd St., Springfield, OR 97477 / 541-741-4118; FAX: 541-988-1097 gunworks@worldnet.att.net www.thegunworks.com

The Gunsight, 1712 North Placentia Ave., Fullerton, CA 92631

The Hanned Line, 4463 Madoc Way, San Jose, CA 95130 smith@hanned.com www.hanned.com

The Hawken Shop, P.O. Box 593, Oak Harbor, WA 98277 / 206-679-4657; FAX: 206-675-1114

The Keller Co., P.O. Box 4057, Port Angeles, WA 98363-0997 / 214-770-8585

The Lewis Lead Remover (See LEM Gun Specialties)

The Midwest Shooting School, Pat LaBoone, 2550 Hwy. 23, Wrenshall, MN 55797 / 218-384-3670 shootingschool@starband.net

The NgraveR Co., 67 Wawecus Hill Rd., Bozrah, CT 06334 / 860-823-1533; FAX: 860-887-6252 ngraver98@aol.com www.ngraver.com

The Orvis Co., Rt. 7, Manchester, VT 05254 / 802-362-3622; FAX: 802-362-3525

The Outdoor Connection, Inc., 7901 Panther Way, Waco, TX 76712-6556 / 800-533-6076 or 254-772-5575; FAX: 254-776-3553 floyd@outdoorconnection.com www.outdoorconnection.com

The Park Rifle Co., Ltd., Unit 6a Dartford Trade Park, Power Mill Lane, Dartford DA7 7NX, ENGLAND / 011-0322-222512

The Paul Co., 27385 Pressonville Rd., Wellsville, KS 66092 / 785-883-4444; FAX: 785-883-2525

The Protector Mfg. Co., Inc., 443 Ashwood Place, Boca Raton, FL 33431 / 407-394-6011

The Robar Co., Inc., 21438 N. 7th Ave., Suite B, Phoenix, AZ 85027 / 623-581-2648; FAX: 623-582-0059 info@robarguns.com www.robarguns.com

The School of Gunsmithing, 6065 Roswell Rd., Atlanta, GA 30328 / 800-223-4542

The Shooting Gallery, 8070 Southern Blvd., Boardman, OH 44512 / 216-726-7788

The Sight Shop, John G. Lawson, 1802 E. Columbia Ave., Tacoma, WA 98404 / 253-474-5465 parahellum9@aol.com www.thesightshop.org

The Southern Armory, 25 Millstone Road, Woodlawn, VA 24381 / 703-238-1343; FAX: 703-238-1453

The Surecase Co., 233 Wilshire Blvd., Ste. 900, Santa Monica, CA 90401 / 800-92ARMLOC

The Swampfire Shop (See Peterson Gun Shop, Inc.)

The Wilson Arms Co., 63 Leetes Island Rd., Branford, CT 06405 / 203-488-7297; FAX: 203-488-0135

Things Unlimited, 235 N. Kimbau, Casper, WY 82601 / 307-234-5277

Thirion Gun Engraving, Denise, PO Box 408, Graton, CA 95444 / 707-829-1876

Thomas, Charles C., 2600 S. First St., Springfield, IL 62704 / 217-789-8980; FAX: 217-789-9130 books@ccthomas.com ccthomas.com

Thompson Bullet Lube Co., P.O. Box 409, Wills Point, TX 75169 / 866-476-1500; FAX: 866-476-1500 thompsonbulletlube.com www.thompsonbulletlube.com

Thompson Precision, 110 Mary St., P.O. Box 251, Warren, IL 61087 / 815-745-3625

Thompson, Randall. See: HIGHLINE MACHINE CO.

Thompson Target Technology, 4804 Sherman Church Ave. S.W., Canton, OH 44710 / 330-484-6480; FAX: 330-491-1087 www.thompsontarget.com

Thompson Tool Mount, 1550 Solomon Rd., Santa Maria, CA 93455 / 805-934-1281 ttm@pronet.net www.thompsontoolmount.com

Thompson/Center Arms, P.O. Box 5002, Rochester, NH 03866 / 603-332-2394; FAX: 603-332-5133 tech@tcarms.com www.tcarms.com

Thunden Ranch, HCR 1, Box 53, Mt. Home, TX 78058 / 830-640-3138

Thurston Sports, Inc., RD 3 Donovan Rd., Auburn, NY 13021 / 315-253-0966

Tiger-Hunt Gunstocks, Box 379, Beaverdale, PA 15921 / 814-472-5161 tigerhunt4@aol.com www.gunstockwood.com

Time Precision, 4 Nicholas Sq., New Milford, CT 06776-3506 / 203-775-8343

Tinks & Ben Lee Hunting Products (See Wellington)

Tink's Safariland Hunting Corp., P.O. Box 244, 1140 Monticello Rd., Madison, GA 30650 / 706-342-4915; FAX: 706-342-7568

Tioga Engineering Co., Inc., P.O. Box 913, 13 Cone St., Wellsboro, PA 16901 / 570-724-3533; FAX: 570-724-3895 tiogaeng@epix.net

Tirelli, Snc Di Tirelli Primo E.C., Via Matteotti No. 359, Gardone V.T. Brescia, I ITALY / 030-8912819; FAX: 030-832240

TM Stockworks, 6355 Maplecrest Rd., Fort Wayne, IN 46835 / 219-485-5389

Tom Forrest, Inc., P.O. Box 326, Lakeside, CA 92040 / 619-561-5800; FAX: 888-GUN-CLIP info@gunmag.com www.gunmags.com

Tombstone Smoke`n' Deals, PO Box 31298, Phoenix, AZ 85046 / 602-905-7013; FAX: 602-443-1998

Tom's Gun Repair, Thomas G. Ivanoff, 76-6 Rt. Southfork Rd., Cody, WY 82414 / 307-587-6949

Tom's Gunshop, 3601 Central Ave., Hot Springs, AR 71913 / 501-624-3856

Torel, Inc., 1708 N. South St., P.O. Box 592, Yoakum, TX 77995 / 512-293-2341; FAX: 512-293-3413

Track of the Wolf, Inc., 18308 Joplin St. NW, Elk River, MN 55330-1773 / 763-633-2500; FAX: 763-633-2550

Traditions Performance Firearms, P.O. Box 776, 1375 Boston Post Rd., Old Saybrook, CT 06475 / 860-388-4656; FAX: 860-388-4657 info@traditionsfirearms.com www.traditionsfirearms.com

Trafalgar Square, P.O. Box 257, N. Pomfret, VT 05053 / 802-457-1911

Trail Visions, 5800 N. Ames Terrace, Glendale, WI 53209 / 414-228-1328

Trax America, Inc., PO Box 898, 1150 Eldridge, Forrest City, AR 72335 / 870-633-0410; or 800-232-2327; FAX: 870-633-4788 trax@ipa.net www.traxamerica.com

Treadlok Gun Safe, Inc., 1764 Granby St. NE, Roanoke, VA 24012 / 800-729-8732; or 703-982-6881; FAX: 703-982-1059

Treemaster, P.O. Box 247, Guntersville, AL 35976 / 205-878-3597

Trevallion Gunstocks, 9 Old Mountain Rd., Cape Neddick, ME 03902 / 207-361-1130

Trico Plastics, 28061 Diaz Rd., Temecula, CA 92590 / 909-676-7714; FAX: 909-676-0267 ustinfo@ustplastics.com www.tricoplastics.com

Trigger Lock Division / Central Specialties Ltd., 220-D Exchange Dr., Crystal Lake, IL 60014 / 847-639-3900; FAX: 847-639-3972

Trijicon, Inc., 49385 Shafer Ave., P.O. Box 930059, Wixom, MI 48393-0059 / 248-960-7700 or 800-338-0563

Trilby Sport Shop, 1623 Hagley Rd., Toledo, OH 43612-2024 / 419-472-6222

Trilux, Inc., P.O. Box 24608, Winston-Salem, NC 27114 / 910-659-9438; FAX: 910-768-7720

Trinidad St. Jr. Col. Gunsmith Dept., 600 Prospect St., Trinidad, CO 81082 / 719-846-5631; FAX: 719-846-5667

Triple-K Mfg. Co., Inc., 2222 Commercial St., San Diego, CA 92113 / 619-232-2066; FAX: 619-232-7675 sales@triplek.com www.triplek.com

Tristar Sporting Arms, Ltd., 1814 Linn St. #16, N. Kansas City, MO 64116-3627 / 816-421-1400; FAX: 816-421-4182 tristar@blitz-it.net www.tristarsportingarms

Tru-Balance Knife Co., P.O. Box 140555, Grand Rapids, MI 49514 / 616-647-1215

True Flight Bullet Co., 5581 Roosevelt St., Whitehall, PA 18052 / 610-262-7630; FAX: 610-262-7806

MANUFACTURER'S DIRECTORY

Truglo, Inc., P.O. Box 1612, McKinna, TX 75070 / 972-774-0300; FAX: 972-774-0323 www.truglosights.com

Trulock Tool, P.O. Box 530, Whigham, GA 31797 / 229-762-4678; FAX: 229-762-4050 trulockchokes@hotmail.com trulockchokes.com

Tru-Square Metal Products, Inc., 640 First St. SW, P.O. Box 585, Auburn, WA 98071 / 253-833-2310; or 800-225-1017; FAX: 253-833-2349 t-tumbler@qwest.net

Tucker, James C., P.O. Box 366, Medford, OR 97501 / 541-245-3887 jctstocker@yahoo.com

Tucson Mold, Inc., 930 S. Plumer Ave., Tucson, AZ 85719 / 520-792-1075; FAX: 520-792-1075

Turk's Head Productions, Mustafa Bilal, 908 NW 50th St., Seattle, WA 98107-3634 / 206-782-4164; FAX: 206-783-5677 info@turkshead.com www.turkshead.com

Turnbull Restoration, Doug, 6680 Rt. 5 & 20, P.O. Box 471, Bloomfield, NY 14469 / 585-657-6338; FAX: 585-657-6338 turnbullrest@mindspring.com www.turnbullrestoration.com

Tuttle, Dale, 4046 Russell Rd., Muskegon, MI 49445 / 616-766-2250

Tyler Manufacturing & Distributing, 3804 S. Eastern, Oklahoma City, OK 73129 / 405-677-1487; or 800-654-8415

U

U.S. Fire Arms Mfg. Co., Inc., 55 Van Dyke Ave., Hartford, CT 06106 / 877-227-6901; FAX: 800-644-7265 usfirearms.com

U.S. Optics, A Division of Zeitz Optics U.S.A., 5900 Dale St., Buena Park, CA 90621 / 714-994-4901; FAX: 714-994-4904 www.usoptics.com

U.S. Repeating Arms Co., Inc., 275 Winchester Ave., Morgan, UT 84050-9333 / 801-876-3440; FAX: 801-876-3737 www.winchester-guns.com

Ultra Dot Distribution, P.O. Box 362, 6304 Riverside Dr., Yankeetown, FL 34498 / 352-447-2255; FAX: 352-447-2266

Ultralux (See U.S. Importer-Keng's Firearms)

UltraSport Arms, Inc., 1955 Norwood Ct., Racine, WI 53403 / 414-554-3237; FAX: 414-554-9731

Uncle Bud's, HCR 81, Box 100, Needmore, PA 17238 / 717-294-6000; FAX: 717-294-6005

Uncle Mike's (See Michaels of Oregon Co.)

Unertl Optical Co., Inc., 103 Grand Avenue, P.O. Box 895, Mars, PA 16046-0895 / 724-625-3810; FAX: 724-625-3819 unertl@nauticom.net www.unertloptics.net

Unique/M.A.P.F., 10 Les Allees, 64700, Hendaye, FRANCE / 33-59 20 71 93

UniTec, 1250 Bedford SW, Canton, OH 44710 / 216-452-4017

United Binocular Co., 9043 S. Western Ave., Chicago, IL 60620

United Cutlery Corp., 1425 United Blvd., Sevierville, TN 37876 / 865-428-2532; or 800-548-0835; FAX: 865-428-2267

United States Products Co., 518 Melwood Ave., Pittsburgh, PA 15213-1136 / 412-621-2130; FAX: 412-621-8740 sales@us-products.com www.us-products.com

Universal Sports, P.O. Box 532, Vincennes, IN 47591 / 812-882-8680; FAX: 812-882-8680

Upper Missouri Trading Co., P.O. Box 100, 304 Harold St., Crofton, NE 68730-0100 / 402-388-4844

USAC, 4500-15th St. East, Tacoma, WA 98424 / 206-922-7589

Uselton/Arms, Inc., 842 Conference Dr., Goodlettsville, TN 37072 / 615-851-4919

Utica Cutlery Co., 820 Noyes St., Utica, NY 13503 / 315-733-4663; FAX: 315-733-6602

V

V.H. Blackinton & Co., Inc., 221 John L. Dietsch, Attleboro Falls, MA 02763-0300 / 508-699-4436; FAX: 508-695-5349

Valdada Enterprises, P.O. Box 773122, 31733 County Road 35, Steamboat Springs, CO 80477 / 970-879-2983; FAX: 970-879-0851 www.valdada.com

Valtro USA, Inc., 1281 Andersen Dr., San Rafael, CA 94901 / 415-256-2575; FAX: 415-256-2576

VAM Distribution Co. LLC, 1141-B Mechanicsburg Rd., Wooster, OH 44691 www.rex10.com

Van Gorden & Son Inc., C. S., 1815 Main St., Bloomer, WI 54724 / 715-568-2612

Van Horn, Gil, P.O. Box 207, Llano, CA 93544

Van Patten, J. W., P.O. Box 145, Foster Hill, Milford, PA 18337 / 717-296-7069

Vann Custom Bullets, 2766 N. Willowside Way, Meridian, ID 83642

Van's Gunsmith Service, 224 Route 69-A, Parish, NY 13131 / 315-625-7251

Vecqueray, Rick. See: VARMINT MASTERS, LLC

Vega Tool Co., c/o T.R. Ross, 4865 Tanglewood Ct., Boulder, CO 80301 / 303-530-0174 clanlaird@aol.com www.vegatool.com

Vektor USA, Mikael Danforth, 5139 Stanart St, Norfolk, VA 23502 / 888-740-0837; or 757-455-8895; FAX: 757-461-9155

Venco Industries, Inc. (See Shooter's Choice Gun Care)

Venus Industries, P.O. Box 246, Sialkot-1, PAKISTAN FAX: 92 432 85579

Vest, John, 1923 NE 7th St., Redmond, OR 97756 / 541-923-8898

VibraShine, Inc., P.O. Box 577, Taylorsville, MS 39168 / 601-785-9854; FAX: 601-785-9874 rdbekevibrashine.com www.vibrashine.com

Vibra-Tek Co., 1844 Arroya Rd., Colorado Springs, CO 80906 / 719-634-8611; FAX: 719-634-6886

Vic's Gun Refinishing, 6 Pineview Dr., Dover, NH 03820-6422 / 603-742-0013

Victory Ammunition, P.O. Box 1022, Milford, PA 18337 / 717-296-5768; FAX: 717-296-9298

Victory USA, P.O. Box 1021, Pine Bush, NY 12566 / 914-744-2060; FAX: 914-744-5181

Vihtavuori Oy, FIN-41330 Vihtavuori, FINLAND, / 358-41-3779211; FAX: 358-41-3771643

Vihtavuori Oy/Kaltron-Pettibone, 1241 Ellis St., Bensenville, IL 60106 / 708-350-1116; FAX: 708-350-1606

Viking Video Productions, P.O. Box 251, Roseburg, OR 97470

Village Restorations & Consulting, Inc., P.O. Box 569, Claysburg, PA 16625 / 814-239-8200; FAX: 814-239-2165 www.villagerestoration@yahoo.com

Vincent's Shop, 210 Antoinette, Fairbanks, AK 99701

Vintage Industries, Inc., 2772 Depot St., Sanford, FL 32773

Viper Bullet and Brass Works, 11 Brock St., Box 582, Norwich, ON N0J 1P0 CANADA

Viramontez Engraving, Ray Viramontez, 601 Springfield Dr., Albany, GA 31721 / 229-432-9683 sgtvira@aol.com

Viramontez, Ray. See: VIRAMONTEZ ENGRAVING

Virgin Valley Custom Guns, 450 E 800 N #20, Hurricane, UT 84737 / 435-635-8941; FAX: 435-635-8943 vvcguns@infowest.com www.virginvalleyguns.com

Visible Impact Targets, Rts. 5 & 20, E. Bloomfield, NY 14443 / 716-657-6161; FAX: 716-657-5405

Vitt/Boos, 1195 Buck Hill Rd., Townsend, VT 05353 / 802-365-9232

Voere-KGH GmbH, Untere Sparchen 56, A-6330 Kufstein, Tirol, AUSTRIA / 0043-5372-62547; FAX: 0043-5372-65752 voere@aon.com www.voere.com

Vorhes, David, 3042 Beecham St., Napa, CA 94558 / 707-226-9116; FAX: 707-253-7334

VSP Publishers (See Heritage/VSP Gun Books), P.O. Box 887, McCall, ID 83638 / 208-634-4104; FAX: 208-634-3101 heritage@gunbooks.com www.gunbooks.com

VTI Gun Parts, P.O. Box 509, Lakeville, CT 06039 / 860-435-8068; FAX: 860-435-8146 mail@vtigunparts.com www.vtigunparts.com

Vulpes Ventures, Inc., Fox Cartridge Division, P.O. Box 1363, Bolingbrook, IL 60440-7363 / 630-759-1229

W

W. Square Enterprises, 9826 Sagedale Dr., Houston, TX 77089 / 281-484-0935; FAX: 281-464-9940 lfdw@pdq.net www.loadammo.com

W. Waller & Son, Inc., 2221 Stoney Brook Rd., Grantham, NH 03753-7706 / 603-863-4177 www.wallerandson.com

W.B. Niemi Engineering, Box 126 Center Road, Greensboro, VT 05841 / 802-533-7180 or 802-533-7141

W.C. Wolff Co., P.O. Box 458, Newtown Square, PA 19073 / 610-359-9600; or 800-545-0077; mail@gunsprings.com www.gunsprings.com

W.E. Birdsong & Assoc., 1435 Monterey Rd., Florence, MS 39073-9748 / 601-366-8270

W.E. Brownell Checkering Tools, 9390 Twin Mountain Cir., San Diego, CA 92126 / 858-695-2479; FAX: 858-695-2479

W.J. Riebe Co., 3434 Tucker Rd., Boise, ID 83703

W.R. Case & Sons Cutlery Co., Owens Way, Bradford, PA 16701 / 814-368-4123; or 800-523-6350; FAX: 814-368-1736 jsullivan@wrcase.com www.wrcase.com

Wagoner, Vernon G., 2325 E. Encanto St., Mesa, AZ 85213-5917 / 480-835-1307

Wakina by Pic, 24813 Alderbrook Dr., Santa Clarita, CA 91321 / 800-295-8194

Waldron, Herman, Box 475, 80 N. 17th St., Pomeroy, WA 99347 / 509-843-1404

Walker Arms Co., Inc., 499 County Rd. 820, Selma, AL 36701 / 334-872-6231; FAX: 334-872-6262

Wallace, Terry, 385 San Marino, Vallejo, CA 94589 / 707-642-7041

Walls Industries, Inc., P.O. Box 98, 1905 N. Main, Cleburne, TX 76033 / 817-645-4366; FAX: 817-645-7946 www.wallsoutdoors.com

Walters Industries, 6226 Park Lane, Dallas, TX 75225 / 214-691-6973

Walther America, P.O. Box 22, Springfield, MA 01102 / 413-747-3443 www.walther-usa.com

Walther GmbH, Carl, B.P. 4325, D-89033 Ulm, GERMANY

Walt's Custom Leather, Walt Whinnery, 1947 Meadow Creek Dr., Louisville, KY 40218 / 502-458-4361

WAMCO-New Mexico, P.O. Box 205, Peralta, NM 87042-0205 / 505-869-0826

Ward & Van Valkenburg, 114 32nd Ave. N., Fargo, ND 58102 / 701-232-2351

Ward Machine, 5620 Lexington Rd., Corpus Christi, TX 78412 / 512-992-1221

Warenski Engraving, Julie Warenski, 590 E. 500 N., Richfield, UT 84701 / 435-896-5319; FAX: 435-896-8333 julie@warenskiknives.com

Warenski, Julie. See: WARENSKI ENGRAVING

Warne Manufacturing Co., 9057 SE Jannsen Rd., Clackamas, OR 97015 / 503-657-5590 or 800-683-5590; FAX: 503-657-5695 info@warnescopemounts.com www.warnescopemounts.com

Warren Muzzleloading Co., Inc., Hwy. 21 North, P.O. Box 100, Ozone, AR 72854 / 501-292-3268

Washita Mountain Whetstone Co., P.O. Box 378, Lake Hamilton, AR 71951 / 501-525-3914

Wasmundt, Jim, P.O. Box 511, Fossil, OR 97830

Watson Bros., 39 Redcross Way, SE1 1H6, London, ENGLAND FAX: 44-171-403-336

Watson Bullets, 231 Allies Pass, Frostproof, FL 33843 / 863-635-7948 cbestbullet@aol.com

Wayne E. Schwartz Custom Guns, 970 E. Britton Rd., Morrice, MI 48857 / 517-625-4079

Wayne Firearms For Collectors & Investors

Wayne Specialty Services, 260 Waterford Drive, Florissant, MO 63033 / 413-831-7083

WD-40 Co., 1061 Cudahy Pl., San Diego, CA 92110 / 619-275-1400; FAX: 619-275-5823

Weatherby, Inc., 3100 El Camino Real, Atascadero, CA 93422 / 805-466-1767; FAX: 805-466-2527 www.weatherby.com

Weaver Products ATK, P.O. Box 39, Onalaska, WI 54650 / 800-648-9624 or 608-781-5800; FAX: 608-781-0368

Weaver Scope Repair Service, 1121 Larry Mahan Dr., Suite B, El Paso, TX 79925 / 915-593-1005

Webb, Bill, 6504 North Bellefontaine, Kansas City, MO 64119 / 816-453-7431

Weber & Markin Custom Gunsmiths, 4-1691 Powick Rd., Kelowna, BC V1X 4L1 CANADA / 250-762-7575; FAX: 250-861-3655 www.weberandmarkinguns.com

Webley and Scott Ltd., Frankley Industrial Park, Tay Rd., Birmingham, B45 0PA ENGLAND / 011-021-453-1864; FAX: 0121-457-7846 guns@webley.co.uk www.webley.co.uk

Webster Scale Mfg. Co., P.O. Box 188, Sebring, FL 33870 / 813-385-6362

Weems, Cecil, 510 W Hubbard St., Mineral Wells, TX 76067-4847 / 817-325-1462

Weihrauch KG, Hermann, Industriestrasse 11, 8744 Mellrichstadt, Mellrichstadt, GERMANY

Welch, Sam. See: SAM WELCH GUN ENGRAVING

Wellington Outdoors, P.O. Box 244, 1140 Monticello Rd., Madison, GA 30650 / 706-342-4915; FAX: 706-342-7568

Wells, Rachel, 110 N. Summit St., Prescott, AZ 86301 / 928-445-3655 wellssportstore@cableone.net wellssportstore@cableone-net

Wells Creek Knife & Gun Works, 32956 State Hwy. 38, Scottsburg, OR 97473 / 541-587-4202; FAX: 541-587-4223

Welsh, Bud. See: HIGH PRECISION

Wenger North America/Precise Int'l., 15 Corporate Dr., Orangeburg, NY 10962 / 800-431-2996; FAX: 914-425-4700

Wenig Custom Gunstocks, 103 N. Market St., P.O. Box 249, Lincoln, MO 65338 / 660-547-3334; FAX: 660-547-2881 gustock@wenig.com www.wenig.com

Werth, T. W., 1203 Woodlawn Rd., Lincoln, IL 62656 / 217-732-1300

Wescombe, Bill (See North Star West)

Wessinger Custom Guns & Engraving, 268 Limestone Rd., Chapin, SC 29036 / 803-345-5677

West, Jack L., 1220 W. Fifth, P.O. Box 427, Arlington, OR 97812

Western Cutlery (See Camillus Cutlery Co.)

Western Design (See Alpha Gunsmith Division)

Western Mfg. Co., 550 Valencia School Rd., Aptos, CA 95003 / 831-688-5884 lotsabears@eathlink.net

Western Missouri Shooters Alliance, P.O. Box 11144, Kansas City, MO 64119 / 816-597-3950; FAX: 816-229-7350

Western Nevada West Coast Bullets, P.O. BOX 2270, DAYTON, NV 89403-2270 / 702-246-3941; FAX: 702-246-0836

Westley Richards & Co. Ltd., 40 Grange Rd., Birmingham, ENGLAND / 010-214722953; FAX: 010-214141138 sales@westleyrichards.com www.westleyrichards.com

Westley Richards Agency USA (See U.S. Importer for Westwind Rifles, Inc., David S. Sullivan, P.O. Box 261, 640 Briggs St., Erie, CO 80516 / 303-828-3823

Weyer International, 2740 Nebraska Ave., Toledo, OH 43607 / 419-534-2020; FAX: 419-534-2697

Whildin & Sons Ltd, E.H., RR 2 Box 119, Tamaqua, PA 18252 / 717-668-6743; FAX: 717-668-6745

Whinnery, Walt (See Walt's Custom Leather)

Whiscombe (See U.S. Importer-Pelaire Products)

White Pine Photographic Services, Hwy. 60, General Delivery, Wilno, ON K0J 2N0 CANADA / 613-756-3452

White Rifles, Inc., 234 S.1250 W., Linden, UT 84042 / 801-932-7950 www.whiterifles.com

White Rock Tool & Die, 6400 N. Brighton Ave., Kansas City, MO 64119 / 816-454-0478

Whitestone Lumber Corp., 148-02 14th Ave., Whitestone, NY 11357 / 718-746-4400; FAX: 718-767-1748 whstco@aol.com

Wichita Arms, Inc., 923 E. Gilbert, P.O. Box 11371, Wichita, KS 67211 / 316-265-0661; FAX: 316-265-0760 sales@wichitaarms.com www.wichitaarms.com

Wick, David E., 1504 Michigan Ave., Columbus, IN 47201 / 812-376-6960

Widener's Reloading & Shooting Supply, Inc., P.O. Box 3009 CRS, Johnson City, TN 37602 / 615-282-6786; FAX: 615-282-6651

Wideview Scope Mount Corp., 13535 S. Hwy. 16, Rapid City, SD 57702 / 605-341-3220; FAX: 605-341-9142 wvdon@rapidnet.com www.jii.to

Wiebe, Duane, 5300 Merchant Cir. #2, Placerville, CA 95667 / 530-344-1357; FAX: 530-344-1357 wiebe@d-wdb.com

Wiest, Marie. See: GUNCRAFT SPORTS, INC.

Wilcox All-Pro Tools & Supply, 4880 147th St., Montezuma, IA 50171 / 515-623-3138; FAX: 515-623-3104

Wilcox Industries Corp., Robert F Guarasi, 53 Durham St., Portsmouth, NH 03801 / 603-431-1331; FAX: 603-431-1221

Wild Bill's Originals, P.O. Box 13037, Burton, WA 98013 / 206-463-5738; FAX: 206-465-5925 wildbill@halcyon.com

Wild West Guns, 7521 Old Seward Hwy., Unit A, Anchorage, AK 99518 / 800-992-4570 or 907-344-4500; FAX: 907-344-4005 wwguns@ak.net www.wildwestguns.com

Wilderness Sound Products Ltd., 4015 Main St. A, Springfield, OR 97478 / 800-47-0006; FAX: 541-741-0263

Wildey, Inc., 45 Angevine Rd, Warren, CT 06754-1818 / 203-355-9000; FAX: 203-354-7759

Wildlife Research Center, Inc., 1050 McKinley St., Anoka, MN 55303 / 763-427-3350; or 800-USE-LURE; FAX: 763-427-8354

Will-Burt Co., 169 S. Main, Orrville, OH 44667

William E. Phillips Firearms, 38 Avondale Rd., Wigston, Leicester, ENGLAND / 0116 2886334; FAX: 0116 2810644 wephillips@aol.com

William Powell Agency, 22 Circle Dr., Bellmore, NY 11710 / 516-679-1158

Williams Gun Sight Co., 7389 Lapeer Rd., Box 329, Davison, MI 48423 / 810-653-2131 or 800-530-9028; FAX: 810-658-2140 williamsgunsight.com

Williams Mfg. of Oregon, 110 East B St., Drain, OR 97435 / 503-836-7461; FAX: 503-836-7245

Williams Shootin' Iron Service, The Lynx-Line, Rt. 2 Box 223A, Mountain Grove, MO 65711 / 417-948-0902; FAX: 417-948-0902

Williamson Precision Gunsmithing, 117 W. Pipeline, Hurst, TX 76053 / 817-285-0064; FAX: 817-280-0044

Willow Bend, P.O. Box 203, Chelmsford, MA 01824 / 978-256-8508; FAX: 978-256-8508

Wilsom Combat, 2234 CR 719, Berryville, AR 72616-4573 / 800-955-4856; FAX: 870-545-3310

Wilson Case, Inc., P.O. Box 1106, Hastings, NE 68902-1106 / 800-322-5493; FAX: 402-463-5276 sales@wilsoncase.com www.wilsoncase.com

Wilson Combat, 2234 CR 719, Berryville, AR 72616-4573 / 800-955-4856

Winchester Div. Olin Corp., 427 N. Shamrock, E. Alton, IL 62024 / 618-258-3566; FAX: 618-258-3599

Winchester Sutler, Inc., The, 270 Shadow Brook Lane, Winchester, VA 22603 / 540-888-3595; FAX: 540-888-4632

Windish, Jim, 2510 Dawn Dr., Alexandria, VA 22306 / 703-765-1994

Winkle Bullets, R.R. 1, Box 316, Heyworth, IL 61745

Winter, Robert M., P.O. Box 484, 42975-287th St., Menno, SD 57045 / 605-387-5322

Wise Custom Guns, 1402 Blanco Rd., San Antonio, TX 78212-2716 / 210-828-3388

Wise Guns, Dale, 1402 Blanco Rd., San Antonio, TX 78212 / 210-734-9999

Wiseman and Co., Bill, P.O. Box 3427, Bryan, TX 77805 / 409-690-3456; FAX: 409-690-0156

Wisners, Inc., P.O. Box 58, Adna, WA 98522 / 360-748-4590; FAX: 360-748-6028 parts@gunpartsspecialist.com www.wisnersinc.com

Wolf (See J.R. Distributing)

Wolfe Publishing Co., 2625 Stearman Rd., Ste. A, Prescott, AZ 86301 / 928-445-7810; or 800-899-7810; FAX: 928-778-5124

Wolf's Western Traders, 1250 Santa Cora Ave. #613, Chula Vista, CA 91913 / 619-482-1701 patwolf4570book@aol.com

Wolverine Footwear Group, 9341 Courtland Dr. NE, Rockford, MI 49351 / 616-866-5500; FAX: 616-866-5658

Wood, Frank (See Classic Guns, Inc.), 5305 Peachtree Ind. Blvd., Norcross, GA 30092 / 404-242-7944

Woodleigh (See Huntington Die Specialties)

Woods Wise Products, P.O. Box 681552, Franklin, TN 37068 / 800-735-8182; FAX: 615-726-2637

Woodstream, P.O. Box 327, Lititz, PA 17543 / 717-626-2125; FAX: 717-626-1912

Woodworker's Supply, 1108 North Glenn Rd., Casper, WY 82601 / 307-237-5354

Woolrich, Inc., Mill St., Woolrich, PA 17701 / 800-995-1299; FAX: 717-769-6234/6259

Working Guns, Jim Coffin, 1224 NW Fernwood Cir., Corvallis, OR 97330-2909 / 541-928-4391

World of Targets (See Birchwood Casey)

World Trek, Inc., 7170 Turkey Creek Rd., Pueblo, CO 81007-1046 / 719-546-2121; FAX: 719-543-6886

Worthy Products, Inc., RR 1, P.O. Box 213, Martville, NY 13111 / 315-324-5298

Wostenholm (See Ibberson [Sheffield] Ltd., George)

Wright's Gunstock Blanks, 8540 SE Kane Rd., Gresham, OR 97080 / 503-666-1705 doyal@wrightsguns.com www.wrightsguns.com

WTA Manufacturing, P.O. Box 164, Kit Carson, CO 80825 / 800-700-3054; FAX: 719-962-3570 wta@rebeltec.net http://www.members.aol.com/ductman249/wta.html

Wyant Bullets, Gen. Del., Swan Lake, MT 59911

Wyant's Outdoor Products, Inc., P.O. Box 9, Broadway, VA 22815

Wyoming Custom Bullets, 1626 21st St., Cody, WY 82414

Wyoming Knife Corp., 101 Commerce Dr., Ft. Collins, CO 80524 / 303-224-3454

X

X-Spand Target Systems, 26-10th St. SE, Medicine Hat, AB T1A 1P7 CANADA / 403-526-7997; FAX: 403-528-2362

Y

Yavapai College, 1100 E. Sheldon St., Prescott, AZ 86301 / 520-776-2353; FAX: 520-776-2355

Yavapai Firearms Academy Ltd., P.O. Box 27290, Prescott Valley, AZ 86312 / 928-772-8262; FAX: 928-772-0062 info@yfainc.corn www.yfainc.com

Yearout, Lewis E. (See Montana Outfitters), 308 Riverview Dr. E., Great Falls, MT 59404 / 406-761-0859; or 406-727-4569

Yellowstone Wilderness Supply, P.O. Box 129, W. Yellowstone, MT 59758 / 406-646-7613

Yesteryear Armory & Supply, P.O. Box 408, Carthage, TN 37030

Young Country Arms, William, 1409 Kuehner Dr. #13, Simi Valley, CA 93063-4478

Z

Zabala Hermanos S.A., P.O. Box 97, 20600 Elbar, Elgueta, Guipuzcoa, 20600 SPAIN / 943-768076; FAX: 943-768201 imanol@zabalahermanos.com www.zabalahermanos.com

Zander's Sporting Goods, 7525 Hwy 154 West, Baldwin, IL 62217-9706 / 800-851-4373; FAX: 618-785-2320

Zanotti Armor, Inc., 123 W. Lone Tree Rd., Cedar Falls, IA 50613 / 319-232-9650 www.zanottiarmor.com

Zeeryp, Russ, 1601 Foard Dr., Lynn Ross Manor, Morristown, TN 37814 / 615-586-2357

Zero Ammunition Co., Inc., 1601 22nd St. SE, P.O. Box 1188, Cullman, AL 35056-1188 / 800-545-9376; FAX: 205-739-4683

Ziegel Engineering, 1390 E. Bunnett St. "F", Signal Hill, CA 90755 / 562-596-9481; FAX: 562-598-4734 ziegel@aol.com www.ziegeleng.com

Zim's, Inc., 4370 S. 3rd West, Salt Lake City, UT 84107 / 801-268-2505

Zufall, Joseph F., P.O. Box 304, Golden, CO 80402-0304